Sarajevo's Holiday Inn on the Frontline
of Politics and War

Kenneth Morrison

Sarajevo's Holiday Inn on the Frontline of Politics and War

Kenneth Morrison
Department of History
De Montfort University
Leicester, UK

ISBN 978-1-137-57717-7 (hardcover)   ISBN 978-1-137-57718-4 (eBook)
ISBN 978-1-349-84653-5 (softcover)
DOI 10.1057/978-1-137-57718-4

Library of Congress Control Number: 2016938713

© The Editor(s) (if applicable) and The Author(s) 2016, First softcover printing 2018
The author(s) has/have asserted their right(s) to be identified as the author(s) of this work in accordance with the Copyright, Designs and Patents Act 1988.
This work is subject to copyright. All rights are solely and exclusively licensed by the Publisher, whether the whole or part of the material is concerned, specifically the rights of translation, reprinting, reuse of illustrations, recitation, broadcasting, reproduction on microfilms or in any other physical way, and transmission or information storage and retrieval, electronic adaptation, computer software, or by similar or dissimilar methodology now known or hereafter developed.
The use of general descriptive names, registered names, trademarks, service marks, etc. in this publication does not imply, even in the absence of a specific statement, that such names are exempt from the relevant protective laws and regulations and therefore free for general use.
The publisher, the authors and the editors are safe to assume that the advice and information in this book are believed to be true and accurate at the date of publication. Neither the publisher nor the authors or the editors give a warranty, express or implied, with respect to the material contained herein or for any errors or omissions that may have been made.

Printed on acid-free paper

This Palgrave Macmillan imprint is published by Springer Nature
The registered company is Macmillan Publishers Ltd. London

For Anne and Grant Simpson

Foreword

Sarajevo's Holiday Inn was the ultimate war-zone hotel. Established as the prestige hotel for the Sarajevo Winter Olympics of 1984, the Holiday Inn was subject to shell and sniper fire for the duration of the 1992–95 Bosnian war, the most brutal of the wars that marked the death of the Yugoslav state. One of the first acts of the war that tore Bosnia and Herzegovina apart took place on 6 April 1992, when shots were fired, probably from the hotel itself, into a crowd of peace demonstrators assembled outside the Bosnian parliament building opposite. The hotel, at the time the headquarters of the 'crisis staff' of Radovan Karadžić's Serbian Democratic Party (SDS), was then stormed by the crowd and ransacked. In the conflict that followed, Sarajevo was placed under siege, and the Holiday Inn would stand only two hundred yards from the frontline and from sniper positions in Grbavica; its south side was rendered uninhabitable by shellfire. Yet it continued to function throughout the siege.

The hotel's history deserves a book to itself, and finally, thanks to Kenneth Morrison, it has one. In this well-researched and fascinating monograph, he pays proper tribute to the local staff who kept the place going in the most dangerous of conditions, and to such estimable journalists as John F. Burns of the *New York Times* and Kurt Schork of Reuters who enjoyed or endured its hospitality. Of course, not everyone thought so fondly of it. A field producer for one of the American TV networks, with a reputation well established in other trouble spots, arrived in Sarajevo one day in the summer of 1992, took one look at the hotel and the war, took against both of them, and fled for safety the next day. Most of us thought otherwise, and we made the Holiday Inn our Sarajevo home when reporting from the city.

Kenneth Morrison's book is full of surprises and incisive observations, revealing even for those veteran correspondents who were regular visitors throughout the siege. And for those correspondents who came to know it well, the Holiday Inn, Sarajevo, will always be what it was: the most special hotel in the world.

Martin Bell, OBE
London

Acknowledgements

This book could not have been written without the help and encouragement of a significant number of people. At the (former) Holiday Inn, Sarajevo, I would like to give thanks to staff past and present, some of whom have worked there since the hotel first opened its doors on 19 October 1983, who have provided me with significant help and valuable insights. Foremost among them is Amira Delalić, now a citizen of Jacksonville, Florida, who worked in the Holiday Inn for a ten-year period between 1985 and 1995. She was a constant source of help, ideas, suggestions, and encouragement at crucial periods in the process of researching and writing this book. I would also like to thank, in particular, Rajko Dragović, Slobodan Kakuća, Ismet 'Crni' Mršević, Esad 'Eso' Bajraktarević, Manuela Ivanković, and Mersija 'Buba' Tutundžić for their help and Alena Bukvić, who arranged for me to access what remains of the hotel's archive. All work, or have worked, at the Holiday Inn, Sarajevo, and collectively they have an intimate knowledge of the hotel and its history. Without their input, this book simply could not have been written. Thanks also to Ivan Štraus (the architect who designed the Holiday Inn and many other remarkable buildings in Bosnia and Herzegovina and beyond) and Dragana Štraus for fascinating insights into the design and construction of the hotel.

    A better understanding of life in the Holiday Inn during the siege of Sarajevo could not have been achieved without the input of the numerous journalists, photojournalists, stringers, and translators from the numerous media organisations and agencies that operated from within the hotel. They provided me with intriguing and unique insights. I am indebted to Joel Brand, Allan Little, and Džemal Bećirević for the patience and time they gave to reading various drafts and engaging in lengthy discussions. Thanks also to Chris Ryder, Janine di Giovanni, Martin Bell, Jeremy Bowen, John F. Burns, Remy Ourdan, Florence Hartmann, Stephane Manièr, Robert King, Ariane Quentier, Marcus Tanner, Maggie O' Kane, Michael Montgomery, Chuck Sudetić, Malcolm Brabant, Tim Judah, Rosie Whitehouse, Kevin Sullivan, Charlotte Eagar, Sean Maguire, Peter Maass, Nic Robertson, Paul Lowe, Sebastian Rich, John Sweeney, Colin Smith, Amra Abadžić-Lowe, Victoria Clark, Phil Davison, Paul Harris, Sabina Ćosić, Samir Korić, Senada Kreso, Zoran Stevanović, Aida Ćerkez, Zoran Kusovac, and Vaughan Smith at the Frontline Club in London. Thanks also to Ismet 'Nuno' Arnautalić at SAGA Film, Sarajevo, and Sam Wilson at BBC News.

Gratitude, too, to many colleagues who have provided assistance and advice throughout. Prof. Robert Donia, Dr Miran Norderland, and Dr Neven Andjelić helped me greatly with advice and contacts and were sources of great encouragement from the outset. During the research process, I drew on the expertise of Dr James Lyon, Prof. Dr Jason Vuić, Prof. Peter Andreas, Dr Damir Arsenijević, Dr Adam Ramadan, Dr Sara Fregonese, Prof. Nigel Osborne, Geert-Hinrich Ahrens, and Chris Bennett throughout the writing process. My colleagues at De Montfort University have, as ever, been supportive throughout.

Thanks also to Eshaan Patel for transcribing the vast amount of audio interviews with such great care and diligence. Thanks to my *kum* Bojan Galić, who was born and spent the early part of his life in Sarajevo, and Ruud Peeten and Neven Pajović for their friendship, advice, knowledge, and enthusiasm for the project. As always, this book could not have been written without the love, support, and patience of my family, in particular Helen and my wonderful daughter Hannah.

Contents

1 Introduction — 1

2 Hotels as Strategic Assets, Prestige Targets, and Sanctuaries — 7

3 Press Hotels in Conflict Zones — 33

4 The Construction of Sarajevo's 'Olympic Hotel' — 47

5 Politics Comes to the Holiday Inn — 71

6 In Residence: Radovan Karadžić and the SDS — 83

7 Crossing the Rubicon: The Outbreak of War in Sarajevo — 103

8 A New Reality, A New Clientele — 117

9 The Hazards of Living on the Frontline — 141

10	Hostelry *in Extremis*	165
11	The Targeting of the Holiday Inn	193
12	The Rebirth and Demise of Sarajevo's Holiday Inn	203

References 217

Index 235

About the Author

Kenneth Morrison is a Reader in Modern Southeast European History and Co-Director of the Jean Monnet Centre for European Governance (JM-CEG) at De Montfort University, Leicester, UK, and was a Senior Visiting Fellow at the European Institute of the London School of Economics and Political Science (LSE) in 2012. He has written extensively on the modern history of the Balkans and is the author of *Montenegro: A Modern History* (2009) and (with Elizabeth Roberts) *The Sandžak: A History* (2013).

ABBREVIATIONS

ABC	American Broadcasting Company
AP	Associated Press
BBC	British Broadcasting Corporation
CANBAT	Canadian Peacekeeping Battalion in Bosnia and Herzegovina
CIA	Central Intelligence Agency
COMINFORM	Communist Information Bureau
CNN	Cable News Network
CSCE	Commission for Security and Cooperation in Europe
DPA	Dayton Peace Agreement
DUTCHBAT	Dutch Peacekeeping Battalion in Bosnia and Herzegovina
EC	European Community
ECMM	European Community Monitoring Mission
EOKA	*Ethniki Organosis Kyprion Agoniston* (National Organisation of Cypriot Fighters)
EU	European Union
FMLN	Farabundo Marti National Liberation Front
FREBAT	French Peacekeeping Battalion in Bosnia and Herzegovina
HDZ-BiH	*Hrvatska demokratska zajednica Bosne i Hercegovine* (Croatian Democratic Community of Bosnia and Herzegovina)
HOS	*Hrvatske obrambene snage* (Croatian Defence Forces)
HVO	*Hrvatsko vijeće obrane* (Croatian Defence Council)
IAHI	International Association of Holiday Inns
ICRC	International Committee of the Red Cross
ICTY	International Criminal Tribunal for the Former Yugoslavia
IDF	Israeli Defence Force
IEBL	Inter-Entity Boundary Line

IFOR	(NATO) Implementation Force
IHG	Intercontinental Hotels Group
IMF	International Monetary Fund
INM	Independent Nasserite Movement
IOC	International Olympic Committee
IRA	Irish Republican Army
ITN	Independent Television News
JNA	*Jugoslovenska narodna armija* (Yugoslav People's Army)
KRF	(Phalange) Kataeb Regulatory Forces
LNM	Lebanese National Movement
MUP	*Ministarstvo unutrašnjih poslova* (Ministry of Internal Affairs)
NATO	North Atlantic Treaty Organisation
NICRA	Northern Ireland Civil Rights Association
OHR	Office of the High Representative
OIC	Organisation of Islamic Countries
OSCE	Organisation for Security and Cooperation in Europe
PIC	Peace Implementation Council
PIRA	Provisional Irish Republican Army
PL	*Patroitska liga* (Patriotic League)
PLO	Palestinian Liberation Organisation
RPG	Rocket-propelled grenade
RS	*Republika Srpska* (Serb Republic)
RTL	*Radio Télévision Luxembourg* (Radio Television Luxembourg)
SAP	Sarajevo Agency Pool
SDA	*Stranka demokratske akcije* (Party of Democratic Action)
SDS	*Srpska demokratska stranka* (Serbian Democratic Party)
SFOR	(NATO) Stabilisation Force
SIPA	(Bosnian) State Investigation and Protection Agency
SFRJ	*Socijalistička Federativna Republika Jugoslavija* (Socialist Federal Republic of Yugoslavia)
SKJ	*Savez komunista Jugoslavije* (Yugoslav League of Communists)
SK-SDP	*Savez komunista Bosne i Hercegovine/Socijaldemokratska Partija Bosne i Hercegovine* (Bosnian League of Communists/Social Democratic Party)
SORA	*Savez omladinska radna akjica* (Youth Voluntary Labour Association)
SPECA	Salvadoran Foreign Press Corps Association
SRS	*Srpska radikalna stranka* (Serbian Radical Party)
SRSJ	*Savez reformskih snaga Jugoslavije* (Alliance of Reform Forces of Yugoslavia)
TORS	*Teritorialna obramba Republike Slovenije* (Territorial Defence of the Republic of Slovenia)

UCSB	University of California Santa Barbara
UDA	Ulster Defence Association
UFF	Ulster Freedom Fighters
UK	United Kingdom
UPI	United Press International
UVF	Ulster Volunteer Force
UN	United Nations
UNAMI	United Nations Assistance Mission in Iraq
UNHCR	United Nations High Commission for Refugees
UNFICYP	United Nations Peacekeeping Force in Cyprus
UKRBAT	Ukrainian Peacekeeping Battalion in Bosnia & Herzegovina
UNPROFOR	United Nations Protection Force
UUP	Ulster Unionist Party
VOPP	Vance–Owen Peace Plan
VRS	*Vojska Republika Srpske* (Army of Republika Srpska)
ZKS	*Zveza komunistov Slovenije* (League of Communists of Slovenia)

List of Figures

Image 1.1	The Holiday Inn during the siege of Sarajevo, January 1993	4
Image 2.1	The Europa's manager, Harper Brown, outside the hotel circa 1972	20
Image 3.1	The Hotel Pelegrin, Kupari, Croatia	42
Image 4.1	Olympic symbols embedded into one of the concrete pillars near the entrance to the hotel—the pockmarks from sniper fire still evident	49
Image 4.2	The Holiday Inn under construction, circa June 1983	53
Image 4.3	The atrium of the Holiday Inn, replete with Štraus's 'big top'	56
Image 4.4	The Holiday Inn hotel, circa June 1984	63
Image 6.1	The view from the Holiday Inn during the *Valter* demonstrations, March 1992	94
Image 8.1	Satellite dishes on the fifth floor of the western side of the hotel, circa July 1992	135
Image 9.1	The view from the (uninhabitable) southern side of the Holiday Inn, circa 1993. Snipers located in the apartment blocks in Grbavica had a clear line of fire into the hotel	152
Image 10.1	Waiting staff preparing to serve the New Year buffet, circa December 1992	173
Image 10.2	One of the CNN rooms at the Holiday Inn, complete with satellite phone, dish, plastic sheeting on the windows, and sleeping bag	183

Image 11.1	The western and southern sides of the Holiday Inn hotel, circa January 1996	197
Image 12.1	Design for the much-lauded 'Grand Media Centre' that was never realised	211

CHAPTER 1

Introduction

Sarajevo, the capital of Bosnia and Herzegovina, basked in the warm sunshine, the cafés and streets full of people enjoying the traditional 1 May holiday. The city was abundant with noise and colour and the small traders in Baščaršija (the old Ottoman quarter) were doing a brisk trade. Tourism seemed to be booming, no doubt bolstered by the global attention the city was receiving during the centenary year of the assassination of Archduke Franz Ferdinand and his wife Sophie von Hohenberg, shot and killed by the Bosnian Serb, Gavrilo Princip. Of course, this snapshot of Sarajevo, tourist Sarajevo, though seductive was both superficial and misleading. Bosnia and Herzegovina remains a country dogged by political, economic, and social problems and burdened by the legacies of the brutal 1992–95 war (during which Sarajevo endured a three-and-a-half-year siege), the legacies of the 1995 Dayton Peace Agreement (DPA) and, more recently, economic crisis and social unrest, peaking, thus far, with the violent protests of February 2014.

Walking westward from Baščaršija towards the Marindvor area, the rattle of the trams packed with people heading into the centre of the city only added to the general sense of well-being. But how sharp the contrast when approaching the entrance to the city's famous Holiday Inn hotel, one of the most iconic buildings in the city (perhaps the most recognisable in Sarajevo during the three-and-a-half-year siege) and something of a metaphor for the fate of the city. Marindvor is now peppered with very modern and expensive shopping centres and fashionable (though somewhat lurid) apartment blocks. Sitting uncomfortably amidst this brash newness is the iconic Holiday Inn, known the world over as the city's 'war hotel', the centre for the international media during the siege. The hotel, an aesthetically challenging modernist structure adorned with a façade of yellow, ochre, and brown, was one of the jewels of the construction boom that preceded the 1984 Winter Olympics, but now it looked run-down. Its rather idiosyncratic appearance seemed something of an anachronism, at odds with the newly built (though equally idiosyncratic) structures that now surround it. I recalled the old photographs that I had seen in the hotel's (depleted) archive during a previous visit. They showed the newly built Holiday Inn glowing in the sunshine, the neat external areas, though constructed from grey concrete, looking every bit the picture of modernity and its clipped gardens providing a welcome contrast to the angular design of the building. These images conveyed confidence and hope; the hotel a symbol of a city on an upward trajectory, a physical manifestation of that positivity.

Now, however, the hotel looked rather dispiriting. Its garden was overgrown and unkempt, the concrete paving leading to the hotel's entrance cracked and crumbling, and what was once pleasant green space was now surrounded by a battered corrugated iron fence covered in graffiti imploring citizens to protest against the economic uncertainty and endemic corruption that has, sadly, characterised post-Dayton Bosnia (and had fuelled the social unrest of February 2014). The feature fountain in front of the hotel's main entrance, which usually transmitted the comforting sound of gently turbulent water, was empty and the flags that flew on the poles in front of the building were dirty and tattered. Upon entering the Holiday Inn, its vast atrium, once *the* place to be (and be seen in), the emptiness, and the acoustics only a vast, empty space can produce, was disconcerting. Footsteps echoed loudly—resonating around the vast, empty atrium. I had been in the hotel many times, but this time the experience was quite different. The atrium had always been cavernous, even when busy, but now it was cold, empty, dark.

It transpired that the hotel was temporarily closed for business for a then unspecified period, as the result of a botched privatisation, lack of investment, years of mismanagement, and a workers' strike. The hotel was not receiving guests and the building was 'occupied' by staff who had not received their salaries for months (and their pension contributions for several years). Their protest was entirely just and driven by their shoddy treatment at the hands of the hotel's owners, once regarded as the saviour of the iconic building. The hotel had been bought by an Austrian company *Alpha Baumanagement* in 2004, and the new owners had promised that the Holiday Inn would not just thrive but would be modernised and would be central to plans to construct the so-called Grand Media Centre, replete with shopping centre, fitness clubs, and a casino, with the hotel as the core of the new complex. Hopes were high that the Holiday Inn would again occupy its rightful place as one of Sarajevo's great hotels in an increasingly competitive market. But it wasn't to be. The promised investment never materialised and the hotel gradually accumulated significant debts. How ironic that having survived the ravages of the siege of Sarajevo and the difficulties of post-war transition, the hotel was now threatened with closure as the result of a privatisation process gone awry.

Upon arrival, it was clear that the striking workers had taken their leave for the day (it was, of course, a holiday across the country), but I was not, in any event, there per se to discuss the protests or the privatisation process that had led to the apparent demise of the hotel, but to meet with a one-time security officer in the hotel; Sarajevo-born but now, like so many of his countrymen, living abroad. We sat in the freezing cold and eerily empty atrium, discussing life in the hotel in the years after its opening in 1983, its many illustrious guests, and its place in the folklore of Sarajevo, before moving on to discuss the disintegration of the Yugoslav state, the war in Bosnia and Herzegovina, the siege of Sarajevo, contemporary political events, the country's troublesome privatisation process, and the consequences of it, consequences that were all too clear right there in the hotel. The discussion went on for several hours, and he lamented the fate of the hotel in which he had spent many years working, and had been proud to work in. The emotional attachment he still has to the building was evident, though he expressed little hope that the future for the hotel was bright.

Then, with the acquiescence of the sole security guard on duty, we walked through the dark and deserted corridors, stairwells, conference rooms, kitchens, and restaurants of the hotel. Dark, cold, empty, and without electricity, it felt like the *Mary Celeste*, as if everyone, guests and staff, had departed in a hurry. Overflowing ashtrays were dotted around, glasses lay uncollected, discarded pieces of clothing were strewn on the backs of chairs. In the large kitchen—once state of the art—pots, pans, and unwashed cutlery lay on the work surfaces, and hastily constructed placards on which staff had written messages imploring the owners to address their concerns lay scattered on the floor. Of course, this was the residue of more recent events, but walking through those dark-

Image 1.1 The Holiday Inn during the siege of Sarajevo, January 1993. The sign reads: 'Danger zone: Run or R.I.P'. (Photo: Paul Lowe)

ened, empty spaces, one could almost feel the ghosts of the past stalking the corridors—because this hotel has, despite its relative infancy, a past (Image 1.1). There was, however, no way to avoid reaching the conclusion that this fascinating past was no guarantor of the hotel's future. It was, therefore, an appropriate time to document the history of the hotel, particularly throughout its most turbulent years, lest the building be closed permanently and the opportunity, perhaps, lost.

The hotel would, however, be given a temporary stay of execution and would again open for guests for the summer of 2014 (though the hotel would again be closed in July 2015, perhaps permanently), but its future was uncertain and the importance of documenting its history remained. Embarking upon such an endeavour was not difficult to justify, because the Holiday Inn was not simply one of Sarajevo's most aesthetically striking and symbolically important buildings, it has been an inanimate and passive witness to some of the key moments in the modern history of a city that has experienced significant social, economic, and political flux and war. If the walls could speak, there would be much to convey, for some of those events took place either *within* or in the immediate environs of the hotel. Consequently, history has left indelible marks on the building—some tangible, others intangible.

Constructed in advance of the 1984 Winter Olympics, primarily to host leading members of the International Olympic Committee, the hotel is only just over thirty years old—relatively youthful for a building with such a rich history. In the first six years of its existence, the Holiday Inn was Sarajevo's finest hotel, hosting many prestigious guests. It would also host domestic political elites. Alija Izetbegović, the wartime president of the Bosnian government, launched the Party of Democratic Action (SDA) at the Holiday Inn, though it was later frequently used by Radovan Karadžić's Serbian Democratic Party (SDS), and was briefly their headquarters. The hotel was at the centre of events during the 'referendum weekend' of February/March 1992, and it was from the hotel that senior members of Karadžić's party launched, in the wake of the referendum, the 'war of the barricades' that brought the city to a temporary standstill. It was also from the hotel that, on 6 April 1992, some of the first shots of the war in Sarajevo were fired into a crowd of peace demonstrators assembled in front of the Bosnian parliament building. After the events of 6 April, the hotel closed, but was reopened as the siege of Sarajevo tightened, thereafter serving as a *press hotel*—frequented, in the main, by the international media that had descended on the city following the outbreak of war in Bosnia and Herzegovina. The Holiday Inn, while *in* Sarajevo was not strictly *of* it—the hotel was detached and subject to a specific set of micro-dynamics; subject to, but in many ways quite different from, the dynamics that existed in the city during the siege. It remained thus until the Bosnian war ended and the siege of Sarajevo was lifted after the signing of the Dayton Agreement in December 1995, whereupon the hotel entered a new era of uncertainty.

However, despite the gravity of events that have taken place either within or in the immediate vicinity of the hotel, there has hitherto been no attempt to document, in sufficient depth, the history of the building and its myriad guests. The Holiday Inn is oft-mentioned in the plethora of written material focusing on the war in Bosnia and Herzegovina and the siege of Sarajevo, be it in academic studies, journalist's memoirs, newspaper reports, or magazine articles, yet it is mentioned, largely, in passing and treated superficially. The following book represents, therefore, an attempt to shed light upon how the hotel was utilised by different individuals and groups before (be they politicians, political parties, journalists, diplomats, aid workers, intellectuals, or peace activists), during and after the siege drawing, in part, on the recollections of those who either worked in or stayed in the hotel for long periods. It analyses how the hotel functioned under siege conditions, despite being located a few hundred yards from the frontline, and how the hotel's guests adapted to these extraordinary circumstances.

However, while this book focuses *on* Sarajevo's Holiday Inn, it is not strictly a history *of* the hotel in the conventional sense. It is not a traditional study of a hotel but, rather, a study of the significant historical events that have taken place within its walls or its immediate environs. And, of course, the scope of the book is necessarily narrow in focus, and it is not, nor can it be, a detailed account of the siege of Sarajevo, or indeed the war in Bosnia and Herzegovina—that has been admirably executed elsewhere and in painstaking detail by other scholars. The book does, nevertheless, provide a unique insight that other books or articles do not. Not only is this a general history of the building and of the events that have taken place there, but it also draws upon the experiences and insights of the hotel's myriad guests, with a particular focus on those who frequented the hotel during the siege. More broadly, however, it is also a book about hotels and hostelry in wartime, how such places function in the context of a war, and how staff and management endeavour to provide the most basic of services while conveying a semblance of normality to guests in the most extraordinary of circumstances. And the history of the Holiday Inn provides us with an example par excellence of a hotel that continued to function in the context of war, but did so despite being located directly on the frontline of the longest siege in modern European history.

CHAPTER 2

Hotels as Strategic Assets, Prestige Targets, and Sanctuaries

Why devote an entire book to something as seemingly mundane as a hotel?[1] Hotels are, after all, as ordinary as they are omnipresent.[2] They exist to provide for the most basic of needs: shelter, sleep, food, and a range of other services that facilitate the paying guests' needs, be they modest or otherwise. In the context of war, however, the mundane and the extraordinary juxtapose, and hotels take on an entirely different significance.[3] Though while ostensibly created specifically for business travel, leisure, and relaxation, hotels have always been part of a security apparatus. They are occasionally requisitioned

---

[1] Hotels have long been the setting for the work of novelists and playwrights; Graham Greene's *The Comedians*, Ernest Hemingway's *The Fifth Column*, Stanisław Lem's *The Futurological Congress*, J.G. Farrell's *Troubles* and Stephen King's *The Shining* being perhaps the best-known novels or plays to be framed within the specific context of the hotel.

[2] For an overview of the specific dynamics of life within hotels, see Caroline Field Levander & Matthew Pratt Guterl, *Hotel Life: The Story of a Place Where Anything Can Happen*, Chapel Hill: University of North Carolina Press, 2015.

[3] During the Second World War, hotels became places of refuge for a myriad of politicians and royal families in exile. Behind the superficial glamour, hotels such as the Ritz, Claridges, and the Dorchester and the Ritz Hotel on the Paris Vendôme (which was, according to Tilar J. Mazzeo, 'the centre of political action' in Europe even before the outbreak of the Second World War) were places of political intrigue and betrayal with a colourful array of guests, the latter hosting an array of guests from Winston Churchill to Coco Chanel. See, for example, Matthew Sweet, *The West End Front: The Wartime Secrets of London's Grand Hotels*, London: Faber & Faber, 2011, and Tilar J. Mazzeo, *The Hotel on Place Vendôme*, New York: HarperCollins, 2014.

as barracks[4] during war or used as locations where warring factions embark upon peace negotiations.[5] They host not only tourists but also politicians, diplomats, spies, journalists, and representatives of military or paramilitary groups. Additionally, in wartime, hotels often become *press hotels*, bases for journalists during conflicts. In so doing, these buildings often become integral parts of the narrative and imagery of those conflicts.[6]

Every conflict or revolution generates memorable examples of the hospitality industry's resourcefulness, courage, and 'grace under fire'.[7] Similarly, each has its own 'war hotel' (or hotels), places that often become among the most recognisable symbols of the respective wars in which they are part. As the writer and journalist Paul Harris notes, when war breaks out 'there will always be certain types of hotel guest for the establishment that keeps its doors open' though in the absence of normal guests, these tend to be journalists, aid workers, intelligence agents, or 'war tourists'.[8] Sarajevo's Holiday Inn, the primary focus of this book, was not the first hotel, nor would it be the last, to become so intrinsically linked with conflict. Hotels such as the Europa in Belfast; the Holiday Inn, the St George's, and Commodore hotels

---

[4] During the 1992–95 war in Bosnia and Herzegovina, for example, numerous hotels were either commandeered by paramilitary groups. The Hotel Višegrad, next to the old bridge made famous by Ivo Andrić's Nobel Prize-winning novel *Na Drini ćuprija* (*The Bridge on the Drina*) and the nearby the Vilina vlas and the Bikavac hotels were commandeered by the murderous Serb paramilitary group known as *Osvetnici* (Avengers) during their murderous campaign against the town's Muslim population. The hitherto unremarkable Hotel Prijedor was used as a base for Serb paramilitaries before the ethnic cleansing of the Prijedor region (during which Muslim males were incarcerated in camps in Omarska and Trnopolje), the Hotel Fontana in Bratunac was the location where General Ratko Mladić and his deputy Radoslav Krstić 'negotiated' the fate of the Muslims of Srebrenica with Colonel Thom Karremans, the commander of DUTCHBAT III (the Dutch United Nations peacekeeping contingent tasked with protecting the 'safe area' of Srebrenica), before the fall of the enclave in July 1995. Serbian paramilitary groups also used the *Hotel* Drina and the *Hotel* Jezero before and during their attack on the city in April 1992. See United Nations Security Council, 'Final Report of the United Nations Commission of Experts Established Pursuant to Security Council Resolution 820: Annex IV – The Policy of Ethnic Cleansing', S/1994/674/Add.2 (Vol.1), 28 December 1994.

[5] Sara Fregonese, 'Between a refuge and a battleground: Beirut's discrepant cosmopolitanisms', *The Geographical Review*, 102(3), pp. 316–336.

[6] *The Times*, London, 23 November 2001, p. 4.

[7] *The Times*, London, 16 February 2015, http://www.thetimes.co.uk/tto/news/world/europe/article4354944.ece?shareToken=7f4199705e7f8aa4dd5e4f82422ad264 (last accessed 17 June 2015).

[8] Paul Harris, *More Thrills than Skills: Adventures in Journalism, War and Terrorism*, Glasgow: Kennedy & Boyd, 2009, p. 160.

in Beirut; the Ledra Palace in Nicosia; the Hotel Aletti (now the Hotel Es Safir) and the El Aurassi in Algiers; the Continental Palace and Caravelle in Saigon (now Ho Chi Minh City); the Meikles Hotel in Salisbury (now Harare); the Al Rashid in Baghdad or, more recently, the Rixos in Tripoli have all been significant 'markers' in their respective conflicts and are synonymous with these conflicts for global television audiences.

Much of what has been written about these hotels in wartime is imbued with over-sentimental musings, and there is, particularly among journalists who frequent these places, a tendency to over-romanticise them, to hail them as extraordinary. Robert Fisk, the veteran correspondent from *The Independent*, noted how there was a distinct mythology surrounding 'war hotels', arguing that there was 'something odd, even unpleasant, about our desire to romanticize these over-expensive and uncomfortable institutions'. Why, he asked 'Have so many of us written so many words about these grubby hotels when the epic tragedies outside their doors should have made such reports both tasteless and inappropriate?' He continues:

> Why must we recreate Casablanca every time we cover wars? Rick's Café has a lot to answer for. Humphrey Bogart was soft-hearted, his pianist a romantic, his barman gentle, the local police chief a rogue but honest at heart, the wartime occupying power villainous. Rick's was the place to go to forget your troubles....But the proprietors of our gloomy wartime homes have little of Bogart's charms.[9]

Fisk's observations are, of course, incisive, but the (albeit overly romanticised) musings of the press corps provide us with some insight into a world that is, at best, obscured. While journalists have written much about their wartime accommodation, the phenomenon of the 'war hotel' (or, rather, the myriad roles that hotels play in wartime) is remarkably understudied by researchers. So why do they matter? Hotels matter because they play a very important function during periods of armed conflict, be they key strategic buildings, prestige targets for terrorist groups, bases for the press, or as places of temporary sanctuary. Yet the history of the hotel during wartime is largely fragmented—observations (or even) footnotes in the memoirs of journalists or politicians, with the hotel merely the backdrop to more significant events outside its doors.

---

[9] *The Independent*, London, 2 June 1993, p. 19.

Hotels as Strategic Assets

Hotels belonging to large international chains are often grand, high-rise structures, intended to invoke a sense of awe, of the *other*, of some untouchable, unattainable luxury. In peacetime, this is seductive and appealing; yet, these impressive and intimidating structures take on an entirely different, much darker, significance during times of conflict. Indeed, hotels in this context are often militarised; their primary utilisation transformed from luxury hostelry into key military-strategic asset. This is particularly the case during urban conflicts, where the high ground becomes coveted and control of it crucial, and thus rival armies or militias engage in fierce battles to ensure that they secure high-rise structures (including hotels) and establish control of the strategic heights. 'Verticality', argue Fregonese and Ramadan, 'represents a military strategic asset during conflict', an advantage that is highly prized. That this dynamic is of huge importance has been most recently evidenced by the cases of Cairo's Ramses Hilton Hotel (where the regime of Hosni Mubarak allegedly placed snipers on the rooftop to target protestors on Tahrir Square during the 2011 demonstrations, part of the so-called Arab Spring); the Safir Hotel (which is perched on the high ground above the Syrian town of Maaloula) where Islamist rebels fought government soldiers; and the Hotel Ukraine on Maidan Square in Kiev, where, it is alleged, anti-government snipers fired from the building in February 2014.[10]

The importance of hotels in the struggle for command of the strategic heights in urban warfare was most evident during the so-called Battle of the Hotels in Beirut, Lebanon, in 1975–76 (during which major hotels in Beirut's hotel district were destroyed was essentially a struggle for control of the city's strategic heights). The city's many hotels, once the very symbol of Beirut's modernity, progress, and economic well-being, would become central to the conflict in Lebanon and in Beirut.[11] Indeed, one of the most potent and visible symbols of Lebanon's 1975–77 Civil War[12] is Beirut's Holiday Inn. Today, the hotel stands deserted and scarred by the conflict(s) which raged in it and around it, a favourite stop on the 'war tourist trail' of the city. The hotel, located in the fashionable and cosmopolitan

---

[10] Fregonese, Sara., & Ramadan, Adam. Hotel Geopolitics: a research agenda. *Geopolitics*, 20(4), 2015, pp. 793–813.

[11] Helena Cobban, *The Making of Modern Lebanon*, Hutchinson, London and New York, p. 130.

[12] For a succinct account of this first phase, see Cobban, *The Making of Modern Lebanon*, pp. 125–149.

Minet-el-Hosn area of Beirut (which housed a complex of high-rise hotels), was designed by the French architect André Wogenscky and his Lebanese collaborator Maurice Hindié, and built by the wealthy businessman Abdal Moshin Kattan in the modernist style that was characteristic of the new Lebanese architecture of the 1960s and 1970s.[13] Construction of the hotel began in 1971 and was completed in 1974. Overlooking the prestigious St George's and the Phoenicia on the beachfront, the Holiday Inn was the most luxurious in the city, and according to Samir Kassir, 'Both its rooftop revolving restaurant and its movie theatre, the most luxurious in the city, were topics of conversation.'[14] As one of the leading hotels in Beirut and one of the best in Lebanon, it was the epitome of modernist glamour. Unfortunately, however, the opening of the hotel coincided with the country's descent into civil war, and it was soon consumed by the so-called Battle of the Hotels.[15]

The battle over the strategically valuable high-rise buildings, the majority of which were hotels, raged for almost five months between late October 1975 and March 1976, and pitted the Christian (conservative) 'Lebanese Front' against the Muslim/Leftist 'Lebanese National Movement' (LNM) and fighters from the Palestinian Liberation Organisation (PLO). There were numerous luxury hotels in close proximity, including the Holiday Inn, the St George's Hotel, the Hilton, the Excelsior, the Phoenicia Intercontinental,[16] and the Palm Beach.[17] The battle, which was never resolved in a 'neat military fashion',[18] began on 24 October (eighteen days after 'Black Saturday')[19] when a small group of fighters known as the

---

[13] Dounia Salamé, 'On Memory and Commemoration in Beirut: The Holiday Inn in Bloom', CUJAH, Concordia University, Vol. IV, Essay 16, p. 1.

[14] Samir Kassir, *Beirut*, pp. 356–366.

[15] For an analysis of the worsening cycle of violence that led to the 'Battle of the Hotels', see Samir Khalaf, *Civil and Uncivil Violence in Lebanon: A History of the Internationalization of Communal Conflict*, pp. 227–238.

[16] For a beautifully illustrated history of the Hotel Phoenicia, see Mehanna T. Hadjithomas, *Le Phoenicia, un hôotel dans l'Histoire*, Tamyras, Beirut, 2012.

[17] Before the civil war (and the subsequent destruction of the hotel), the St George Hotel was reputed to be a key meeting place for intelligence agents, diplomats, journalists, wealthy businessmen, and politicians. For a detailed analysis of life in the hotel and the plots hatched there, see Said Aburish, *Beirut Spy: International Intrigue at the St. George Hotel Bar*, Bloomsbury Press, London, 1989.

[18] Edgar O' Balance, *The Civil War in Lebanon, 1975–1992*, London: MacMillan Press, 1998, p. 27.

[19] 'Black Saturday' (6 December 1975) marked a significant escalation in Lebanon's civil war, which had been raging since April 1975. On the morning of 6 December 1975, the

'Hawks of Zeidani', a faction of the *Al-Murabitoun*, the armed militia of the 'Independent Nasserite Movement' (INM) occupied the high-rise (and unfinished) *Burj Al-Murr* (Murr Tower), known more recently as the 'Rizk Tower', and used their base there as a position from which to attack Christian-held neighbourhoods in East Beirut.[20] By way of response, mainly Christian Maronite militias, known as the Phalange 'Kataeb Regulatory Forces' (KRF), took up positions around the hotel complex and in the nearby Holiday Inn, the Phoenicia Intercontinental, and the St George's Hotel.[21] The fierce and intense clashes went on for three days with little respite—the fighting intensifying after the Holiday Inn was attacked by the INM and the Muslim/Leftist militias (for whom the hotels represented symbols of social disparity and economic privilege).[22] Those staff and guests who were not as well prepared were pinned-down in the hotel during the clashes, and they were unable to leave. After a prolonged agony, they were, on 28 October, eventually evacuated.[23] Thereafter, clashes continued though a short ceasefire allowed guests and staff to retrieve their valuables from the hotel.[24] It was estimated that there were 200 people trapped in the Holiday Inn during the first five days of fighting, and once their evacu-

bodies of four senior members of the (predominantly Maronite Christian) Kataeb Party were discovered in an abandoned car in the mainly Christian East Beirut. The shocking discovery unleashed a wave of violence and murder carried out by Phalangist militiamen, who blamed the Muslim/Leftist militias for the killings. They established roadblocks in the parts of Beirut they controlled and stopped cars to identify Muslims. It remains unknown exactly how many Palestinians or Lebanese Muslims (mainly civilians) were killed by the Phalangists, but some estimates claim the number could be as high as 300. See Robert Fisk, *Pity the Nation: The Abduction of Lebanon* (Fourth Edition), Nation Books, New York, 2002, pp. 78–79.

[20] According to David Hirst, the one-time Middle East correspondent of the *Guardian*, 'They [the Muslim/Leftists] chose those targets mainly for strategic reasons: the hotels constituted the head of a Phalangist salient that projected into Muslim West Beirut.' See David Hirst, *Beware of Small States: Lebanon, Battleground of the Middle East*, Nation Books, New York, 2010, p. 111.

[21] *The Guardian*, London, 15 December 1975, p. 2.

[22] *The Guardian*, London, 12 December 1975, p. 2. According to Antoine J. Abraham, '[The Holiday Inn was] as symbol of Lebanon's pro-Western posture, economic prosperity and capitalism, which the leftists rejected. To them, it was a manifestation, or symbol, of American imperialism.' See Antoine J. Abraham, *The Lebanon War*, Westport: Praeger Publishers, 1996, p. 1.

[23] Beirut Domestic Service, 29 October 1975, Foreign Broadcast Information Service (FBIS), FBIS-MEA-75-210, p. 2.

[24] Cairo NEMA News Service, 2 November 1975, (FBIS), FBIS-MEA-75-212.

ation was complete, hostilities quickly resumed, despite attempts by the Lebanese government to demilitarise the hotel complex.[25]

By then, the St George's, the Phoenicia, and the Holiday Inn were in the hands of KRF, in spite of the mounting pressure from the INM and the Muslim/Leftists, who controlled the Excelsior and the Palm Beach hotels; Phoenicia Street, hitherto a glittering strip of nightclubs and discotheques, formed the frontline.[26] In November, the battle intensified, with the Phoenicia Hotel being the focus of the rival militias' attention. In an attempt to seize the building, the Lebanese Army engaged but was, ultimately, pushed back, while the KRF and the Muslim/Leftists continued with their attempts to wrest control of the Phoenicia Hotel and maintain control of the Alcazar Hotel.[27] In mid-December, the INM and the Muslim/Leftists achieved their objective.[28] During these battles, Hans Teufl, the general manager of the Phoenicia, was with staff when a shell was fired into the building, igniting a fire in the hotel's auditorium (which had been used as a store for mattresses). Teufl was among a number of staff killed. (In a further cruel twist, Bob Kulka, Teufl's predecessor, was killed in a plane crash in the same month.)[29]

With the Muslim/Leftists taking control of the Phoenicia and the approaches to the St George's Hotel, the KRF remained holed up in the Holiday Inn under constant fire from the Muslim/Leftist militias in the Phoenicia. The KRF still had access to electricity and supplies of food (which could be kept refrigerated), but the besieging Muslim/Leftists had no such luxuries; the Phoenicia had no electricity and, as a consequence, any food left in the hotel had long expired.[30] On 15 December 1975, the Lebanese Army again attempted to separate the warring factions and again met with little success, though the PLO leader, Yasser Arafat, eventually persuaded Muslim militias to leave the Rizk Tower and allow the Lebanese Army to occupy the building. The KRF, however, held their positions at the Holiday Inn, while the Muslim/Leftists remained in the St George's Hotel,[31] though the Lebanese Army would eventually take control of the hotel. By then, it was empty and battle-scarred. Today, most of the hotels

---

[25] Edgar O' Balance, *The Civil War in Lebanon, 1975–1992*, p. 28.
[26] *The Guardian*, London, 2 November 1975, p. 3.
[27] Edgar O' Balance, *The Civil War in Lebanon, 1975–1992*, p. 37.
[28] *The Guardian*, London, 15 December 1975, p. 2.
[29] James Potter, *World of Difference: 50 Years of Intercontinental Hotels and Its People*, London: Weidenfeld Nicholson, 1996, p. 159.
[30] *The Guardian*, London, 15 December 1975, p. 2.
[31] Edgar O' Balance, *The Civil War in Lebanon, 1975–1992*, p. 38.

have been fully reconstructed, though the Holiday Inn remains as it was at the end of the 'Battle of the Hotels', a stark symbolic reminder of the country's civil war.[32]

THE PRESTIGE OR POLITICAL TARGET

In addition to being of strategic importance, hotels represent 'prestige targets' for terrorist groups, the bombing of which is likely to generate significant publicity. Frequently, the targets are not the hotels per se but the guests, deemed to represent an occupying force, perhaps because the hotel has been commandeered by them or is utilised by the 'ex-patriot' community. In the decade following the end of the Second World War, representatives of the British government, often located in or frequenting hotels, were considered legitimate targets for domestic armed groups. In the postwar British colonies (or mandates), numerous hotels came under attack.

The 1946 bombing of the King David Hotel in Jerusalem, then the headquarters of the British Mandate authorities in Palestine, by the Zionist paramilitary organisation, *The Irgun*, was a direct attack on what the latter deemed an occupying force. Similarly, the bombing of the Semiramis Hotel by the Jewish paramilitary organisation (that would later become the core of the Israeli Defence Force—IDF), *Haganah*, was an explicit attempt to undermine the British. And in other areas where British troops were stationed attacks on hotels were commonplace. A British delegation was also attacked, not for the first time, by the Greek Cypriot 'National Organisation of Cypriot Fighters' (*Ethniki Organosis Kyprion Agonastin*—EOKA) at the Ledra Palace Hotel in Nicosia, Cyprus, on 26 November 1955, during the annual 'Caledonian Society Ball', when a bomb exploded inside the hotel's ballroom. And while there were no casualties (though a number of guests were injured), the Caledonian Ball bomb sent a message of intent from EOKA, who were determined to drive out of Cyprus. It was symbolic because it was 'a psychological attack on some of the cultural assumptions that underpinned the colonial way of life' and was executed at a place frequented by the British.[33]

---

[32] The Holiday Inn may well be reconstructed in the future, as the Phoenicia was in 2000 (only to be badly damaged again in 2005, when a large car bomb, which killed Rafiq Hariri, the Lebanese Prime Minister, was detonated outside the hotel). The St George's was also very badly damaged in the same explosion.

[33] Tabitha Morgan, *A Sweet and Bitter Island: A History of the British in Cyprus*, London: IB Tauris, 2010, p. 222.

In the 1970s and 1980s, attacks on hotels, seen by the assailants as legitimate targets, continued. The Provisional Irish Republican Army (PIRA—more commonly abbreviated to IRA) bombings of the Europa Hotel in Belfast were an attempt to generate publicity, and their leadership were acutely aware that the press and, often, politicians were in the hotel, and any assault on it would guarantee front-page news (the 1984 bombing of the Grand Hotel in Brighton, however, was a more audacious and explicit attempt to murder the leadership of the then British government, though it also served such a purpose). As a consequence, the Europa Hotel became a frequent target, awarding the hotel the distinctly dubious honour of being 'Europe's most bombed' hotel. Some of its regular guests dubbed the Europa 'the hardboard hotel', its windows frequently boarded up after a bombing.

The Europa played an important role, being a networking hub for journalists, politicians, and representatives of paramilitary groups. Described by Chris Ryder, the *Sunday Times* journalist, as 'the crossroads of intrigue', it was a place where myriad political, military, and paramilitary figures converged.[34] But it functioned in the midst of a conflict where there was no distinct frontline, only an *invisible* frontline in a conflict in which armed groups operated in the shadows and was thus exposed. While in this context, the sources of that danger may not have been immediately evident but they were chillingly omnipresent. In just over two decades, the hotel was bombed thirty-three times by the IRA, with intermittent attacks taking place between the opening of the hotel in 1971 and the IRA/Loyalist paramilitary ceasefire in August 1994.[35]

The Europa was, however, originally conceived in a more positive social, political, and economic environment. When the Grand Metropolitan Hotels Group[36] announced in 1966 that they would construct a large new hotel on Great Victoria Street in the centre of the city (on the site of the former Great Northern Railway station), it was envisaged that the Europa would be a

---

[34] A key component in Belfast's commercial development, the Europa was targeted because it represented both a crucial asset of the city's business community and a symbol of the British government's attempts to weaken the sentiment for conflict by promoting economic development and prosperity in Belfast.

[35] *The Independent*, London, 30 November 2011, p. 30.

[36] Grand Metropolitan Hotels was founded by the London-born entrepreneur Maxwell Joseph who having owned his own estate agent's company and spent a stint in the Royal Engineers during the Second World War, bought the Mandeville Hotel in London before going on to acquire a number of other hotels under the umbrella of the Grand Metropolitan Hotels PLC.

shining example of Belfast's 'urban renaissance' and a physical manifestation of a city 'on the up'.[37] The architects, the London-based firm, Sidney Kaye, Eric Firkin and Partners, were commissioned to design the hotel in 1968, and construction commenced in the autumn of 1969. When the hotel was conceived, relations between the Protestant and Catholic communities, despite historical enmity, were generally stable, but by the time construction commenced, a matter of weeks after the British Army had been deployed to maintain law and order in Northern Ireland, the political landscape had changed significantly.

It would be almost two years before the hotel opened its doors to its first paying guests, but in July 1971, the 12-storey, 210-room Europa opened to significant fanfare.[38] The interior of the hotel was undoubtedly luxurious for the standards of the time, with en suite bathrooms in every room and impressive spaces for business meetings, weddings, and large social gatherings.[39] Reviews of the building's design—quite revolutionary for Belfast—were largely positive, and Grand Metropolitan went to significant lengths to emphasise not only the revolutionary design of the building but also the unique services offered within. The Europa was, according to their then public relations officer, 'a visually attractive and dramatic addition to the [Belfast] skyline'.[40] Not everyone agreed. Some of the hotel's more vociferous critics regarded it with outright disdain, one commentator from the *Irish Times* denouncing the Europa's modern-

---

[37] The roots of the Europa Hotel can be traced back to 1966 when the Grand Metropolitan Hotels group purchased, through the Northern Ireland (Stormont) government, six hotels which had been the property of the Ulster Transport Authority (UTA)—the Midland in Belfast, the City in Derry, the Slieve Donard in Newcastle, the Northern Counties in Portrush, the Laharna in Larne, and the Rostrevor Hotel—were sold for £600,000, on the basis that the Grand Metropolitan Group would build a major hotel in Belfast. The transaction caused some controversy, with opposition MPs in the Stormont parliament arguing that the six hotels had been 'given away'. The same six hotels were sold to the Hastings Hotel Group (who would purchase in Europa in 1994) in May 1971 prior to the opening of the Hotel Europa, which cost an estimated £2.5 million to build. See *The Irish Times*, Dublin, 8 May 1971, p. 9.

[38] Clive Scoular, *In the Headlines: The Story of the Belfast Europa Hotel*, Appletree Press, Belfast, 2003, p. 23.

[39] *Ibid*, p. 25.

[40] Briefing note by Lynn Stewart (Public Relations Officer for the Hotel Europa) entitled 'Above All Else: The Belfast Europa', May 1971, Hotel Europa archives.

ist architectural style as 'a symbol of alien decadence' and 'an extravagant affront to a working class city'.[41]

But by the time the Europa opened its doors, however, the polished grandeur of the building stood in stark contrast to the shifting economic and political context in Belfast (and throughout Northern Ireland), which had changed substantially since work on the building had begun in 1969. 'The Troubles' that emerged in the late 1960s were a result of the tensions generated by the political system of Northern Ireland: they were complex, fluid, and involved myriad actors. They lasted, at least formally, until the signing of the 'Good Friday Agreement' in April 1998, and involved violent campaigns by Catholic paramilitary groups, in particular the Irish Republican Army (IRA),[42] Loyalist paramilitaries such as the Ulster Volunteer Force (UVF) and the Ulster Freedom Fighters (UFF), the British Army, the Army of the Republic of Ireland, and a plethora of political parties and groups. It was a conflict in which the Europa Hotel found itself, on occasion, at the epicentre. Nevertheless, throughout 'The Troubles' and the numerous attacks on the hotel, the management and staff stubbornly refused to yield, and the hotel remained (largely) open to guests even in the worst of times.

The construction of the Europa coincided with the rise of the 'Civil Rights Campaign', which had gained momentum by the mid- to late 1960s. The Northern Ireland Civil Rights Association (NICRA), an organisation influenced by the Civil Rights Movement in the USA, had embarked upon a campaign increasingly characterised by street protests. While the core of their campaigns was essentially grounded in grievances driven by discrimination against Catholics, NICRA was perceived by many Protestant Loyalists as simply a Trojan horse for nationalist Republicans to further a nationalist political agenda—their real aim, it was alleged, was to reunite Ulster with the 'Free State' to the south.

Loyalist paramilitary groups were created (or reformed) in the mid-1960s, as a response to what they argued was a rising Irish nationalism among the Catholic communities of Ulster. The most prominent of these was the UVF, led by Gusty Spence, a former British soldier, who had served in Cyprus in the 1950s before returning to Belfast where he worked as a stager (he built the scaffolding, inside which ships were constructed)

---

[41] *The Irish Times*, Dublin, 1 July 1981, p. 9.
[42] For an objective and readable account of the history of the IRA, see Peter Taylor, *The Provos: The IRA and Sinn Fein*, Bloomsbury Books, London, 1997.

in the Harland and Wolff shipyard, famous for having built the *Titanic* during the golden years of shipbuilding in the city.[43] The group, formed in 1965, took their name from the Ulster Volunteer militia which had been created by Edward Carson, the leader of the Ulster Unionist Party (UUP), in 1912 to resist 'Home Rule' for Ireland (which was then formally part of the UK). Loyal to Edward Carson, the leader of the UUP, the UV—comprising various groups of volunteers—was synthesised into the 'UVF' in 1913.[44] Stepping up their resistance to Dublin, each member signed the 'Ulster Covenant', which committed each and every UVF member to the struggle to depend on (Protestant) Ulster and the province's place within the UK. The UVF grew to approximately 90,000 members, well organised and committed.[45] However, with the outbreak of the First World War in August 1914, many members of the UVF went to fight for the British Army (embedded into the thirty-sixth 'Ulster Division') on the Western Front. Collectively, they paid a high price.

By 1969, clashes between NICRA demonstrators and the Protestant-dominated police force, the Royal Ulster Constabulary (RUC), and Loyalists were commonplace; the worst of these taking place in the Bogside area of Derry/Londonderry in August 1969. By the middle of the month, the British Army were deployed in Derry and Belfast in an attempt to stem the rising tide of violence and to protect the Catholic community from Loyalist attacks. However, while initially welcomed by the Catholic community, relations between the British Army and those they were ostensibly protecting quickly deteriorated into mutual distrust and, eventually, mutual loathing. To the militant elements within the Catholic community, the presence of British troops was interpreted as the return of a force that had traditionally oppressed Republicans. As a consequence, a revitalised

---

[43] According to Steve Bruce, Gusty Spence came from 'a staunch Orange Order family, well known and well connected on the Shankill Road. His brother, William Spence, was a major figure in the local Unionist Party and was election agent for James Kilfedder, who won the West Belfast Westminster seat in 1964.' See Steve Bruce, *The Red Hand: Protestant Paramilitaries in Northern Ireland*, Oxford University Press, Oxford, 1992, p. 15.

[44] For a detailed history of the UV and UVF between 1910 and 1922, see Timothy Bowman, *Carson's Army: The Ulster Volunteer Force, 1910–1922*, Manchester University Press, Manchester, 2007. For the UVF role in the First World War, see Richard S. Grayson, *Belfast Boys: How Unionists and Nationalists Fought and Died Together in the First World War*, Continuum, London, 2009.

[45] Steve Bruce, *The Red Hand: Protestant Paramilitaries in Northern Ireland*, p. 9.

and militant republicanism, in the form of the Provisional IRA, re-emerged and by 1970 they were essentially at war with the British Army.

The Europa would not remain immune to the deteriorating political situation. Indeed, the hotel was directly targeted by the IRA, who saw it as a symbol of a Belfast (and of a British imperialism) that they despised.[46] (As Robert Fisk pointed out, 'from the Falls Road area you can look down the grubby streets of Catholic Belfast and there, in the distance is the hotel, with its nightclub lights blazing'.)[47] The first bombing of the Europa, one month prior to its opening, was to be the first of many. That the hotel was to be targeted so frequently by the IRA was no surprise; as a symbol of the Northern Ireland government's policy of investing in the economic development in the centre of Belfast, the hotel became an attractive target, and attacking the hotel would not only impact upon the (predominantly Protestant) business community but also generate the publicity the IRA craved. The first explosion, on 3 July 1971 (prior to the hotel's opening), did little real damage, though one member of staff was seriously injured.[48] It was a dark portent of things to come—the Europa would go on to be bombed on more than thirty occasions.

The hotel's first manager was the charismatic Harper Brown, a man with two decades of experience in catering and hostelry. He would become a central figure in the drama played out in the hotel throughout the 1970s, personifying the Europa's struggle to remain viable.[49] Described in *The Guardian* as 'a dapper, moustachioed man who could have stepped from the pages of a Graham Greene novel', Brown was a bon vivant, well groomed, and with a passion for sharp dressing and jazz music. He was an ever-present in the hotel, staying permanently in a suite on the seventh floor.[50] But Brown may have got more than he had bargained for when

[46] *The Irish Times*, Dublin, 21 December 1976, p. 5. See also Martin Dillon 'The Europa Hotel: A Symbol', *The European Magazine*, London, May 2003, p. 66.

[47] *The Times*, London, 23 July 1972, p. 2.

[48] *The Guardian*, London, 3 July 1971, p. 18.

[49] Briefing note by Lynn Stewart (Public Relations Officer for the Hotel Europa) entitled 'Above All Else: The Belfast Europa', May 1971, Hotel Europa archives.

[50] *The Guardian*, London, 14 July 1993 (Supplement), p. A2. The Graham Greene character the article refers to is almost certainly a reference to Harper Brown's namesake, known simply as 'Brown' in Greene's 'The Comedians'. Set in Papa Doc Duvalier's Haiti, Brown is the novel's main protagonist and narrator. He is the owner of the Hotel Trianon in Port-au-Prince (which was, allegedly, inspired by the Hotel Oloffson in the city), which is the venue for a numerous political intrigues. Brown eventually finds himself out of favour with the government and has to develop his own, often cunning strategies to survive, though he,

Image 2.1 The Europa's manager, Harper Brown, outside the hotel circa 1972. (Photo: The Hotel Europa, Belfast)

he accepted the post of general manager at the Europa, and subsequent events would stretch his management skills more than he might have expected (Image 2.1).

The first indication that the Hotel Europa might become more than simply a random target for the IRA came two months after opening.[51] On

unlike Harper Brown, is eventually forced to leave the hotel. See Graham Greene, *The Comedians*, The Bodley Head, London, 1966.

[51] *The Guardian*, London, 23 October 1971, p. 1.

22 October 1972, a bomb was planted in the Europa by two IRA operatives, who had driven to the front of the hotel and entered the reception area where they held eight people at gunpoint while they deposited an 'anti-handling' bomb at the hotel's reception.[52] A British Army disposal team, led by Major George Styles, was then called in to defuse the device, which they succeeded in doing after a seven-hour operation.[53]

Of course, the worsening security situation in Belfast dictated that the 'normal' guests were becoming a far less regular fixture. They were, instead, replaced by a small army of journalists, mainly from mainland UK, who would use the hotel as a base. Most would check in and opt for rooms on the upper floors of the hotel, with many avoiding rooms that faced Great Victoria Street (where many of the bombs had exploded) or the first four floors of the building where their windows were likely to be blown out by a blast. The hotel, with its twenty telephone lines and a tenth-floor darkroom for developing photographs, which could be utilised by journalists to send their daily dispatches, became Northern Ireland's link with the outside world.[54] Alongside the journalists, the lobby and the bars of the Europa filled with myriad guests, from plain-clothes police officers to politicians to representatives of paramilitary groups.[55] On occasions when events in Northern Ireland were headline news, the hotel would be full—and almost entirely with journalists and TV crews.[56]

While staying at the Europa, the guests could enjoy all that the hotel had to offer. The 'Beefeater' restaurant (replete with a 'sumptuous scarlet décor [which] makes this an exceptionally elegant restaurant') was a particular favourite; guests would be served by waiting staff adorned in mock Beefeater outfits.[57] Those seeking to wind down after a tough day on the streets of Belfast could do so by sinking a few pints of the Europa's own beer (Europa Bass Ale) in the 'Whip and Saddle' public bar, and for entertainment into the early morning hours, there was also a surprising touch of glamour in the shape of the 'The Penthouse', a bar on the top floor of the

---

[52] *The Times,* London, 23 October 1971, p. 1.

[53] Major Styles was awarded the George Cross in January 1972 for his bravery. See *The Times,* London, 12 January 1972, p. 1. For a profile of Major Styles, see *The Guardian,* London, 31 October 1971, p. 2.

[54] *The People,* Dublin, 19 August 1974, p. 4.

[55] Interview with Chris Ryder (*Sunday Times*) in BBC Northern Ireland documentary 'Bombs, Bullets and Business as Usual', Director: Richard Weller, Waddell Media Productions, 2011.

[56] *The Irish Times,* Dublin, 4 July 1974, p. 5.

[57] Text from Hotel Europa guest information pack from 1974, Hotel Europa archive.

hotel, where guests could enjoy 'the most sophisticated scene in town'.[58] Serving cocktails there were the rather scantily clad (at least, for the standards of the time) 'Penthouse Poppets', a less risqué variant of the Playboy bunnies.[59] The 'Carriage Room', conversely, served mainly tea and coffee and was a more modest and sobering affair.

But these distractions did not, ultimately, detract from the fact that the Europa could be targeted at any time. The hotel was bombed several times in 1974, and matters worsened throughout 1975, with the first major attack on the hotel taking place on 23 January, causing extensive damage.[60] On 1 December 1975, a devastating blast on Great Victoria Street badly damaged the front of the hotel, buckled the lift shafts, and almost completely destroyed the second and third floors.[61] As a consequence, the Europa was forced to close for more than a year, and the cost of refurbishment was estimated by Harper Brown to be in the region of £2.4 million, almost as much as the hotel had cost to build six years earlier.[62] Security was subsequently the order of the day, and by the time the hotel had reopened 'Fortress Europa' was surrounded by barricades and barbed wire to stop unidentified cars driving up to the front entrance. Security inside the building was also tightened with guests frequently being subject to body searches upon entering to the hotel.[63] Remarkably, however, no one was killed in the hotel as a result of the IRA bombs, a fact the hotel management did their best to emphasise.[64]

The mid-1970s represented a nadir for the Europa, but while the political circumstances in Northern Ireland remained dire as the 1980s dawned, the situation for the hotel (and for the commercial centre of Belfast) generally improved. The death of hunger striker (and British MP)

---

[58] *Ibid*, Text from Hotel Europa guest information pack from 1974, Hotel Europa archive.

[59] Scoular, *In the Headlines: The Story of the Belfast Europa Hotel*, pp. 25–26.

[60] RUC Police Report in respect of Malicious Damage to Property: Grand Metropolitan Hotels: Belfast Europa Hotel—Great Victoria Street, Belfast, 23 January 1975, PRONI File No: NIO/24/1/22 A.

[61] Memorandum from A T Bateman Esq (Loss Adjusters) to Northern Ireland Office, 'Subject: Grand Metropolitan Hotels Ltd.: Belfast Europa Hotel', 29 December 1975, PRONI File No: NIO/24/1/22 A.

[62] *The Irish Times*, Dublin, 21 December 1976, p. 5.

[63] Martin Dillon 'The Europa Hotel: A Symbol', p. 68.

[64] In an interview with the Irish magazine, *The People* (their correspondent claiming that Brown 'runs the Europa more like a command post than a hotel') in the wake of the July attacks, Brown defiantly stated that 'We haven't lost a guest yet…we're proud of that', *The People*, Dublin, 19 August 1974, p. 4.

Bobby Sands in May 1981 produced a major political and security crisis in which the Europa was again at the epicentre, but it was not the only hotel in the IRA's sights. They would hit a number of prestige targets on the British mainland, perhaps the most 'prestigious' being the Grand Hotel on the seafront in Brighton during the 1984 Conservative Party Conference (which was taking place in the nearby Brighton Centre). The IRA had already detonated bombs in central London in the years preceding the Brighton bombing (Hyde Park and Regent's Park in July 1982 and the Harrods department store in December 1982 being the most high profile), but this was by far their most audacious attempt—to strike at the very heart of a British government.[65]

Their target would be the prestigious Grand Hotel (built in 1864 and designed by the English architect John Whichcord Jr), one of the jewels of the Brighton seafront. It was here where senior members of the cabinet, including Margaret Thatcher, were residing during the conference, oblivious of the dangers that would soon become evident. The bomb, fitted with a 'long-delay timer', had been concealed in bathroom of room 629 by the IRA operative Patrick Magee (who checked into the hotel under a pseudonym, Roy Walsh) during a short stay in the hotel between 14 and 17 September, almost a month before the conference.[66] On the morning of 12 October 1984, the bomb detonated. Earlier that evening, party delegates had gathered for the 'Agent's Ball', which was attended briefly by Margaret Thatcher. At the party's end, some continued the merriment in the hotel bar. At just before 3.00 am, however, the bomb detonated,

---

[65] It was not, however, the first time that the British political elite had been targeted by Irish nationalist groups. In June 1974, the IRA detonated a bomb near the Houses of Parliament, and on 30 March 1979 one of Margaret Thatcher's closest confidants (and a man who was predicted by many to be the next Northern Ireland Secretary in the event of a Conservative Party victory in the forthcoming general election), Airey Neave, was killed by a bomb placed under the rear of his car by the Irish National Liberation Army (INLA). The bomb exploded as he exited the Palace of Westminster car park and he died soon after being freed from the wreckage of the car.

[66] Patrick Magee was born in Belfast in 1951 but left the city at the age of four when his parents moved to Norwich in England. He returned to Belfast in 1969, joined the IRA, and was interned between 1973 and 1975 for his activities. Following his release, he developed an expertise in bomb making, making him a perfect candidate for IRA operations in the UK. He was originally based in Blackpool in the north-west of England, where he had been tasked with attacking a British Army barracks, but he soon realised he was under surveillance by British Intelligence (MI5), so did not execute the operation. He subsequently played a key role in planning and executing the Brighton bombing.

blowing a gaping hole in the upper floors of the building and collapsing a chimney stack, the weight of which sent debris crashing through the lower floors. On the first-floor suite, the British Prime Minister Margaret Thatcher (who was still awake) and her husband Denis narrowly avoided injury.[67] Other colleagues were less fortunate. Thatcher's close associate, Norman Tebbit (then Trade and Industry Secretary), was badly injured, while his wife, Margaret, was left paralysed. Others fared even worse; five lost their lives and thirty-one were injured, some seriously.

The events shook Margaret Thatcher, and she was quickly spirited away to a nearby police station. While there, however, she announced to the waiting press corps that the conference would go on. Alasdair McAlpine, the Conservative Party treasurer who had hosted the previous evening's party, arranged for the local branch of Marks and Spencer to open early so that conference delegates could be provided with new clothing to replace those rendered unobtainable by the blast. Margaret Thatcher, despite receiving advice from her security detail not to do so, insisted upon walking to the conference—a demonstration of defiance to the IRA. Her subsequent conference speech, in which she declared that 'The fact that we are gathered here now, shocked but composed and determined, is a sign that not only that this attack has failed, but that all attempts to destroy democracy by terrorism will fail', remains one of the defining moments of her long premiership.[68] Her handling of the bombing, and her determination to continue with the conference in its wake, ensured that her popularity increased to levels akin to those she enjoyed in the immediate period following the 1982 Falklands War. Eight months after the bombing, in June 1985, Patrick Magee, dubbed by the British media as 'The Brighton Bomber', was arrested in Glasgow and sentenced to serve eight life sentences (though he would serve only fourteen years in prison, released as part of the 1998 'Good Friday Agreement').[69]

---

[67] Margaret Thatcher, *The Downing Street Years*, HarperCollins, London, p. 380.

[68] *Ibid*, p. 382.

[69] Andy McSmith, *No Such Thing as Society: A History of Britain in the 1980s*, London: Constable Press, 2010. Magee was eventually released from prison in 1999 as part of the 'Good Friday Agreement'. While in prison he married the American novelist Barbara Byer (the two had initially struck up a relationship by means of written correspondence) and completed a PhD thesis on fictional representations of 'The Troubles'. He expressed regret that 'people got hurt and killed because of actions taken in a war time situation' but maintained that he was acting as any soldier would during wartime. He was later 'forgiven' for the Brighton bombing by the Conservative MP and committed Christian, Harvey Thomas, who

By the time of the events in Brighton, the situation for the Europa had improved markedly. But in the latter years of the 1980s, the hotel's then owners (Northern Emerald) appeared to be bringing the Europa back to life, but the company, following an ambitious (and unsuccessful) expansion, went into receivership in April 1991. The future of the Europa was again thrown into doubt. The receivers were making good progress in their negotiations with a number of international hotel brands (such as the Marriot, Jury's Inn, and the Holiday Inn group), and were confident that a sale could be concluded. But during these negotiations, the Europa was targeted by the IRA once again. On 4 December 1991, an IRA bomb concealed in a hijacked van in Glengall Street blew a gaping hole in the side of the building, severely damaging the lower floors and rendering the hotel's function rooms completely out of service.[70] The hotel was badly damaged again on 20 May 1993, the day after local council elections, when a 1000-lb bomb was detonated on Glengall Street.[71] The bomb badly damaged the Europa and the headquarters of the UUP, and blew a hole in the newly restored Grand Opera House.[72] The receivers were now desperate to confirm a buyer, and William Hastings stepped forward as the hotel's saviour. The Europa was formally bought by the Hastings Hotel Group on 3 August 1993, but such was the additional damage wrought by the May IRA bombing that it was sold for a mere £4.4 million (it had been valued, prior to the May bombing, at around £10 million).[73] It was a significant risk for Hastings, but it was one that would prove his instincts were right. After a major refurbishment, the Europa partially reopened its doors for guests in February 1994.[74] It

---

was in the Grand Hotel during the bombing. See BBC News, 'Brighton bomb victim: Why I forgive', BBC News website, 8 August 2011, http://news.bbc.co.uk/1/hi/uk/1480081.stm (last accessed 21 June 2014).

[70] *The Guardian*, London, 6 December 1991, p. 6. See also *The Irish Times*, Dublin, 10 December 1991, p. 15.

[71] J. Bowyer Bell, *The Secret Army: The IRA*, Transaction Publishers, New Jersey, 1997, p. 642.

[72] *The Guardian*, London, 21 May 1993, p. 22. The Europa was not the only hotel to be bombed that week. On 22 May, the Drumkeen Hotel in south Belfast was attacked. In the early morning of the 22nd, the hotel's night porter, Tommy Black, had received a warning from the IRA informing him that a car bomb would detonate outside the hotel in 30 min. The hotel was then evacuated and the guests, including a couple who had been married, were led to safety. See *The Guardian*, London, 24 May 1993, p. 4.

[73] *The Belfast Telegraph*, Belfast, 25 August 2011, p. 16.

[74] Hotel Europa Marketing Strategy, June 1994–March 1995 (prepared by P. Wilson, M. Williamson, J. Toner), June 1994, Hotel Europa archives, p. 1.

was a fortuitous time to do so. After twenty-five years of conflict, the IRA announced, on 31 August, 'a complete cessation of military operations'; by October, the UVF, UDA, and the 'Red Hand Commando' announced that they, too, had called a ceasefire.

The Europa would, again, play a key role in the political life of Northern Ireland—though this time it would be the forum for peace negotiations. (An unprecedented meeting between the representative of the Loyalist paramilitaries, Gusty Spence, and the Irish Deputy Prime Minister, Dick Spring, took place in the Europa soon after.) So the Europa would, as before, be rather central to events in Belfast and Northern Ireland. The first major event of the 'new era' was the Flax Trust Ball, a gala evening for around 500 local and international dignitaries. In December 1994, the then British Prime Minister John Major; the US Commerce Secretary Ron Brown; and several US politicians held a 'black tie dinner' in the hotel as part of a two-day international investment conference.[75] The Clinton administration placed the Democrat Senator George Mitchell in Belfast to chair the peace talks, and he thus began a four-year 'residency' in the Europa. In November 1995, the then US President, Bill Clinton (and his wife Hilary) checked into the hotel for their stay in Belfast, albeit only for one night. That Clinton chose to stay in the 'most bombed hotel in Europe' was symbolically and politically significant. A suite on the tenth floor was redecorated in advance of his visit and was subsequently named 'The Clinton Suite' in honour of his night spent at the Europa.[76]

Another hotel that found itself at the heart of intercommunal conflict involving the British Army was the elegant colonial-style Ledra Palace, once the most exclusive hotel in the Cypriot capital, Nicosia. Designed by the German Jewish architect Benjamin Günsberg and built by the Cyprus Hotels Group, construction of the hotel began in 1947 and took two years to complete. The Ledra Palace's opening in October 1949 attended by numerous dignitaries, such as the British Governor of Cyprus, Sir Andrew Wright, and the Vice-Mayor of Nicosia, George Poulios. The Ledra was the island's first 'deluxe' hotel, with centrally heated rooms, telephones in each room, and a wide range of facilities, such as conference and reading rooms and a ballroom. The addition of a swimming pool, a children's play area, and tennis courts served only to increase the reputation of the Ledra Palace. The hotel did, however, acquire the reputation of being a haven for British colonialists and was the target of the (aforementioned) attack by EOKA in November 1955.

---

[75] *The Irish Times*, Dublin, 14 December 1994, p. 7.
[76] *The Irish Times*, Dublin, 4 December 1995, p. 4.

By 1963, however, the political dynamics had changed, and as the intercommunal troubles between the island's Greeks and Turks worsened, the hotel became the base for foreign journalists. The following year, the United Nations Peacekeeping Force in Cyprus (UNFICYP) arrived in Cyprus in attempt to impose some semblance of stability and order. On occasion, the hotel would be at the centre of events. In April 1964, for example, scuffles broke out between UNFICYP and Greek Cypriot police (both with and without uniforms) over the erection of Greek Cypriot barricades which the UNFICYP had insisted be removed.[77] And the hotel was again central to events following the Turkish airborne invasion of northern Cyprus in July 1974 (ostensibly to create a 'zone of safety' for the Turkish Cypriot community). The UNFICYP received information that the hotel was to be attacked, as it was alleged by the Turks that Greek Cypriot paramilitary forces were operating from the hotel. Seven hours after the invasion, a number of armed Greek Cypriots belonging to the 'Greek Cypriot National Guard' remained in the hotel. Having raised the Greek flag and set up sniping positions on the four corners of the hotel, they embarked upon a firefight which lasted throughout the evening of 20 July (the remaining guests cowered in the basement throughout).[78] In order to avoid further bloodshed, the UNFICYP moved in, evacuated the remaining guests, and placed the Ledra Palace under their control.[79] As the guests had fled quickly, they had no time to settle their bills, so the hotel management sent them an invoice reminding them of the need to pay regardless. The letter was published in *The Observer* newspaper and read:

> We hope that you have had a pleasant journey back home and that your stay at the Ledra Palace Hotel was an enjoyable one, up to the unfortunate moment when the Turkish invasion broke out on Saturday, 20 July 1974, for which I am sure we will all have a memorable experience. You will appreciate that the hotel guests had to be evacuated with the assistance of the United Nations peacekeeping force on Sunday, 21 July, and we have therefore invoiced your account up to 19 July 1974....Enclosed please find your hotel invoice to the amount of....for which an early settlement will be much appreciated. Thanking you in advance, and we look forward to welcoming you back at the Ledra Palace Hotel on [sic] better conditions in due course.[80]

---

[77] *The Guardian*, London, 18 April 1964, p. 9.
[78] *The Observer*, London, 21 July 1974, p. 2.
[79] Olga Demetriou, 'The Militarization of Opulence: Engendering a Conflict Heritage Site', *International Feminist Journal of Politics*, Vol. 1, No. 14, 2012, p. 63.
[80] *The Observer*, London, 15 September 1974, p. 36.

Thereafter, the Ledra Palace fell directly within the boundaries of the 'UN Buffer Zone', and was thus largely used as a barracks for peacekeepers. The hotel remained a UN base between 1974 and 1997, hosting, on occasion, high-level meetings between Greek Cypriot and Turkish Cypriot leaders and foreign delegations.[81] These days, the hotel hosts numerous peace-building projects that bring both sides of the Cypriot divide together. From 2008 onward, the Ledra played a new role—a designated crossing point on the 'Green Line' still separating the Republic of Cyprus from the Turkish Republic of Northern Cyprus.

The attacks on the aforementioned hotels had at their heart a political logic in that they were attempts to damage or destroy prestige (economic) targets or key political figures. The targets were, in many respects, 'part of the game', engaged, to a greater or lesser extent, in the politics of these conflicts, and this has been true of some of the more recent attacks on hotels. Al-Qaeda's attack on the Canal Hotel in Baghdad in 2003,[82] which was then the headquarters of the United Nations Assistance Mission in Iraq (UNAMI), the January 2008 attack on the Serena Hotel in Kabul, the June 2009 terrorist attacks on the Pearl Continental Hotel in Peshawar, and the June 2011 attack on the Intercontinental Hotel in Kabul were motivated by the presence within the buildings of staff belonging to international organisations.[83] Hotels hosting these 'internationals' were thus frequently targeted, and in 2009 a *Stratfor* report highlighted the growing risk to staff working for international organisations, noting that terrorists would likely identify the hotels that hosted meetings, parties, or conferences and that they 'offer the best chance for militants in many countries to kill or injure large numbers of Westerners in a single attack...the casual-

---

[81] On one such occasion in October 1993, the British Prime Minister John Major spoke at the Ledra Palace Hotel about the need to find a solution to the 'Cyprus Question'. The British delegation was led by Queen Elizabeth, who had her car windscreen smashed by a Greek Cypriot protestor. She was still reviled among some within the community for failing to commute the sentences of nine EOKA fighters who were hanged by the British during the anti-colonial struggles of the 1950s. See *The Times*, London, 21 October 1993, p. 5.

[82] The attack on the Canal Hotel resulted in the deaths of 22 people, the vast majority of which were UNAMI staff. Those killed included the UN Special Representative in Iraq, Sergio Vieira de Mello, an esteemed Brazilian UN diplomat who had served in Bangladesh, Cambodia, Bosnia and East Timor, among others. Another attack on a UNAMI base three days later hastened the UN's withdrawal from Iraq.

[83] *The Times*, London, 29 June 2011, p. 5.

ties could even include local business and government leaders, considered high-value targets especially if they are seen as collaborators'.[84]

Increasingly, however, hotels that do not fit this model (the hotel as a *political space* which hosts political actors) have become legitimate targets for terrorist groups. The strategy of attacking hotels to generate publicity or strike at the heart of 'agents of colonialism' has long existed, but the more recent Islamist attacks on 'soft targets', essentially hostelries that host tourists with no explicit political involvement, are of a quite different character. The attacks on the Paradise Hotel Resort in Mombasa; the Moevenpick and Ghazala Gardens hotels in Sharm el-Sheikh, Egypt, in 2005; the Taj Mahal Palace and Oberoi Trident in Mumbai, India, in 2008; the Corinthia Hotel in Tripoli, Libya, in January 2015; and the Imperial Hotel and Hotel Club Riu Bellevue in Sousse, Tunisia, in June of the same year are the most striking examples of the targeting of tourist hotels with no apparent political character other than the fact they host Western guests.[85]

While hotels have become frequent targets, they can, conversely, serve a more positive function in times of crisis. They can be forums for negotiations, serving a function as *neutral spaces* that can facilitate meetings and negotiations between warring factions and diplomats attempting to broker peace. Fregonese and Ramadan have noted how hotels play a function as part of the 'infrastructure of peace-building', citing the examples of the Geneva Intercontinental Hotel (utilised as the base for negotiations between the Islamic Republic of Iran and the P5 + 1 countries); hotels in the Egyptian Red Sea resort of Sharm el-Sheik, which hosted Israeli-Palestinian peace talks in the 1990s; and Nicosia's (defunct) Ledra Palace, which has played a new role as a space that has facilitated discussions about the 'Cyprus problem'.[86]

Hotels can also serve as temporary sanctuaries for refugees fleeing fighting; places where large number can be accommodated in a time of crisis (often in cellars or large function rooms). In recent times, hotels have again been used to house refugees, with some, such as the 'Captain Elias

---

[84] Stratfor, 'Special Security Report: The Militant Threat to Hotels', 8 September 2009, p. 5.

[85] BBC News, 'Libya hotel attack: five foreigners among nine killed', 28 January 2015, http://www.bbc.co.uk/news/world-africa-31001094 [last accessed on 16 February 2015]. For the subsequent securitisation of hotels, see Debbie Lisle, Debbie, 'Frontline leisure: Securitizing tourism in the War on Terror', *Security Dialogue*, 2013, Vol. 44 No. 2, pp. 134–136.

[86] Sara Fregonese & Adam Ramadan, 'Hotel Geopolitics', p. 795.

Hotel' on the Greek island of Kos being used to shelter refugees from Syria, Iraq, Afghanistan, and Bangladesh, though such a pattern is not unusual in times of conflict.[87] During the JNA/Montenegrin attack on Dubrovnik and its environs in 1991, for example, the basements of some of the hotels on the coast, such as the Libertas (now owned by the Rixos chain), were used as shelters for civilians fleeing the JNA/Montenegrin attack on the city and its environs.[88] Once one of the most prestigious hotels on the Dalmatian coast, the Libertas was completely destroyed, and six people were killed in the grounds of the hotel. But the large basement became a temporary home of hundreds of refugees from around the area in which the hotel is located. And as the Yugoslav wars continued, hotels were also used as 'transit centres' and temporary accommodation for 'internally displaced people' (IDPs) and refugees after the war.[89]

But the role of the 'hotel as sanctuary' was most clearly demonstrated in the case of the Hotel Milles des Collines in Kigali during the 1994 Rwandan genocide. Hitherto one of the city's most prestigious hotels, it became a place of temporary sanctuary; the hotel's manager Paul Rusesabagina (whose endeavours were dramatised in the film *Hotel Rwanda*) sheltering over a thousand Tutsis and moderate Hutus from the murderous *Interahamwe*, a Hutu paramilitary organisation. Rusesabagina recalled brighter days in the hotel, during which 'it would hold weddings, conferences and diplomatic receptions', but by mid-April 1994, the hotel hosted guests who were 'exhausted refugees in dirty clothes, some with machete wounds, many who had seen their friends turn into killers and

---

[87] *The Globe and Mail* (Toronto), 'Abandoned Greek hotel a reminder of migrants' economic struggle', www.theglobeandmail.com/news/world/abandoned-greek-hotel-a-reminder-of-migrants-economic-struggle/article26246390/ [last accessed 8 September 2015].

[88] The Libertas, which was heavily bombed on 6 December 1991, was almost completely destroyed (only one solid metal sculpture—which remains in the main lobby of the hotel to this day—survived the firestorm that engulfed the hotel), and six people were killed in the onslaught. For an excellent analysis of the course of events that led to the Montenegrin/JNA attack on Dubrovnik, see Srdja Pavlović, 'Reckoning: The Siege of Dubrovnik and the Consequences of the 'War for Peace,' Spaces of Identity 5, 2005: 1–47. See also United Nations Security Council, 'Final Report of the United Nations Commission of Experts Established Pursuant to Security Council Resolution 780: Annex XI.A: The Battle of Dubrovnik and the Law of Armed Conflict', S/1994/674/Add. 2 (Vol. V), December 28, 1994. For the role of the Montenegrin political elite and media in forging war see Živko Andrijašević, *Nacrt za ideologiju jedne vlasti*, Bar: Conteco, 1999.

[89] AIM Press, Paris, 'Refugees: Hotels as Alternative Shelter', 27 February 2001.

their families turned into corpses'.[90] In his memoirs, he described the scene inside the Milles des Collines. 'Each room' he said, 'held an average of eight frightened and brutalized people....The hotel rooms were like death-row prison cells, but we knew they were all that kept us from joining the ranks of the murdered for one more day.' He worried that there would be no more space in the hotel but Rusesabagina persisted, making more room for people. 'I would have ordered my guests to start lying on top of one another if it had meant saving a few more lives. And I don't think anyone in the Mille Collines would have objected,' he said.[91]

REFERENCES

Abraham, A. J. (1996). *The Lebanon War*. Westport: Praeger Publishers.
Aburish, S. (1989). *Beirut Spy: International Intrigue at the St. George Hotel Bar*. London: Bloomsbury Press.
Bowman, T. (2007). *Carson's Army: The Ulster Volunteer Force, 1910–1922*. Manchester: Manchester University Press.
Bowyer Bell, J. (1997). *The Secret Army: The IRA*. New Jersey: Transaction Publishers.
Bruce, S. (1992). *The Red Hand: Protestant Paramilitaries in Northern Ireland*. Oxford: Oxford University Press.
Demetriou, O. (2012). The militarization of opulence: Engendering a conflict heritage site. *International Feminist Journal of Politics, 1*(14), 56–77.
Dillon, M. (2003). The Europa hotel: A symbol. *The European Magazine*, London, 66–70.
Fisk, R. (2002). *Pity the Nation: The Abduction of Lebanon* (4th ed.). New York: Nation Books.
Grayson, R. S. (2009). *Belfast boys: How Unionists and Nationalists Fought and Died Together in the First World War*. London: Continuum.
Greene, G. (1966). *The Comedians*. London: The Bodley Head.
Harris, P. (2009). *More Thrills than Skills: Adventures in Journalism, War and Terrorism*. Glasgow: Kennedy & Boyd.
Hirst, D. (2010). *Beware of Small States: Lebanon, Battleground of the Middle East*. New York: Nation Books.
Levander, C. F., & Guterl, M. P. (2015). *Hotel Life: The Story of a Place Where Anything Can Happen*. Chappel Hill: University of North Carolina Press.

---

[90] Paul Rusesabagina, *An Ordinary Man: The True Story Behind Hotel Rwanda*, London: Bloomsbury Press, 2006, p. 145.
[91] *Ibid*, p. 141.

Lisle, D. (2013). Frontline leisure: Securitizing tourism in the war on Terror. *Security Dialogue, 44*(2), 127–146.
Mazzeo, T. J. (2014). *The Hotel on Place Vendome: Life, Death and Betrayal at the Hotel Ritz in Paris.* New York: HarperCollins.
McSmith, A. (2010). *No Such Thing as Society: A History of Britain in the 1980s.* London: Constable Press.
Morgan, T. (2010). *A Sweet and Bitter Island: A History of the British in Cyprus.* London: IB Tauris.
O'Ballance, E. (1998). *The Civil War in Lebanon, 1975–1992.* London: MacMillan Press.
Potter, J. (1996). *World of Difference: 50 Years of Intercontinental Hotels and Its People.* London: Weidenfeld Nicholson.
Rusesabagina, P. (2006). *An Ordinary Man: The True Story Behind Hotel Rwanda.* London: Bloomsbury Press.
Scoular, C. (2003). *In the Headlines: The Story of the Belfast Europa Hotel.* Belfast: Appletree Press.
Stratfor Global Intelligence. (2009). Special security report: The militant threat to hotels.
Sweet, M. (2011). *The West End Front: The Wartime Secrets of London's Grand Hotels.* London: Faber & Faber.
Taylor, P. (1997). *The Provos: The IRA and Sinn Fein.* London: Bloomsbury Press.

CHAPTER 3

Press Hotels in Conflict Zones

In addition to being strategic assets, prestige targets, forums for political negotiations, and temporary sanctuaries, hotels also serve as bases for the media during times of conflict. These *press hotels* were, not infrequently, culturally insulated, detached spaces for diplomats, aid workers or peacekeepers in the midst of war, some located some distance from the frontline, others closer in proximity. Journalists naturally gravitate towards them because they can set up their equipment and gain access to the basic tools of the trade: food, water, laundry, electricity, and city maps—necessities that are difficult to source elsewhere in a conflict zone. Before, and to some extent after, the advent of the Internet, the primary method for journalists to 'plug-in' was to identify the press hotel, join colleagues, garner and share information about the latest developments and discern where was (or was not) accessible. In this respect, hotels served as crucial networking nodes in a context within which operating independently could be both difficult and dangerous, while providing a relatively safe base from which journalists could work effectively. These hotels would, further, provide not simply a professional function, but a social one. The lobbies and (particularly) bars of these hotels were places to socialise, to decompress, to connect with peers, to share experiences, and, when appropriate or possible, to drown sorrows.

The press hotel is not an entirely modern phenomenon. Since the Crimean War, foreign correspondents had travelled to the proximity of the conflict to convey their impressions in the burgeoning print media.[1] Many of these correspondents would stay in the finest hotels, some close to the frontline, others detached from it. But it was not until the Spanish Civil War (1936–39) that the press hotel began to play such an important role in the lives of foreign correspondents. Ernest Hemingway, Martha Gellhorn (later Hemingway's third wife), Robert Capa, Gerda Taro (dubbed 'The Lost Generation'), and other notable correspondents of the time had made the Hotel Florida on the *Plaza de Callao* in Madrid (sadly destroyed in the 1960s to make way for a department store) their base for covering the Spanish Civil War; hotels served as important bases for broadcasting news.[2] This hotel was, according to Amanda Vaill, targeted regularly by Franco's Nationalists and was one of the few places in Madrid with a supply of hot water. The spacious front rooms of the hotel, facing the Plaza, were considerably cheaper (and more dangerous) than the rooms without a view, but the building nevertheless played an important role in that it provided a relatively safe haven for journalists who were in close proximity to battle.[3]

The advent of television news, however, dictated that hotels played an increasingly important role. Given that television news required access to on-site operations equipment, they became important bases from which the media operated. Thus these often exotic hotels became increasingly familiar to Western domestic audiences, and be it in Vietnam, Cambodia, Bangladesh, Biafra, Lebanon, Iraq, or (the former) Yugoslavia, reporters would frequently provide the overview of the day's events from the balconies or roofs of their 'war hotels'. By extension, these hotels often became inextricably linked to public perceptions of the conflicts.[4] In Saigon (Ho Chi Mihn City), during the Vietnam War (the first 'televised war') there was not one, but several press hotels, located primarily within 'District 1' of the city. Designed by the French architect Ernest Hébrard, and built by the French businessman Pierre Cazeau, the Palace Continental Hotel,

---

[1] See Phillip Knightley, *The First Casualty of War: The War Correspondent as Hero, Propagandist and Myth Maker from Crimea to the Gulf War II*, (Third Edition) London: Carlton Books, 2003, pp. 1–17.

[2] For an excellent account of the journalists who frequented the Hotel Florida during the Spanish Civil War see Amanda Vaill, *Hotel Florida: Truth, Love and Death in the Spanish Civil War*, Bloomsbury Press, London and New York, 2014.

[3] Amanda Vaill, *Hotel Florida: Truth, Love and Death in the Spanish Civil War*, p. 124.

[4] Al Jazeera, 'Iconic war hotels', 21 September 2011, http://www.aljazeera.com/indepth/features/2011/09/20119121275757209.html [last accessed 23 May 2014].

which had opened in 1880, was perhaps the most important.[5] The elegant colonial-style building was frequented by the French writer, André Malreaux, and was where Grahame Greene wrote his novel *The Quiet American* (while 'stringing' for MI6)[6] and the 'Continental shelf' terrace bar was where main protagonist of the novel, Thomas Fowler, meets Alden Pyle. It was relatively safe and sufficiently culturally detached to become a home from home for many correspondents. Indeed, according to Mark Frankland of *The Observer*, 'Anyone who thought that the Continental was Vietnam was kidding himself. It was simply a ghost from the French colonial days.'[7] During the First Indochina War (1946–50) the hotel became colloquially known as *Radio Catinat*, the main place in the city where journalists, political elites, and businessmen would discuss 'Vietnamese affairs of the state', while during the Vietnam War, American and European journalists would also use the hotel as a base.[8] Thus the 'Continental shelf' became *the* place to gather intelligence. According to Martin Woollacot, 'Unless you were plugged into The Shelf at least once a day, you were likely to miss what was going on. If you passed The Shelf at a normally busy time and saw it was empty, you *knew* you had missed something.'[9]

Its location, in addition to its clientele, was also a key factor. It was located close to the South Vietnamese parliament building and to the nearby Rex Hotel (also built by a French businessman—though its initial function was as a garage),[10] which was used by the US Army to give press briefings.[11] These briefings, which always took place at 5.00 pm and often in the rooftop garden of the hotel, became known among the increasingly cynical US press corps as the 'five o'clock follies'. (Richard Pyle, the Associated Press Saigon bureau chief, described them as 'the longest-playing tragicomedy in Southeast Asia's theatre of the absurd'.)[12]

---

[5] For a history of the Continental Hotel in Saigon from the 1880s to the end of the Second World War, see Srilata Ravi, 'Moderntiy, imperialism and the pleasures of travel: The continental hotel in Saigon', *Asian Studies Review*, December 2008, Vol. 32, pp. 475–490.

[6] See Richard West, 'Graham Greene and the quiet American', *The New York Review of Books*, 16 May 1991.

[7] *The Observer*, London, 28 December 1980, p. 21.

[8] *The Guardian*, London, 4 July 1972, p. 16.

[9] *The Guardian*, London, 14 July 1993, (Supplement) p. A2.

[10] William McGurd, 'Putting on the Rex', *The American Spectator*, February 1998, Vol. 31, Issue 2, p. 12.

[11] *The New York Times*, New York, 25 January 1988, p. 23.

[12] *Time Magazine*, New York, 12 February 1973, p. 12.

There were other hotels that played an equally important role for journalists during the Vietnam War. In addition to the Continental and the Rex, the Majestic, the Caravelle (which had functioning air-conditioning and a rooftop that would provide an excellent view of events as the city fell into the hands of the Viet Cong),[13] and the Royal Hotel (the latter run by Jean Ottavj, a Corsican with an opium addiction) were also regular haunts for journalists, diplomats, aid workers, and spies.[14] These hotels were also frequented by the thousands of US workers who came to Vietnam after the signing (in January 1973) of the Paris Peace Accord, which brought the US military engagement in Vietnam to an end. Business was good until the fall of Saigon to the North Vietnamese in late April 1975, whereupon all US personnel were evacuated from Vietnam.

In subsequent wars in South East Asia, hotels also provided crucial bases (and temporary sanctuary) for journalists and aid workers. In Phnom Penh (Cambodia), for example, *Le Royal* (The Royal), known during the war simply as *Le Phnom*, played such a role, hosting many foreign correspondents. Located in the affluent Duan Penh area of the city, the hotel opened in 1929 and its previous guests included the likes of Charlie Chaplin and W. Somerset Maugham, among others. The prestigious guests that had once graced the hotel were long gone, but even when they were replaced by journalists and aid workers, the hotel nevertheless retained something of its colonial grandeur. By 1974, as the war closed in on Phnom Penh, journalists, such as Sydney Schanberg of the *New York Times* and Jon Swain from the *Sunday Times*, would, when in the city, use the hotel as a base and a sanctuary (of sorts) from the fighting. The hotel was something of an oasis, retaining, according to Swain, 'something of the lazy charm of the pre-war days'.[15] But as the city's fall became inevitable, there was no avoiding, even within the gilded walls of the *Le Phnom*, the reality that the hotel could be a sanctuary no more. By early March 1975 food supplies were diminishing within the capital and the hotel was struggling to provide the level of service that its guests, in many ways isolated from the war, had become accustomed to.[16] In April 1975, two weeks before the US evacuation from Saigon, the communist *Khmer Rouge* overran Phnom Penh, taking control of key buildings

---

[13] *The Observer*, London, 16 April 2000, p. 23.
[14] *The Independent*, London, 30 November 2011, p. 30.
[15] Jon Swain, *The River of Time*, London: Minerva Books, 1996, p. 90.
[16] *The Observer*, London, 2 March 1975, p. 9.

within the city. Jon Swain vividly recounted the final moments in the hotel as it was surrounded and overrun by the Khmer Rouge. 'Pandemonium gripped the hotel', he said, as 'people ran in all directions'. He described the sorrow he felt as the hotel staff begged the journalists in the hotel not to abandon them. 'Their words', said Swain, 'come back to haunt me now, for most of them are dead'.[17] (These events are dramatised in the film *The Killing Fields*.)

In Lebanon, after the 'Battle of the Hotels' had rendered the luxury hotels in the *Minet-el-Hosn* complex an unviable option, the rather less salubrious *Le Commodore* (The Commodore) in West Beirut became the favoured haunt for foreign correspondents. 'Every war has its hotel', said Thomas Friedman of the *New York Times*, 'and the Lebanese wars [of the 1980s] had the Commodore'.[18] The hotel had been frequented by journalists since the outbreak of war in 1975, but was particularly busy during the Israeli siege of West Beirut in the summer of 1982, which attracted significant media attention.[19] On 6 June 1982, Israel began military operations known as 'Operation Peace in Galilee', with the core objective of eliminating the PLO in Lebanon and pushing Palestinian militias out of southern Lebanon, from where they would launch attacks on Israeli towns and cities with rockets. It was a significant military operation that went beyond stated objectives and culminated with the 73-day siege of West Beirut.[20] During this time, correspondents flocked to the Commodore. Located in the *Hamra* area of the Muslim-held west of the city, it was somewhat more secure, if only because it was tucked in between a number of taller buildings, which would take the brunt of any incoming fire.[21] Nevertheless, the hotel was hit several times, the first time being 4 August 1982 (the day of the heaviest fighting of the siege).[22] Another popular

---

[17] Jon Swain, *The River of Time*, p. 145.

[18] Thomas Friedman, *From Beirut to Jerusalem*, New York: Doubleday, 1995, p. 64.

[19] For an analysis of Israeli objectives in advance of their military offensive into Lebanon see Martin van Creveld, *The Land of Blood and Honey: The Rise of Modern Israel*, St. Martin's Press, New York, 2010, pp. 203–205.

[20] Edgar O'Ballance. *The Civil War in Lebanon, 1975–1992*, p. 114.

[21] *The Guardian*, London, 13 July 1993, (Supplement), p. A2.

[22] John Laffin, *The war of desperation: Lebanon 1982–1985*, Osprey Press, London, 1985, p. 106. The Commodore and the Alexandre were not the only West Beirut hotels to be damaged during the 1982 Israeli bombardment. In August 1982 the Summerland Hotel, West Beirut's most fashionable and 'only a few hundred yards from poverty-stricken areas', was destroyed by Israeli air strikes. The hotel was refurbished and re-opened in the spring of 1983 but was again attacked by 'two carloads of armed men' who shot dead two guards

centre for the press was the Alexandre Hotel in East Beirut, which had also been attacked, albeit from Palestinian positions, on 12 July, and by a car bomb in August.[23] But despite the dangers, the Commodore and the Alexandre remained the safest places to be while still being able to have a decent view of the fighting (indeed, much of the TV footage of the Israeli bombardment of West Beirut was filmed from the rooftops of the Commodore and the Alexandre).[24]

The Commodore became notorious for being a place of hard-drinking (despite its West Beirut location), frequented by a colourful clientele. Its lush garden and swimming pool was often graced by a strange mix of foreign correspondents, intelligence officers, diplomats, and militias from the PLO. (The PLO held press conferences there.) The Commodore was not, according to one veteran correspondent, 'a relaxed hotel at which to stay— there were eyes everywhere'.[25] Correspondents checking into the hotel would, apparently, be asked by the receptionist whether they wanted a room 'on the shelling side or the car bomb side of the hotel?'[26] Once settled, they would find that the hotel, for all its hazards, functioned remarkably well. Water was always available and the electrical supply power for the journalist's telex machines was consistent, in addition to the usual services expected of a hotel. Moreover, the hotel's management understood what mattered to journalists and how to cater for them. According to Thomas Friedman, the management understood 'that there is only one thing journalists appreciate more than luxury and that is functioning communications equipment with which to file their stories or television spots'. By paying bribes, he claimed, one could 'maintain live international telex and telephone lines into his hotel, no matter how bad the combat became'.[27] Additionally, the laundry service, available almost constantly, was said to be 'exemplary'.[28] There was also no shortage of alcohol to oil the wheels (though this, sometimes, had to be smuggled from Christian East Beirut), but access to it became more problematic by 1984, when Shi'ite *Hezbollah* (Party of God)

outside the hotel before rolling a car full of explosives into the hotel entrance. See *The Guardian*, London, 21 July 1983, p. 7.

[23] *Ibid*, p. 153.
[24] *Ibid*, p. 153.
[25] John Laffin, *The War of Desperation: Lebanon 1982–1985*, p. 153.
[26] *The New York Times*, New York, 6 November 1983, p. 6. Robert Fisk of *The Independent*, however, argues that '[This] legend is a lie'. Journalists simply took the filthy rooms allotted to them. See *The Independent*, London, 17 May 1992, p. 10.
[27] Thomas Friedman, *From Beirut to Jerusalem*, p. 66.
[28] *The Guardian*, London, 14 July 1993 (Supplement), p. A2.

militias held sway in West Beirut.[29] The hotel's bar boasted of an African Grey parrot called 'Coco', which had belonged to a BBC correspondent (Chris Drake).[30] The parrot became rather accomplished at two particular 'imitations', the first being one of the victory phrases from Beethoven's Fifth Symphony, the other the sound of an incoming mortar shell.[31]

But the Commodore, claimed Robert Fisk of *The Independent*, was ultimately 'a trap', which insulated journalists and detached them from the world outside. It was, he said, home to 'a breed of journalistic lounge lizard, reporters who rarely left the building—or the downstairs bar—and who culled their information from the wire machines in the lobby'. Located firmly within the confines of the hotel, they would simply 'write about the hotel, about other reporters, about the parrot that imitated the sound of incoming shells'.[32] In February 1987, the Commodore was badly damaged following a vicious gun battle between rival militias, though it was rebuilt and reopened in the early 1990s.

Another conflict that persisted throughout the 1980s was the 1979–92 war in El Salvador, one fought between the US-backed government and the *Farabundo Marti National Liberation Front* (FMLN), essentially a conglomerate of left-wing guerrilla groups. For journalists, several hotels in the capital, San Salvador, would provide a base from which to cover the war. The Sheraton Hotel housed, though not exclusively, 'US military trainers, State Department and CIA types', while the Camino Real, in the main, housed the international press, among them the so-called Salvadoran Foreign Press Corps Association (SPECA).[33] When not in their second floor suites-cum-offices, the press would sit around the lobby of the hotel 'waiting for something "big" to happen'.[34] But when the American writer Joan Didion (who had 'always wanted to go to Vietnam' but had been unable to do so), visited San Salvador and stayed in the hotel (in Didion 1982a, b) and found that many of the journalists had moved on to cover wars in Lebanon, Iran-Iraq or the aftermath of the British task force re-establishing control of the Falklands Islands after the Argentinian invasion in April 1982.[35] 'So many journalists had departed', she said, 'the

---

[29] *The Irish Times*, Dublin, 9 February 1984, p. 5.
[30] *The Guardian*, London, 14 July 1993 (Supplement), p. A2.
[31] *Ibid*, p. A2.
[32] Robert Fisk, *Pity the Nation: The Abduction of Lebanon*, p. 217.
[33] P.J. O' Rourke, *Holidays in Hell*, New York: Picador, 1988, pp. 136–137.
[34] Mark Pedelty, *War Stories: The Culture of Foreign Correspondents*, Abingdon: Routledge, 1995, p. 125.
[35] *The Guardian*, London, 6 April 1983, p. 6.

dining room had discontinued its breakfast buffet, a fact often remarked upon: no breakfast buffet meant no action, little bang-bang, a period of editorial indifference in which stories were field and held, and film rarely made the network news'.[36] Coverage of the war was periodic, but the hotel was busy in November 1989 when the FMLN launched one of their largest offensives. The BBC's Jeremy Bowen, then a young journalist covering his first war, described the atmosphere in the hotel throughout the offensive:

> Every room was packed with news people. TV editors had set up their gear in the rooms. The screeching gabble of tapes being played fast, backwards and forwards, filled the corridors. Cables dangled out of windows to generators and live positions. You couldn't go out because of the shoot-on-sight curfew, so we ate and drank on the terrace. Multi-coloured tracer looped around the volcano that dominates the city. The war went on as dinner was served.[37]

With the collapse of communism in 1989–91 in Europe, many journalists now found themselves not covering Cold War proxy conflicts in Africa, Asia, or the Americas, but a continent that had, though subject to the tensions of the Cold War, been largely peaceful since the end of the Second World War. However, as communist systems in Central and Eastern Europe, the legitimacy of which had weakened throughout the 1980s, collapsed, revolutions, some of which were violent, erupted. During the 1989 Romanian Revolution, for example, the Continental in Bucharest and the Hotel Continental in Timişoara served as bases for the press covering the downfall of the communist regime of Nicolae Ceauseşu.

Events in Eastern Europe were, however, soon eclipsed by events in the Middle East, and following Iraq's invasion of Kuwait in August 1990 much of the focus shifted towards the 'First Gulf War'. During the Gulf War, hotels again became crucial to the functioning of television news. Most news agencies established bases in Riyadh, from where they would report on events and cover the US Army (or coalition) press briefings. Most journalists were more or less forced into 'pools', where they would be given whatever access the US military deemed appropriate, though others attempted to forge their own independent path. A number of journalists (who were roundly condemned by the US military) reported from Baghdad, establishing their operational base in the Al Rashid Hotel. The BBC's John Simpson, ITV's Brent Sadler, and CNN's Peter Arnett

---

[36] Joan Didion, *Salvador*, London: Granta Books, 2006, p. 49.
[37] Jeremy Bowen, *War Stories*, Simon & Schuster, London, 2006, p. 130.

brought to Western audiences, according to Phillip Knightley, 'vivid film of night skies alight with explosions and the exhaust fumes of missiles, on a soundtrack of explosions and anti-aircraft fire, interspersed with breathless commentary'.[38] CNN, in particular, consolidated their reputation as a leading global media agency during their reporting from Baghdad.[39] It was impossible for networks or agencies to transmit live pictures from the Iraqi capital, but CNN established a rather rudimentary (but functional) direct audio link between Baghdad and Amman in Jordan, thus facilitating a satellite link to the world. Thereafter, CNN's reporters in the city (Peter Arnett, Bernard Shaw, and John Holliman) gave an 'eyewitness, real-time account of the American air attack' from their ninth-floor suite in the Al Rashid Hotel.[40] After the end of the war, a mosaic of the US President, George Bush, was installed on the floor of the hotel's lobby—anyone entering the hotel would have to walk over Bush's face (doing so is considered an insult in Arab culture).

As the Gulf War ended, the Balkans would be the next port of call for many correspondents. In 1991, during the collapse of communism in Albania, and again in 1997, during the subsequent collapse of the Albanian state, the International and Dajti hotels (the latter of which had hitherto been, until 1991, strictly for the communist elite) became the bases for journalists.[41] And as the Yugoslav state began its violent disintegration in 1991, journalists flocked to hotels in Slovenia, Croatia, and Bosnia and Herzegovina (and later Kosovo). Sarajevo's Holiday Inn became the most infamous, but others, such as the Intercontinental (formerly the Esplanade) in Zagreb (which housed the 'International Press Centre' and became the meeting place for journalists going to, or coming from, conflict zones in Croatia), the Hotel Osijek (Osijek), and the Hotel Argentina (near Dubrovnik, Croatia), with its balcony view of the medieval city's old town (and the shelling of it), served

---

[38] Phillip Knightley, *The First Casualty of War: The War Correspondent as Hero, Propagandist and Myth Maker from Crimea to the Gulf War II*, p. 492.

[39] *The Sunday Times*, London, 27 January 1991, p. 6.

[40] John Owen (ed.), *International News Reporting: Frontlines and Deadlines*, Chichester: Wiley-Blackwell, 2009, p. 31. For Arnett's personal account of CNN's operations from the Al Rashid see Peter Arnett, *Live from the Battlefield*, New York: Touchstone, 1994.

[41] During the period of the Enver Hoxha regime in Albania, the Hotel Dajti, set in the 'Blok' district (which housed most of the communist elite, including Hoxha, was 'out of bounds' for ordinary Albanians. Only after the death of Hoxha in 1985 did the clientele include foreigners (who tended to stay at the Tirana International Hotel). By the early 1990s, foreign businessmen, along with trade and political delegations, formed the bulk of the Dajti's clientele'. Although being recognised as an important building of cultural significance in 2002, the hotel was closed in 2005.

as *press hotels*, while the Hotel Libertas and the Hotel Imperial were among a number of hotels that housed refugees during the attack on the Dubrovnik region by Serb/Montenegrin and Yugoslav Army (JNA) forces in 1991, during which some hotels were completely destroyed. The entire Kupari hotel resort, which included the Hotel Pelegrin, was completely destroyed, as was the Libertas (though the latter has since been rebuilt) (Image 3.1).

Before and during the 1998–99 Kosovo conflict, the Grand Hotel in Prishtina, Kosovo, served as both a Serb enclave within the city and a crucial meeting place for journalists and politicians.[42] Similarly, the Hyatt and Intercontinental Hotels (now the Crowne Plaza) in Belgrade, Serbia, were centres for the international media and frequented by various Serbian political party and paramilitary leaders during the NATO bombing of the Federal Republic of Yugoslavia (FRY) in 1999. In the lobbies and bars of these *Novi Beograd* (New Belgrade) hotels, journalists would rub shoulders with the Belgrade *Mafiosi*, among them the Serbian paramilitary leader turned politician, Željko Ražnatović 'Arkan', who would himself be shot and killed in the lobby of the Intercontinental Hotel in January 2000.[43]

Image 3.1 The Hotel Pelegrin, Kupari, Croatia. (Photograph: Kenneth Morrison)

---

[42] James Pettifer, *Kosova Express: A Journey in Wartime*, Hurst & Co., London, 2005, p. 37.

[43] For a more detailed account of the assassination of Arkan, see Christopher S. Stewart, *Hunting the tiger: The Fast Life and Violent Death of the Balkans' Most Dangerous Man*, New York: St Martin's Press, 2007, pp. 276–284.

(The *Hotel Jugoslavija*, of which Arkan was then part-owner, was hit by two missiles and badly damaged by NATO's bombing of targets in Belgrade.)[44]

Following the US-led coalition invasion of Afghanistan in 2001, the Intercontinental and the Serena became the hostelries of choice, while the Al Hamra and the Palestine in Baghdad (Iraq) became temporary bases for journalists during the US-led coalition's invasion of Iraq in 2003. During the war in Libya, the Corinthia Hotel and the Rixos-owned Hotel al-Nasr in Tripoli were the bases for many of the foreign correspondents covering the fall of the regime of Muammar Gaddafi. In August 2011, during the so-called Rixos Crisis, thirty-five of them, including correspondents from CNN, the BBC, Reuters, and Sky News, were trapped in the hotel, the 'guests' of pro-Gaddafi militiamen, whose behaviour became increasingly erratic as it became clear that the regime had fallen and that the hotel was being slowly encircled. Journalists inside the building feared that they would be 'used as human shields' against attacks by Libyan rebels.[45] They eventually escaped, transported from the hotel by the International Committee of the Red Cross (ICRC), though preparations were in progress by NATO forces to storm the hotel if necessary.[46] But the fall of the Gaddafi regime did not bring an end to hostilities in Libya. In 2014, as the country descended into further instability and chaos, hotels again played an important role. The Al-Masira Hotel in Torbuk, Libya, became the base for one of Libya's two rival governments, with the hotel's conference hall being where their 'parliament' assembled.[47]

In Syria, the Four Seasons in Damascus became the base for the press covering the chaos that engulfed the country following the anti-government protests in 2011 and the outbreak of armed hostilities between the Assad government and anti-government rebels. In the contested city of Aleppo, two of the city's finest hotels—the Carlton Citadel Hotel and the Baron (the latter of which had hosted both Charles de Gaulle and Kemal Ataturk

---

[44] Opened in 1969, the Hotel Jugoslavija was then the most prestigious hotel in Yugoslavia. Located near the Yugoslav Federal Parliament building, the hotel hosted many of Josip Broz Tito's foreign guests. The hotel played host to Queen Elizabeth II, the West German Chancellor Willy Brandt, US Presidents Richard Nixon and Jimmy Carter, and US astronauts Neil Armstrong and Buzz Aldrin. For the urban development of New Belgrade see Brigette Le Normand, *Designing Tito's Capital: Urban Planning, Modernism, and Socialism in Belgrade*, Pittsburgh: University of Pittsburgh Press, 2014.

[45] BBC News, 'Libya unrest: Journalists' Rixos Hotel ordeal described, 24 August 2011, http://www.bbc.co.uk/news/world-africa-14654958 [last accessed, 23 June 2014].

[46] *The Daily Telegraph*, London, 25 August 2011, p. 5.

[47] BBC News, 'Libya's government holed-up in a 1970s hotel', 16 October 2014, http://www.bbc.co.uk/news/magazine-29603393 [last accessed 2 March 2015].

and was where, in room 203 of the hotel, Agatha Christie had written *Murder on the Orient Express*)—were both badly damaged, the Carlton Citadel almost completely destroyed by a large blast on 8 May 2014.[48] In Crimea, the Best Western in Sevastopol and the Hotel Marakand in Simferopol (both in Crimea) were press hotels during the Russian annexation of the peninsula by Russia. In the later conflict between the Ukrainian Army and Russian-backed separatists in eastern Ukraine, the Hotel Ramada in Donetsk became yet another in a longlist of press hotels. According to *The Times* correspondent Ben Hoyle:

> The sign on the doors of the Ramada hotel in Donetsk reminds you that you are somewhere unusual….Back in the summer, when the city first came under artillery attack, there were far, far too many separatist fighters drinking beer and clowning around with loaded AK-74s on the Ramada's pleasant veranda. Evening firearms etiquette seems to have improved though. The Ramada's restaurant—used by reporters, aid workers, mafia types, overdressed women and separatist fighters—remains a source of indispensable up-to-date knowledge about what is happening in the conflict zone. [It's] impossible to forget the war in there.[49]

The story of the Donetsk Ramada has been repeated many times, and in many places. The Holiday Inn, Sarajevo, the primary subject of this book, is merely one of a plethora of 'war hotels'. What differentiates Sarajevo's Holiday Inn, however, is that unlike many of the hotels utilised by the press during wartime, it was no safe haven and there was no detachment from the conflict. The hotel was not only *within* siege lines, but in one of the most exposed and dangerous parts of Sarajevo, directly *on* the frontline and a few hundred yards from the besieging Bosnian Serb positions in Grbavica. Residing in the Holiday Inn during the siege of Sarajevo offered little of the protection that hotels previously frequented by journalists could, to a greater or lesser extent, provide. Exposed and subject to regular assault it became, in the words of the veteran BBC correspondent Martin Bell, 'the ultimate war hotel' from where 'you didn't go to the war, the war came in to you'.[50]

---

[48] *The Independent*, London, 10 November 2001, p. 4.
[49] *The Times*, London, 16 February 2015, p. 32.
[50] Martin Bell, *In Harm's Way*. See also *The Independent*, London (Travel Supplement), p. 24.

References

Arnett, P. (1994). *Live from the Battlefield*. New York: Touchstone.
Bowen, J. (2006). *War Stories*. London: Simon & Schuster.
Didion, J. (1982a). In El Salvador. *The New York Review of Books*.
Didion, J. (1982b). In El Salvador: Soluciones. *The New York Review of Books*.
Donia, R. J. (2006). *Sarajevo: A Biography*. London: Hurst & Co..
Friedman, T. (1995). *From Beirut to Jerusalem*. New York: Doubleday.
Knightley, P. (2003). *The First Casualty of War: The War Correspondent as Hero, Propagandist and Myth Maker from Crimea to the Gulf War II* (3rd ed.). London: Carlton Books.
Laffin, J. (1985). *The War of Desperation: Lebanon 1982–1985*. London: Osprey Press.
Le Normand, B. (2014). *Designing Tito's Capital: Urban Planning, Modernism, and Socialism in Belgrade*. Pittsburgh: University of Pttsburgh Press.
McGurn, W. (1998). Putting on the Rex. *American Spectator, 31*(2).
Owen, J. (Ed.) (2009). *International News Reporting: Frontlines and Deadlines*. Chichester: Wiley-Blackwell.
O'Rourke, P. J. (1988). *Holidays in Hell*. New York: The Atlantic Monthly Press.
Pedelty, M. (1995). *War Stories: The Culture of Foreign Correspondents*. Abingdon: Routledge.
Pettifer, J. (2005). *Kosova Express: A Journey in Wartime*. London: Hurst & Co..
Ravi, S. (2008). Moderntiy, imperialism and the pleasures of travel: The continental hotel in Saigon. *Asian Studies Review, 32*, 475–490.
Stewart, C. S. (2007). *Hunting the Tiger: The Fast Life and Violent Death of the Balkans' Most Dangerous Man*. New York: St. Martin's Press.
Swain, J. (1996). *The River of Time*. London: Minerva Books.
Vaill, A. (2014). *Hotel Florida: Truth, Love and Death in the Spanish Civil War*. London and New York: Bloomsbury Press.
C. M., V. (2010). *The Land of Blood and Honey: The Rise of Modern Israel*. New York: St. Martin's Press.
West, R., Graham Greene and the Quiet American (1991). *The New York Review of Books*.

CHAPTER 4

The Construction of Sarajevo's 'Olympic Hotel'

Standing on the roof of Sarajevo's Holiday Inn hotel, surveying the high ground once held by the Bosnian Serb Army (*Vojska Repulike Srpske—*VRS) that had surrounded the city, placed heavy weapons on Mount Trebević, and subjected the city to a three-and-a-half-year siege, one cannot fail to understand just how exposed it was, and how dangerous it had been to enter, exit, or even stay within the confines of the hotel during the siege. From this elevated position, one can look almost directly into the upper floors of the apartment buildings in Grbavica, from where much of the sniper fire directed at the Holiday Inn emanated from. Despite the fact that the Holiday Inn was not as badly damaged as the nearby UNIS (now UNITIC) towers and the Bosnian parliament building (both of which had been gutted by incendiary shells in the early summer of 1992), the Holiday Inn was highly exposed, surrounded by space on all sides and located on one of the widest thoroughfares in the city. During the siege, this was one of the most exposed and dangerous parts of Sarajevo.[1] The image of the hotel became scarred into public consciousness during the siege, its battered yellow, ochre, and brown exterior of the building, an anomalous block of lurid colour, in the midst of a grim, isolated, war-torn, and decaying city.[2] As the only functioning hotel in the city, large enough

---

[1] See Ivan Štraus, *Arhitekt i barbari*, and Sarajevo: Međunarodni centar za mir, pp. 98–99.
[2] The Holiday Inn's exterior (and interior) provided the visual backdrop to myriad news reports being broadcast the world over. Many of the most famous images of the conflict were photographed from the hotel. Subsequently, the hotel has featured in numerous films, such

to cater for the demands of its wartime guests (largely foreign correspondents, aid workers, and diplomats), the Holiday Inn became the city's 'war hotel', thereby becoming the most renowned (or notorious) hostelry in Sarajevo.[3] It would provide the backdrop for a plethora of television news reports and features throughout the siege, becoming a familiar sight to viewers across the globe.

While the Holiday Inn has become an iconic symbol of the siege, for citizens of Sarajevo it represents something altogether more positive—a symbol of happier times, before the violent disintegration of the Socialist Federal Republic of Yugoslavia (SFRJ), the Bosnian war, and the siege. The hotel was conceived during a period which marked the zenith in the modern history of Sarajevo—the preparations for and the successful execution of the 14th Winter Olympic Games (*Zimskih Olimpijskih Igara*—ZOI), held in February 1984. In May 1978, during the eightieth session of the International Olympic Committee (IOC), held at the Hotel Caravel in Athens, Sarajevo had beaten both Sapporo and Gothenburg to win the right to host the 14th Winter Olympics (Image 4.1).[4]

The games were, however, organised and held in an increasingly troubled political and economic context; a time of great flux in the SFRJ. Josip Broz Tito had died on 4 May 1980, and while the vast majority of his countrymen lamented his death, he left behind a dubious legacy. Constitutional changes, particularly the wide-ranging, decentralising reforms of the 1974 constitution, had ensured peace throughout his twilight years but would create what proved to be insurmountable problems in the immediate years following his death. It was to be the Yugoslav League of Communists (*Savez komunista Jugoslavije*—SKJ) as a whole that would endeavour to maintain the status quo in his wake—the slogan, *I Poslije Tita, Tito!* (After Tito, Tito!), underpinning this vision. No obvious successor was groomed, and the Yugoslav Presidency, in the wake of Tito's death, rotated between the republics, a system that proved, ultimately, dysfunctional. In the years following Tito's death, the SFRJ slid into an acute economic

as Michael Winterbottom's *Welcome to Sarajevo* and Arturo Pérez-Reverte's *Territorio Comanche* (both dramas about foreign correspondents in Bosnia during the war), Richard Shepard's *The Hunting Party*, novels such as Charlotte Eagar's *The Girl in the Film*; Kevin Sullivan's *Sleeping With* Angels, and even graphic novels, such as Joe Sacco's *The Fixer: A Story from Sarajevo* and Joe Kubert's *Fax From Sarajevo*.

[3] FAMA, *Sarajevo Survival Guide*, Sarajevo: FAMA, p. 84.

[4] Kate Meehan Pedrotty, 'Yugoslav Unity and Olympic Ideology', in Hannes Grandits & Karin Taylor (eds.), *Yugoslavia's Sunny Side: A History of Tourism in Socialism (1950s–1980s)*, Budapest-New York: Central European University Press, 2010, p. 342.

Image 4.1 Olympic symbols embedded into one of the concrete pillars near the entrance to the hotel—the pockmarks from sniper fire still evident. (Photo: Kenneth Morrison)

crisis, one that would put the federation under significant pressure. That the economy was in difficulty was made clear by the effects of the 1979 'Oil Crisis', but the political implications would become clear only later. The first clear manifestation of the seriousness of the post-Tito political crisis within the SFRJ came during student demonstrations in Kosovo in 1981, which led to a violent crackdown by Yugoslav authorities, in which eleven were killed.[5] Throughout the 1980s embattled communist elites, operating within a political structure that was effective only while Tito

---

[5] *The Times*, London, 7 April 1981, p. 7. Relations between Yugoslavia and Albanian worsened considerably after the events of April 1981. One month later, two bombs were thrown onto the terrace of the Yugoslav Embassy in Tirana provoking a sharp diplomatic protest. See *The Times*, London, 24 May 1981, p. 9.

was alive, seemed powerless to effectively tackle the economic crisis. They would also be powerless in the face of the rising tide of nationalism, which re-emerged as the dominant political ideology in Serbia and, as a consequence, throughout the SFRJ.[6] In the immediate years after Tito's death, however, it was the economy that presented the greatest challenge. Loans that had funded the 'good times' in the 1960s and 1970s were called in, as investors became nervous about the country's ability to repay its debts. The economy laboured under a growing trade deficit, a significant balance of payments deficit, and a burgeoning foreign debt.[7] By 1983, the International Monetary Fund (IMF) demanded that the Yugoslav leadership make the structural economic reforms necessary to contain the country's spiralling debt.[8] The economic medicine given by the IMF was reluctantly administered by a federal government only too aware of the potentially negative impact on social stability. The organisation of the Winter Olympics, therefore, took place within a context of growing economic crisis and rising conflicts between the republics of the SFRJ, albeit largely fuelled by economic issues, and debates over the financing of the games would further expose fissures between Yugoslavia's republics.[9]

It was within this problematic context that the building that Sarajevo's Holiday Inn was conceived. The construction of the 'Olympic Hotel' (Holiday Inn) was part of a wider process of building that facilitated a more effective infrastructure, one that could cater for the thousands of foreign visitors that would inevitably descend upon the city during the Winter Olympics. Equally important was to provide a post-games legacy that would benefit the citizens of Sarajevo. Put simply, the objective of the organising committee was to construct world-class sporting facilities and transform Sarajevo into a modern 'Olympic' city, while vastly improving the city's infrastructure and improving the city's future tourism prospects.[10] The new 'Olympic Road', built to the city's south, became the principal east–west traffic axis which connected mountains to the south of Sarajevo (with the

---

[6] For a detailed analysis of rising anti-Yugoslav rhetoric going back to 1966, see Helsinški odbor za ljudska prava u Srbiji, *Kovane antijugoslovenske zavere*, Svedočanstva Br. 26, Knjiga 1, Zagorac, Beograd, 2006.

[7] Milica Uvalić, *Serbia's Transition: Towards a Better Future*, London: Palgrave Macmillan, 2010, p. 24.

[8] Branka Magaš, *The Destruction of Yugoslavia*, London: Verso Press, 1993, p. 170.

[9] Kate Meehan Pedrotty, 'Yugoslav Unity and Olympic Ideology', p. 338.

[10] Aziz Hadžihasanović, *1984: Olimpijada trijumfa i šansi*, Sarajevo: Rabic, 2010, pp. 11–12.

bob sleigh, ski jumping, and skiing facilities constructed on their slopes). A new north–west axis within the city was also established after the construction of the Skenderija sports centre on the southern bank of the Miljacka River and the Zetra sports hall next to the refurbished Koševo Stadium, where the opening ceremony of the games took place. Accommodation, designed to host the athletes, was built in Mojmilo, while journalists from around the world were housed in newly constructed 'bland yet functional' buildings in Dobrinja.[11] (Both would later be utilised as new suburbs to house Sarajevo's growing population, which had determined that the city was expanding west towards Ilidža.) To commemorate the Sarajevo games a Habsburg-era villa in the northern part of the Austro-Hungarian part of town was refurbished into the 'Museum of 14th Winter Olympic Games' and the snowflake logo of the games was imprinted into the pavements and the facades of several buildings, including the Holiday Inn.

The Holiday Inn became immediately iconic. An unconventional, boxy, angular, modernist structure, it stood in sharp contrast to the older, more subtle constructs in Marindvor, though it should not, ostensibly, have stood in striking juxtaposition to the other modernist buildings in the area. It was the striking façade of yellow, ochre, and brown that set it apart from an aesthetic perspective, somewhat apart from a city bestowed, on its eastern side, with the subtle and seductive grace of Oriental (Ottoman) and the grandeur of Occidental (Austro-Hungarian) architecture and, on its western side, typically drab socialist residential buildings (in areas such as Grbavica, Hrasno, Čengić Vila, Otoka, Dolac Malta, and, later, Mojmilo and Dobrinja) characteristic of the urban planning of the 1960s, 1970s, and early 1980s.[12] Marindvor, the area in which the Holiday Inn is located was, according to Robert Donia, 'the modernist counterpoint to Baščaršija traditionalism'. Since the late 1950s, numerous modernist structures, such as the Faculty of Philosophy, the Faculty of Natural Sciences and Mathematics buildings, the Museum of the Revolution, and the government offices of the Assembly of Bosnia and Herzegovina, had been built.[13] But even among the existing modernist structures in Marindvor the Holiday Inn stood out.

---

[11] Jason Vuić, *The Sarajevo Olympics: A History of the 1984 Winter Games*, University of Massachusetts Press, 2015, p. 55.

[12] See James Lyon, 'Habsburg Sarajevo 1914: A Social Picture', *Prilozi/Contributions*, Institut za istoriju u Sarajevu, No. 43, Sarajevo, 2014, pp. 23–40.

[13] Robert Donia, *Sarajevo: A Biography*, London: Hurst & Co., 2006, p. 233.

Designed by the Bosnian architect (of Slovenian origin), Ivan Štraus, whose work had already been widely acclaimed throughout Yugoslavia.[14] Štraus's best-known works included the *Muzej avijacije* (Museum of Aviation) near Belgrade airport (for which he was awarded the prestigious *Borba* award for architectural achievement), the *Hotel Onogošt* in Nikšić, Montenegro, the *Hotel Slano* in Osmine on the Dalmatian coast, the *Dom vojske* (Army Hall) in Derventa, the *Župa Sveti Franje* Catholic church in Zovik (near Brčko), the building of *Elektropriveda BiH* (Electric Company of Bosnia and Herzegovina) in New Sarajevo, the—now-destroyed—Olympic Press Centre in Bjelašnica (near Sarajevo), and the UNIS towers (now named the UNITIC[15] towers), known locally as *Momo* and *Uzeir*, which was built in 1986.[16] Štraus's designs, however, could be found in the most unlikely of places; throughout his illustrious career his designs were commissioned in such cities as Addis Ababa (Ethiopia) and Sofia (Bulgaria), though the vast majority of his work is to be found in Bosnia and Herzegovina (with a more limited number across former Yugoslav republics).

Having studied architecture in Zagreb, Štraus completed his training at the Technical University of Sarajevo in 1958. Within a decade, he developed into a respected master of his craft, winning numerous high-profile commissions and prizes for his bold, innovative designs. By 1965, only seven years after completing his training as an architect, he was awarded the 'City of Sarajevo April 6th Award' in 1965, and in 1978 he was given the 'Republic of Bosnia & Herzegovina Award' for his architectural achievements.[17] Thus, by the time he had been commissioned, having won first place in the competition, to build the 'Olympic Hotel'[18] (which subsequently became the Holiday Inn), he was Bosnia's foremost architect and one of the most celebrated modernist architects in Yugoslavia, alongside

---

[14] Jason Vuić, *The Sarajevo Olympics: A History of the 1984 Winter Games*, p. 55.

[15] UNITIC is an acronym for the 'United Investment and Trading Company' (a joint venture between UNIS Holding and the Kuwait Consulting and Investment Company). Utilised to house a conglomerate of military enterprises before the war in Bosnia and Herzegovina, the building now houses a diverse range of 'tenants', from charitable organisations, media organisations to businesses.

[16] See Adnan Pašić, *Arhitekt Ivan Štraus*, Arhitektonski fakultet u Sarajevu, Sarajevo Green Design, Sarajevo, 2011. Momo and Uzeir were a Bosnian comedy duo comprising Rejhan Demiridžić (a Muslim) and Rudi Alvadj (a Serb).

[17] By his own admission, some of Ivan Štraus's most important architectural prizes were won for collaborative projects with his fellow architects Zdravko Kovačević, Halid Muhašilović and Štraus's brother, Tihomr. See Adnan Pašić, *Arhitekt Ivan Štraus*, p. 39.

[18] Štraus had previously designed (in 1962) with Zdravko Kovačević the *Dom Štampe I gradki hotel* for the same plot in Marindvor, though the project was never realised. See Ivan Štraus, *Arhiteky i barbari*, p. 101.

Image 4.2 The Holiday Inn under construction, circa June 1983. (Photo: The Holiday Inn, Sarajevo)

the likes of the Serbian architect (and one-time mayor of Belgrade) Bogdan Bogdanović, and other esteemed peers in the field, such as Edvard Ravnikar, Stanko Kristl, Živorad Janković, and Branko Bulić. Having already designed a number of buildings in Sarajevo, his adopted home, Štraus would have ample opportunity to put his own stamp on the cityscape following the announcement that Sarajevo would host the 1984 Winter Olympics. 'By accepting Sarajevo's candidacy as a host for the Winter Olympics', he said, 'an exceptional investment into construction and execution of a series of functionally different venues and facilities necessary for the operation of the greatest winter sports manifestation in the world started'.[19] The reconstruction of the city—Olympic Sarajevo—began in earnest, and the Štraus-designed hotel was one of the most important buildings to be erected during this new infrastructural investment (Image 4.2).

Construction of the Holiday Inn commenced in 1981.[20] Štraus committed himself fully to overseeing the project, even giving up another

---

[19] Ivan Štraus, *Arkitektura Bosne i Herzegovine, 1945–1995*, Sarajevo: Oko, p. 101.

[20] The Holiday Inn was one of a number of hotels built for the Winter Olympics. Others included the ŽTO hotel in Sarajevo, the Bistrica, Košuta, Vučko, and Ferolelectric hotels on Jahorina, the Koran and Panorama hotels in Pale, the Hotel Igman on Mount Igman (which doubled as 'Olympic Village 'B'), and the Famos hotel on Mount Bjelašica. There were a

prestigious project—the redesign and reconstruction of the *Hotel Crna Gora* (Hotel Montenegro) in Titograd (Podrorica), Montenegro.[21] The building of the Holiday Inn involved both professional building firms and volunteers in the Youth Voluntary Labour Association (*Savez omladinska radna akcija*—SORA; sometimes abridged to *Omladinska radna akcija*—ORA).[22] The hotel was built on a plot of land known as the *Bulgaren Äcker*, which had been, during the Austro-Hungarian period known locally as the *Cirkus plac*—a place where visiting circuses, often leading Russian performers, would visit Sarajevo[23]—directly across from the Faculty of Philosophy building and the National Parliament and State Administration buildings (both designed by Juraj Neidhardt) which had hitherto dominated the area.[24] With the design of the Holiday Inn, Štraus demonstrated that he was a bold innovator, though he himself acknowledged that the design of the Holiday Inn was, even by his standards, an 'architectural risk'.[25] Though many compared his work to that of the American architect John Portman, Štraus's design for the Holiday Inn was, he asserted, influenced by Bosnian architectural styles and was based on 'a space organisation scheme of Sarajevo's Morića Han from the seventeenth century (a well-known hotel from that period) in a modern style, as a ten-story cube panelled with surprising yellow aluminium façade square plates'.[26] The design for the hotel had been envisaged by Štraus for many

number of existing hotels that were reconstructed—including the Evropa, Bosna, and Stojčevac hotels in Sarajevo, the Yugoslav Army (JNA) hotel (Borik) on Jahorina, the Turist hotel in Pale, and the Mrazište hotel on Mount Igman. See 'Završni izvještaj—Organizacionog komiteta XIV zimskih olimpijskih igara Sarajevo, 1984', Sarajevo: Oslobodjenje, 1984, p. 106 and Ivan Štraus, *Arkitektura Bosne i Hercegovine, 1945–1995*, p. 105.

[21] Author's interview with Ivan Štraus, September 2013.

[22] For an overview of the history and the activities of SORA/ORA see Dragan Popović, 'Youth Labor Action as Ideological Holiday-Making' in Hannes Grandits & Karin Taylor (eds.), *Yugoslavia's Sunny Side: A History of Tourism in Socialism (1950s–1980s)*, Budapest-New York: Central European University Press, 2010, pp. 279–302.

[23] For a fascinating overview of life in Habsburg Sarajevo see James Lyon, 'Habsburg Sarajevo 1914: A Social Picture', *Prilozi/Contributions*, Institut za istoriju u Sarajevu, No. 43, Sarajevo, 2014, pp. 23–40.

[24] Ivan Štraus, *Arkitektura Bosne i Hercegovine*, p. 113.

[25] Ivan Štraus, *Arhitekt i barbari*, p. 118.

[26] Ivan Štraus, *Arkitektura Bosne i Hercegovine*, p. 102. In their book *Modernism In-Between: The Mediatory Architectures of Socialist Yugoslavia* the architectural historians, Vladimir Kulić, Maroje Mrdjulaš and Wolfgang Thaler argue that many of the hotels, conference centres, and public buildings that were constructed for the numerous events that Yugoslavia hosted in the 1970s and 1980s (such as the 1979 Mediterranean Games in Split,

years, though it had taken many years to be realised. The preliminary design had been drawn up in 1969, for the same plot, though for a different investor.[27] But the context of the approaching Winter Olympics, and the need to create a distinct, modern image for the city, represented a perfect backdrop in which Štraus and other Yugoslav architects could express their considerable talents and, on occasion, their undoubted eccentricity.[28]

Štraus, by his own admission, was given 'a lot of freedom in terms of the design' of the building, took the liberty of 'using colour to the fullest, since its content allowed this'.[29] Every Monday Štraus would meet with party officials, including some of the most powerful people in Bosnia and Herzegovina (such as Branko Mikulić, Milanko Renovica, and Hamdija Pozderac), to discuss the progress of the building and would use a scale model to outline his vision.[30] 'The scale model was yellow', he said, 'but no-one expected that the *actual* exterior of the hotel would be same colour. The construction workers were shocked when the brown, ochre and yellow façade blocks arrived at the site—they thought it was a joke.'[31] So why yellow? 'The purpose of having a yellow façade' said Štraus, 'was to advertise the building—to make it stand out. Of course, it wouldn't be appropriate to build a yellow hospital, but this is a *hotel*, a place for leisure—why would it not be yellow?'.[32]

In a context where Yugoslav architects were given significant scope for creativity (particularly after the 1948 Tito–Stalin split, when Yugoslavia was

the 1984 Winter Olympics in Sarajevo, and the 1987 University Games in Zagreb) evoked 'Fredric Jameson's famous analysis of John Portman's Bonaventura Hotel in Los Angeles, which Jameson casts as an example of the postmodernist "cultural logic of late capitalism": sprawling, self-contained quasi-public interior worlds that repel the outside city, with inconspicuous entrances and the urban presence that stresses surface effect. Indeed, with its atrium lobby equipped with exposed glass elevators, the Holiday Inn Hotel in Sarajevo, built for the 1984 Winter Olympics, directly relied on the models established by Portman, and its aluminium façade in yellow and ochre offered a pop-art celebration of pure surface.' The authors acknowledge, however, that Štraus rejects this, claiming instead that he 'arrived at the atrium solution independently of Portman and that the cantilevered floors on the exterior refer to Bosnian vernacular architecture'. See Kulić et al., *Modernism In-Between: The Mediatory Architectures of Socialist Yugoslavia*, Jovis, Zagreb & Vienna, 2013, p. 48.

[27] Author's interview with Ivan Štraus, September 2013.
[28] Zoran Manević et al., *Arhitektura XX vijeka*, Prosveta, Beograd, 1986, p. 64.
[29] Adnan Pašić, *Arhitekt Ivan Štraus*, p. 33.
[30] *Slobodna Bosna*, Sarajevo, 25 April 2013, p. 65.
[31] Author's interview with Ivan Štraus, September 2013.
[32] Author's interview with Ivan Štraus, Sarajevo, September 2013. See also *Slobodna Bosna*, Sarajevo, 25 April 2013, p. 65.

Image 4.3 The atrium of the Holiday Inn, replete with Štraus's 'big top'. (Photo: Kenneth Morrison)

expelled from Communist Information Bureau [COMINFORM]), Štraus's design was revolutionary. The exterior aesthetic did not, however, hold universal appeal and divided opinion sharply among *Sarajlije* (Sarajevans).[33] Many stood aghast as the bold colours of the exterior became gradually evident. Sarajevans awarded the building a number of equally colourful 'terms of endearment' such as *žutica* (jaundice) to describe the new and distinctive building, which would become the most distinctive landmark in Sarajevo.

Further surprises were in store when the hotel formally opened its door to guests in January 1984, and those sceptical about the exterior of the building were equally so with the interior, which was strikingly different from the exterior. 'When you look at the Holiday Inn', said Štraus, 'the first thing that strikes you is the fact that it is yellow, though inside there is no such dramatic colouring—this duality of architecture is created, intentionally, on both the visual and functional level'.[34] The interior contained a number of eccentric features, characteristic of Štraus's idiosyncratic style. A range of catering spaces and a large, open atrium which included a parasol designed to resemble a circus 'big top', an acknowledgement of the historical utilisation of the plot on which the hotel had been built (Image 4.3). The atrium, originally

---

[33] For an excellent analysis of the 1948 Tito–Stalin split, Yugoslavia's expulsion from COMINFORM and the internal consequences, see Ivo Banac, *With Stalin Against Tito: Cominformist Splits in Yugoslav Communism*, Ithica and London: Cornell University Press, 1988.

[34] Author's interview with Ivan Štraus, September 2013.

conceived by Štraus as a large indoor space, was also bold and striking with surrounding galleries fronted by reflective glass, creating the 'optical illusion of unlimited space' which created a 'good visual effect by casting changing reflections, contributed to the privacy of the guests and helped to alleviate one's fear of height when looking down at the lobby' (Štraus was later upset when the hotel management 'despotically' decided to remove these glass panels).[35] The vast expanse of the large central atrium was offset by grey and red brick walls, green panelling, marble flooring with a distinctive 'zig-zag' pattern, a rather lurid purple carpet, and matching purple chairs and sofas on a raised level that also featured a small marble fountain. The rear wall of the atrium contained a large wooden sculpture known as the 'heavenly chariot'.

Aesthetics aside, the Holiday Inn was a multifunctional building, comprising 336 rooms, 16 suites, and 714 beds.[36] From the rooms, which included, integrated radios and telephones, guests could enjoy good views of Sarajevo, particularly from the eastern side. The 'Olympic Hotel' now needed an international brand. There existed a number of international hotel brands in the SFRJ, including the Intercontinental and Hyatt hotels in Belgrade and the Intercontinental in Zagreb (the latter was the first international brand hotel in the country)[37]; but by the early 1980s there were none in Bosnia and Herzegovina, so the Holiday Inn (known before the agreement was signed with the Holiday Inn group as 'The Olympic Hotel') would be the republic's first.[38] The Holiday Inn brand was perhaps not as most prestigious as the Hilton or the Intercontinental, but they had rapidly become one of the biggest in the world since its inception in 1952, and were, by the 1970s, extending their franchise operation worldwide. According to Sabahudin Selesković, one of the key members of the 1984 Winter Olympics organising committee, 'We wanted a nicer chain, such as Hilton, but Hilton wanted more money, so we chose the Holiday Inn. We knew Holiday Inn was a mid-level hotel in America, a hotel for motorists, but visitors were floored when they saw it. It was really nice.'[39]

---

[35] Ivan Štraus, *Arhitekt i barbari*, p. 118. See also Adnan Pašić, *Arhitekt Ivan Štraus*, p. 33.
[36] *Olimpijski informator*, Broj 22, Sarajevo, Oktobar 1983, p. 2.
[37] James Potter, *World of Difference: 50 Years of Intercontinental Hotels and Its People*, p. 73.
[38] The most modern hotel in Sarajevo at the time was the Hotel Bristol, which was built in the early 1970s and used frequently by the communist elite; but in terms of luxury and modern conveniences, the Holiday Inn was in a class of its own.
[39] Interview with Sabahudin Selesković in Jason Vuić, *The Sarajevo Olympics: A History of the 1984 Winter Games*, p. 55.

The Holiday Inn brand, though clearly an 'all-American' brand, carried less ideological baggage than the Hilton brand (Conrad Hilton, the founder of Hilton International Hotels, made no secret of his anti-communist leanings).[40] The company, essentially the brainchild of Kemmons Wilson (a businessman and entrepreneur based in Memphis, Tennessee), had humble roots.[41] Wilson already owned and ran a successful real estate business, but in 1951 he had a simple idea that would transform the hotel industry in the USA. At the beginning of the 1950s, hotels in the larger US cities tended to be lavish, expensive, and out of reach of most people, and in rural areas the quality of hotels varied considerably—there was clearly a gap in the market that had not yet been exploited. That summer, while taking his family on vacation in Washington D.C, he became increasingly disenchanted with the standard of accommodation available during his travels. Wilson identified the emerging market for good quality but affordable family hotels and the increasing 'democratisation of travel'. Having done so, he set out to establish his own chain of hotels that would offer increasingly aspirational consumers—many of whom were now enjoying the fruits of the post-war consumer boom and regularly taking family holidays—a level of accommodation and service that was in step with their rising expectations. The improved economic conditions, more secure employment (many workers enjoyed, for the first time, paid holidays), and the 'baby boom' following the end of the Second World War produced a record number of 'nuclear families' who would use their paid leave to holiday with their families.

The 'Holiday Inn' was born. The company, named after the 1942 Hollywood movie (of the same name), which starred Bing Crosby and Fred Astaire (with music, including the first introduction of 'White Christmas', by Irving Berlin), grew quickly.[42] The first Holiday Inn hotel was opened

---

[40] Conrad Hilton stated that the Cold War could not be won with satellites and H-bombs and that the building of hotels provided an opportunity to sow the communist world 'the other side of the coin'. For Conrad Hilton's political views, see Annabel Jane Wharton, *Building the Cold War: Hilton International Hotels and Modern Architecture*, Chicago: University of Chicago Press, 2001, pp. 8–11.

[41] The story of Kemmons Wilson's endeavours to create the Holiday Inn Hotels Group; see Kemmons Wilson, *Half Luck and Half Brains: The Kemmons Wilson, Holiday Inn Story*, Memphis: Hambleton Hill, 1996.

[42] The name 'Holiday Inn' was not Wilson's idea. In a speech he gave in Tennessee in 1998, he said that his draughtsman, Eddy Bluestein, had written the name on some rough drawings of the hotel Wilson proposed to build. When he was given the drawings, he saw the words 'Holiday Inn' and the brand was born. 'I asked him where the name came from and

in Memphis in 1952, and comprised 120 rooms, a swimming pool, and a range of other amenities regarded as rather novel for the time, but by the mid-1950s, Wilson had standardised the style of the hotel and franchised it to other business owners. The franchised chain hotel, now omnipresent, was born—the Holiday Inn brand thrived. Offering bright colours, clean rooms, efficient service, and a swimming pool for families, they became genuine destinations of choice for the new aspiring and upwardly mobile working class. And the distinct identity of the Holiday Inn brand was consolidated by the brightly lit roadside corporate logo in green and yellow, known as the 'Great Sign'. It became central to the identity of the brand, and adaptations of it were rolled out across the rapidly growing number of Holiday Inn hotels across the USA. The US franchise (which was to become the corporate model for the Holiday Inn's operations) was opened in Clarksdale, Mississippi in 1954, and by 1959 there were more than hundred Holiday Inns across the USA. The following year the first Holiday Inn outside the USA was opened in Montreal, Canada.

The Holiday Inn franchise operation thrived throughout the 1960s, and the company was listed on the New York Stock Exchange in 1963.[43] Occupancy rates were generally higher than their competitors, due in large part to the IBM-developed HOLIDEX booking system (adopted in 1965), then the world's largest computerised reservation system. The chain then began an expansion of their franchise operation, branching out beyond the USA and into Europe. An international franchise under the umbrella of the 'International Association of Holiday Inns' (IAHI) was created, and the first European Holiday Inn opened in Leiden in The Netherlands in 1968.[44] The European franchise continued to expand throughout the 1970s, with the first Holiday Inn opened in the UK in 1971 (in Leicester, England). And while the Holiday Inn brand retained their image of being 'family friendly' hotels, their European and (later) worldwide franchise adopted a different business model, focusing predominantly on business travel.[45] By then, Kemmons Wilson was regarded as one of the USA's great entrepreneurs—he even featured on the cover of *Time Magazine* in

---

he said he had seen a Bing Crosby movie on television the night before. In the movie the inn was only open on holidays. I said "Eddie, that's a great name—we'll use it".' Speech by Kemmons Wilson, Tennessee Governor's School for Hospitality and Tourism, 8 June 1998.

[43] *The Independent*, London (Travel Supplement), 13 February 2010, p. 6.
[44] *The Times*, London, 9 August 1972, p. 13.
[45] *The Times*, London, 3 November 1980, p. 16.

1972, described as 'The Man with 300,000 Beds.'[46] He retired in 1979, having suffered a heart attack, but the Holiday Inn franchise continued to thrive and expand in his absence.

Such was the omnipotence of Holiday Inn hotels by the late 1970s that they became something of an object of ridicule, dismissed as uniform, characterless, and lacking in architectural merit. During a visit to Beirut the American writer, P.J. O'Rourke, described the city's devastated Holiday Inn (destroyed during the 1975–76 'Battle of the Hotels') as a 'delight to the eye'. Who, he asked, 'when travelling around the earth faced with endless Holiday Inns, has not fantasised blowing one to flinders?'[47] Much of this derision emanated from the fact they tended to architecturally standardise, at least in the USA; a manifestation of the bland set in stone. Sarajevo's Holiday Inn, however, was not designed to be one, and was certainly not typical of the architectural standardisation that characterised Holiday Inn hotels. One of the most unusual in the franchise, the Sarajevo Holiday Inn became part of the growing global franchise in 1983 (which by then extended as far afield as Kyoto in Japan and Beijing in China), and was equipped with more facilities than one might have expected from a standard Holiday Inn.

Of course, Sarajevo's Holiday Inn was more than merely a functional hotel to be used for business or leisure. The hotel was a symbol of modern Sarajevo, a city that was hosting the Winter Olympics. And the initial purpose of the hotel was to provide accommodation for the 'Olympic Family', comprising the IOC and their esteemed guests; thus it was the benchmark in modernity and luxury. Those fortunate enough to have been recruited to work in the hotel began preparations for opening in August 1983, two months in advance of the formal opening on 6 October 1983, cleaning and preparing the hotel to the highest of standards.[48] On that day, Juan Antonio Samaranch, the then President of the Olympic Committee (IOC), arrived at Sarajevo Airport to be met by Branko Mikulić, the President of the ZOI Organising Committee, Anton Šućić (the President of the Executive Committee of the ZOI), and Uglješa Uzelac (the Mayor of Sarajevo) before being taken to the Holiday Inn. There he was greeted by the hotel's management and presented with the *zlatni ključ* (golden key), as the Holiday Inn's first guest, before being taken to the fifth-floor

---

[46] *Time Magazine*, New York, 12 June 1972, p. 1.
[47] P.J. O' Rourke, *Holidays in Hell*, p. 27.
[48] Author's interview with Holiday Inn (Sarajevo) employee, September 2013.

suite, named 'The Presidential Suite', in his honour.⁴⁹ Addressing gathered journalists, Samaranch expressed his delight at the hotel and Sarajevo's preparation for the games.⁵⁰ 'The IOC', he said, 'carefully watches over the preparation for the Games in Sarajevo. And on each occasion I've had the pleasure of seeing the great progress in these preparations. A prime example of these successes is the opening of the Holiday Inn.'⁵¹

Sarajevo's Holiday Inn was, by the standards of the time, very impressive. As Ivan Štraus had intended, the large atrium and surrounding dining and shopping facilities gave the impression of an 'indoor city'.⁵² Guests need never leave the hotel, and could choose from a number of restaurants in which to dine. The *Noćni* (Night), the *Nacionalni* (National) served Bosnian and Western food, while guests seeking something less formal could eat at the *Piccolo*, which served pizza and pasta. The hotel also boasted a hairdressing salon, a travel agency—which had representatives of Yugoslav Airlines (JAT), *Putnik* and *Kompas*—two clothing boutiques, a commercial art gallery, a souvenir shop, and a newspaper/tobacco shop (a *Hertz* car rental office would open later in the decade). For those inclined to gamble, one could do so in the casino on the ground floor, and for those with an inclination to drink and dance there was *Diskoteka '84* in the basement, where the 'latest international sounds' could be enjoyed (or endured).⁵³ The majority of visitors to the Holiday Inn would, however, simply sit in the large atrium lobby drinking coffee or alcoholic beverages (though both staff and guests complained that the large atrium was often cold).⁵⁴

⁴⁹ 'Samaranch Itinerary in Sarajevo', 6 September 1983, International Olympic Committee Archives, Lausanne, Switzerland (CIO JO-1984W-HEBER, folder 204627).
⁵⁰ Sabahudin Selimić, *Sarajevo '84*, Organazacioni komitet XIV zimskih olimpijskih igara Jugoslavija, Sarajevo, 1984, p. 2.
⁵¹ *Olimpijski informator*, Broj 22, Sarajevo, Oktobar 1983, p. 2.
⁵² Author's interview with Ivan Štraus, September 2013.
⁵³ Holiday Inn, Sarajevo, brochure from 1984 (courtesy of Amira Delalić).
⁵⁴ The district of Marindvor comprises four blocks positioned at the intersection of the main boulevard (Zmaja od Bosne) and the streets that encircle the Ottoman and Austro-Hungarian sections of the city. The area possesses several public buildings from different periods of Sarajevo's history, amongst which the Communist Party of Yugoslavia (KPJ) commissioned and built a number of modernist landmarks (such as the Bosnian parliament, the Faculty of Philosophy building, the UNIS towers, and the Holiday Inn), though there have been new developments in the forms of the 'Sarajevo Centar' and 'Alta' shopping centres since the late 2000s. The residential suburbs to the west of Marindvor (Alipašino polje, Otoka, Socijalno Grbavica, and Dolac Malta) were built as neighbourhoods composed of free-standing high-rise apartment buildings constructed around open spaces and public facilities, including squares, playgrounds, schools, nurseries, and sport halls. Robert Donia argues

Samaranch and the leadership of the IOC would stay in the luxurious rooms and suites. But in addition to hosting the IOC, the heads of International Sports Federations (such as FIFA), the National Olympic Committee, and the delegations of the Organising Committees of the Games,[55] the hotel would also host various other esteemed guests—such as King Olaf V of Norway, King Carl XVI Gustav, the US and British Ambassadors to Yugoslavia, Premier Peter Lougheed of Alberta, Canada (the host of the 1988 Calgary Winter Olympics), Amadou Mahtar M'Bow, Director General of the of the United Nations Educational, Scientific and Cultural Organization (UNESCO), and the American actor, Kirk Douglas (a personal friend of Tito, who was known to admire Douglas's films).[56] Corporate sponsors such as PAN-AM Airlines (who had an existing 'referral arrangement' with the global Holiday Inn franchise) and Coca Cola also held events at the hotel.[57] One member of staff recalled that, 'the hotel was full of important guests, both foreign and domestic; many journalists, the Olympic Committee and, of course, Juan Antonio Samaranch in the Presidential Suite. It was the place where the most important people came from the world of film and entertainment, sport, politics and business. It was really something new and special for Sarajevo.'[58]

The hotel was the location of choice for anyone of note visiting Sarajevo; numerous high-level delegations visited the hotel and royalty from the UK, Norway, and Sweden stayed there throughout the 1980s. Other famous faces came and went. The American actor Kirk Douglas stayed in the hotel during the Winter Olympics (local stories tell of him spending liberally in the casino). Such esteemed guests required (and expected) the highest of standards, and the hotel's director, Danilo Dursun, made sure that these standards were reached and maintained. He oversaw a hugely successful period during which the plaudits of both the hotel and the

---

that these suburbs brought a revolution to Sarajevo's everyday residential life because unlike the Ottoman period *mahalas*, which were ethnically segregated neighbourhoods composed around a religious building, the socialist-period suburbs built west of Marindvor were ethnically and religiously mixed neighbourhoods concentrated around places for public gathering, (interethnic) socialising, and living. See Robert Donia, *Sarajevo: A Biography*, p. 231.

[55] 'Accommodation of Olympic Family', 6 September 1983, International Olympic Committee Archives, Lausanne, Switzerland (CIO JO-1984W-HEBER, folder 204627).

[56] See Jason Vuić, *The Sarajevo Olympics. A History of the 1984 Winter Games*, p. 55.

[57] "Holiday Inn, Sarajevo: Receptions, dinners, cocktails and buffets in the hotel during the Olympic Games", 30 January 1984, International Olympic Committee Archives, Lausanne, Switzerland (CIO JO-1989W-RP, folder 204755).

[58] Author's interview with Holiday Inn (Sarajevo) employee, September 2013.

Image 4.4 The Holiday Inn hotel, circa June 1984. (Photo: The Holiday Inn, Sarajevo)

service provided there were manifold. Even today, the hotel's staff (many of whom have worked there since the opening day) speak with immense pride about the role that the Holiday Inn played as an important centre for international guests and the excellent standards that were maintained in the hotel throughout these early years (Image 4.4).[59]

The 1984 Winter Olympics was an unmitigated success for Sarajevo, and, according to Vuić, 'financing, construction, transportation, security: contrary to all expectations…everything worked'.[60] The gold medal performances of the UK ice-dancing partnership of Torvill and Dean, the US figure skater Scott Hamilton, the German figure skater Katarina Witt, and the remarkable seven-game winning streak of the Soviet ice hockey team were etched in the memories of those that witnessed them.[61] Yet, the

---

[59] Author's interviews with Holiday Inn (Sarajevo) employees, September 2013 and April/May 2014.

[60] Jason Vuić, *The Sarajevo Olympics: A History of the 1984 Winter Games*, p. 9.

[61] Maurice Ravel's 'Boléro' will forever be associated with the 1984 Winter Olympics. The music was a key element of Jane Torvill and Christopher Dean's performance of the same name. The British ice dancers would return to Sarajevo in 1999 to make a documentary with National Broadcasting Company (NBC) crew. They also returned to perform their 'Boléro' routine in 2014, marking the thirtieth anniversary of their gold medal performance. See *The Telegraph*, London, 14 February 2014, p. 31.

games also exposed the fractures in unity between Yugoslavia's republics. According to Kate Meehan Pedrotty:

> The Sarajevo Olympic Games opened up a dangerous space in Yugoslav society, a space that exposed some of the economic and political issues that would become tragically unworkable by the end of the decade. Inter-republican rivalries, suspicion of corruption and financial malfeasance, accusations of nationalism, fascism, and "anti-communism", and exasperation with the federal system all emerged during Yugoslavia's Olympic experience.[62]

In the wake of the 1984 Winter Games, the Olympic star faded, but the Holiday Inn remained at the centre of Sarajevo's social and cultural life. Elton John stayed there in April 1984 during his 'European Express' (part of his wider 'Breaking Hearts' tour), the concert taking place at the Zetra sports hall. (While in Sarajevo he also attended a football match between FK Željezničar and FK Red Star Belgrade at the Grbavica stadium.) Likewise, Rory Gallagher, once of the British blues-rock group *Taste*, stayed at the hotel while playing in Sarajevo. Of course, in addition to the occasional global celebrity, local personalities, sportsmen (and sport's teams), and the Bosnian communist elite would often be seen in the hotel's lobby. It was, according to Silvija Jestrović, a time when 'the 'suits of Socialism' were 'literally rubbing shoulders with Western pop culture'.[63]

For many ordinary Sarajevans, however, the hotel was a world apart, a place considered far too expensive for the majority to stay in or dine in—it was widely regarded as an elite hotel, so many Sarajevans preferred to drink coffee or eat in the city's more traditional hostelries.[64] So despite the success of the Holiday Inn, other hotels, such as the Europa in the Baščaršija district, built in 1882 by Gligorije Jeftanović, and with its famed *Bečka kafana* (Viennese café), remained

---

[62] Kate Meehan Pedrotty, 'Yugoslav Unity and Olympic Ideology', pp. 337–338.

[63] Silvija Jestrović, *Performances, Space, Utopia: Cities of War, Cities of Exile*, Basingstoke: Palgrave MacMillan, 2013, p. 110. For an excellent study of Yugoslav rock music and the many Sarajevo-based bands, see Dalibor Mišina, *Shake, Rattle and Roll: Yugoslav Rock Music and the Poetics of Social Critique*, Farnham: Ashgate Press, 2013.

[64] For an overview of the construction of hotels during the Austro-Hungarian period, see Mary Sparks, *The Development of Austro-Hungarian Sarajevo, 1878–1918: An Urban History*, Bloomsbury Press, London & New York, 2014, pp. 171–173.

one of the major cultural confluences in the city.⁶⁵ The nearby Hotel Bristol was popular with the Bosnian communist elite, though it lacked the 'international glamour' of the Holiday Inn, which represented a modern, progressive, outward-looking Sarajevo. Indeed, the hotel also became a location of choice for the city's fashionable youth. In 1988, a club night in the pool (situated in a building across from the hotel's main entrance) known as *zenba*, a play on the word *bazen* (pool), attracted Sarajevo's young hipsters. The hotel was also used in a number of domestic films (long before it appeared in Western films such as Michael Winterbottom's *Welcome to Sarajevo*, Richard Shepard's *The Hunting Party*, or Gerardo Herrero's *Territorio Comanche*), such as Benjamin Filipović's *Praznik u Sarajevu* (Holiday in Sarajevo), in which the New Year party scene was filmed in the atrium of the hotel.

But the apparent glamour of the Holiday Inn masked the difficult economic situation in Bosnia and Herzegovina and throughout the SFRJ.⁶⁶ Economic turmoil was felt in all parts of Yugoslavia but was more acute in the poorer republic. Living standards dropped as ordinary Yugoslavs began to feel the effects of the government's austerity policy. In an attempt to rescue the economy, the government took drastic measures, closing down unviable enterprises while reducing manpower costs in others. For the increasingly beleaguered communist elite, the official line remained that nationalism was counter-revolutionary and a danger to the principles of national equality and *bratstvo i jedinstvo* (brotherhood and unity). Yet the Yugoslav League of Communists (SKJ) grew increasingly impotent in their attempts to stem the rising tide of nationalism, and as the crisis worsened, their legitimacy (and communism as the ideological underpinning of the Yugoslav political system)

---

⁶⁵ The Hotel Europa was, according to Dževad Karahasan, 'The semantic centre of Sarajevo. Bearing elements of both the East and Central Europe, this hotel is like a prism that gathers within itself the diffuse rays of what Sarajevo really is… To know Sarajevo means to need to go to the Hotel Europa quite regularly.' See Dževdad Karahasan, *Sarajevo: Exodus of a City*, Kodansha International, New York, 1994. p. 91. The Europa was, in July 1995, destroyed by artillery fire by Bosnian Serb forces who claimed that the hotel was being used by a Muslim paramilitary group *Zelene beretke* (Green Berets). See *Dani*, Sarajevo, 12 December 2008, p. 11.

⁶⁶ For the Central Intelligence Agency's then view on the economic crisis, see Central Intelligence Agency (CIA), Directorate of Intelligence, 'Yugoslavia: Key Questions and Answers on the Debt Crisis: An Intelligence Assessment', Document No. (FOIA)/ESDN (CREST): 0005361799.

eroded. Nationalism, largely dormant since 1945, now became an alternative ideological basis for those who would ultimately destroy the SFRJ.

The disintegration of the SFRJ was gradual, complex, and multidimensional, and there is no single causal factor.[67] The economic crisis of the 1980s, however, created a context in which anti-communist forces could thrive. Serb nationalists, for example, sought to exploit the economic instability, arguing that Serbs were disadvantaged within the SFRJ, helping to reawaken ethnic urges that would ultimately triumph over economic reform and political pluralisation. The first pivotal event was the emergence of the so-called *Memorandum*, an unpublished manuscript that had emanated from the Serbian Academy of Arts and Sciences (*Srpska akademija nauka i umetnosti*—SANU). Though similar studies had been conducted before, the Memorandum had a distinctly political edge.[68] But while the Memorandum was the work of nationalist intellectuals, the first politician of significance to understand (and exploit) the opportunities presented by these shifting political currents was Slobodan Milošević. A former banker and seemingly unremarkable party *apparatchik*, he had risen through the ranks of the League of Communists of Serbia (*Savez komunista Srbije*—SKS) through the mid-1980s, largely as a result of his close relationship with Ivan Stambolić, his friend, political mentor, and nephew of Petar Stambolić (an esteemed Yugoslav communist). Milošević's visit to Kosovo in April 1987, whereupon he told Serbs that they 'would not be beaten again', was a pivotal moment. Thereafter, following the Eighth Session of the Central Committee of the SKS in 1987, Milošević used the issue of Serb rights in Kosovo to undermine Stambolić, a strategy that ultimately succeeded. In the wake of Stambolić's downfall, Milošević quickly became the undisputed leader of the SKS and the 'saviour of the Serbs'.[69]

---

[67] The disintegration of the SFRJ can only be dealt with superficially in this book. However, for a succinct explanation of the contributory dynamics and a review of relevant literature, see Dejan Jović, 'The Disintegration of Yugoslavia: A Critical Review of Explanatory Approaches', *European Journal of Social Theory*, 4(1): 101–120.

[68] See, for example, Ruža Petrović & Marina Blagojević, *The Migration of Serbs and Montenegrins from Kosovo and Metohija: Results of the Survey Conducted in 1985–1986*, Serbian Academy of Arts and Sciences (SANU), Demographic Studies, Volume III, Belgrade, (English translation) 1992.

[69] For an analysis of the events surrounding the Eighth Session of the League of Communists of Serbia see Dejan Jović, *Yugoslavia: A State that Withered Away*, Purdue University Press, West Lafayette, Indiana, 2009, pp. 268–272.

Promising to revise the 'anti-Serb' 1974 constitution, which had decentralised power to the SFRJ's republics and autonomous regions', and stem the 'counter-revolution' in Kosovo, Milošević sent the JNA into Kosovo and set about re-establishing control in Kosovo and Vojvodina (the two provinces of Serbia that had been given significant autonomy) and Montenegro (traditionally a close ally of Serbia). The instrument used to achieve this objective being the so-called anti-bureaucratic revolution.[70] Ostensibly, demonstrations about the status of Serbs and Montenegrins in Kosovo, the real aim was to undermine, and eventually force out, the tottering communist leaderships there (giving Milošević control of four of the eight Yugoslav federal presidency votes). The Milošević-manipulated 'politics of the streets' were used with some efficacy in Vojvodina, where a series of well-organised rallies dubbed 'The Yoghurt Revolution' (due to protestors throwing yoghurt at the government buildings in Novi Sad) brought the province's leadership to its knees. In Montenegro, the (Kosovo Serb-led) 'Meetings of Truth' took place across the republic, with rallies taking place throughout August and September in Nikšić, Andrijevica, Kolašin, and Cetinje. Seeking to capitalise from the popular discontent fuelled by Montenegro's grim economic situation, they took their demonstrations to Titograd, the republic's capital.[71] A series of rallies outside the parliament building forced the communist authorities to submit, and by January 1989, the old guards were replaced by the *mladi, lijepi i pametni* (young, handsome, and intelligent) troika of Momir Bulatović, Milo Djukanović, and Svetozar Marović. But for all their perceived merits, they were inexperienced and, given the rhetorical (and logistical) support

---

[70] See Nebojša Vladisavljević, *Serbia's Antibureaucratic Revolution: Milošević, the Fall of Communism and Nationalist Mobilisation*, Palgrave MacMillan, Basingstoke, 2008 and (by the same author) 'The Break-up of Yugoslavia: The role of popular politics', in Djokić & Ker-Lindsay, *New Perspectives on Yugoslavia: Key Issues and Controversies*, Routledge, London & New York, 2011, pp. 143–160.

[71] The demonstrations in Montenegro were primarily driven by economic discontent. They were, however, quickly manipulated by Milošević's supporters to replace the Montenegrin communist leadership with younger elites (within the party) who were more inclined towards Belgrade. See Kenneth Morrison, *Montenegro, A Modern History*, pp. 81–88. See also Srdjan Darmanović, 'The Peculiarities of Transition in Serbia and Montenegro', in Dragica Vujadinović et al., *Between Authoritarianism and Democracy: Serbia, Montenegro, Croatia*, CEDET, Belgrade, 2003, and Nebojša Vladisavljević, *Serbia's Antibureaucratic Revolution: Milošević, the Fall of Communism and Nationalist Mobilisation*, pp. 160–166.

they received from Belgrade, they owed their rapid rise to power in some measure to Milošević.

These developments were watched with growing anxiety in Slovenia and Croatia, and in January 1990, amidst increasing tension between the Yugoslav republics, Slovenian delegates left the "Fourteenth Special Congress' of SKJ held in the Sava Centre in Belgrade'. They were followed thereafter by the Croatian delegation. In the spring of 1990, multiparty elections were held in both Slovenia and Croatia. In the former, Milan Kučan, the former leader of the Slovenian League of Communists (*Zveza komunistov Slovenije*—ZKS), became president, while in the latter, Franjo Tudjman of the nationalist Croatian Democratic Community (*Hrvatska demokratska zajednica*—HDZ) triumphed over Ivica Račan's Social Democratic Party of Croatia (*Socijaldemokratska partija Hrvatske*—SDP), albeit narrowly, in the Croatian elections.

In Slovenia there was a tiny Serb minority, thus Milošević was less concerned about Slovenia's secession from the SFRJ. Slovenia held an independence referendum on 23 December 1990, resulting in an overwhelming majority in favour of leaving the SFRJ. Slovenia declared independence on 25 June 1991, resulting in a short conflict between the Slovenian Territorial Defence (*Teritorialna obramba Republike Slovenije*—TORS) and the JNA, before the latter departed Slovenian territory. The declaration of Croatian independence on the same day was, however, a different matter. There, the significant Serb minority, the vast majority of whom opposed the HDZ, feared that the party was preparing to secede from the SFRJ, and they sought help from Belgrade. The Milošević government in Belgrade thereafter continued to stoke the fears of Croatia's Serbs, and the Serb rebellion against the Tudjman government, emanating from the *Krajina* and led by Milan Babić, the mayor of Knin, and Milan Martić, a local police chief, thus began in earnest. It would culminate in a full-scale war pitting Croatian government forces and paramilitaries against Serb rebels, Serb paramilitaries, and the JNA.[72]

---

[72] For the events leading to the war in Croatia, see Hannes Grandits & Carolin Leutloff, 'Discourses, actors, violence: the organisation of war-escalation in the Krajina region of Croatia, 1990–1991', in Jan Koehler & Christopher Zürcher (eds.), *Potentials of Disorder*, Manchester and New York: Manchester University Press, 2003, pp. 23–45. Branka Magaš & Ivo Žanić, *The War in Croatia and Bosnia-Herzegovina 1991–1995*, London: Frank Cass, 2001.

References

Djokić, D., & Ker-Lindsay, J. (2011). *New Perspectives on Yugoslavia: Key Issues and Controversies*. New York & London: Routledge.
Grandits, H., & Leutloff, C. (2003). Discourses, actors, violence: The organisation of war-escalation in the Krajina region of Croatia, 1990–1991. In J. Koehler, & C. Zürcher (Eds.), *Potentials of Disorder* (pp. 23–45). Manchester and New York: Manchester University Press.
Grandits, H., & Taylor, K. (Eds.) (2010). *Yugoslavia's Sunny Side: A History of Tourism in Socialism (1950s–1980s)*. Budapest: Central European University Press.
Hadžihasanović, A. (2010). *1984: Olimpijada trijumfa i šansi*. Sarajevo: Rabic.
Jestrović, S. (2013). *Performances, Space, Utopia: Cities of War, Cities of Exile*. Basingstoke: Palgrave MacMillan.
Jović, D. (2009). *Yugoslavia: A State that Withered Away*. West Lafayette, Indiana: Purdue University Press.
Karahasan, D. (1994). *Sarajevo, Exodus of a City*. Tokyo & London: Kodansha International.
Kulić, V., et al. (2013). *Modernism In-Between: The Mediatory Architectures of Socialist Yugoslavia*. Zagreb & Vienna: Jovis.
Lyon, J. (2014). Habsburg Sarajevo 1914: A social picture, *Prilozi/Contributions*, Institut za istoriju u Sarajevu, 43, Sarajevo, 23–40.
Magaš, B. (1993). *The Destruction of Yugoslavia*. London: Verso Press.
Magaš, B., & Žanić, I. (Eds.) (2001). *The War in Croatia and Bosnia-Herzegovina 1991–1995*. London: Frank Cass.
Manević, Z., et al. (1986). *Arhitektura XX vijeka*. Beograd: Prosveta.
Mišina, D. (2013). *Shake, Rattle and Roll: Yugoslav Rock Music and the Poetics of Social Critique*. Farnham: Ashgate Press.
Organizacionog komiteta XIV zimskih olimpijskih igara Sarajevo (1984). *Završni izvještaj—Organizacionog komiteta XIV zimskih olimpijskih igara Sarajevo, 1984*. Sarajevo: Oslobodjenje.
Petrović, R., & Blagojević, M. (1992). *The Migration of Serbs and Montenegrins from Kosovo and Metohija: Results of the Survey Conducted in 1985–1986*, Serbian Academy of Arts and Sciences (SANU), Demographic Studies, Volume III, Belgrade, (English translation).
Sparks, M. (2014). *The Development of Austro-Hungarian Sarajevo, 1878–1918: An Urban History*. London & New York: Bloomsbury Press.
Vladisavljević, N. (2008). *Serbia's Antibureaucratic Revolution: Milošević, the Fall of Communism and Nationalist Mobilisation*. Basingstoke: Palgrave MacMillan.
Vuić, J. (2015). *The Sarajevo Olympics: A History of the 1984 Winter Games*, University of Massachusetts Press.
Wharton, A. J. (2001). *Building the Cold War: Hilton International Hotels and Modern Architecture*. Chicago: University of Chicago Press.
Wilson, K. (1996). *Half Luck and Half Brains: The Kemmons Wilson, Holiday Inn Story*. Memphis: Hambleton Hill.

CHAPTER 5

Politics Comes to the Holiday Inn

Bosnia and Herzegovina was not, of course, immune from the events taking place in Slovenia and neighbouring Croatia. The most multi-ethnic of the SFRJ's republics, it would also enter into a new period of multiparty politics as the federal state continued its demise, though the ethnic dynamics there were far more complex than in the cases of Slovenia or Croatia. Bosnia and Herzegovina was akin to Yugoslavia in microcosm, with a mixed population of Muslims, Serbs, and Croats, and thus the disintegration of the SFRJ would have significant consequences for the republic. Here, too, political parties would emerge to challenge the League of Communists of Bosnia and Herzegovina (*Savez komunista Bosne i Hercegovine*—SK-BiH), then led by Nijaz Duraković. Political parties were first registered in Bosnia and Herzegovina in early 1990, the first being minor ones emerging in Mostar and none of them being of any real significance.[1] In Sarajevo, however, parties that would become powerful forces in Bosnian politics would also emerge. Problematically, they were of a predominantly mono-ethnic character (despite a republic-wide ban on parties deemed by the ruling communists to be overtly nationalist), organised along ethnic lines and their interpretation of events viewed through an ethnic lens.

The Holiday Inn's extensive conference facilities made it a popular venue for the political gatherings of those parties that emerged following the demise of the SKJ in January 1990. From 1990, the hotel played host

[1] Neven Andjelić, *Bosnia-Herzegovina: The End of a Legacy*, p. 135.

to newly formed political parties, who would hold their launch events there. Thus, the Holiday Inn increasingly became a *political space*, often at the epicentre of the political events. As Bosnia and Herzegovina moved towards the republic's first multiparty elections, held in November 1990, the hotel became a regular meeting place for the numerous political parties that were formed in advance of those fateful elections. In the new 'democratic' environment, the Holiday Inn would become the forum for political activity, with a plethora of meetings and party launches taking place in the hotel throughout 1990. The first of these took place on 27 March 1990[2] in the 'Vrbas Hall'[3] of the Holiday Inn, whereupon the (predominantly Muslim) SDA (*Stranka demokratske akcije*) held their founding congress.[4] The party was led by its then de facto leader, Alija Izetbegović, a Muslim lawyer and scholar who had, as a member of *Mladi Muslimani* (Young Muslims), been jailed in 1946 for anti-communist activities and again in 1983 during the so-called *Sarajevski proces* (The Sarajevo Trials) for writing and disseminating 'hostile propaganda' and engaging in 'counter-revolutionary acts'.[5] A key part of the accusations directed against Izetbegović was that he had propagated the idea of a Muslim-dominated Bosnia and Herzegovina (in which Islamic law could be practised) in his *Islamska deklaracija* (Islamic Declaration), which had originally been published in 1970. The book made no specific reference to Bosnia per se, but this made little difference.[6] He was, nevertheless, sentenced to fourteen years in prison, but was released in 1988. The SDA was, according to Izetbegović, 'a political union of Yugoslav citizens belonging to the Muslim cultural and historical traditions, as well as other

---

[2] The leaders of the nascent SDA were not the only 'prestigious' guests in the hotel on that day. The British heavy metal band 'Motorhead' were also guests (they played at Zetra on 27 March 1990), though they were almost certainly unaware of the gravity of political events that were taking place in the hotel on that day.

[3] All of the conference halls in the Holiday Inn were named after rivers in Bosnia and Herzegovina: Vrbas, Una, Neretva, and Drina.

[4] Tanjug Domestic Service, Belgrade, FBIS-LD270323490, 27 March 1990. For an analysis of the formation of the SDA in the Sandžak region, see Kenneth Morrison & Elizabeth Roberts, *The Sandžak: A History*, London: Hurst & Co, 2013, pp. 134–139.

[5] For a detailed analysis of the trial see Rajko Danilović, *Sarajevski proces 1983*, Tuzla: Bosanka riječ, 2006.

[6] Noel Malcolm, *Bosnia: A Short History*, Pan-MacMillan, 1994, p. 208. Malcolm goes on to note that 'The treatise, written in the late 1960s, is a general treatise that on politics and Islam, addressed to the whole Muslim world; it is not about Bosnia and does not even mention Bosnia.' See *Ibid*, p. 219.

citizens of the country', but Izetbegović had a history, and the SDA never transcended beyond a predominantly Muslim party.

At the launch event in the Holiday Inn, Alija Izetbegović, flanked by the core members of the SDA, read out the 'Statement of the Forty', the programmatic underpinning for the party.[7] Two months later, on 26 May 1990, the 'Constituent Assembly' of the SDA was held in the hotel, and this time the room was packed.[8] The party's programme was still in its infancy and not clearly articulated at this stage, but the SDA essentially brought together key Muslims (businessmen, intellectuals, and nationalists) under its banner. Alija Izetbegović, an intellectual and political activist, was clearly the leading figure in the party, though also in attendance at the 26 May meeting at the Holiday Inn was Adil Zulfikarpašić, a wealthy Bosnian Muslim exile living in Switzerland since the late 1940s, who had arrived in Sarajevo and taken a suite at the Holiday Inn.[9] He would, in the coming weeks and months, emerge as an alternative and competing centre of power within the SDA. The 'liberal' wing of the party was essentially supportive of Adil Zulfikarpašić, a founding member of the party who had become increasingly concerned by the direction in which Alija Izetbegović was taking the SDA.[10] Gradually, it became evident that a bifurcation was taking place within the party leadership, which would soon consolidate into two competing factions heading inexorably towards conflict.[11] In the early days of the party, the more conservative factions (led by Alija Izetbegović in Bosnia, Sulejman Ugljanin in Serbia, and Harun Hadžić in Montenegro) were in the ascendancy, and many Muslims gravitated towards parties and institutions—the SDA and the Islamic Community (*Islamska zajednica*—IZ)—that claimed to be their protectors. Zulfikarpašić, claiming he was unable to find common ground

---

[7] For the full text of the SDA's 'Statement of the Forty', see Alija Izetbegović, *Inescapable Questions: Autobiographical Notes*, Leicester: The Islamic Foundation, 2003, pp. 66–74.

[8] Alija Izetbegović, *Inescapable Questions: Autobiographical Notes*, p. 75.

[9] Adil Zulfikarpašić (in dialogue with Milovan Djilas and Nadežda Gaće), *The Bosniak*, London: Hurst & Co., 1998, p. 130.

[10] *Demokratija*, Belgrade, 13 October 1990, p. 4.

[11] Born in Foča in the then Kingdom of Yugoslavia, Adil Zulfikarpašić was the descendant of a longline of prominent Muslim *beys* (lords). He was a member of the Yugoslav Communist Party during the Second World War, and was, in 1942, arrested and jailed in Sarajevo by the Ustaše. Upon his release, he became a prominent member of the party, and was awarded the post of Deputy Minister for Trade. However, he gradually became disillusioned with Tito and fled Yugoslavia for exile in Switzerland in 1946. He returned to Bosnia in 1990 and was a key early member of the SDA. See Adil Zulfikarpašić, *The Bosniak*, London: Hurst & Co., 1998.

with Izetbegović, would later leave the SDA to create the Muslim Bosniak Organisation (MBO) with Muhamed Filipović.

Also present at the Holiday Inn meeting was the Chairman of the Croatian Democratic Union (HDZ), Dalibor Brozović. Though based in Zagreb, he had been born in Sarajevo and came with a message that Croatia respected Bosnia's borders and their government would not accept 'possible offers concerning the division of Bosnia', but that 'this standpoint should not provoke any suspicion or anxiety' among Bosnia's Serb community.[12] But, of course, the sight of Muslim and Croat leaders sharing the same platform did animate the more nationalistic elements within the Bosnian Serb community.[13] Two months after the 26 May SDA meeting, in August 1990, the Bosnian branch of the HDZ, known as the Croatian Democratic Union of Bosnia and Herzegovina (*Hrvatskademokratska zajednica Bosne i Hercegovine*—HDZ-BiH) was formed. They held their launch event at *Dom mladih* in Skenderija, where delegates reiterated their commitment to a unified Bosnian state in which Croats enjoyed equal status.[14] The party was originally led by Davorin Perinović, but was soon replaced by Stjepan Kljuić. The latter was a moderate, with pro-Bosnia leanings and would later come into conflict with the more nationalist strands within the HDZ-BiH and the 'Herzegovinan lobby' within the Croatian HDZ. He would eventually be replaced as leader of the HDZ-BiH by the more hard-line Mate Boban in January 1992, a Herzegovinan Croat who was the architect of the *Hrvastska republika Herceg-Bosna* (the Croatian Republic of Herceg-Bosna).[15]

---

[12] Tanjug Domestic Service, Belgrade, FBIS-LD2705131490, 26 May 1990. For Brožović's speech at the SDA meeting see also Neven Andjelić, *Bosnia-Herzegovina: The End of a Legacy*, p. 163.

[13] During a meeting of the Assembly of the SDS on 24 October 1991, Dr Dragan Djukanović reminded the audience that 'The sufferings of Serbs in Bosnia were actually prepared when the HDZ-BiH was formed. What many assumed would happen was confirmed by Mr. Brožović at the founding of the Party of Democratic Action, across the street from here in the Holiday Inn hotel in late May last year. You remember very well that he said that Croatia would be defended on the River Drina, and his speech received frenetic applause.' See 'Serbian Democratic Party of Bosnia & Herzegovina: Stenograph of the constituting session of the Assemble of the Serbian People in Bosnia and Herzegovina', 24 October 1991, UN-ICTY Doc No. SA02-2055-SA02-2164/SA01-2055-SA01-2164/MP, p. 28.

[14] Mario Pejić, *HVO Sarajevo*, Sarajevo: Libertas, 2008, p. 17.

[15] According to Stjepan Kljuić, he was replaced by Boban because he would not execute 'this dirty mission of the partition of Bosnia and Herzegovina'. Speaking of Boban, he said, 'Boban, who was anonymous in the HDZ, never gave us a single speech at [HDZ] meetings.

The SDS was formed in July 1990 and led by the psychiatrist (and amateur poet) Radovan Karadžić, a Montenegrin by birth.[16] Karadžić was, according to Neven Andjelić, the 'last-ditch choice' after other respected Serbs (such as the then Rector of Sarajevo University, Nenad Kecmanović) had declined to lead the party.[17] Like HDZ-BiH, they held their launch event at *Dom mladih*. The audience, which included both Alija Izetbegović and Muhamed Filipović, heard Karadžić inform the crowd that the SDS would be a party that was both 'social democratic' and 'patriotic'.[18] Karadžić, the man who would come to personify the SDS, was born in June 1945 in the village of Petnjica, in the present-day municipality of Šavnik (traditionally one of the poorest municipalities in Montenegro) and hailed from a well-known family.[19] His father, Vuk, had fought for both the Chetniks and the Communist-led Partisans during the 1941–45 war that ravaged Yugoslavia, but had been arrested by the communists in 1945 and sentenced to fifteen years in prison (though he would serve only five).[20] Thus, Radovan Karadžić was brought up without his father for the first five years of his life, and he developed a much stronger bond with his mother, Jovanka, who would remain a central figure in

---

He was a deputy in our parliament [but] he was known for the fact that he was the only one who kept silent' (Kljuić suggests this was the case because Boban possessed an 'inferiority complex'). See Transcript of interview with Stjepan Kljuić, in 'Death of Yugoslavia Archive', 3/39, UBIT, 035-038, p. 3.

[16] For an excellent and detailed assessment of Radovan Karadžić's political life, see Robert Donia, *Radovan Karadžić: Architect of the Bosnian Genocide*, Cambridge: Cambridge University Press, 2015. See also Nick Hawton, *The Quest for Radovan Karadžić*, London: Hutchinson, 2009. For a more sympathetic assessment see Lijljana Bulatović (ed.), *Radovan*, Belgrade: EVRO, 2002.

[17] Neven Andjelić, *Bosnia-Herzegovina: The End of a Legacy*, p. 163.

[18] *Naši Dani*, Sarajevo, 20 July 1990, p. 12. See also Neven Andjelić, *Bosnia-Herzegovina: The End of a Legacy*, p. 166.

[19] Radovan Karadžić always played up to his family name, on occasion implying that he was directly related to the Serbian linguist who codified the Serbian language. Commenting on footage of Karadžić from a BBC documentary entitled 'Serbian Epics', the Serbian sociologist, Ivan Čolović noted that 'Karadžić can be seen in Vuk's house in his birthplace of Tršić [Serbia] demonstrating his skill in the playing the *gusle* [a traditional Serbian instrument— though it is played by other nations in the Balkans]. But the strongest part of this film is a scene in which the Karadžić of our day points to a portrait of the old Karadžić, asking us to note a detail which discloses the remarkable working of the genes: a dimple on the chin of the old Karadžić which is identical to the one embellishing the chin of his professed descendant.' See Ivan Čolović, *The Politics of Symbol in Serbia*, London: Hurst & Co., 2002, p. 17.

[20] Robert Donia, *Radovan Karadžić: Architect of the Bosnian Genocide*, p. 27.

his life. In 1956, the Karadžić family moved to Nikšić, where Radovan attended *srednja škola* (middle school).[21] He performed well in his studies, and at the age of sixteen left Nikšić to embark upon studies in psychiatry at Sarajevo University (he would also later study in both Norway and the USA). While there he surrounded himself with a small group of like-minded young Serbs with nationalist leanings. He revelled in his Montenegrin roots. Montenegro was, according to their own folklore, the *Srspka Sparta* (Serbian Sparta), and Montenegrins 'the best of Serbs', those who had fought the Turks for centuries while carving out a meagre existence in the rocky crags around *Stara Crna Gora* (Old Montenegro) around Cetinje, thereby preserving the flame of Serbdom, Orthodoxy, and freedom while building their nascent state under the Petrović dynasty.[22] In the tradition of some of the great Montenegrin leaders, such as Petar II Petrović 'Njegoš' (*Vladika* and author of the epic poem *Gorski vijenac*—'The Mountain Wreath'), Karadžić developed a love of poetry, which he began to write while a student in Sarajevo.[23]

His one-time friend, the writer Marko Vešović (a fellow Montenegrin), described the young Karadžić as 'charming, bright and popular—always at the centre of everything' though he seemed to be 'a man in a hurry—the first to marry and first to start a family'.[24] He wed Ljiljana Zelen, a medical student from Sarajevo, in 1967 and had their first daughter, Sonja, in the same year. But marriage did not get in the way of his growing interest in politics. His activities while as a student involved engagement with the 1968 protests in Sarajevo, where he would mingle with other influential figures in the movement, such as Slavko Leovac and Milorad Ekmečić (an historian at the University of Sarajevo), both of whom would later hold positions within the SDS.[25] After graduating from university, how-

---

[21] *Ibid*, p. 27.

[22] For the emergence and consolidation of the Montenegrin state in the nineteenth century, see Kenneth Morrison, *Montenegro: A Modern History*, London: IB Tauris, 2009, pp. 18–38, and Elizabeth Roberts, *Realm of the Black Mountain: A History of Montenegro*, London: Hurst & Co., 2007, pp. 186–250.

[23] For the poetry of Njegoš see Andrew Wachtel, *Making a Nation, Breaking a Nation: Literature and Cultural Politics in Yugoslavia*, California: Stanford University Press, 1998 and Edward D. Goy, *The Sabre and the Song: Njegoš, the Mountain Wreath*, Belgrade: PEN Serbia, 1995. For a biography of Njegoš see Milovan Djilas, *Njegoš*, London: Harcourt, 1966.

[24] *Monitor*, Podgorica, 23 August 2008, p. 14.

[25] Robert Donia, *Radovan Karadžić: Architect of the Bosnian Genocide*, p. 32.

ever, Karadžić began work in the psychiatric clinic within Koševo hospital. So despite his humble roots, he began to settle into a seemingly stable middle-class life in Sarajevo. He also developed a number of business interests, though it was in this regard he ran into trouble with the authorities in the early 1980s.

In November 1984, he and his friend and business partner Momčilo Krajišnik (who would later become a key figure within the SDS) went on trial and were eventually sentenced to three years for misappropriating funds from the Sarajevo-based Enegroinvest firm (of which Krajišnik was an employee).[26] Karadžić always maintained that he was innocent of the charges and that the case against him was 'politically motivated'. Upon his release from prison, Karadžić left Sarajevo and moved to Belgrade, where he became an acquaintance of Dobrica Ćosić, widely regarded as the 'Father of Serb Nationalism'. Details of the relationship between the men are sketchy, but Karadžić was watched closely by Bosnian authorities when he returned to Sarajevo in 1988. He was one of the founders of the SDS (in 1990) and would become the party's leader soon after, though others, such as Vladimir Srebrov (also one of the founders of the party) had been in the running to lead the SDS, though he later fell out of favour.[27] Karadžić was thus selected to become the leader of the SDS; the man to lead Bosnian Serbs through 'historic times'.[28] The SDS was a Serb nationalist party, yet there was little in Karadžić's early pronouncements to suggest that either he or the SDS more broadly were capable of the crimes they would subsequently commit,[29] though, as Edina Bećirević notes,

---

[26] *Ibid*, p. 40.

[27] Srebrov would later say that when the SDS was formed he believed that the party would evolve into a civic party. 'I was', he said, 'too much of an optimist because I believed that the nationalist phase would last only for a short time and that SDS would transform itself in a civic party which would support the development of Bosnia & Herzegovina into a secular, civic state'. See *Vreme*, Belgrade, 30 October 1995, p. 16.

[28] In a 1994 interview, the SDP leader, Zlatko Lagumdžija, claimed that Karadžić, while the symbolic head of the SDS, was not the real power within it. According to Lagumdžija, that honour belonged to the historian and head of the SDS Political Council, Milorad Ekmečić. 'We knew', said Lagumdžija, 'that Ekmečić was the man behind the strategy of the [SDS] project. At one moment he said [to] forget about what Karadžić is saying, because he has no right to say it...it was quite an unusual situation'. See Transcript of interview with Zlatko Lagumdžija, in 'Death of Yugoslavia Archive', 3/47, UBIT 046-048-297, p. 2.

[29] See, for example, an early interview given to the Belgrade weekly *NIN* in July 1990. The nationalist tone is certainly present, but the language is rather moderate in comparison to many of his later interviews. See *NIN*, Belgrade, 17 September 1990, pp. 10–16.

'Karadžić's rhetoric towards Muslims was to change dramatically after the elections'.³⁰ In an interview for the Belgrade weekly *NIN*, Karadžić assured voters that the SDS was 'a party of peace and tolerance' but that the SDS was 'committed to [the continuation of] a federal Yugoslavia'.³¹

The SDS operated from offices on *Ulica Titova* (Tito's Street) and from there they ran their campaign for the 1990 elections (though they later, from March 1991, had an office on the tenth floor of the Holiday Inn). In those elections, held in November 1990, Nijaz Duraković's League of Communists (SK-SDP) and Nenad Kecmanović's Alliance of Reform Forces (SRSJ) were both expected to perform well, and polls conducted suggested that their share of the vote would far outstrip that of the nationalist parties.³² It was not to be. The citizens of Sarajevo voted, in the main, for the nationalist parties, though the percentage of those voting for non-nationalist parties was higher in the city than throughout Bosnia.³³ Seven members were elected to the republic's 'presidium', two Bosnian Muslims (Alija Izetbegović and Fikret Abdić), two Bosnian Serbs (Biljana Plavšić and Nikola Koljević—both academics who held posts at the University of Sarajevo), two Bosnian Croats (Franjo Boras and Stjepan Kljuić), and an 'other' (SDA member Ejup Ganić, a Muslim from the Sandžak, who had run as a 'Yugoslav'). Alija Izetbegović became the president of the presidium, after Fikret Abdić, who had won more votes than any other candidate

---

³⁰ Edina Bećirević, *Genocide on the Drina River*, New Haven and London: Yale University Press, 2014, p. 52.

³¹ *NIN*, Belgrade, 17 September 1990, p. 14.

³² For an overview of the pre-election campaigns and the predictions in advance of the elections, see Neven Andjelić, *Bosnia-Herzegovina: The End of a Legacy*, pp. 156–184.

³³ Suad Arnautović, *Izbori u Bosni i Hercegovini '90: Analaiza izborni procesa*, Sarajevo: Promocult, 1996, p. 112. The victory of the nationalist parties came as a shock to many observers, though Zoran Pajić noted that 'After so many years of a comfortable collective identity within the [Yugoslav] system, the common man was simply unprepared to take on the responsibility to exercise his individual freedom. The easiest option was therefore to seek another form of collective identity, another protective shield against the confusion. This was nationalism. Many politicians quickly realised that the nationalist ticket was a lifeboat for them also. It was an instrument for the homogenisation of people and the creation of the constituency that, in the one-party system, they had never had.' See Zoran Pajić, 'Bosnia-Herzegovina: From Multi-ethnic Co-existence to "Apartheid"...and Back', in Payam Akhavan (ed.), *Yugoslavia: The Former and the Future—Reflections by Scholars from the Region*, The Brookings Institute, Washington, and the United Nations Research Institute for Social Development, Geneva, 1995, p. 153.

agreed to stand aside. In any event, the SDS/SDA/HDZ-BiH coalition that was formed after the elections comprised uncomfortable bedfellows; problems were evident from the outset. Fundamentally, they disagreed on the future of the state. The SDS were absolutely committed to the preservation of the Yugoslav state, while the SDA and HDZ-BiH were less so (although they did not express an explicit desire for independence at this early stage). Relations between the parties had become so strained that opposition parties, such as the SDP, attempted to 'moderate' in an attempt to bridge the growing divide.[34]

As the SFRJ further fragmented, relations between the newly elected governments in the country's republics became increasingly strained. These republican governments had little respect for the Yugoslav federal government and the federal state, and tended to behave as independent states in an increasingly hostile political context.[35] But the short (ten-day) war following Slovenia's declaration of independence on 25 June 1991 and the subsequent Serb rebellion in Croatia, which intensified after Croatia's declaration of independence on the same day, poisoned the political atmosphere in Bosnia. Strains became more acute among the coalition's nationalist partners.

As war raged in Croatia, the reverberations were felt strongly in Bosnia and Herzegovina. By this time the Holiday Inn had become the venue for many of the large SDS meetings that took place from the summer of 1991, and it was here that they discussed their plans for carving out large swathes of Bosnia in the event of the republic seceding from the SFRJ. In July 1991, however, the hotel was also full of Yugoslavia's best-known musicians and rock stars (such as Rade Šerbedžija, Indexi, Plavi Orkestar, Haris Džinović, Dino Merlin, EKV, Crvena Jabuka, and Goran Bregović, among others). The 'Yutel za mir' (Yutel for Peace) concert was scheduled to take place in front of the hotel, but heavy rain dictated that the

---

[34] According to Zlatko Lagumdžija, the then leader of the SDP, the three ruling parties were very antagonistic in their differing perception of the future of Bosnia and Herzegovina and that this required the opposition to act as moderators. 'I must admit', he said, 'it sounds ridiculous that the opposition party is a moderator between the ruling parties, but we tried exactly that'. See Transcript of interview with Zlatko Lagumdžija, in 'Death of Yugoslavia Archive', 3/47, UBIT 046-048-297, p. 1.

[35] Neven Andjelić, *Bosnia-Herzegovina: The End of a Legacy*, p. 197.

concert had to be held, instead, in the Zetra sports hall.[36] But the Holiday Inn increasingly became a *political space*, used less for entertainment and more as a meeting place for politicians (primarily from the SDS), though it continued, of course, to function as a 'normal' hotel.

That political matters had reached a very serious juncture was manifest during a session of the Bosnian parliament on 14 October 1991, whereupon HDZ-BiH and SDA deputies proposed a declaration of sovereignty and stated their intention to hold a referendum on independence. Karadžić's now notorious response was that such actions would put Bosnia on 'the same highway to hell and suffering that Slovenia and Croatia have already taken' and 'Do not think that you will not take Bosnia & Herzegovina to hell and the Muslim people maybe into extinction; because if there is a war, the Muslim people will not be able to defend themselves.' At approximately 2.00 am on the morning of the 15 October, the SDS delegates then left the parliament and the motion was passed in their absence.

Following their boycott of the Bosnian parliament, the SDS would, throughout late 1991 and early 1992, continue to use the Holiday Inn for their meetings and conferences, and the hotel would come to play a central role in the months ahead. In response to the HDZ-BiH declaration of sovereignty, the SDS scheduled a plebiscite which, when it took place on 9 and 10 November 1991, asked (Serb) voters whether they wished to 'remain in a common state of Yugoslavia with Serbia, Montenegro, SAO Krajina, SAO Slavonia, Baranja and Western Srem, and all others wishing the same?' The subsequent result confirmed that the majority of Serbs wished to remain in Yugoslavia, in whatever form.[37] Perhaps the most controversial meeting to take place at the hotel was held on 19 December

---

[36] The entire 'Yutel za mir' concert can be found on YouTube at https://www.youtube.com/watch?v=sx2Hl0xeliI [last accessed 19 June 2015].

[37] During an SDS meeting at the Holiday Inn on 21 December 1991, Karadžić insisted that 'We have the right to prevent anyone on the territories where we conducted our referendum to secede from Yugoslavia. In all the territories where Serbs took part in the referendum, regardless of whether they make 5 % or 55 % of the population, they are a constituent element of that town or that Republic. All the territories where we voted in our referendum to remain within Yugoslavia must stay within Yugoslavia if we decide so.' 4th SDS Session, 21 December 1991, in Robert Donia, *Iz Skupštine Republike Srpske 1991–1996: Izvodi iz izlaganja poslanika skupštine Republike Srpske kao dokazni material ns medjunarodnom krivičnom tribunal u Hagu*, Sarajevo: University Press, 2012, p. 32.

1991, with SDS municipal chiefs and SDS deputies present in the Bosnian parliament. A document was distributed at this meeting which included the so-called Variant A (areas where Serbs were a majority) and 'Variant B' (areas in which Serbs were a minority), which contained instructions on seizing power in the towns (whether the Serbs were a majority there or not) with the help of the JNA and volunteers from Serbia. The SDS had already begun their encirclement of Sarajevo by creating 'Serb Autonomous Districts' (*Srpske autonomne olbasti*—SOA), but this document took plans a step further.[38]

By December 1991, the republic's Foreign Minister, Haris Silajdžić, was appealing for a United Nations (UN) peacekeeping force to be deployed across Bosnia and Herzegovina.[39] A Central Intelligence Agency (CIA) report from the same month echoed these concerns, claiming that Bosnia and Herzegovina was already 'on the edge of the Abyss'.[40] The Commission on Security and Cooperation (CSCE) were, however, already in Sarajevo, led by the senior German diplomat, Geert-Hinrich Ahrens and by Professor Thomas Fleiner, a constitutional expert based at the University of Fribourg. They met with, among others, Karadžić and other members of the SDS leadership in the Holiday Inn and established a cordial, working relationship within which some common ground could be found. (Ahrens, knowledgeable about Yugoslav culture having spent many years in the country as a young diplomat, sought to ease tension by discussing Yugoslav literature with them.) However cordial, their political resolve was, said Ahrens, 'somewhat alarming'.[41] And that resolve was not merely rhetorical. According to Edina Bećirević, the (increasingly Serb-dominated) JNA had already begun 'to distribute weapons to areas with a majority Serb population via the SDS party structure'.[42]

---

[38] For a detailed analysis of the creation of SAO's and the SDS encirclement of Sarajevo, see Robert Donia, *Sarajevo: A Biography*, pp. 264–274.

[39] *The Times*, London, 24 December 1991, p. 6.

[40] Central Intelligence Agency (CIA), CIA Directorate of Intelligence Memorandum: Bosnia and Herzegovina on the Edge of the Abyss, 19 December 1991, Document No. (FOIA)/ESDN (CREST): 5235e50c9329405d174d7.

[41] Geert-Hinrich Ahrnes, *Diplomacy on the Edge: Containment of Ethnic Conflict and the Minorities Working Group of the Conferences on Yugoslavia*, Washington: Wilson Centre Press, 2008, p. 203.

[42] Edina Bećirević, *Genocide on the Drina River*, p. 53.

References

Ahrens, G. H. (2008). *Diplomacy on the Edge: Containment of Ethnic Conflict and the Minorities Working Group of the Conferences on Yugoslavia*. Washington: Wilson Centre Press.
Arnautović, S. (1996). *Izbori u Bosni i Hercegovini '90: Analaiza izborni procesa*. Sarajevo: Promocult.
Bulatović, L. (Ed.) (2002). *Radovan*. Belgrade: EVRO.
Čolović, I. (2002). *The Politics of Symbol in Serbia*. London: Hurst & Co..
Donia, R. J. (2015). *Radovan Karadžić: Architect of the Bosnian Genocide*. Cambridge: Cambridge University Press.
Hawton, N. (2009). *The Quest for Radovan Karadžić*. London: Hutchinson.
Izetbegović, A. (2003). *Inescapable Questions: Autobiographical Notes* (pp. 66–74). Leicester: The Islamic Foundation.
Malcolm, N. (1994). *Bosnia: A Short History*. London: MacMillan Press.
Morrison, K., & Roberts, E. R. (2013). *The Sandžak: A History*. London: Hurst & Co..
Pejić, M. (2008). *HVO Sarajevo*. Sarajevo: Libertas.
Zulfikarpašić, Adil (in dialogue with Milovan Djilas and Nadežda Gaće) (1998). *The Bosniak: Adil Zulfikarpašić*. London: Hurst & Co..

CHAPTER 6

In Residence: Radovan Karadžić and the SDS

The Holiday Inn had become, by January 1992, something of an SDS stronghold; indeed, since their boycott of parliament in October 1991, it had become their primary base in Sarajevo. It possessed excellent conference facilities, could provide accommodation for SDS members from outside Sarajevo, and could facilitate large meetings and allow SDS members to congregate among their own and in a relatively safe environment that was 'their territory'. The party held all major events in the hotel, and these happened with increasing regularity throughout the early months of 1992. It was in the hotel that, on 9 January 1992, the SDS proclaimed that the 'Serb Republic of Bosnia & Herzegovina' (later *Republika Srpska*) would be activated in the event of the international community's recognition of an independent Bosnia and Herzegovina. As well as having boycotted the parliament, the SDS largely vacated their offices in Tito Street and instead rented offices on the seventh floor of the Holiday Inn, from where they directed their Sarajevo operations.[1] And as relations between the SDS on one side and the SDA and HDZ-BiH on the other worsened, the seventh floor of the Holiday Inn (formally the office of a company called *Boksit*)

---

[1] Many of the Holiday Inn staff interviewed stated that they remembered clearly the way the hotel quickly became used by the SDS as a base, although many noted that they had used the hotel often for events and 'holiday celebrations'. Nevertheless, almost all said they felt very uncomfortable about the increasing presence of armed SDS men and bodyguards sitting around the hotel lobby.

would become the centre of SDS activities and their de facto headquarters until they were obliged to evacuate the hotel on 6 April 1992.[2] With the acquiescence of the hotel's director and SDS sympathiser, Danilo Dursun (whose brother was a member of the party),[3] the party's leader, Radovan Karadžić, and his increasingly well-armed entourage became part of the furniture in a hotel whose regular business clientele were fast disappearing, and by January 1992 it was dominated by the SDS.[4] Seemingly ever ebullient, Karadžić would frequently hold court in the hotel lobby, giving interviews to the media about the worsening political crisis in the SFRJ and in Bosnia and Herzegovina while, albeit less frequently, pontificating about all manner of issues from politics to poetry and literature. His party intensified their activities on 9 January 1992, with the first major event of the New Year being the 'Assembly of the Serbian People of Bosnia & Herzegovina', which was held in the hotel. The meeting, ostensibly called to discuss the position of the Serbs in Bosnia and Herzegovina, was opened by the 'President of the Assembly of the Serbian People', Momčilo Krajišnik. Striking a sombre note, he bemoaned the Muslim–Croat decision to schedule an independence referendum before reading out a declaration stating that the 'Serbian Republic of Bosnia & Herzegovina' was to come into existence henceforth, that it was envisaged that it would remain within the SFRJ, and that Sarajevo would be its capital.[5]

In the days following the declaration, a little time was set aside for relaxation. The Holiday Inn was an ideal venue for the party. The sweeping

[2] Citing a report in *Oslobodjenje* from 5 March 1992, Donia noted that the Holiday Inn's 'expensive restaurant became the mess hall for SDS paramilitaries, who moved freely about the hotel with their weapons in full view of the other guests'. See Robert Donia, *Sarajevo: A Biography*, p. 273.

[3] *Ibid*, p. 273. According to Smail Čekić, Danilo Dursun was an SDS member and close associate of Radovan Karadžić, hence the SDS being able to use the hotel as frequently and easily as they did. He also claims that as early as June 1991, Dursun and other leading figures in the SDS were provided with arms by the JNA. Dursun, he claims, was given a *Scorpion* and ninety bullets. See Čekić, Smail, *The Aggression against the Republic of Bosnia & Herzegovina: Planning, Preparation, Execution* (Book One), Institute for the Research of Crimes Against Humanity and International Law, Sarajevo, 2005a, p. 695. Similar allegations were made in the Sarajevo daily *Oslobodjenje*. See *Oslobodjenje*, Sarajevo, 25 February 1993, p. 5.

[4] The leadership of the SDS had more of a passing interest in the Holiday Inn. In 'writings from prison', published under the name of *Svedočim: Knjiga pisana u zatvoru*, Biljana Plavšić claims that during a meeting of the SDS in October 1991, she discovered that Karadžić was interested, in concert with others from the SDS, in investing (and possibly purchasing) the hotel. When she expressed surprise that he would be doing so, he replied that he had 'to make a living'. See Biljana Plavšić, *Svedočim: Knjiga pisana u zatvoru*, Banja Luka: Trioprint, 2005. See also *Oslobodjenje*, Sarajevo, 26 July 2008, p. 5.

[5] See *Radio Belgrade Network*, 9 January 1992, FBIS AU0901134092.

function rooms of the hotel were, after all, perfect venues for relaxation. On the evening of 13 January 1992, senior SDS members gathered in the hotel to celebrate Orthodox New Year.[6] On an evening of drinking, dancing, and general merriment, Karadžić and other SDS 'notables' appeared in high spirits, dancing the *kolo* to the patriotic sound of Serbian folk music. But the superficial joviality belied the increasing paranoia among the SDS leadership and their plans for Sarajevo. Their part in the trajectory of events in the subsequent months would ensure that this was the last time that the SDS would celebrate New Year in Sarajevo.[7] Indeed, within months it would become impossible for the SDS leadership and many of the party faithful to remain in the city.

At this stage, however, the SDS pressed on with their planning, and on 14 February 1992, the *glavni odbor* (Main Board) of the party met in the Holiday Inn.[8] Radovan Karadžić gave a lengthy speech to board members, outlining the increasingly febrile political situation in Bosnia and Herzegovina, and the worsening relations between Serbs and the Croats and Muslims.[9] In terms of the former he was more guarded, though regarding the latter he was more hostile, stating that 'The moment Muslims get hold of fundamentalism, they cannot live anywhere, with anybody....We [Serbs] really are something other, something different, and we should not hide that. We are not brothers...we must know that.'[10]

With the formal recognition of Slovenia and Croatia by the European Community (EC) on 15 January 1992, the seemingly inexorable

[6] These 'Instructions for the Organisation and Activities of the Organs of the Serb People in Bosnia and Herzegovina in a State of Emergency' were distributed to SDS delegates at a party meeting at the Holiday Inn on 19 December 1991. In the document, SDS from across Bosnia were instructed to make arrangements for the implementation of plans for taking control of areas in which the Serbs were a majority (Variant A) and some where they were not (Variant B). This document represents the first insight into plans for carving out 'Serb-dominated' territory within Bosnia in the event of independence.

[7] Footage of the New Year celebrations at the Holiday Inn can be found in Avdo Huseinović's documentary film *Krvavi ples po šeheru*, http://www.youtube.com/watch?v=ry9_8DN9trw.

[8] For a detailed analysis of the structure of the leadership of the SDS and the role played by key individuals since the formation of the party in 1990, see Patrick J. Treanor, 'Lideri Srpske demokratske stranke: Rukovodstvo bosanskih Srba, 1990–1992, (Izvještaj o istraživanju pripremljen za predmet KRAJIŠNIK i PLAVŠIĆ (IT-00-39 & 40), 30 jula 2002, in Helsinški odbor za ljudska prava u Srbiji, *Jezgro velikosrpskog projekta*, Svedočanstva Br. 27, Zagorac, Beograd, 2006b, pp. 201–392.

[9] For an assessment of the SDS strategy of creating SAOs, see *Dani*, Sarajevo, 25 February 2011, pp. 30–32.

[10] UN-ICTY, 'Mićo Stanišić and the Bosnian Serb Leadership 1990–1992 (Addendum to the Bosnian Serb Leadership, 1990–1992), Patrick J. Treanor, Research report prepared for the case of Mićo Stanišić (IT-04-79), 21 February 2008, p. 10.

downward spiral gained even greater momentum. The Bosnian government were now faced with a dilemma: stay in a Yugoslav state dominated by the Serbs, or opt to hold a referendum which would determine whether or not they have the mandate to declare independence. Despite the proclamation of the 'Serbian Republic of Bosnia & Herzegovina' and increasingly dire warnings of the consequences emanating from the SDS leadership should the referendum be held, it was scheduled nevertheless, on the suggestion of the EC, for the weekend of 29 February and 1 March 1992. This would determine whether independence was the will of the majority of the citizens of Bosnia and Herzegovina.

The referendum, claimed Karadžić, was 'not a referendum of all citizens only the Muslim and Croat communities', and that Serbs had already expressed their will through their own plebiscite.[11] In advance of the 'referendum weekend', the SDS held numerous meetings at the Holiday Inn to discuss the referendum and its potential implications. On 25 February, the '8th Session of the Assembly of the Serbian People in Bosnia & Herzegovina' was held in the hotel. The meeting was opened by Momčilo Krajišnik, who welcomed the delegates, which included a member of the Serbian royal family (Princess Linda Karadjordjević). Her presence was, he said, 'the best proof that just as our Karadjordjević family has not forgotten the Serbian people, just as the Serbian people have not forgotten the Karadjordjević's'. On 28 February, the day before the referendum voting began, the SDS 'Club of Parliamentary Representatives' met in the Holiday Inn.[12] On the agenda was the Lisbon Conference and related implications. Radovan Karadžić and Nikola Koljević began by telling the gathered delegates of the progress made during the negotiations and the issues that remained unresolved. The main purpose of the meeting, however, was the adoption of the 'Constitution of the Serb Republic of Bosnia & Herzegovina' in which it was declared this 'entity' included Serb autonomous regions, municipalities, and other Serbian ethnic entities in Bosnia and Herzegovina. The constitution was passed by the SDS just one day before 'referendum weekend' began in earnest.

---

[11] Quote by Radovan Karadžić in *Borba*, Belgrade, 31 January 1992, in Helsinški odbor za ljudska prava u Srbiji, *Jezgro velikosrpskog projekta*, p. 22.

[12] For the full transcript of the meeting, see UN-ICTY Case No. IT-95-5/18-T, 'The Prosecutor V. Radovan Karadžić (ET SA01-1505-SA01-1571.doc), 'Club of Parliament Representatives, Serb Democratic Party, Bosnia and Herzegovina: Transcript from the meeting of the Club, Sarajevo 28 February 1992.

The Referendum Weekend and the 'War of the Barricades'

The referendum weekend of 29 February and 1 March 1992 was characterised by growing tensions across Bosnia and Herzegovina, in Sarajevo, and the Holiday Inn (as the SDS base) would be at the centre of events throughout the referendum weekend. The hotel was fully booked, bringing together in close proximity the most unusual of 'bedfellows'—EC election monitors, foreign journalists, and a growing number of armed SDS men, who could be seen stalking the lobby, bars, corridors, and stairs of the hotel.[13] SDS leaders could often be seen drinking coffee and chatting, surrounded by their bodyguards, on the first-floor mezzanine level (under the 'big top').[14] Visible to all guests, these bodyguards monitored who entered and exited the building. It was clear, according to reports in the Sarajevo daily *Oslobodjenje*, that (in full view of the international press and EC monitors) the hotel had become the nerve centre for SDS operations in Sarajevo, as the referendum votes were being cast and counted.[15]

The vast majority of Serbs boycotted the referendum (as instructed by the SDS), while the vast majority of Muslims and Croats voted in favour of independence. On Sunday 1 March, the tension was already palpable in Sarajevo even before a Serb wedding party was fired upon outside the Serbian Orthodox Church in the Baščaršija area of the city. Nikola Gardović, the father of the bridegroom, was killed and a Serbian Orthodox priest, Radenko Mirović, injured in the attack. The SDS leadership immediately blamed the SDA for organising the shooting, which they alleged to have been carried out by a Sarajevo underworld figure, Ramiz Delalić 'Ćelo', who was originally from the Sandžak region (which straddles the border between Serbia and Montenegro, and where tensions between Serbs and Muslims were also acute),[16] who, they argued, was

---

[13] *Oslobodjenje*, Sarajevo, 3 March 1992, p. 3.
[14] Author's interview with Senada Kreso, April 2014.
[15] *Oslobodjenje*, Sarajevo, 3 March 1992, p. 3.
[16] For an analysis of events in the Sandžak region during this period, see Kenneth Morrison & Elizabeth Roberts, *The Sandžak: A History*, Hurst & Co., London, 2013, pp. 132–145. Ramiz Delalić remained a powerful figure throughout the Bosnian war. Unlike a number of Sarajevo's criminals (such as Jusuf 'Juka' Prazina), he remained loyal to the Bosnian government throughout. He was charged with the murder of Nikola Gardović through the court although the accusations against him were not proven. He was murdered in what appeared to be a 'gangland hit' in Sarajevo in June 2007. For the events that led to his court case, see *Slobodna Bosna*, Sarajevo, 3 February 2005, pp. 20–23.

under the protection of the SDA.[17] The murder was, according to the SDS's de facto spokesman (in Karadžić's absence), Rajko Dukić, evidence that Serbs in Sarajevo were in mortal danger, and would be further so in an independent Bosnia.[18] This, however, was rejected by Šefer Halilović, who in 1991 had formed the paramilitary group, the Patriotic League (*Patriotska liga*—PL), who claimed it 'wasn't really a wedding' but a provocation, and that the wedding party were SDS activists. They wanted, he said, 'to go through Baščaršija with the cars, with the flags, with the banners, to provoke us and to see how we would react'.[19]

In any event, the shootings further fuelled the tensions, and early the following morning, within a few hours of the completion of referendum voting, barricades appeared at key transit points across the city, manned by armed and masked SDS supporters. According to a report by the CSCE, the blockade of the city 'turned from spontaneous protests provoked by the wedding incident to an SDS-controlled effort'.[20] Thus, the barricades appeared not simply to 'protect Serbs' in the wake of the Baščaršija shooting but to demonstrate that the SDS would not accept lightly a declaration of independence in the event of a 'yes' vote. According to a report by the Bosnian (*Ministarstvo unutrašnjih poslova*—MUP) from 6 March 1992, 'Snipers were provided to protect the SDS Crisis Staff, who were stationed on top of the Holiday Inn hotel before the setting of the barricades.'[21] And while the SDS spokesman Rajko Dukić would claim that the erection of the barricades was 'a spontaneous event',[22]

[17] Robert Donia, *Sarajevo: A Biography*, p. 278.

[18] *Slobodna Bosna*, Sarajevo, 28 November 1998, p. 16. According to a witness statement of Miroslav Deronjić (the one-time Chairman of the Executive Committee of the SDS and later member of the Main Board of the party) given to the International Criminal Tribunal for the Former Yugoslavia (ICTY) in 2003, Dukić was 'A highly influential figure, both politically and economically, a man well known even before the war, who maintained good relations with former communist and economic officialdom. He was a man who enjoyed extensive political prestige both in Belgrade and in the SDS leadership.' ICTY Doc. No. 0344-7914-0344-7981, November 2003.

[19] Transcript of interview with Šefer Halilović, in 'Death of Yugoslavia Archive', 3/28, UBIT 295-297, p. 4. In May 1992 Halilović became the Commander of the Bosnian Territorial Defence (*Teritorijalna odbrana*—TO), which was later incorporated in the Army of Bosnia and Herzegovina (ARBiH).

[20] CSCE, 'The Referendum on Independence of Bosnia-Herzegovina, February 29–1 March, 1992', CSCE Report, March 1992, p. 19.

[21] UN-ICTY Document, 'Socialist Republic of Bosnia & Herzegovina: Ministry of the Interior State Security Service, Sarajevo, 'Security Information in Relation to the Events of 01.03/02.03 and 303.03/04.03.1992 in Sarajevo', 6 March 1992, ET 0323-7746-0323-7757, p. 4.

[22] *Slobodna Bosna*, Sarajevo, 28 November 1998, p. 16.

the same report stated that 'the fact that most of the barricades organised by the Serbs were set up on strategic locations in Sarajevo' and that 'the weapons and radio equipment available, the organised distribution of weapons and food to the people at the barricades, the time and manner of setting and withdrawing the barricades it can be concluded they were not a spontaneous reaction'.[23] Likewise, Kemal Kurspahić, the editor of *Oslobodjenje* observed that 'It was obvious that such a comprehensive blockade of a city of half a million people had not been conjured out of the thin night air without prior organisation and planning—there was not a whiff of spontaneity about it.'[24] Alija Izetbegović learned of the barricades while celebrating the end of the referendum voting (which the SDA had predicted a successful 'yes' vote) at party headquarters in Sarajevo, a move which had forced he and his closest advisors to consider whether to resist the SDS barricades. He opted not to, because he 'wanted to avoid street fighting in the parts of the city where we did not have enough forces'.[25]

In the interim, however, two large groups of demonstrators (one gathering at the Catholic Church in the city centre, the other coming from the western suburbs of Sarajevo) converged and made their way towards the parliament building directly across from the Holiday Inn.[26] The peace demonstrators achieved their objective only after shots were fired over their heads from a barricade (next to the Maršal Tito barracks) manned not by SDS gunmen but by JNA soldiers. Several shots were fired; some reports claimed that two people were wounded.[27] Soon after 8.00 pm that evening, a group of around twenty people, who had been participating in the demonstrations against the barricades outside the parliament and had fled the shooting outside the barricades near the Maršal Tito barracks, entered the hotel to use the public telephones. They were immediately identified by the armed SDS men watching from the first-floor mezzanine level as unwelcome guests. On the

---

[23] UN-ICTY Document, 'Socialist Republic of Bosnia & Herzegovina: Ministry of the Interior State Security Service, Sarajevo, 'Security Information in Relation to the Events of 01.03/02.03 and 303.03/04.03.1992 in Sarajevo', 6 March 1992, ET 0323-7746-0323-7757, p. 3.
[24] Kemal Kurspahić, *As Long as Sarajevo Exists*, The Pamphleteers Press, Connecticut, 1997, p. 121.
[25] Transcript of interview with Alija Izetbegović, in 'Death of Yugoslavia Archive', 3/32, UBIT 286-288, p. 7.
[26] Robert Donia, *Sarajevo: A Biography*, p. 280.
[27] *Belgrade RTB Television Network*, 2 March 1992, FBIS AU0203222093.

ground floor, the lobby bar was relatively busy with foreign journalists who had been covering the independence referendum and who had stayed on after the EC monitors had departed.[28] The group's presence did little to attract the attention of the journalists, but they did not go unnoticed by the SDS gunmen, who were present in the hotel at the time. (At the time, Karadžić,[29] Koljević, and Krajišnik were not in Sarajevo but in Belgrade discussing developments with the Serbian President, Slobodan Milošević.)[30] The hotel was, according to Florence Hartmann of the French daily *Le Monde*, 'evidently entirely under the control of the SDS, many of whom were armed and carrying Motorola's; obviously to communicate with those manning the barricades', and the group had, unwittingly, walked into a danger equal to that on the streets outside.[31] As a warning, one of the armed SDS guards fired a shotgun into the air, shattering suspended roof lamps and showering the atrium with glass.[32] While the journalists and other guests in the atrium bar threw themselves to the ground or

---

[28] According to Joel Brand (later of *The Times and Newsweek* when the group entered the hotel, 'there was an immediate increase in tension before what I think was a shotgun blast—one of the SDS gunmen had fired straight into the ceiling, sending broken glass flying.' Author's interview with Joel Brand (The Times/Newsweek), April 2014.

[29] On the evening of the 1 March, Ejup Ganić spoke by telephone to Karadžić. The SDS leader claimed that he did not have information about who ordered the erection of the barricades, but that the problem should be resolved by senior members of the SDS in Sarajevo. See Ejup Ganić, *Razgovori i svjedočenja 1990–1994*, Sarajevo: Svjetlost, 2007, p. 260.

[30] In a 1998 interview for the Bosnian weekly *Slobodan Bosna*, Rajko Dukić—the director of the 'Boksit' company which had an office in the Holiday Inn and was seen as a cover for channelling SDS funds—claimed that the atmosphere in the hotel during 1 March had darkened significantly. 'I came to the party office [at the Holiday Inn] and found three priests and another man there who were very agitated. They told me they had been shot at near the church…Party [SDS] members started gathering. Information circulated that Green Berets had been seen, and that an attack was imminent. People spontaneously started to volunteer for defence. They informed me that they had put up barricades; it was a spontaneous event. That night, we wrote a proclamation which we sent to the Presidency and to the government. I could not get in touch with Karadžić and the people in Belgrade until the following morning. At first I did not know where they were. The Holiday Inn was full of people…we were all afraid of what might happen.' See *Slobodna Bosna*, Sarajevo, 28 November 1998, p. 16.

[31] According to Hartmann, the SDS members were being treated well in the hotel and were provided with three course dinners while the group she was with had to make do with cheese and bread. 'I was horrified. After all, we were paying guests, but it became clear that we were not the most important guests in the hotel.' Author's interview with Florence Hartmann (Le Monde), April 2015.

[32] Author's interviews with Joel Brand (*The Times/Newsweek*) and Michael Montgomery (*Daily Telegraph*), April 2014.

behind the furniture, the group were chased from the lobby of the hotel by a number of SDS gunmen before fleeing in different directions, some towards the *Karingtonka* apartment block, the others towards the adjacent technical school, with shots being fired over their heads.[33] The incident, led the Sarajevo daily *Oslobodjenje* to question whether the Holiday Inn was a 'hotel or a barracks'. Indeed, the paper quoted Florence Hartmann, who had been standing just outside the hotel entrance as the group entered, and her observations confirmed what many in Sarajevo already knew—that armed groups linked to the SDS were using the hotel as a base for their operations (organising the erecting and guarding of barricades) in Sarajevo city centre. Evidently, the SDS gunmen had been angered by the group of those who were demonstrating against the roadblocks entering 'their' hotel. In an interview for *Oslobodjenje* she described the events that were unravelling on the evening of Sunday 1 March:

> It all began somewhere around 9.30 pm, when a group of men arrived at the hotel…they were mostly very young people. I was standing at the entrance gate, I passed them and I could see that they were not armed. I thought maybe they came to have a drink or something. When I went outside, I approached one of the two police cars that were parked in front of the hotel and started to talk to one of the policemen. At that moment, I heard gunfire in the hotel, so I entered the car to get away. Then the group of civilians that I had passed came running out of the hotel and immediately behind them were several armed men who were firing over their heads. Part of the group escaped to the left of the exit while the rest ran across the parking lot and turned left. As they escaped, the armed men continued to fire and I saw one of them climbing on to a large flower pot from where he continued to fire over the heads of those who were fleeing. I quickly re-entered the hotel, where I found a large number of frightened people.[34]

While Hartman and other foreign correspondents in the Holiday Inn acknowledged that the situation calmed down relatively quickly thereafter, it was a sign, if one was needed, of the tension surrounding the referendum weekend and the 'war of the barricades'. Shaken by the appearance of the barricades and the armed SDS gunmen, the EC election monitors gathered in the Holiday Inn, awaiting permission to leave Sarajevo. A group of German elections monitors, among them Bundestag deputies

---

[33] Author's interview with Florence Hartmann (*Le Monde*), April 2015.
[34] *Oslobodjenje*, Sarajevo, 5 March 1992, p. 3.

Stefan Schwarz and Joerg van Essen, were forbidden from leaving their hotel rooms by the SDS, though they were later allowed to move to the lobby.[35] A Bosnian government translator, Senada Kreso (who was tasked with liaising with the monitors), joined them, doing her best to provide assurances (and be provided with assurances by the JNA general, Milutin Kukanjac) that they would be safely transported from the hotel to the airport. It was, according to Kreso, a 'very dramatic' situation.[36] 'The whole morning', she said, 'people were in a panic; I remember, I came into the [Holiday Inn] foyer and found all of the EC observers gathered there, because they had been told that the hotel foyer was the safest place to be. They were all on the floor because a second before we had heard some shooting...three SDS gunmen had entered the hotel and fired shots into the air.'[37] Panic gripped the EC monitors, who expressed a desire to leave the hotel (and Sarajevo) as quickly as possible, and buses were arranged to take them to Sarajevo airport. They were advised to return to their rooms until the buses arrived, which they duly did. While waiting for the buses, however, Kreso was approached by one of the EC monitors and told that when he had returned to his room, as advised, there was a man standing in it wearing a stocking over his head. When the monitor asked what was going on, the man simply left.[38] For those who had returned to their rooms, it was an agonising wait. One of those sitting in their rooms waiting to be evacuated was Rosie Whitehouse (the wife of *The Times* correspondent Tim Judah) and their two young children, Ben and Esther. She recalled the chaos when the first bus arrived:

> I remember running downstairs with the children just as the bus was preparing to leave. It was completely full and I can clearly remember so many dark thoughts running through my head at that moment. There was complete silence on the bus; everybody was petrified. I remember clearly that among all of these EC monitors, was this one woman, I don't know who she was, but she certainly wasn't an EC monitor. She looked rather glamorous and

[35] Hamburg DPA, Hamburg, FBIS-LD0203193592, 2 March 1992, p. 1.
[36] Kreso also noted that while the terrified EC monitors were having breakfast in the hotel, 'the manager was in the restaurant hurriedly making lunch packets for the [SDS] people on the barricades'. See interview with Senada Kreso in Suada Kapić, *The Siege of Sarajevo: 1992–1996*, Sarajevo: FAMA, 2000, p. 144. A report in *Oslobodjenje* also makes this claim, stating that a white van was parked in front of the hotel and was being used to take food to the 'boys on the barricades'. See *Oslobodjenje*, Sarajevo, 3 March 1992, p. 3.
[37] Author's interview with Senada Kreso, April 2014.
[38] Interview with Senada Kreso in Suada Kapić, *The Siege of Sarajevo: 1992–1996*, p. 144.

was wearing a big fur coat and I remember she was visibly shaking, so all these furs on her coat were quivering. The tension was palpable...it was really a dramatic moment.[39]

The EC monitors were taken by the JNA to Sarajevo airport (through six SDS barricades) and were subsequently flown to Belgrade and to safety.[40] The following day, an *Oslobodjenje* journalist entered the Holiday Inn to assess Hartmann's claims that the hotel had become an 'SDS barracks'. He walked into the hotel, through the lobby, got in the lift and stopped at the third floor. While walking along the corridor, he saw one of the doors of a nearby room open. When he approached he saw 'many armed men in camouflage clothing'.[41] Whatever was being planned by the SDS, it was being plotted in the Holiday Inn.

Despite the ongoing tensions in Sarajevo throughout 2 March, the international press corps, in the main, departed the Holiday Inn and Sarajevo in the wake of the referendum result (though a small number remained to monitor and report on post-referendum developments). The result of the referendum was, after all, clear—63.4 % of the population had voted, of which 99.7 % had done so in favour of Bosnia's independence. Nevertheless, Sarajevo remained extremely tense throughout 2 and 3 March, by which time, according to Robert Donia, the SDS had turned the Holiday Inn into 'a stronghold for Bosnian Serb leaders and a billet for the growing contingent of Karadžić's bodyguards'.[42] Indeed, the Holiday Inn was now, informally, the *križni stab* (crisis headquarters) of the SDS. On that day, Rajko Dukić and Velibor Ostojić (in Karadžić's absence) gave an SDS press conference at the hotel, stating that the barricades were a reaction by the 'Serbian people in Bosnia & Herzegovina' to the shooting in Baščaršija and the 'illegal referendum', the result of which the SDS would not accept.[43]

Yet despite the tensions and the threats from the SDS, those calling for peace and further dialogue (those who marched on the barricades) won a small, though hollow, victory that evening. Negotiations between

[39] Author's interview with Rosie Whitehouse, April 2014. See also Rosie Whitehouse, *Are We There Yet? Travels with My Frontline Family*, London: Reportage Press, 2007, pp. 97–100.
[40] CSCE, 'The Referendum on Independence of Bosnia-Herzegovina, February 29–1 March, 1992', CSCE Report, March 1992, pp. 19–20.
[41] *Ibid*, p. 3.
[42] Robert Donia, Radovan Karadžić: Architect of the Bosnian Genocide, p. 164.
[43] *Oslobodjenje*, Sarajevo, 3 March 1992, p. 12.

Image 6.1 The view from the Holiday Inn during the *Valter* demonstrations, March 1992. (Photo: Joel Brand)

Izetbegović and Karadžić, brokered by the JNA, led to the barricades coming down and 'joint patrols' being established. Thereafter, citizens of Sarajevo began to mobilise. In the early days of March, the so-called *Valter* (Walter) demonstrations—named (Image 6.1) after the Partisan resistance fighter, Vladimir Perić-Valter, lionised in the 1972 film *Valter brani Sarajevo* (Walter Defends Sarajevo)[44]—organised protests against the barricades and the dangerous rhetoric of the nationalist parties. The protests were partially organised by the SDP, but was also citizens' movement with no clear leadership structure. They had their successes, though their endeavours to have the barricades dismantled were ultimately a hollow victory. Nevertheless, in his memoirs, the architect of the Holiday Inn, Ivan Štraus, described the scene as the barricades were deserted by the SDS gunmen:

> Citizens of Sarajevo, some from the east, others from the west—in the early evening, with children and candles, walked to wards the barricades demanding that peace return to the city. The heroes on the barricades ran away in

---

[44] *Valter brani Sarajevo* was made in 1972 and directed by the Sarajevo-born Hajrudin 'Šiba' Krvavac, who was notable for a number of 'Partisan films'. He died of a heart attack in Sarajevo in July 1992. For a fascinating overview of the 'Partisan Genre' and the work of AVALA Films (the studio that created most of the Partisan films), see the documentary film 'Cinema Komunisto', Dir: Mila Turajlić, Dribbling Pictures, Belgrade, 2010.

panic, in all directions, most of them to the slopes of Trebević. And in the night throughout Sarajevo walked citizens, old and young, happy that the bloodshed had been stopped.[45]

It had not been stopped, merely delayed. (In the month before the outbreak of armed hostilities in Sarajevo, the SDS and SDA/HDZ-BiH used the subsequent weeks to prepare for war.)[46] Events in the Holiday Inn on the evening of Sunday 1 March may have been obscured by the Baščaršija shooting and the subsequent appearance of the SDS barricades, the Valter protests, and the citizens' efforts to dismantle the barricades, but they were, nevertheless, equally demonstrative of the febrile atmosphere in Sarajevo. Aware of the continuing tension and in an attempt to bring the key political players together to discuss ways ahead, the European Community Monitoring Mission (ECMM) representative Colm Doyle (who noted 'a rise in tension among the Serb community') left his hotel in Ilidža to drive through the barricades to the Holiday Inn in an effort to engage the SDS leadership (who were, according to Doyle, 'operating their own crisis committee, which was setting [their] demands)'.[47]

The following day, 3 March, in the Bosnian parliament, the SDA leader Alija Izetbegović declared the Republic of Bosnia and Herzegovina to be an independent state, a declaration immediately ratified by the parliament (the SDS had, of course, boycotted the session). Just across the street in the Holiday Inn, Karadžić, giving an interview to Associated Press (AP), told journalists that Bosnia's independence was 'a unilateral decision that Serbs will oppose'.[48] Tensions were high, with the possibility of armed conflict increasing with every act of brinkmanship—Sarajevo and, indeed, Bosnia and Herzegovina remained extremely tense. Life in the hotel went on as usual—SDS members came and went, and Karadžić continued to give statements and interviews regularly in the hotel lobby or in his suite. However, the arrival of new 'guests' two weeks later did much to ease the tension, at least temporarily. It had been decided by the UN, despite objections being raised in New York by senior UNPROFOR officials, that the headquarters for the Croatia peacekeeping operations would be based in Sarajevo, 350 km away. Not only would this prove logistically

[45] Ivan Štraus, *Arhitek i barbari*, p. 62.
[46] Robert Donia, *Sarajevo: A Biography*, p. 281.
[47] See UN-ICTY, The Prosecutor v. Ratko Mladić, Prosecution 92 TER MOTION: RM114(Colm Doyle), Case No. IT-09-92-T, 23 July 2012, p. 25.
[48] *Dani*, Sarajevo, April 2008, p. 87.

problematic, the new base for UNPROFR operations was itself becoming increasingly unstable, and the organisation's staff would soon find themselves in the Holiday Inn (sharing the facilities with the SDS) and, subsequently, in the midst of the chaos that would consume Sarajevo.

Uncomfortable Bedfellows: Clan Karadžić and UNPROFOR at the Holiday Inn

Almost two weeks later, on 13 March 1992, the UNPROFOR team, including the Canadian General Lewis MacKenzie and the Indian General Satish Nambiar (the elder brother of Vijay Nambiar, who would later become UN Under-Secretary General and the UN Secretary General Ban Ki Moon's Chief of Staff), and a small contingent of Swedish peacekeepers arrived in Sarajevo and were based (initially) in the Holiday Inn.[49] Upon arrival, the ECMM's representative, Colm Doyle, noticed that the hotel was 'full of heavily armed Serbs, who were Dr Karadžić's henchmen and bodyguards'.[50] MacKenzie, too, immediately noticed the grim atmosphere in the building. 'The hotel's reception area', he said, 'was packed with hundreds of people resembling extras from a KGB film. The bulges under their arms were a little obvious, and some of them were carrying automatic weapons in plain sight, although wearing civilian attire. There was a definite feeling of tension throughout the hotel.'[51] According to a member of the Holiday Inn's reception staff, 'I remember clearly the day that UN troops showed up to stay with us. I was told by one of the UN officers that "you have lots of weapons in this hotel". I was genuinely not aware of this. I guess I was so naïve back then, so it came as a real shock.'[52]

The UNPROFOR team would soon begin to 'demilitarise' the hotel and improve security, and the newly arrived UNPROFOR team met with Cedric Thornberry, UNPROFOR's political adviser, and the EC's main negotiator in Sarajevo, Jose Cutileiro, who briefed them on the situation in the city. The latter had become convinced that the UN would have

---

[49] *Oslobodjenje*, Sarajevo, 14 March 1992, p. 3.

[50] *Oslobodjenje*, Sarajevo, 21 March 1992, p. 1. For Colm Doyle's assessment of the situation in Sarajevo during March 1992, see UN-ICTY, The Prosecutor v. Ratko Mladić, Prosecution 92 TER MOTION: RM114(Colm Doyle), Case No. IT-09-92-T, 23 July 2012, p. 25.

[51] Lewis MacKenzie, *Peacekeeper: The Road to Sarajevo*, Vancouver/Toronto: Douglas & McIntyre, 1993, p. 120.

[52] Author's interview with Holiday Inn (Sarajevo), September 2013.

no role if the latest peace proposal worked and that they should expect a quiet time in the city. 'We were delighted to hear that' stated MacKenzie; 'In fact we quite wondered why we were there, because we really didn't want to put our headquarters in Sarajevo.'[53] Yet their arrival appeared to calm the tensions, the Sarajevo daily *Oslobodjene* observing the change in atmosphere in the hotel after UNPROFOR's arrival:

> Instead of armed civilians, under whose coats the most modern battle weapons protrude, an airport checkpoint for guests and passers-by has been set up at the main entrance to the hotel. All the world's languages are being spoken, and the two large letters 'UN', with the well-known insignia of this world organisation dominate the hotel's parking lot. The 'Holiday Inn' is the temporary location of the General Staff of UNPROFR, with General Satish Nambiar at the head. The hotel that had recently become the headquarters of the paramilitary units of one national party [the SDS] was transformed overnight into a multi-national shelter. It is evident that the cold Swedes warmly received the task of disarming visitors to the Holiday Inn and very carefully checked all entrances to the headquarters of the General Staff.[54]

Such an easing of tensions was encouraging, though Nambiar's response, when asked by an *Oslobodjenje* journalist whether his family would be joining him in the hotel and in Sarajevo, was less so. His reply was, at best, non-committal and did little to assuage the growing fears of Sarajevo's citizens that war was approaching.[55] And while many of them put their faith in UNPROFOR's presence negating the possibility of such a dark scenario unfolding, unbeknown to them the UNPROFOR team in the Holiday Inn were already engaged in organising a 'pool' to place bets on when the shooting war would begin.[56] For the meantime, however,

---

[53] Transcript of interview with General Lewis MacKenzie in 'Death of Yugoslavia Archive', UBIT, p. 1.

[54] *Oslobodjenje*, Sarajevo, 21 March 1992, p. 3.

[55] *Ibid*, p. 3. According to MacKenzie, Nambiar was delighted when he was eventually relocated to a hotel complex called Stojčevac 2 km southwest of Sarajevo. 'General Nambiar' he said, 'could not wait to move in. He hated living in the Holiday Inn.' See Lewis MacKenzie, *Peacekeeper: The Road to Sarajevo*, p. 125.

[56] Transcript of interview with General Lewis MacKenzie in 'Death of Yugoslavia Archive', UBIT, p. 1. In a speech published in the Canadian Journal of Military and Strategic Studies, MacKenzie said, 'One of my Majors won 1200 bucks US for picking 2.30 pm on the afternoon of the 6th of April when snipers opened up at the Holiday Inn at the crowd in front of the Presidency. I had 2.32 pm, others had 2.31 pm, 2.28 pm. It didn't take 20 years in the diplomatic corps or a PhD in Political Science to see it coming.' See Lewis MacKenzie,

UNPROFOR's presence in the hotel provided a semblance of hope to the citizens of Sarajevo, despite the cynicism of the UNPROFOR team. Surely now, optimists hoped, with the presence of an international force, however small, war could be avoided. But UNPROFOR now shared their accommodation with those who harboured very different intentions.

Throughout March 1992, the lobby of the hotel would be full of ECMM and UNPROFOR staff, journalists, TV crews, SDS members, and the personal bodyguards of Radovan Karadžić, who had moved into the Holiday Inn. In late February 1992, fearing (after the proclamation of the Serbian Republic of Bosnia and Herzegovina) that his family were potentially endangered in their apartment in *Ulica Sutjeska* (Sutjeska street) in central Sarajevo, he had moved himself, his wife Ljiljana, and his two children, Sonja and Aleksandar (Saša), into the hotel. The Karadžić family occupied rooms 526–530 on the fifth-floor 'Presidential Suite' (the first occupant of room 530 had been the IOC President, Juan Antonio Samaranch, in January 1984 in advance of the 1984 Winter Olympics). They would remain ensconced there, Karadžić's family rarely venturing beyond the confines of their suite and the hotel lobby.[57] Be it in the SDS offices or the atrium, Radovan Karadžić or other key figures in the SDS, almost always flanked by Todor Dutina,[58] the party's 'press officer', provided daily statements and interviews to the press from all over Europe, and regardless of the 'stabilising' presence of the ECMM delegation (the majority of the UNPROFOR were preparing to move to the *Dom penzionera*—known to the UNPROFOR troops as the 'Hotel Rainbow'—near the *Oslobodjenje* building), the Holiday Inn remained the centre of SDS activity.

Radovan Karadžić, though based in the Holiday Inn, spent much of March involved in the so-called Carrington-Cutileiro Plan negotiations.[59]

'Canada's Army—Post Peacekeeping', *The Canadian Journal of Military and Strategic Studies*, Volume 12, Issue 1, Fall 2009, p. 8.

[57] According to a member of the housekeeping staff, the cleaners became increasingly displeased with the Karadžić family's cats urinating on the floor of the suite. Author's interview with Holiday Inn (Sarajevo) employee, April 2014.

[58] Before joining the SDS, Todor Dutina was an editor at the Svjetlost publishing house in Sarajevo. He was the first director of the 'Serb News Agency' (SRNA) established in Pale in April 1992, before becoming Deputy Foreign Minister of Republika Srpska in 1993, then being sent to Moscow as an envoy in 1994. After the war he became Bosnia's ambassador to the United Nations in Geneva.

[59] For more detail on the Lisbon negotiations see Stephen L. Burg, & Paul Shoup, *The War in Bosnia-Herzegovina: Ethnic Conflict and International Intervention*, New York: M.E. Sharpe, 2000, pp. 108–117.

The plan, also known as the *Lisabonski sporazum* (the Lisbon Agreement), envisaged a cantonised Bosnia comprising small autonomous units that reflected the ethnic balance in each canton (though there was some ambiguity over which ethnic group was dominant in each canton). It went through a number of revisions and was rejected, in the first instance, by the Bosnian Serbs. By the time of the fourth revision, however (which envisaged a division of Bosnia into three ethnic units—Serb, Croat, and Muslim), agreement appeared closer. The plan was signed by Karadžić, Boban, and Izetbegović respectively on 18 March 1992. Ten days later, on 28 March, Izetbegović withdrew his signature and reverted to type, insisting that he would not accept a territorial division of Bosnia. The 'Lisbon Agreement' was thus annulled, and war drew closer, though it remains unclear how well the plan would have functioned if implemented.

On the same day, members of the 'Congress of Serbian Intellectuals in Bosnia & Herzegovina' gathered at the Holiday Inn for their first annual congress, during which they planned to discuss the predicament of Serbs in Bosnia and Herzegovina. The invitation sent out to delegates stated that the event was being held in a context where 'The Serbian nation is facing the [sic] threat aimed at its annulling, even destruction.'[60] Alongside the SDS personnel, billed to speak on the topic of 'The Yugoslav Crisis and the Serbian Question', were the likes of the writer and 'father' of Serb nationalism Dobrica Ćosić; Prince Tomislav Karadjordjević; the leader of the Serbian Radical Party (*Srpska radikalna stranka*—SRS) Vojislav Šešelj; and the Montenegrin poet Matija Bećković, although none of them, apparently due to ill health or previous commitments, attended. Their written statements were, instead, read out to those who were present.[61] At the meeting's end, the congress put forward their *Deklaracija* (Declaration), which, among other things, stated that 'the fate of the Serbs in indivisible' and that 'anything that happens on one country relates to Serbs wherever they live'.[62] The meeting, organised to with the objective of finding ways

---

[60] SDS—President's Cabinet, Number 617-011-1/92, Sarajevo, 17 March 1992. ICTY document no: ETSA03-0331-SA03-0331.

[61] *Borba*, Belgrade, 30 March 1992, p. 5. In a letter to SDS members sent on 17 March (although the document incorrectly states 17 May), Karadžić sent a letter imploring them to both attend the 'Congress of Serbian Intellectuals' meeting and donate money for its realisation. The letter claimed the meeting was being held at a moment when 'the struggle for the unity of the Serbian nation is of decisive historical importance'. See UN-ICTY Case No. IT-95-5/18-T, 'The Prosecutor V. Radovan Karadžić (ET SA03-0331-SA03-03311.doc).

[62] The 'Declaration of the Congress of Serbian Intellectuals in Bosnia & Herzegovina' and the letter to the Congress from Dobrica Ćosić were published in the Belgrade daily *Borba*,

for 'the Serbian nation to surmount the on-going crisis', would be the last SDS-sponsored event of any significance (barring a seemingly mundane meeting of the SDS main board on 3 April) to take place in the hotel before the subsequent events of 5 and 6 April.[63]

The SDS leadership were now almost permanently in the Holiday Inn, and they were becoming increasingly paranoid, particularly Radovan Karadžić.[64] The SDS (in conjunction with Serb members of MUP) developed their own communication code (they would have assumed that their phone calls were being tapped, and thus needed to develop their own coded communications). The five leading figures in the SDS were numbered one to five—Karadžić, for example, was '01'—while various key buildings were also given codes. The Holiday Inn was '024', while Sarajevo airport was '032', Code number '017' was 'armed attack—help needed'.[65] That the leadership of the SDS were nervous was not lost on those who interviewed him in the days leading up to the outbreak of war. Writing in the *Spectator* magazine, Robin Lodge stated that the Holiday Inn, 'run by Serbs and doubling up as public relations office for Radovan Karadžić's SDS', was gripped by real tension in the days leading to the outbreak of war in Sarajevo. Walking around the hotel were young, armed SDS activists; 'Sour-faced, puppy-fat youths hang around the gloomy corridors, fondling the safety-catches of their automatic rifles, daring you to ask them to step aside.'[66] Maggie O' Kane of *The Guardian* described meeting him in the Holiday Inn as akin to 'an audience with a Mafia don; Young men with Kalashnikov's knocked on the door…announcing that Dr Karadžić was ready to receive. In the Olympic suite, the boys in the anteroom frisked the visitors before entering.' Karadžić was, she said, 'a genial host; a nice guy with a sting in his tail, who was paranoid about his own security'.[67] Likewise, the correspondent for the Slovenian daily

and the transcripts of both were republished in Helsinški odbor za ljudska prava u Srbiji, *Jezgro velikosrpskog projekta*, pp. 281–283.

[63] SDS Main Board, Number 700-02/92, Sarajevo, 3 April 1992, ICTY doc. Number: ET SA04-2503-SA04-2504.

[64] A member of the hotel's housekeeping staff in 1992 (who requested anonymity) claimed that Karadžić became increasingly nervous in March/April 1992, and that his state of mind was evidenced by his 'heavy drinking and frequent bed-wetting'. Author's interviews with Holiday Inn staff, Sarajevo, September 2013.

[65] 'Code Communication System for the SDS, MUP-BiH, CBS Sarajevo', UN-ICTY Doc No. SA02-1378-SAO3-1379.

[66] *The Spectator*, London, 18 July 1992, p. 10.

[67] *The Guardian*, London, 10 August 1992, p. 19.

Novi Tednik (in an article entitled 'Clan Karadžić at the Holiday Inn') also noted that armed bodyguards who served the Karadžić family could be seen 'strutting around the hotel's lobby' and that these new 'guests' were 'making the senior management of the Holiday Inn Hotels Group (based in Atlanta, Georgia) increasing nervous'. Indeed, according to the same article, they were seeking to terminate the franchise agreement with their Sarajevo concern (though, in the same article, the hotel's manager, Danilo Dursun, strenuously denied this).[68] Steve Crawshaw of *The Independent*, who noted that, 'The gunmen usually only chat...[but] when Radovan Karadžić turns up they jab their guns at anyone who fails to keep a respectful distance', gave a particularly striking account of the atmosphere in the Holiday Inn in March 1992:

> There are strange hotels, and there are very strange hotels. The Holiday Inn in Sarajevo undoubtedly falls into to the latter category...This must be one of the few Holiday Inn's in the world where guests share the foyer with large numbers of armed men who stroll around as if they owned the place. They occupy the hotel all day, every day. The gunmen's favourite resting place is on the mezzanine balcony in the atrium-style hotel. They crook their guns on their knees and gaze over the balcony....The hotel staff smile and are courteous in several languages, while affecting not to notice the gun-toting men in leather jackets and jeans.[69]

Staying in the Holiday Inn, added Crawshaw, presented the journalists with a genuine dilemma: 'On one hand', he said, 'guests do not regard a man wielding a Kalashnikov as an essential part of the scenery; on the other, it is the only Sarajevo hotel which has international direct dialling'.[70] Thus, despite the disconcerting presence of armed SDS men, growing legions of foreign journalists and delegations visited the hotel in the weeks following the independence referendum, largely seeking an audience with Karadžić (or ECMM and UNPROFOR staff), eager to determine the SDS leader's intentions as international recognition of Bosnia and Herzegovina drew closer, and how the international community's representatives would attempt to stem the seemingly inexorable slide to armed conflict. The failure to reach agreement (the so-called Lisbon Agreement—which envisaged a division of the republic into three ethnic areas) brought

---

[68] *Novi Tednik*, Ljubljana, 9 April 1992, p. 14.
[69] *The Independent*, London, 7 March 1992, p. 10.
[70] *Ibid*, p. 10.

such conflict even closer. Upon his return from the Lisbon negotiations, Karadžić, when in Sarajevo, or Dutina (when Karadžić was absent) were always available to be interviewed, or give a statement, in the lobby of the hotel. But the Holiday Inn would not remain an 'SDS hotel' for long; the events of 5 and 6 April would ensure that the leadership of the SDS based there would be forced to leave the Holiday Inn and Sarajevo forever.

References

Burg, S. L., & Shoup, P. (2000). *The War in Bosnia-Herzegovina: Ethnic Conflict and International Intervention*. New York: M.E. Sharpe.

CSCE. (1992). The referendum on independence in Bosnia-Herzegovina, February 29–March 1, 1992, CSCE report.

Čekić, S. (2005). *The Aggression against the Republic of Bosnia & Herzegovina: Planning, Preparation, Execution* (Book One). Sarajevo: Institute for the Research of Crimes Against Humanity and International Law.

Ganić, E. (2007). *Razgovori i svjedočenja 1990–1994*. Sarajevo: Svjetlost.

Kapić, S. (2000). *The Siege of Sarajevo: 1992–1996*. Sarajevo: FAMA.

Kurspahić, K. (1997). *As Long as Sarajevo Exists*. Connecticut: The Pamphleteers Press.

MacKenzie, L. (1993). *Peacekeeper: The Road to Sarajevo*. Vancouver/Toronto: Douglas & McIntyre.

MacKenzie, L. (2009). Canada's Army—Post Peacekeeping. *The Canadian Journal of Military and Strategic Studies, 12*(1).

Morrison, K., & Roberts, E. R. (2013). *The Sandžak: A History*. London: Hurst & Co..

Pavlović, S. (2005). Reckoning: The Siege of Dubrovnik and the consequences of the 'War for Peace'. *Spaces of Identity, 5*, 1–47.

UN-ICTY Case No. IT-95-5/18-T. (1992). The Prosecutor V. Radovan Karadžić (ET SA01-1505-SA01-1571.doc), Club of Parliament Representatives, Serb Democratic Party, Bosnia and Herzegovina: Transcript from the meeting of the Club, Sarajevo.

UN-ICTY Case No. IT-09-92-T. (2012). The Prosecutor v. Ratko Mladić, Prosecution 92 *TER* MOTION: RM114 (Colm Doyle).

Whitehouse, R. (2007). *Are We There Yet? Travels with my Frontline Family*. London: Reportage Press.

CHAPTER 7

Crossing the Rubicon: The Outbreak of War in Sarajevo

Clashes in Bosanski Brod and the Serb attack on Bijeljina (in eastern Bosnia) led by the *Srpska dobrovoljačka garda* (Serbian Volunteer Guard), better known as *Arkanovi tigrovi* (Arkan's Tigers—after their leader, Željko Ražnatović 'Arkan'), were dark portents of things to come.[1] War had ostensibly begun, though such conflicts had thus far been avoided in Sarajevo. But on 4 April, as information about the killings started to trickle out from Bijeljina, the Bosnian government announced a general mobilisation call.[2] The SDS response was that armed conflict in Sarajevo had moved a step closer with the announcement of the mobilisation. Karadžić's reaction to the mobilisation call was one of outrage. He stated that this gave Bosnia's Serbs a clear indication of Izetbegović's true intentions. 4 April 1992, he would later say, 'Was the last day of Ramadan'. According to the Koran, the Muslims must not wage war during the Ramadan, but immediately after it finishes, their duty is to kill the infidels. When we heard that Izetbegović had issued a mobilisation call, he knew 'that this would lead to war'.[3] In response, the SDS announced

---

[1] *Oslobodjenje*, Sarajevo, 3 April 1992, p. 1. For a detailed analysis of the ethnic cleansing of eastern Bosnia in 1992, see Edina Bećirević, *Na Drini genocid: istraživanje organiziranog zločina u istočnoj Bosni*, Sarajevo: Buy book, 2009. For a succinct analysis of the period between 1 and 10 April (in Bijeljina, Foča, Višegrad, Vlasenica, and Zvornik), see *Dani*, Sarajevo, 12 December 2010, pp. 38–41.
[2] *Oslobodjenje*, Sarajevo, 5 April 1992, p. 3.
[3] Transcript of interview with Radovan Karadžić in 'Death of Yugoslavia Archive', UBIT 177, p. 6.

the creation of an exclusively Serb Interior Ministry (*Ministarstvo unutrašnjih polova*—MUP) as the SDS considered the Bosnian MUP an instrument of the SDA and (in part) the HDZ-BiH.[4] Once again, barricades appeared across Sarajevo.[5]

The atmosphere in Sarajevo was tense. Karadžić would later claim that the evening of 4 April was one of fear, anxiety, and tension; the streets, he said, 'were deserted, and we could see from our offices in the Holiday Inn Muslim Green Berets' snipers placed on the top of high buildings… Everything was blocked and we could not leave the hotel. So we waited to see what would happen.'[6] The citizens of Sarajevo, too, could see that war was becoming, at best, increasingly inevitable and, at worst, unavoidable— though for many *Sarajlije* it was simply unimaginable. All that was needed for that scenario to be realised, however, was a spark to light the fuse. The following day, 5 April, SDS gunmen attacked the police academy in Vraca (a key strategic target for the Serbs), while the (Muslim) Green Berets took control of a number of key buildings in the city centre. According to the testimony of Aleksandar Vasiljević, the former chief of the Yugoslav counter-intelligence service (*Kontra-obavještajna služba*—KOS), the Green Berets invaded military buildings in search of weapons, began looting Serb shops, and sought to initiate armed conflict.[7] The Bosnian MUP, conversely, claimed that Serb and Montenegrin militias, in concert with the JNA, were preparing an assault on Sarajevo.[8]

---

[4] The plans for creating an exclusively Serb MUP had been ongoing for over six months. In an SDS document entitled *Mogućnosti organizovanja Srpskog ministarstva za unutrašnje poslove* (Possibilities of Organising a Serbian Ministry of the Interior) from October 1991, basic plans were drawn up that envisaged its creation, which involved either a Bosnian Serb MUP being incorporated into the Serbian MUP (in Serbia proper) or an independent Bosnian Serb MUP being established. At the time of the report being circulated to SDS members, the former option was judged most desirable. See SDS document SA02/3707, Sarajevo, 17 oktobra 1991 godine, p. 2. See also Robert Donia, *Iz Skupštine Republike Srpske 1991–1996*, Sarajevo: University Press, 2012, pp. 141–143. For the SDS perspective on the ethnic division of MUP, see the English translation of the interview with Momčilo Mandić in *Slobodna Bosna*, Sarajevo, 10 April 1994. UN-ICTY Doc No. ET ERN 0215-5771 0215-5776 Doc.

[5] *Oslobodjenje*, Sarajevo, 5 April 1992, p. 2.

[6] Transcript of interview with Radovan Karadžić in 'Death of Yugoslavia Archive', UBIT 177, p. 7.

[7] See UN-ICTY Case No. IT-95-5/18-T, 'The Prosecutor V. Radovan Karadžić: Revised Notification of Submission of Written Evidence Pursuant to Rule 92 *ter*: Aleksandar Vasiljević' (KW527), p. 69.

[8] For an overview of the events of 5 and 6 April 1992 and the movements of different armed groups in Sarajevo, see *Oslobodjenje*, Sarajevo, 7 April 2008, p. 5.

Meanwhile, a demonstration began in the Sarajevo suburb of Dobrinja, and the numbers grew as the demonstrators reached the centre of the city. As a group of peace demonstrators crossed the Vrbanja bridge in the direction of the Bosnian parliament building, shots were fired by SDS gunmen behind the *Unionvest* building (though it has been alleged that the shots came from the Holiday Inn) and they shot and killed Suada Dilberović, a young medical student from Dubrovnik, and Olga Sučić from Sarajevo.[9] Shocked but unbowed, the demonstrators continued towards the parliament building, directly across from the Holiday Inn where the SDS leadership and their armed guards were ensconced. They arrived at the parliament just after 3.00 pm, stressed the need for unity and understanding, while appealing to the national leaders, in particular Izetbegović and Karadžić, to find a solution that would reverse what appeared to be an inevitable and inexorable trajectory towards war. Some of Sarajevo's best-known actors, artists, and intellectuals were there, each making emotional pleas and calls for calm. The celebrated actor, Rade Šerbedžija, filmed by a YUTEL[10] film crew outside the parliament, stated that, 'These people are no longer defending Yugoslavia. These people will defend their own lives, their lives as citizens, as civilians, their freedom, their right to life; the lives of their children.'[11]

Despite the quixotic and increasingly desperate pleas for the respective leaders to work towards finding a way out of the crisis, any form of constructive dialogue proved impossible. Even ostensibly straightforward matters, such as deciding upon a location for the leaders to meet, proved problematic. The former suggested the *Konak* in the Old Town as a meeting place, a suggestion immediately rejected by Karadžić, largely on the basis of symbolism. 'I could not go there', he said, 'because he [Izetbegović] wanted to humiliate me. His idea was probably to sit there on some sort of a

---

[9] *Oslobodjenje*, Sarajevo, 6 April 1992, p. 1.

[10] YUTEL, which was often criticised by the SDS, was funded in part by the Yugoslav 'Federal Executive Council', under the presidency of Ante Marković. The organisation was based in Sarajevo and was, according to its Director General, Bato Tomašević, a channel designed to provide a more balanced view of events than could be found on the TV stations in the Yugoslav republics. The channel would, he claimed, 'give every side a chance to put forward their views calmly and debate then in a civilised manner'. YUTEL functioned from October 1990 until May 1992. See Bato Tomašević, *Life and Death in the Balkans: A Family Saga in a Century of Conflict*, London: Hurst & Co., 2008, p. 458.

[11] Senad Hadžifejzović, *Rat užvo: ratni teevizijski dnevnik*, Mladinska knjiga, Ljubljana, 2002, p. 38.

platform, so that his seat would be elevated in relation to mine, and I, being a Christian slave, would have to salute to him as if he were a [Ottoman] vizier.'[12] In response, Izetbegović refused to meet at the Holiday Inn (which was known to all in Sarajevo as an 'SDS hotel'), and thus Karadžić and his entourage remained in the hotel throughout the evening of 5 April. They became increasingly convinced that they were encircled and endangered by the Bosnian government forces and the Muslim *Zelene beretke* (Green Berets), who had raided and looted Karadžić's flat in Sutjeska Street earlier in the day, only adding to the existing paranoia.[13] Throughout the night, the crowds remained in the parliament building across the road from the Holiday Inn. Declaring themselves 'The People's Assembly', they hastily elected a *Komitet nacionalnog spasa* (Committee of National Salvation), which pledged to organise and schedule a new round of elections. Speaker after speaker conveyed the same message: It was imperative to avoid intensification of the crisis and that Sarajevo's citizens should remain united. The city was paralysed, with traffic and public transport at a standstill.[14] Sarajevo TV relayed the events continuously to a bewildered and frightened population, who were hard pressed to absorb the gravity and speed of the events which were unfolding on their television screens. In the meantime, however, the sound of mortar and machine-gun fire could be heard in Baščaršija.

The following morning, 6 April (the forty-seventh anniversary of Sarajevo's liberation from German and Ustaša occupation in 1945), the EC recognised Bosnia and Herzegovina as an independent state, while the USA followed suit the following day. Having repeatedly declared that they would not recognise the legitimacy of an independent Bosnia and Herzegovina, it would be the pretext the SDS needed. In the meantime, the demonstrators who had been in the parliament throughout the night were bolstered the following morning by greater numbers, some, having seen the events of the previous day, coming from beyond Sarajevo to lend their support. By 12.00 pm, the majority of them (which Karadžić described as 'Izetbegović's armed peace activists') had reached the

---

[12] Transcript of interview with Radovan Karadžić in 'Death of Yugoslavia Archive', UBIT 177, pp. 7–8. Karadžić, despite expressing an aversion to meeting in the *Konak*, had in fact attended numerous meetings there in February 1992 as part of an SDS delegation during EC-sponsored negotiations. See Steven L. Burg and Paul Shoup, *The War in Bosnia–Herzegovina: Ethnic Conflict and International Intervention*, p. 108.

[13] *Oslobodjenje*, Sarajevo, 6 April 1992, p. 3.

[14] *Ibid*, p. 3.

parliament building across the street from the Holiday Inn.[15] The crowds numbering, according to the estimates of the Sarajevo daily *Oslobodjenje*, 100,000 people, assembled outside the parliament building.[16] They carried banners bearing messages such as *Mižel̦imo mir* (We want peace) and *Mi smo Titovi, Tito je nas* (We are Tito's, Tito is ours) while chanting *Dolje vlada!* (Down with the government).

Those among the SDS leadership that were in the Holiday Inn perceived this as something more sinister than merely a peace rally organised and led by the citizens of Sarajevo. Karadžić and his armed entourage had, according to Robert Donia, 'a front row seat' to watch the events unfold from across the street in the Holiday Inn (his suite had a direct view of the large terrace outside the parliament).[17] According to Karadžić's own account, he became increasingly convinced that the events were being organised by his political opponents. 'Buses started arriving [near the parliament] with workers and miners from central Bosnia. Everything had a communist and Bolshevik flair, and it was evident that the whole thing was staged...these miners were armed and you could see automatic rifles and other weapons under their jackets.'[18] As the demonstrations intensified, Momčilo Krajišnik, who was at home watching

[15] Transcript of interview with Radovan Karadžić in 'Death of Yugoslavia Archive', UBIT 177, p. 7.
[16] *Oslobodjenje*, Sarajevo, 8 April 1992, p. 3.
[17] Robert Donia, *Radovan Karadžić: Architect of the Bosnian Genocide*, p. 189.
[18] Transcript of interview with Radovan Karadžić in 'Death of Yugoslavia Archive', UBIT 177, p. 7. In his testimony to the ICTY, the former chief of Yugoslav Military Counter-Intelligence, Aleksandar Vasiljević, claimed that the shots had not been fired by SDS snipers, but by Muslim snipers in the nearby (adjacent) Secondary Technical School. 'There were a number of [SDS] people there [in the Holiday Inn] at the time, working on the archives. According to our information, the firing positions of the Muslim paramilitary formations at the Technical School near the Holiday Inn were held by Juka Prazina. These positions were behind the mass of people, facing in the direction of the Government of Bosnia & Herzegovina, across from the Holiday Inn. From there they opened fire at the people, wounding one or two, and after that they spread misinformation that the Chetniks were opening fire from the Holiday Inn. At the same time, a special unit of the Bosnia & Herzegovina MUP, led by Mirza Jamaković, whose members were dressed in workers' overalls, was on stand-by. They burst into the premises of the SDS at the Holiday Inn, capturing four or five persons who were packing things at the time, and declared that the Chetniks had fired at the people. This was a planned operation to radicalise the situation, to be used as an excuse to take over the BH territorial defence headquarters.' See UN-ICTY Case No. IT-95-5/18-T, 'The Prosecutor v. Radovan Karadžić: Revised Notification of Submission of Written Evidence Pursuant to Rule 92 *ter*: Aleksandar Vasiljević' (KW527), p. 69.

the events unfold on television, advised Karadžić to leave the Holiday Inn: 'Mr Karadžić was in the Holiday Inn during the great demonstrations. He was there at the time and they could easily arrest him. I remember talking on the phone with him and suggesting that he leave the hotel...this peace movement was very dangerous. They later attacked the Holiday Inn as the place where the Serbs were meeting. Because of this association to the Serbs they later tried to destroy the Holiday Inn.'[19]

In the Holiday Inn, Karadžić waited nervously. The crowd, he later said, 'could turn against the Holiday Inn at any moment and take me prisoner. [So] I insisted upon staying in the Holiday Inn, because I thought that if they attacked us the Serbs would come and defend us because they knew that we were there.'[20] The paranoia of the SDS crisis staff who remained in the hotel only grew as, at around 2.00 pm, part of the crowd surged towards the Holiday Inn to directly confront them.[21] Civilian UNPROFOR staff, who were watching events unfold on television in their rooms in the hotel, quickly realised that they, too, were about to be unwillingly thrust into the eye of the storm. The crowd, who were advancing rapidly towards the hotel, may have expected some resistance from the SDS guards in the Holiday Inn, but they did not expect that they would fire indiscriminately into their midst. According to Kemal Kurspahić, the editor of *Oslobodjenje*, the demonstrations were of a peaceful nature, an 'extraordinary and unprecedented demonstration of unity' but 'then the shots rang out. Serb snipers from Karadžić's headquarters [the Holiday Inn] were shooting at unarmed demonstrators.'[22]

Witnesses claim that SDS gunmen located in the upper floors moved from window to window (accounts vary with regard to which floor the snipers were located) firing directly into the crowd, killing six and wounding many more.[23] Those who were exposed in the large, open space between the

---

[19] Transcript of interview with Momčilo Krajišnik in 'Death of Yugoslavia Archive', UBIT 050, p. 4.

[20] Transcript of interview with Radovan Karadžić in 'Death of Yugoslavia Archive', UBIT 177, p. 7.

[21] According to the Sarajevo daily *Oslobodjenje*, the protestors who approached the Holiday Inn were unarmed and were later brave enough to 'take on the snipers with their bare hands'. See *Oslobodjenje*, 7 April 1992, p. 24.

[22] Kemal Kurspahić, *As Long as Sarajevo Exists*, p. 121.

[23] Robert Donia, *Sarajevo: A Biography*, p. 285. See also Sibler and Little, *The Death of Yugoslavia*, London: Penguin Books, p. 229. A 'Radio Sarajevo' report from 6 April (by Zdenko Jendruh), provided a succinct description of the atmosphere in Sarajevo on 6 April. 'Few cars and 'passers-by' can be seen in the streets of Sarajevo today...Firms in the city are

Bosnian parliament building and the Holiday Inn ran for cover, cowered behind bins, cars, or anything else that would provide them a semblance of protection from the sniper fire. Ibrahim Spahić, a citizen of Sarajevo, described the approach to the Holiday Inn as walking straight into 'the snake's nest', though many of those who were approaching the hotel were unaware of what was about to happen.[24] The shootings destroyed the hitherto positive mood of the gathering, and the atmosphere darkened markedly.[25] Armoured police cars fired into the fourth and fifth floors of the Holiday Inn before, enraged by the audacity of the SDS snipers, a group of protestors led by a Bosnian MUP 'Special Unit' led by Dragan Vikić—known also as *Vikićevi specijalci* (Vikić's Specials)—who were ostensibly there to provide security during the rally at the adjacent Assembly building, bore down on the hotel.[26] This time, however, they successfully burst into the hotel lobby with a view to apprehending the snipers. Chaos ensued. According to a UN report, UNPROFOR staff witnessed windows being smashed and smoke bombs and tear gas canisters being thrown into the lobby of the hotel.[27] One of the British journalists in the hotel lobby at the time was *The Independent* correspondent Marcus Tanner, who was made aware of the imminent attack by Cedric Thornberry, the Director of UNPROFOR's Civil Affairs, who was quickly leaving the hotel after a bullet had shattered the window in his room. In Tanner's report for the newspaper, the following day he described the chaos that ensued when the hotel was stormed by the Bosnian MUP Special Unit:

> My decision to stay at the Holiday Inn turned out to be a mistake when Serb snipers on the upper floors opened fire on thousands of Muslim demonstrators in the streets below. As I tried to telephone London,

not working today and schools are closed. The shops are also closed and as of this morning all supplies have stopped. The medical centre has sent an appeal to enable the supply of food for the patients and the supply of hospitals with medical materials, of which there are less and less. There were no daily papers in Sarajevo today. Many shops and tobacco shops have been looted. Postal and telephone links with Sarajevo are interrupted. Trains arrive and leave with delays and the inter-city bus service has been interrupted.' See *Sarajevo Radio Network*, 6 April 1992, FBIS OU604143092.

[24] Interview with Ibro Spahić in Suada Kapić, *The Siege of Sarajevo: 1992–1996*, Sarajevo: FAMA, 2000, p. 153.

[25] Mirko Pejanović, *Through Bosnian Eyes*, p. 54.

[26] Interview with Ibro Spahić in Suada Kapić, *The Siege of Sarajevo: 1992–1996*, p. 153.

[27] Final Report of the United Nations Commission of Experts, 'Study of the Battle and Siege of Sarajevo', Part 1/10, S/1994/674/Add.2 (Vol. II), 27 May 1994, p. 16.

seconds after the civil head of the United Nations peace-keeping operation [UNPROFOR] in Yugoslavia had pulled out of the hotel, a group of Bosnian police and Muslim fighters attacked the building, blasting out the windows by hurling grenades into the reception area and spraying it with machine-gun fire. With half a dozen other journalists, I crawled to safety in a corner of the reception area under the stairs, waiting for the battle between Serbs and Muslims for control over this strategically important building in the city center to finish. After half an hour Muslim fighters [MUP] in control of the lower floors found us. They told us to escape across the adjacent square, ducking the heavy machine-gun fire all around us on the way.[28]

The Times correspondent, Tim Judah, leaped over the reception into an adjacent cloakroom, where he and a few others waited for the shooting to stop. 'We were afraid', he said, 'that they [MUP] would burst 'into' the room, shoot, and ask questions later...the tension was palpable; but soon after we heard someone shouting for the journalists to leave the hotel, which we duly did'.[29] As the journalists and some members of the hotel staff fled, a number were apprehended and taken to local police stations where they were questioned about the alleged shootings. What Judah described as the 'sack of the Holiday Inn' now began.[30] The MUP units then began a room-by-room search of the hotel to identify and apprehend the gunmen. The hotel's guests, workers, and the journalists located inside the building, terrified by the unfolding events, emerged from behind the reception counter, the stairwells, the ground-floor hairdressing salon, and the atrium's concrete pillars where they had been sheltering.[31]

During the storming of the hotel, eight alleged SDS snipers (the number was later confirmed by *Oslobodjenje* as three), who had attempted to evade their pursuers by climbing to the roof of the building, were overwhelmed by sheer numbers, apprehended and beaten before being taken to the lobby and briefly questioned members of the MUP.[32] Frightened and claiming to have no knowledge of the shootings, they were, according to the UNPROFOR General Lewis MacKenzie, 'in a mess by the time

---

[28] *The Independent*, London, 7 April 1992, p. 1.
[29] Author's interview with Tim Judah, London (The Times), April 2014.
[30] *The Times*, London, 9 April 1992, p. 28.
[31] Author's interview with Holiday Inn (Sarajevo) employee, May 2014. See also Tom Gjelten, *Sarajevo Daily: A City and Its Newspaper Under Siege*, New York, HarperCollins, 1995, p. 23.
[32] *Oslobodjenje*, Sarajevo, 8 April 1992, p. 3.

they reached the lobby of the hotel'.[33] They were then dragged from the hotel to face a baying crowd and an uncertain fate.[34] Fortunately for the alleged gunmen, however, they represented valuable bargaining chips for the Bosnian government, and were later exchanged for Bosnian police cadets who had been held prisoner at the Vraca police academy, which had been overrun by SDS militia the previous day.[35] By the time the SDS snipers had been arrested, however, the party's leadership, including Radovan Karadžić, had fled.[36] According to one member of the hotel's staff who was present in the hotel at the time, 'Karadžić and his people had just left; it was all very quick. I could see there was a sense of alarm, but I had no idea what their sudden departure meant. I just couldn't believe, nor could I bring myself to believe, that war was possible until it was already upon us.'[37]

Karadžić had indeed escaped the Holiday Inn. Some witnesses claim that he had been helped to do so by masked bodyguards who escorted him to a waiting car in the basement car park and subsequently whisked away. Karadžić was then taken to nearby Serb-held Ilidža, where he briefly settled in the *Hotel Srbija* (Hotel Serbia) in the hotel complex near *Vrelo Bosne* (the Spring of Bosnia)[38] Karadžić, however, claimed that he had

---

[33] Lewis MacKenzie, *Peacekeeper: The Road to Sarajevo*, p. 140. See also *Oslobodjenje*, Sarajevo, 7 April 1992, p. 3.

[34] Laura Sibler and Allan Little, *The Death of Yugoslavia*, BBC/Penguin Books, Second Edition, London, 1996, p. 229.

[35] According to Kemal Kurspahić, the editor-in-chief of *Oslobodjenje*, one of the snipers arrested was Rajko Kušić, the personal bodyguard of Radovan Karadžić's close associate of Nikola Koljević. See Kemal Kurspahić, *As Long as Sarajevo Exists*, p. 136. Hasan Efendić claims that one of the snipes was 'the deputy secretary for national defence of Sarajevo, Branko Kovačević, previously Radovan Karadžić's personal secretary'. See Hasan Efendić, *Ko je branio Bosnu*, Sarajevo: Udruženje gradjana plemićkog porijekla BiH, 1999, p. 103. According to Smail Čekić, the eventual evacuation of the snipers was organised by the 'Security Department of the Command of the 2nd District' of the JNA. See Smail Čeki, *The Aggression against the Republic of Bosnia & Herzegovina: Planning, Preparation, Execution* (Book 1), Institute for the Research of Crimes against Humanity and International Law, Sarajevo, 2005a, p. 929. See also Vreme News Digest Agency, No. 29, 13 April 1992. For the SDS's precise demands, see *Oslobodjenje*, Sarajevo, 8 April 1992, p. 8.

[36] Author's interview with Holiday Inn (Sarajevo) employee, April 2014.

[37] Author's interview with Holiday Inn (Sarajevo) employee, May 2014.

[38] The Ilidža hotel and spa complex had been built by the Austro-Hungarians in 1910. It comprised of three hotels—'Austria', 'Hungary', and 'Bosnia'—that were considered some of the finest in Bosnia. It was here that the Archduke Franz Ferdinand and his wife Sophie had stayed the night before their fateful assassination on 28 June 1914. See James Lyon, 'Habsburg Sarajevo 1914: A Social Picture', pp. 36–38.

already left the hotel before the shots were fired, having been taken to the Sarajevo TV station to meet with Izetbegović and Kljuić before being instructed by his security detail not to return to the Holiday Inn and instead he was taken to Lukavica.[39] Robert Donia noted that telephone intercepts (used during Karadžić's trial at the ICTY) demonstrate that, at the time of the shootings he was finding a safe route out of Sarajevo.[40] In any event, when Karadžić did leave the city, he would stay at the Hotel Serbia (where he was warmly greeted by local SDS officials) for only a few days before establishing a permanent base in Pale, the small mountain town in which wealthy Sarajevans would have *vikendicas* (weekend houses).[41] There the SDS would use, most frequently, the *Hotel Panorama* as their base (though they would also use the *Hotel Bistrica* on Jahorina, built for the 1984 Winter Olympic Games).[42] Some even claimed that a helicopter in the nearby Maršal Tito barracks was used to evacuate him from Sarajevo, though this would appear to be unfounded.[43] Whatever the method of transportation, Karadžić escaped, leaving a number of SDS members and his armed guard to an uncertain fate. In an interview for Radio Belgrade following his escape from the Holiday Inn, Karadžić denied that SDS snipers had been responsible, and that the whole incident had been staged, placing the blame for the shootings and the subsequent storming of the hotel on 'Muslim militia' shooting from the UNIS towers.[44] This view was

---

[39] Transcript of interview with Radovan Karadžić in 'Death of Yugoslavia Archive', UBIT 177, p. 7.

[40] Robert Donia, Radovan Karadžić: Architect of the Bosnian Genocide, p. 189.

[41] BSA (Bosnian Serb Assembly), 17th Session, 24–26 July 1992, Nedeljko Prstojević, BCS 0214-9561, quoted in Robert Donia, Robert Donia, Radovan Karadžić: Architect of the Bosnian Genocide, p. 190.

[42] UN ICTY: Robert Donia, 'From Election to Stalemate: The Making of the Siege of Sarajevo, 1990–1994', Statement of Expert Witness in Case No. IT-98-29-1, The Prosecutor V. Dragomir Milošević, December 2006, p. 20. The SDS leadership stayed for a short period at the Hotel Srbija (Hotel Serbia). According to the witness statement of Radomir Kezunović, given to the ICTY, Nikola Koljević was permanently based in the hotel, while Karadžić and Krajišnik came 'from time to time'. After internal SDS discussions on the security situation in and around Ilidža, it was decided that the Serb 'government bodies' could not function there it was decided that Pale should be the base of the SDS's operations. Thereafter, none of this troika spent much time in Ilidža. See UN-ICTY, The Prosecutor v. Radovan Karadžić, Case No. IT-95-5/18-T, 27 May 2011, p. 4.

[43] Author's interview with Holiday Inn (Sarajevo) employee, September 2013.

[44] *Oslobodjenje*, Sarajevo, 8 April 1992, p. 5. According to Donia, 'Responsibility for the killing of demonstrators on the afternoon of April 6 remains contested. Serb apologists point

later supported by the General Milutin Kukanjac, the JNA's Commander in Sarajevo. According to him, 'Everything was staged... Izetbegović was behind it all. There were some honest people there—Muslims, Croats and Serbs alike, and they thought the rally was organised to seek protection for all the people in Bosnia. But they were actually skilfully manipulated. And then there was that shooting on the Holiday Inn hotel, for which the Muslims were responsible.'[45]

As Karadžić made his way out of Sarajevo, a number of the hotel's staff, particularly those suspected of being SDS members, having connections to the party or those suspected to have information about Karadžić's whereabouts, were led away for questioning by the Bosnian MUP (the majority were released almost immediately).[46] In the aftermath, some of them would remain in Sarajevo, while others left the city with their families, never to return—most went to Serbia, others to Montenegro. For those that chose to remain, it would be their last day at work for two months. After the staff had been 'evacuated', many of the foreign journalists who had been pinned down in the hotel were also forced by the Bosnian MUP to leave, though some tentatively returned two or three hours later to find their possessions had been either stolen or destroyed.[47] Tim Judah of *The Times* had returned to the hotel to collect his belongings from his room and discovered that his camera, computer, and suitcase were stolen. He managed, however, to gather what remained of his possessions, bundling them into a bed sheet (his suitcases had been used to carry off an assortment of cameras and laptop computers from neighbouring rooms).[48] As he approached the front entrance of the hotel, he was stopped by a gunman, and realised that he might be mistaken for a looter. The gunmen demanded the key to his car

---

to reports of shots coming from buildings to the east, suggesting that Muslim gunmen may have fired on the crowd. The possibility of shooting from other locations cannot be excluded, but, as recorded by television cameras, those in the crowd reacted to gunfire from the Holiday Inn's top floor.' See Robert Donia, *Sarajevo: A Biography*, pp. 285–286.

[45] Transcript of interview with Milutin Kukanjac in 'Death of Yugoslavia Archive', UBIT 166 (2), p. 15.

[46] Author's interview with Holiday Inn (Sarajevo) employee, September 2013.

[47] *The Times*, London, 7 May 1992, p. 2.

[48] *The Independent*, London, 18 April 1992, p. 16. Tanner would later admit that he 'should have seen it coming' when he saw Radovan Karadžić's wife, Ljilijana, and daughter, Sonja, dragging their suitcases down to the hotel reception and checking out the day before. See *The Independent*, London, 15 October 1995, p. 12.

(a black Fiat Uno parked in the basement garage) but he said, 'they had no interest in it—it was a right hand drive, and was clearly not the car of choice for a Sarajevo gunman—so thankfully the car was safe'.[49] He then joined a group of the journalists who were then taken in convoy to the *Hotel Evropa* (Hotel Europe) where they spent the next few days before leaving the city.[50]

In the hours following the events at the Holiday Inn, Sarajevo descended into a menacing anarchy; MUP fighters in the hotel exchanged fire with Serb militia located in nearby Grbavica and Skenderija, and further skirmishes broke in other parts of the city. Roadblocks were again re-erected, and by nightfall an air of grim uncertainty and terrifying anticipation of darker events hung heavily over the city. Sarajevo was gripped with uncertainty. In such a situation, Sarajevans headed for the 'safety' of their homes, hoping for the best but fearing the worst.[51]

The following day, 7 April, Nikola Koljević and Biljana Plavšić resigned from their posts in the collective Bosnian Presidency to assume new positions in their own self-proclaimed Serb republic. In the *Hotel Bosna* (Hotel Bosnia) in Banja Luka, the leadership of the SDS gathered to proclaim that the 'Serbian Republic of Bosnia & Herzegovina' (later Republika Srpska) was now an independent state.[52] One last attempt, however, was made to avert war. On that evening, Momčilo Krajišnik travelled into the centre of Sarajevo, at significant personal risk, to meet with Alija Izetbegović at the deserted Bosnian parliament, where just hours earlier the area between the parliament building and the Holiday Inn had been teeming with demonstrators. Krajišnik implored Izetbegović to make a proposal with regard to the division of the city;[53] the latter responded that he would

---

[49] Author's interview with Tim Judah (The Times), April 2014. See also *The Times*, London, 9 April 1992, p. 28.

[50] Built in 1882, the Hotel Europa was completely destroyed during the siege of Sarajevo. The building was targeted in July and August 1992 (the Bosnian Serbs claimed that the hotel was the headquarters of the 'Green Berets') and was nothing more than a shell thereafter, despite the best efforts of the Sarajevo Fire Service. Its cellar was used as a shelter during the subsequent three-and-a-half-year siege. The Europa was reconstructed after the siege and remains one of Sarajevo's finest hostelries. See also interview with Huso Ćesko (Sarajevo Fire Service) in Sauda Kapić, *The Siege of Sarajevo 1992–1996*, Sarajevo: FAMA, 2000, p. 224.

[51] Kerim Lučarević, *The Battle for Sarajevo: Sentenced to Victory*, Sarajevo: TZU, 2000, p. 49.

[52] *Oslobodjenje*, Sarajevo, 8 April 1992, p. 5.

[53] Recalling conversations over Sarajevo with Radovan Karadžić in the Spring of 1992, the then US Ambassador to the SFRJ, Warren Zimmermann, said that 'Karadžić told me...that Sarajevo was going to be the Serbian capital, and I expressed some surprise, since it's largely

rather Krajišnik forward a proposal first.⁵⁴ The resulting impasse dictated that their meeting ended with no progress being made on an agreement on Sarajevo. The three-and-a-half-year siege of Sarajevo by the Bosnian Serbs would soon commence. In her diary entry of 8 April, Elma Softić, a citizen of Sarajevo, wrote that, 'In the buildings and passageways patrols are being organised. Basements are being fixed up. The radio and TV are reporting that Sarajevo is swarming with snipers. People are besieging the bus depot and the airport. People are fleeing in panic.'⁵⁵ Indeed, thousands of Sarajevans begin to leave the city using whatever means they could; many travelled by plane (the airport remains open for the next month though it is controlled by the JNA), others by car, bus, or train.⁵⁶

References

Bećirević, E. (2009). *Na Drini genocid: istraživanje organiziranog zločina u istočnoj Bosni*. Sarajevo: Buybook.
Donia, R. J. (2006). *Sarajevo: A Biography*. London: Hurst & Co..
Donia, R. (2012). *Iz Skupštine Republike Srpske 1991–1996: Izvodi iz izlaganja poslanika skupštine Republike Srpske kao dokazni material ns medjunarodnom krivičnom tribunal u Hagu*. Sarajevo: University Press.
Efendić, H. (1999). *Ko je branio Bosnu*. Sarajevo: Udruženje gradjana plemićkog porijekla BiH.
Gjelten, T. (1995). *Sarajevo Daily: A City and Its Newspaper Under Siege*. New York: HarperCollins.
Hadžifejzović, S. (2002). *Rat užvo: Ratni teevizijski dnevnik*. Mladinska Kniga: Ljubljana.

---

a Moslem city. He said "Well, we're going to divide it up" and that "We will have the Serbian area, and that will be part of the Serbian Republic, we will have a Moslem area, and we will have a Croatian area, so nobody will have to live next to another ethnic group. There will be divisions."….I asked him about [these] divisions. He said "Yes, we are going to build walls that will separate all of these areas." I said, 'Well that means Serbs can't see Croats – what if they're in a mixed marriage, or something? And he said "Oh yes, they can go through the checkpoints in the walls, with permission of course, to go to the other side and see members of other ethnic groups."' Transcript of interview with Warren Zimmermann, in 'Death of Yugoslavia Archive', 3/87 UBIT 677-678, pp. 9–10.

⁵⁴ Transcript of interview with Momčilo Krajišnik in 'Death of Yugoslavia Archive', UBIT 050, p. 5.
⁵⁵ Elma Softić, *Sarajevo Days, Sarajevo Nights*, Saint Paul, Minnesota: Hungry Mind Press, 1996, p. 10.
⁵⁶ See Mile Jovičić, *Two Days Till Peace: A Sarajevo Airport Story*, Bloomington, Indiana: Author House, 2011.

Jovičić, M. (2011). *Two Days Till Peace: A Sarajevo Airport Story.* Bloomington: Author House.
Kapić, S. (2000). *The Siege of Sarajevo: 1992–1996.* Sarajevo: FAMA.
Lučarević, K. (2000). *The Battle for Sarajevo: Sentenced to Victory.* Sarajevo: TZU.
Sibler, L., & Little, A. (1996). *The Death of Yugoslavia.* London: Penguin Books.
Softić, E. (1996). *Sarajevo Days, Sarajevo Nights.* Saint Paul, Minnesota: Hungry Mind Press.
Tomašević, B. (2008). *Life and Death in the Balkans: A Family Saga in a Century of Conflict.* London: Hurst & Co..
UN Final Report of the United Nations Commission of Experts. (1994). Study of the Battle and Siege of Sarajevo, Part 1/10, S/1994/674/Add.2 (Vol. II).

CHAPTER 8

A New Reality, A New Clientele

The Holiday Inn, the centre of SDS activities throughout the early part of 1992, would close after 6 April, the interior of the building badly damaged by the events of that day. By the time it reopened in late June 1992, it would be transformed from normal hotel, albeit one utilised partially as a *political space* (controlled, in large part, by the SDS), to a *press hotel*, a headquarters for the media that would descend on the city; one directly facing one of the most dangerous parts of the frontline. The Holiday Inn now became the city's 'war hotel', serving as a base for journalists *within* the lines of the siege and entirely subject to the economic dynamics of it. As Peter Maass observed, from 6 April 'it was all downhill for the Holiday Inn. Once fighting began, executives at corporate headquarters [in Atlanta, Georgia] must have been floored by the things happening at their Sarajevo franchise.'[1] The hotel, for so many citizens of Sarajevo a positive symbol of the 1984 Winter Games would now become notorious as the place where some of the first shots of the war in Sarajevo emanated. Thereafter, the Holiday Inn would join the conspicuous list of 'war hotels' alongside such places as Nicosia's Ledra Palace Hotel (also a frontline hotel, albeit for a much shorter period), Belfast's Hotel Europa, and Beirut's Commodore Hotel. Of course, Sarajevo's Holiday Inn would not be the only hotel that gained notoriety during the 1991–99 wars of Yugoslav succession, though none would become as infamous as the Holiday Inn.

---

[1] Peter Maass, *Love Thy Neighbour: A Story of War*, London: Papermac, 1996, p. 122.

In the immediate period following the events of 6 April, however, it was not evident that the Holiday Inn could realistically function as a working hotel. From an external perspective, the Holiday Inn's location dictated that it feel into an area that was in the middle of an emerging frontline (though this was not wholly evident at this point), while the interior of the building, in particular the atrium and the ground-floor windows, had been badly damaged by the storming of the building by MUP and the subsequent room-by-room searches (many of these rooms had been ransacked). The Olympic crest, embedded in the concrete pillar near the front door of the hotel, was pockmarked by bullets (there would be many more added in the coming years). One member of staff who dared to venture into the hotel on 7 April found 'a really ugly scene', with 'many windows and doors smashed or broken'.[2] In addition, looting continued on 7 and 8 April and, with the hotel essentially unstaffed and unprotected, everything from food and alcoholic beverages to computers and cutlery was taken by looters. The Holiday Inn, for a number of weeks, became a meeting place and operational centre for the Bosnian Territorial Defence (*Teritorijalna odbrana*—TO). Thus, following 6 April it would take a significant clean-up operation before the building could revert to its normal function.[3]

The period before the Holiday Inn reopened in June 1992 was characterised by uncertainty, with street battles, and sporadic sniping and shelling from the Serb gunners from their 'strategic positions' on the mountains surrounding Sarajevo. According to the account of Kerim Lučarević, one of the key organisers of the defence of the city, 'Sarajevo had become a city in which everyone was shooting, but no one knew who was shooting. Shots would be heard, the Sarajevans would desert the streets and markets; disappear from the streets.'[4] For these defenders, the lack of arms (due in large part to the UN Security Council Resolution 713, which had, in September 1991, imposed a Yugoslavia-wide arms embargo) was their greatest challenge. Bombardments of Baščaršija were becoming a regular occurrence, with this part of Sarajevo taking the brunt of the shelling.[5] Fierce fighting also took place in Skenderija, around the airport at Butmir and in Ilidža. Heavier fighting broke out between the Bosnian Serbs and

[2] Author's interview with Holiday Inn (Sarajevo) employee, June 2015.
[3] *Dani*, Sarajevo, April 2008, p. 87.
[4] Kerim Lučarević, *The Battle for Sarajevo: Sentenced to Victory*, Sarajevo: TZU, 2000, p. 49.
[5] Final Report of the United Nations Commission of Experts, 'Study of the Battle and Siege of Sarajevo', p. 18.

the JNA and the armed groups defending Sarajevo raged in the early days of May 1992.[6] Sarajevo was bombarded by shells and mortars, while some fire also emanated from within the JNA barracks in the city in which there were still soldiers. On the first day of May, the nascent Army of Bosnia and Herzegovina (*Armija Republike Bosne i Herzegovine*—ARBiH) surrounded JNA barracks, a move which was, according to Donia was 'the first step in holding these troops hostage'.[7] The next day, the JNA responded and the de facto siege of Sarajevo began. On 2 May 1992, the remnants of the JNA, now an army in essentially a foreign country[8] and becoming transformed into the Army of Republika Srpska (*Vojska Republika Srpske*—VRS), intensified their onslaught upon the city.[9]

Battles raged in Sarajevo were raging, with the JNA pushing towards the centre of the city and meeting fierce resistance at the Skenderija and Vrbanje bridges. In addition, there were intense exchanges in areas such as Ilidža, Sokolović kolonija, Butmir, Dobrinja, and other areas surrounding the city's airport. Both sides blamed each other for the intensification. The whole spectacle was shown live on television, with the Sarajevo TV anchorman, Senad Hadžifejzović playing a mediatory role between those witnessing events from within Sarajevo and the JNA who were firing upon

---

[6] For a detailed account of the defence of Sarajevo, the myriad groups who were involved and the eventual creation of the Army of Bosnia and Herzegovina, see Marko Attila Hoare, *How Bosnia Armed*, London: Saqi Books, 2004.

[7] Robert Donia, *Sarajevo: A Biography*, p. 294.

[8] The republics of Serbia and Montenegro remained united in the 'Federal Republic of Yugoslavia', a successor state comprising of only these two republics. The creation of the state was not without controversy. A referendum was held in Montenegro (on 1 March 1992) but not in Serbia. Despite a boycott by Montenegrin opposition parties and their members, 95.7 % of Montenegrins who voted (the turnout was approximately 66 %) approved the creation of the new state. The new constitution of the FRY was scornfully referred to as 'The Žabljak Constitution' by Montenegrin opposition, after the town where the *nomenklatura* from Serbia and Montenegro wrote a new constitution with little or no public consultation. See Kenneth Morrison, 'Montenegro: A Polity in Flux, 1989-2000' in Charles Ingrao & Thomas Emmert, *Confronting the Yugoslav Controversies: A Scholars' Initiative*, West Lafayette, Indiana: Purdue University Press, 2013, pp. 437–438.

[9] The VRS incorporated forces from Knin, Bihać, Tuzla, Sarajevo, and Banja Luka was created on 22 May 1992 under the command of General Ratko Mladić. The commanders (of the Romanija-Sarajevo corps) who directed the siege of Sarajevo were Stanislav Galić (1992–94) and Dragomir Milošević (1994–95). Both were later convicted by the ICTY for responsibility for targeting civilians and civilian infrastructure in Sarajevo.

the city.[10] But this was about to be eclipsed by subsequent events later in the evening of 2 May during the 'Battle for Sarajevo'.[11] While the fighting raged, the Bosnian president, Alija Izetbegović, was returning from the latest round of peace talks in Lisbon, Portugal. Upon arrival he and his travelling companions (Zlatko Lagumdžija, Izetbegović's daughter, Sabina, and the president's bodyguard) were supposed to be given safe passage into Sarajevo by a UNPROFR guard, but was instead metby the airport's manger, Mile Jovičić, who escorted Izetbegović to his office.[12] They were subsequently joined by the JNA Colonel, Magazin, who instructed Izetbegović that he and his companions would be taken to the JNA barracks in Lukavica. After complex negotiations, in which Kukanjac and the JNA sought safe passage out of their barracks in the Bistrik area of Sarajevo (and to Lukavica) in exchange for Izetbegović and his party being transferred to the Presidency building. But things went awry from the outset. The JNA convoy was ambushed by elements of Sarajevo's armed defenders. The number of JNA soldiers killed remains hotly debated, with some figures suggesting the number was as high as forty-two. Ultimately, the exchange was executed, but it came at a high price—seven JNA soldiers were killed.

After the JNA advance of 2 May and the subsequent Dobrovoljačka incident, the JNA and Serb nationalist forces consolidated their control of Sarajevo's Western approaches; they now sought to cut off the city much closer to the centre, just west of the Holiday Inn and the Bosnian parliament.[13] At an SDS Assembly session on 12 May, Radovan Karadžić asserted that 'We hold all our areas, all the municipalities and the settlements around Sarajevo, and we hold our enemies—now I must and can say—we hold our enemies in complete encirclement, so that they cannot receive military assistance, either in manpower or in weapons.'[14]

---

[10] For a transcript of these exchanges, see Senad Hadžifejzović, *Rat užvo: ratni teevizijski dnevnik*, pp. 74–98.

[11] For a succinct overview of the battle, see Marko Attila Hoare, 'Civil-Military Relations in Bosnia-Herzegovina 1992–1995' in Branka Magaš & Ivo Žanić, *The War in Croatia and Bosnia-Herzegovina 1991–1995*, London: Frank Cass, 2001, pp. 186–188.

[12] Mile Jovičić, *Two Days Till Peace: A Sarajevo Airport Story*, p. 189.

[13] 'Background, Politics and Strategy of the Sarajevo Siege, 1991–1995', Statement of expert witness in the case IT-09-92, 'The Prosecutor V. Ratko Mladić', 18 February, 2013, p. 73.

[14] Robert Donia, *Iz Skupštine Republike Srpske 1991–1996*, Sarajevo: University Press, 2012, p. 171.

The Holiday Inn's exterior escaped the intense bombardments of early May, which saw some of Sarajevo's most notable buildings—the Vijećnica (which housed the National Library), the Oriental Institute, the Hotel Europa, the Olympic Museum, and the Zetra Sports Hall—destroyed by artillery fire.[15] (Sarajevo had become, according to the Belgrade weekly *NIN*, a 'Yugo-Beirut'.)[16] But the events of those days would have significant implications for the hotel and all of those, staff and guests, who would subsequently work or stay there. Despite having temporarily crossed the Miljacka River at both the Skenderija and Vrbanja bridges, the attack had failed to divide Sarajevo at Skenderija (the stated objective of the SDS) but the area of Grbavica (directly facing the hotel across the Miljacka River and an area that had traditionally housed many JNA officers and their families) fell under Serb control.[17] And it was from Grbavica that much of the danger to the hotel and its guests would emanate during the siege. Subsequently, the hotel was shelled, quite heavily, on 23 May, rendering parts of the building, particularly the southern part (which directly faced Serb-held Grbavica), uninhabitable.[18]

The hotel was located in a key strategic area that was coveted by the Serbs, who made no secret of their wish to divide Sarajevo in two parts, severing the link between the Ottoman and Austro-Hungarian parts of the city and the western suburbs.[19] The (SDS) leadership of the RS exerted pressure on the Bosnian Government to accept the division of the city (during peace negotiations in Geneva in September 1992, Biljana Plavšić, vice president of the RS, stated that the Bosnian Serbs intended to take the entire city 'west of the Holiday Inn').[20] While there is little evidence that the Bosnian Serbs aimed to conquer Sarajevo in its entirety, Karadžić openly declared that one of the Bosnian Serb's six core war aims was to divide Sarajevo into Serb and Muslim parts which would become the parallel 'capitals' of two new ethnically pure states.[21] A dividing line, similar to the so-called Green Lines in Beirut (Lebanon) and Nicosia (Cyprus), was, seemingly, an acceptable solution for

---

[15] Robert Donia, *Sarajevo: A Biography*, p. 314.
[16] *NIN*, Belgrade, 27 November 1992, p. 23.
[17] Marko Attila Hoare, *How Bosnia Armed*, London: Saqi Books, 2004, p. 73.
[18] Miroslav Prstojević, *Sarajevo: ranjeni grad*, Sarajevo: Ideja, 1994, p. 55. See also Ivan Štraus, *Arhiteky i barbari*, p. 91.
[19] Robert Donia, *Sarajevo: A Biography*, p. 294. For a personal account of the fighting around Sarajevo airport and how it impacted on operational aspects, see Mile Jovičić, *Two Days Till Peace: A Sarajevo Airport Story*.
[20] *The New York Times*, New York, 27 September 1992, p. 3.
[21] Robert Donia, *Sarajevo: A Biography*, p. 290.

the Bosnian Serbs, as if Beirut and Nicosia were shining examples of how to settle such matters.[22] The RS leadership proposed that Muslims and Croats be given the *čaršija*, the surrounding *mahalas* and a part of the Austro-Hungarian town, meaning that the Muslim/Croat part of Sarajevo would include the Ottoman and Austro-Hungarian parts of the city that represented an 'ethnically impure' area (as it contained a mixture of different religious buildings—including the Serbian Orthodox Church). The Serb section of a divided Sarajevo would, it was proposed, include those western parts of the city built mainly in the 1960s and 1970s (extending from the Holiday Inn all the way to Ilidža) and would represent an ethnically pure (Serb) zone, absent of so-called ethnic markers of the eastern part of the city.

During late April and early May the hotel's staff stayed away, though in the early weeks of the siege many people, remarkably, continued with their routines as best they could, often risking their lives to attend their jobs (though the work had all but stopped) and clinging to the hope that the war would be short-lived.[23] Tentatively, the remaining staff of the Holiday Inn, too, began to return with a view to reopening, though their numbers were depleted. Some of the previous members of staff (particularly those deemed to have been close to the SDS), including the hotel's manager, Danilo Dursun, departed Sarajevo in the wake of the MUP storming of the hotel on 6 April; some to Serbia or Montenegro, others merely to Serb-held parts of Sarajevo.[24] When a small number of staff returned to clean and repair, they found the place pretty much as it was after the events of 6 April. According to one member of staff who was tasked with repairing the damage:

[22] *The Observer*, London, 27 December 1992, p. 27. For a detailed analysis of the 'Green Lines' and impact of division on both Beirut and Nicosia, see Jon Calame & Esther Charlesworth, *Divided Cities: Belfast, Beirut, Jerusalem, Mostar and Nicosia*, Pennsylvania: University of Pennsylvania Press, 2009.

[23] After a chance meeting with Jonathan Landay (UPI, later the *Christian Science Monitor*) and Blaine Harden (*The Washington Post*) Džemal Bećirević, who would be hired as a fixer and translator. He recalled that 'In the first weeks of the siege, people just carried on with their routines, going to work. There was nothing to do when they got there, but people held on to their normal routines nevertheless. I lived day by day, as much as normal, going to town to meet friends. I even went to the bank to pay off my overdraft! We thought it would all be over in days or weeks and that we would soon be down on the coast having our regular summer holiday—we never imagined then that it would last over three years.' Author's interview with Džemal Bećirević (UPI/Washington Post), April 2015.

[24] Towards the end of the Bosnian war, Danilo Dursun would become the 'acting director' of the Republika Srpska Bureau in Serbia, which was based in Moše Pijade Street in Belgrade. He would later (in 1997) be on the SDS's list of proposed ambassadors in the (post-Dayton) Bosnian state. See ONASA, Sarajevo, 3 August 1997.

When we returned to the hotel in May, myself and another colleague were repairing doors on some of the rooms and offices on the upper floors. We found some items from which we could conclude that these guests were not from Sarajevo, but had been in the company of members of the SDS. I remember being on the sixth floor and we found the clothes of one of these people. Everything was more or less intact, so it's clear they had left in a hurry.[25]

After the initial clean-up had been completed, the hotel could now be prepared for reopening. It was the hotel's former accounts manager, Željko Juričić, who persuaded those staff that remained in Sarajevo to return to the hotel to begin a clean-up operation with a view to opening its doors to the only prospective guests in the city—journalists. He appeared on Sarajevo TV in June to appeal to staff to return to work, and under his guidance the hotel was made 'habitable', though much of the building was out of use.[26]

The hotel's prospective clientele, with no city-centre hotel to stay in, were scattered throughout the city, and as the bombardment of Sarajevo intensified, the majority (though not all) of them had departed the centre of Sarajevo and retreated to the outskirts of the city. Very few foreign journalists stayed in the city centre, and the remaining, such as those working for Associated Press (AP) and the BBC (and a few that worked for newspapers), were based in the *Hotel Bosna* in Serb-held Ilidža, from where they would make daytime trips into Bosnian government-held (and, occasionally, Serb-held) parts of Sarajevo. The hotel was used by journalists, in the main, because it was a functioning hotel with food, electricity, and international dialling.[27] The BBC crew, for example, had stayed at the Holiday Inn when reporting from Bosnia before the events of 5 and 6 April, but when returning to Sarajevo from Belgrade (on 10 April) they set up in the Hotel Bosna in Ilidža, judging that being there was more desirable than being in the centre of the city. But the intensification of clashes around the hotel complex in Ilidža[28] rendered their residency there increasingly treacherous. The small BBC team, which included the veteran correspondent Martin Bell, operated from the Hotel Bosna, one

---

[25] Author's interview with Holiday Inn (Sarajevo) employee, June 2015.
[26] Author's interview with Holiday Inn (Sarajevo) employee, September 2013.
[27] Author's interview with Joel Brand (*The Times/Newsweek*), April 2014.
[28] Final Report of the United Nations Commission of Experts, 'Study of the Battle and Siege of Sarajevo', p. 29.

of numerous hotels set in the picturesque parkland around *Vrelo Bosne* (Spring of Bosnia), a popular destination for tourists (and where Radovan Karadžić had fled to after the Holiday Inn shootings on 6 April). Bosnian fighters were attempting to break the siege and reach Sarajevo airport and thus fighting around the hotel complex would begin on 22 April and continue throughout the next two weeks, so the BBC (and other journalists in the hotel) would eventually be forced to evacuate their seemingly pleasant semi-rural lodgings. Bosnian government forces had launched a fierce attack on Ilidža from nearby Sokolivić kolonija, and had surrounded the hotel, pinning down the retreating Serb soldiers.

As the battle raged around the hotel, the journalists were unable to leave. The BBC Radio journalist, Misha Glenny, described the atmosphere among the journalists in the hotel as one of 'controlled chaos'. A mortar then landed in the BBC TV's editing suite, and although there was damage, no one was injured. The journalists in the hotel were pinned down while the fighting raged around them.[29] The following morning, the BBC crew (and the British ITV crew) were ordered by their superiors in London to leave their Ilidža base, leaving behind their editing equipment (which was subsequently taken by the Bosnian Serbs). It was, said Martin Bell, 'The BBC's Dunkirk'.[30] Thereafter, the crew headed south via (Croat-held) Kiseljak through the harsh, arid, and mountainous landscape of Herzegovina towards the Croatian border and, eventually, to the port city of Split on the Dalmatian coast. A few journalists stayed on—such as the young Catalan journalist, Jordi Puyol, who was killed by a mortar in Ilidža a few days after the BBC and ITV crews left.

As the BBC crew were departing, the shelling in Sarajevo intensified. Some of the journalists who had returned to the centre of Sarajevo pitched up at the Hotel Belvedere, others at private apartments or at the 'Delegates Club' (a one-time meeting place for Bosnia's communist elite and later a UN base) in the Ciglane area.[31] The heavy shelling in the days after their return forced UNPROFOR to withdraw from Sarajevo. The 'Rainbow Hotel' (as it became known to UNPROFOR staff, though it was, in fact, a retirement home) was in many ways an even more conspicu-

---

[29] Misha Glenny, *The Fall of Yugoslavia*, Penguin Books, London, (3rd edition), 1996, p. 178.

[30] Martin Bell, *In Harm's Way*, p. 150. According to Bell, the BBC's editing equipment was '"liberated" by the grateful Serbs, together with a great quantity of videotape, and became the foundation of their TV service in Pale'. See *Ibid*, pp. 150–151.

[31] *The Guardian*, London, 21 May 1992, p. 17.

ous landmark than the Holiday Inn—its exterior was bright yellow, red, and green could be seen from miles around. Located to the *Oslobodjenje* building and home to a group of UNPROFOR soldiers, it was heavily bombarded on the 14 May. UNPROFOR withdrew their personnel from the city on the following day. Some of the journalists, who would later occupy the Holiday Inn, also withdrew—though some remained to cover the increasingly heavy bombardments throughout May and June 1992.

The Holiday Inn would eventually reopen in June 1992, albeit under new management, a significantly reduced staff and an extremely difficult operational environment. The hotel's management and staff faced significant challenges in their endeavours to run a viable hotel. There was a change of guard at the hotel, and it now had two directors: Dinko Ćorić (a Bosnian Croat and essentially a HDZ-BiH appointee) and Sabahudin Resić (a Bosnian Muslim and SDA appointee, who had been the hotel's chief of security before April 1992),[32] and two assistant managers: Milan Knežević (a Bosnian Serb) and Nermin Halepović (a Bosnian Muslim).[33] They led a staff, though greatly reduced in numbers, which was multi-ethnic, comprising of Serbs, Croats and Muslims (though many of the Serbs working in the hotel had left on 6 April and never returned), and committed to providing a normal service, despite the difficult circumstances. The staff had remained 'employees' while the hotel had been closed during April, May, and June, and many had returned to work rather than be isolated in their homes.[34] Their first job was to repair the damage, as best they could, that had been incurred during the 6 April and the subsequent shelling, before making the hotel habitable for the growing number of press agencies that had arrived in Sarajevo.

---

[32] Sabahudin Resić would later be appointed the director of 'FK Sarajevo' football club. He passed away in 2005 at the age of just 48.

[33] The changing management structure between 1992 and 1996 reflected the changing dynamics of the war. Before the war, the Holiday Inn had a Serb director (Danilo Dursun). Upon reopening, there were two directors (one Croat/one Muslim). With the outbreak of hostilities between the Muslims and Croats in late 1992, the hotel had (thereafter) Bosnian Muslim (SDA) directors.

[34] The premised of many of Sarajevo's largest firms were targeted throughout the siege, thereby destroying much of the commercial infrastructure of the city. For an overview of the impact of the siege on these businesses, see Kemal Grebo, *Privreda u opkoljenom Sarajevu*, Sarajevo: OKO, 1998. For an overview of how some of these firms endeavoured to function and provide basic services for citizens during the siege, see Muhamed Kreševljaković (ed.), *I oni brane Sarajevo*, Sarajevo: Zlatni ljiljani, 1998.

Dinko Ćorić, through his contacts in the Bosnian government, arranged for the journalists to be informed of the reopening of the Holiday Inn, which was now operating again.[35] Running a hotel under such circumstances, however, represented a considerable task. Milan Knežević, one of the deputy managers, said that the hotel had 'lost seventy five percent of its windows and only 100 of 330 rooms were now usable. Before the war started we had almost 500 staff. Now we make do with 70. The staff work in shifts of three days or more at a time, to reduce the number of people who have to run in and out of the building under sniper fire.'[36] Many of the staff lived on the western side of the city, meaning that they had to run the gauntlet towards the hotel along some of the most dangerous and exposed parts of the city, sometimes walking and sometimes (if lucky) finding someone to take them there.[37] As one of them recalled:

> Most of the time I walked, especially in the beginning; I simply refused to run. It was scary, and perhaps a bit stupid, but it's amazing how one adjusts to new reality of constant danger. There was a joke where people would say 'look your best and make sure you wear new underwear—if you get shot and end up in the hospital you wouldn't want to be wearing old underwear'. Anyway, if I was lucky I would get a ride from and to hotel. A lot of people knew me and if they had a car, they would take me. Some journalists and their drivers and translators (mostly local people) were generous in that department too. In that regard I was lucky.[38]

It was extremely dangerous for staff working in the hotel, and these dangers were apparent on a near daily basis. Three Holiday Inn staff (a gardener, a porter, and a chef) were seriously injured in the grounds of the hotel between May, when staff were preparing for reopening, and late June 1992.[39] Running such risks simply to attend their workplace, the staff became the foundation upon which everything else at the siege-era Holiday Inn was built, and most worked without pay, very little pay, or often simply cigarettes or small packets of food that they could bring home to their families.[40] Tips from the hotel's guests helped bolster what little pay they received, though these were entirely dependent on how full the hotel was and how generous the guests were.[41]

---

[35] Author's interview with Holiday Inn (Sarajevo) employee, June 2015.
[36] *The Independent*, London, 11 July 1992, p. 10.
[37] Author's interview with Holiday Inn (Sarajevo) employee, September 2013.
[38] Author's interview with Holiday Inn (Sarajevo) employee, September 2013.
[39] *The Daily Mail*, London, 10 July 1992, p. 10.
[40] Author's interviews with Holiday Inn (Sarajevo) employees, September 2013, April/May 2014 and April 2015.
[41] Author's interview with Holiday Inn (Sarajevo) employee, September 2013.

Under the new management (and extraordinary new circumstances), the Holiday Inn gradually filled with journalists, aid workers, and, less frequently, politicians or diplomats. (Indeed, according to the freelance journalist, Paul Harris, 'the hotel became something akin to an exclusive private club' for the new guests.)[42] Bosnia, unlike many war zones was relatively accessible to journalists, either by car or (depending upon whether the airport was open) by plane. Some of the more recent conflicts (the 1990 Gulf War being a case in point) had been characterised by 'hotel journalism', where correspondents were often far from the frontlines, and largely reporting on (or relaying) US Army press briefings held in the hotels where the media were concentrated. The war in Bosnia afforded journalists a degree of freedom that had been impossible during the Gulf War. Thus, in April 1992 the 'press pack' began to arrive, though the Holiday Inn was closed. Journalists began to return to the city in late May, though most had travelled from Belgrade by car. By late June, however, following the reopening of Sarajevo airport, which was now under the control of UNPROFOR. The first to fly in to Sarajevo's reopened airport was the French President François Mitterand (he did so on 28 June—*Vidovdan*), and the following day the first UN flights arrived. In the coming days, more journalists arrived on UN flights from Zagreb or Ancona (Italy), and those arriving then found that the Holiday Inn had reopened. Within weeks the hotel would become something of a 'home from home' for the many foreign correspondents covering events in Sarajevo, and while its charms were generally lost on all but those seeking a satellite phone or some other access to communications equipment, the Holiday Inn became a 'strangely comfortable, almost familial retreat' for the journalists that were compelled to live and work there.[43] According to Robert Donia, the continued functioning of the Holiday Inn throughout the subsequent three-and-a-half-year siege allowed for an 'army of privileged observers get in and out of the city, stay in relative comfort in the Holiday Inn (the sole hostelry that functioned throughout the war), ride in armoured vehicles along the city's most dangerous routes, and send dispatches to the outside world using the latest communications technology'.[44]

---

[42] Paul Harris, *More Thrills than Skills: Adventures in Journalism, War and Terrorism*, p. 182.
[43] *The Los Angeles Times*, Los Angeles, 22 March 1994, p. 21.
[44] Robert Donia, *Sarajevo: A Biography*, p. 287.

But the Holiday Inn, while providing for many of the journalists' needs, was by no means a safe haven. Many parts of the building were exposed to sniper fire, the lobby windows were no more than dangling shards of glass or open spaces covered with tarpaulin, and virtually every window on the building had been damaged by gunfire; dust and debris covered the discarded pieces of unusable furniture. Marcus Tanner, writing in *The Independent* noted that the newly opened Holiday Inn was 'pummelled and blasted with shells' but that it 'still retained a certain dignity'.[45] Similarly, Robin Lodge, one of the first foreign correspondents to stay at the hotel after it reopened, noted that 'Every room is bullet-scarred, no one is stupid enough to turn on the lights, but there is hot water and the sheets are clean.'[46]

Martin Bell, who would come to know the hotel well, returned to Sarajevo in early July, after the airport was reopened. He was joined by the BBC Radio correspondent Allan Little. Upon arrival, Bell and his crew arranged to stay in a private flat, while Little arranged to stay at the nearby Delegates Club. Rumours were abundant among the journalists already in the city that the Holiday Inn had reopened, but, according to Allan Little, this was viewed with some scepticism. 'Its location made it so exposed, so risky. I didn't like the idea of operating from the Holiday Inn for the simple reason that it seemed too exposed and that, therefore, you couldn't really walk out of the building—you had to drive in and out in (if you were lucky) your armoured car—although at the start of the siege none of us had those.'[47] However, Little's colleague, Malcolm Brabant, did not consider the Delegates Club to be sufficiently protected from incoming fire. 'I took a look out of the window', he said, 'and had a clear view of

---

[45] *The Independent,* London, 11 July 1992, p. 10.

[46] *The Spectator*, London, 17 July 1992, p. 10. The housekeeping staff found innovative ways of dealing with these problems. They would, if they had electricity, launder sheets before, on occasion, hanging them to dry in the hotel's empty pool. Author's interview with Holiday Inn (Sarajevo) employee, September 2013.

[47] Author's interview with Allan Little (BBC), March 2015. According to the photojournalist Paul Lowe, staying at the Holiday Inn had drawbacks (it was exposed), but 'on another level it became quite a convenient place to operate from. It was in the middle of the city, half way between the Old Town and the airport and reasonably close to the TV station and the PTT building. So although the southern side of the hotel was very exposed, it presented good opportunities—you could, from the Holiday Inn, sprint across the road to the museum and towards the front line at Grbavica, if you were feeling sufficiently brave and were trying to do a story about that small pocket there. So it had its positives.' Author's interview with Paul Lowe (The Daily Telegraph/The European), June 2015.

Trebević where the Serb guns were stationed. If I could see them, they could see me. I didn't like it…one mortar and the roof would have a skylight.' So the decision was taken to move to the Holiday Inn. 'It was little more than a hundred metres from the nearest Serb sniper on the opposite bank of the Mijacka River', said Brabant, 'but it was solidly built and there were familiar faces in the lobby'.[48]

The Holiday Inn would soon become the main centre for foreign correspondents, despite the rather unfavourable location. The hotel's reopening meant that the correspondents, who had been scattered across different parts of the city, were now located in the same building—they could cooperate, share intelligence, knowledge, and draw upon their collective experience of a city that many of them barely knew. In July 1992, Martin Bell (who prided himself on being 'something of a connoisseur of war hotels') left the BBC flat and took a room at the Holiday Inn. It was to be quite a new experience in hostelry for the veteran correspondent. 'War hotels', he said, tend to 'defy their surroundings and provide a measure of calm and luxury in a turbulent world. The Holiday Inn offered neither…It was, and remained, the ultimate war hotel, like living at ground zero. From there you didn't go out to the war, the war came into you'.[49] But it was the sole hostelry in Sarajevo with the capacity to cater for the burgeoning press corps, and while life there was not, strictly speaking, a comfortable one, it was the only viable option (the city's other major hotels—the Bristol, the Europa and the Central—had all been badly damaged in the early days of the siege).

Either by good luck or by good judgement, Bell came through the early months of the siege; he and his crew capturing some memorable images of the embattled defenders of Sarajevo repelling the onslaught from the JNA in April and May 1992. Having spent a further two weeks in Sarajevo and at the newly reopened Holiday Inn, Martin Bell handed the baton to his successor, Jeremy Bowen. The BBC continued to pay rent on the flat (though Bell had stayed there only intermittently) so Bowen was initially located there. He was enthusiastic about his posting to Sarajevo, but was less enthused by the flat, which he described as 'pretty grim, stuffy, uncomfortable and had a poor water supply'.[50] After a night tossing and turning on a dusty couch, Bowen decided that his 'huge respect for

---

[48] Author's interview with Malcolm Brabant (BBC), August 2015.
[49] Martin Bell, *In Harm's Way*, p. 63.
[50] Author's interview with Jeremy Bowen (BBC), March 2014.

Martin did not extend to sharing his sleeping arrangements'.[51] And while the accommodation was not to his liking, Bowen felt detached and isolated there. 'Every other press agency or organisation, with the exception of Associated Press (AP) who were based in the privately-owned Belvedere Hotel near the Koševo medical centre, was based in the Holiday Inn, so I checked in there, and the crew soon joined me.'[52] By the time had Bowen arrived at the Holiday Inn, a number of journalists had already established a semi-permanent base, despite the fact that only one hundred of its rooms were inhabitable and that it had lost around 75 % of its windows during the heavy shelling in early May.[53] The hotel, he said, was 'gloomy, often without electricity or water, it did not have a bar and there was also a constant soundtrack of gunfire and explosions to accompany the depressing atmosphere'.[54] Bowen had previously covered conflicts in El Salvador and Croatia (among others) but soon learned that Sarajevo (and residing in the Holiday Inn) was uniquely dangerous. That danger, he said, was not just present on the streets or in exposed areas but *inside* the hotel: 'Bullets fired into the front of the building [The Holiday Inn] occasionally penetrated through to the six-storey atrium in the middle of it, smashing the glass panels around it which showered down into the lobby—it was, to put it mildly, lively.'[55]

For many journalists, even the experienced among them, living on the frontline was different and challenging—quite unlike covering other war zones, where the hotels they resided and worked in were some distance

[51] Jeremy Bowen, *War Stories*, p. 130.

[52] Author's interview with Jeremy Bowen (BBC), March 2014. The Holiday Inn was, strictly speaking, not the only hotel that functioned during the siege. Both the Belvedere on Visnjik 2 and the nearby Hondo on Zaima Šarca (which opened in 1993) were among the very few functioning hotels in Sarajevo. They were, of course, smaller and cheaper, but could not provide the same facilities as the Holiday Inn. Nevertheless, both continued to function in difficult circumstances, though they were far less exposed to (particularly sniper fire) than the Holiday Inn.

[53] *The Independent*, London, 11 July 1992, p. 16.

[54] Jeremy Bowen, *War Stories*, p. 131.

[55] Author's interview with Jeremy Bowen (BBC), March 2014. Bowen also stated that he had made the mistake of using the lifts (which almost never functioned) on one of this first visits to the Holiday Inn. 'Before I knew better, I got into the lift, which was at the front of the hotel facing the Serb positions. The moment the doors opened at my floor and I stepped out…two shots came in and hit the doorframe where I was standing. They missed. A sniper on the Serb side of the front line must have been aiming at the light as the doors opened. After that, the lift stopped working most of the time, and I used the stairs at the back.' See *Ibid*, p. 131.

from the frontline. Anderson Cooper (who worked for the American agency *Channel One* at the time of his first visit to Sarajevo), noted that 'During the 1984 Winter Olympics the location of the hotel was ideal; it was in the heart of the city, near the river, with views of the mountains. During the war, however, the location couldn't be worse.'[56] Indeed, the location could not have been worse; being not only on the frontline but within what became known as 'Sniper's Corner', the most dangerous part of *Aleja snajpera* (Sniper's Alley) and surrounded by high ground controlled by the VRS and just across the Miljacka River from Grbavica. Indeed, from the Bosnia Serb-held *Metalka* building (located on the end of Franje Račkog street), the *Invest Bank* building and other high-rise structures in Grbavica (mainly those located on Lenjinova Street), snipers had a direct line of sight towards the Holiday Inn.[57] Sniper fire would also emanate from the Jewish cemetery in Vraca. According to Remy Ourdan of *RTL*: 'There was a vast difference between covering events in Sarajevo (and living in the Holiday Inn) and other war zones. We were stuck, just like everyone else, though life was, of course, slightly easier in the Holiday Inn. Nevertheless, you are living on the frontline, and constantly at risk of coming under sniper fire. In other war zones, you cover the stories but you move around—staying at the Holiday Inn, you were *within* siege lines, very close the frontline.'[58]

For locals who would work for the press corps their first experience of life in the siege-era Holiday Inn was also a disconcerting experience. Amra Abadžić (now Abadžić-Lowe) began working as a translator for Reuters in June 1992, and remembers vividly the atmosphere in the Holiday Inn:

> It was surreal. The hotel was absolutely full of journalists and photographers. They had plenty of war experience and were, it appeared to me, tough characters that had been to many wars. It was quite frightening to see them in Sarajevo, my home. I remember, too, that there was food in the hotel, and to me this was very strange because the rest of the time we didn't have electricity (and thus no refrigeration), so the food went bad quickly. Stranger still was that the waiters were serving drinks, dressed in jackets and bowties...as if nothing untoward was happening outside.[59]

---

[56] Anderson Cooper, *Dispatches From the Edge: A Memoir of War, Disasters and Survival*, New York: HarperCollins, 2006, p. 54.
[57] ICTY Case No. IT-98-29/1-T, The Prosecutor vs. Dragomir Milošević, Doc. No. 5765, 12 December 2007, p. 77.
[58] Author's interview with Remy Ourdan (Le Monde), 5 November 2013.
[59] Author's interview with Amra Abadžić-Lowe (Reuters), May 2014.

The Holiday Inn was functioning well below its pre-war capacity and could provide only the most basic of services, but, as Peter Andreas notes, it could provide these and 'a central location that could make the daily routine of a foreign journalist much more comfortable than one might imagine possible in the middle of a war zone'.[60] They were, of course, *on* the frontline, but, on the plus side, they had access to basic resources and the ability to send despatches globally using state-of-the-art communication technology (though most dictated their despatches orally over the phone) that could be powered by generators.[61] Additionally, according to Zoran Kusovac, then of Sky News, 'In the Holiday Inn you could find, if you needed one, a fixer, a translator, a driver; it worked both ways. Bosnians would come to the hotel to offer their services, and thus the foreign press had easy access to them.'[62] Likewise, Vaughan Smith of *Frontline News* would visit the Holiday Inn, even if not staying there, to make people aware that his crew was around. 'The big agencies had crews, but not every journalist did, so we would be hired to film for them. Most of this was done over the phone from our office in London, but it was important to be in the Holiday Inn to network and generate business.'[63] So the very fact that the hotel could provide even the most basic functions and additional services that they often needed made it an invaluable location for foreign journalists. The 'big hitters', such as Reuters (who were originally based on the west side of the hotel but later occupied the 'Olympic Suite' on the fifth floor, previously occupied by Juan Antonio Samaranch and Radovan Karadžić, among others), the Cable News Network (CNN), the British Broadcasting Corporation (BBC), the American Broadcasting Company (ABC), and numerous major newspapers, simply could not do their jobs as effectively anywhere else in Sarajevo.[64]

The Holiday Inn would thus soon host some of international journalism's biggest names, with TV networks, press agencies, and journalists from the USA and Europe staying in the hotel, often for long periods. Among them was John F. Burns of the *New York Times*, who was to become

---

[60] Peter Andreas, *Blue Helmets and Black Markets: The Business of Survival in the Siege of Sarajevo*, Ithaca and London: Cornell University Press, 2008, p. 75.
[61] Robert Donia, *Sarajevo: A Biography*, p. 287.
[62] Author's interview with Zoran Kusovac (Sky News), March 2015.
[63] Author's interview with Vaughan Smith (Frontline News), June 2015.
[64] There were other hotels (or motels) functioning in Sarajevo, such as the *Belvedere* (where Associated Press were based), the Hotel Hondo (where a number of journalists moved to in 1993) and the *Monik* (which was used by UPI until October 1992).

something of a fixture in the hotel in the subsequent years. Burns's personal journey to Sarajevo and the Holiday Inn had been wrought with difficulty and personal trauma. An experienced foreign correspondent, Burns was something of an anomaly in the USA, being one of few leading foreign correspondents not from the USA. He had worked at the Canadian *Globe and Mail* before moving on to the *New York Times* in 1975. In the 1980s, he was the paper's bureau chief in both Moscow and Beijing (he was, in the latter, arrested and accused of espionage, and although charges were dropped, he was subsequently expelled from China).

In the midst of a meteoric rise, however, he was, in 1990, diagnosed with cancer while in the UK. Having exhausted the available treatment in the UK, he was, he said, 'resigned to placing a deck chair in the garden and enjoying whatever time was left to me, with my children and reading a good book'.[65] He was, however, persuaded by friends to return to the USA to receive treatment, whereupon he underwent intensive chemotherapy at the Sloan-Kettering Memorial Hospital in New York. Following this treatment, he 'could barely walk from one side of the room to the other', sensed that the treatment had been unsuccessful, and held no expectation that he would be returning to work. However, his editor at the *New York Times* offered Burns a posting in the Balkans, one he felt he had to take (the paper had, he said 'looked after me and my family, so I felt an obligation').[66] He left New York to travel to London and upon arrival felt so unwell that he could go no further, though he pressed on to Belgrade. Two days later he went to Vukovar, where he witnessed the aftermath of the fall of the town—oddly, he started to feel rejuvenated. 'It may seem odd to say so', said Burns, 'but the former Yugoslavia, and particularly Sarajevo, was my recovery ward'.[67]

After covering the latter stages of the war in Croatia, Burns moved between Belgarde and Sarajevo, covering the early days of the siege. Like many of those who had covered events on the immediate period after 6 April, he, too, joined those who had relocated to Ilidža as the UN began their withdrawal from the city. He decided, however (against the wishes of his employers and after heated discussions with his fellow journalists), not to join the convoy out of Sarajevo but to remain in Ilidža with Andrew Reid, a photojournalist from New Zealand. Having several days there, the

---

[65] Author's interview with John F. Burns (New York Times), September 2013.
[66] Author's interview with John F. Burns (New York Times), September 2013.
[67] Author's interview with John F. Burns (New York Times), September 2013.

pair decided to attempt to re-enter the centre of Sarajevo for the weekend. Burns knew this was defying the request to leave the city from his editors in New York. But, he said, 'Most of my editors at the *New York Times* would have been away for the weekend, so if I could get in and out quick, they would not have known what was going on—and if I *could* get in, get the story and get it on the front page of the paper, there would be no arguing over whether I had done the right thing.'[68] But the journey back was fraught.

> We decided to fill our vehicle with as much food as we could muster before attempting to re-enter Sarajevo. We made a dash for the city centre and it was the most horrendous passage. On the first night my car was very badly damaged by mortar fire, so the 'return option' was well and truly gone. So I spent the next few weeks in the city, covering the story and attempting to get my stories out, often using the most rudimentary methods.[69]

Continuing to reject requests from his newspaper to leave Sarajevo, he found accommodation first with a family who lived in the Old Town and then in the Presidency building, where he slept in the office of Jovan Divjak (the then Deputy Commander of the Bosnian TO) before moving to the reopened Holiday Inn in July 1992. There, Burns quickly established himself as a key figure among the press corps in the hotel and he would go on to write some memorable dispatches from Sarajevo, for which he was (in 1993) awarded the Pulitzer Prize (he would subsequently win another Pulitzer for his coverage of the rise of the Taliban in Afghanistan in 1997) (Image 8.1).

While less experienced than Burns, the forty-five-year-old American journalist Kurt Schork would make his name in Sarajevo. Kurt Schork came late to journalism, and his trajectory towards a career as a war correspondent was quite unlike many of his contemporaries, but his commitment to the job and the quality of his reporting meant that he became highly regarded among his peers. Having been a Rhodes Scholar at Oxford University (where he had been a contemporary of Bill Clinton), he worked as an aide to the Democratic Governor Michael Dukakis, before carrying out similar roles with both the Democratic Representative Michael Harrington and the Democratic Senator Bill Bradley. Increasingly disillu-

---

[68] Author's interview with John F. Burns (New York Times), July 2015.
[69] Author's interview with John F. Burns (New York Times), July 2015.

Image 8.1 Satellite dishes on the fifth floor of the western side of the hotel, circa July 1992. (Photo: The Holiday Inn, Sarajevo)

sioned with politics, he left to work instead for the 'New York Metropolitan Transit Authority', essentially running the city's subway. His relationship with Deborah Wong, herself a journalist who would later work for ABC, convinced Schork that a change of career was required.[70] He began as a freelancer in Asia, covering, for example, the war in Sri Lanka, before joining Reuters. But it was in Sarajevo that he made his name as serious journalist. Schork not only worked hard, he was willing to take significant risks and had a clear sense of moral purpose, helping civilians when he could.

Sarajevo (and thus the Holiday Inn) also became a magnet for younger journalists eager to make a name for themselves, some as stringers (who were paid only for whatever stories they published), 'super-stringers' (who were paid an additional retainer) and freelancers who did not have a string, but were hoping to pick one up. According to Vaughan Smith, 'Journalism was becoming increasingly democratised and many young journalists could get to Bosnia by bus or by car. Moreover, technology made it possible to get travel independently with your gear...so it was accessible in a way that previous conflicts were not.'[71] This accessibility determined that many aspiring journalists made their way to Sarajevo in the hope of getting their break. When in Sarajevo, few freelancers could

---

[70] *The Scotsman*, Edinburgh, 29 May 2000, p. 16.
[71] Author's interview with Vaughan Smith (Frontline News), June 2015.

afford to stay in the hotel, though many hung around to network, make themselves available and (sometimes) 'camp-out' in the upper floors of the hotel in some of the damaged rooms, hoping not to be noticed by staff. Some paid, but without the clout of a large agency behind them, were given unfavourable rooms in the hotel. Paul Harris, a freelancer who had various strings (mainly for *The Scotsman* and *Scotland on Sunday*), found himself 'staying in rooms that had been completely boarded-up'.[72]

Among the freelancers who may have appeared, at least at first glance, a young, inexperienced, and ill-equipped correspondent was Joel Brand, who would spend most of the next three years living in the Holiday Inn. He made an unlikely war correspondent. As a student attending the University of California Santa Barbara (UCSB), his main interest was surfing, and prior to his arrival in Yugoslavia in 1991 he had no previous experience as a journalist (notwithstanding his work for the UCSB student newspaper—the *Daily Nexus*). In 1991, having failed to secure an internship at a US newspaper, he had taken some time off from his university studies and was travelling around Europe, writing short dispatches as he went. Enthused by his trip, he decided to take a further break from his studies and join some former UCSB students who had started an English-language newspaper in Prague. Before reaching the Czechoslovak capital, however, he called upon the offices of some of the leading US news organisations. He briefly met the Paris bureau chief of the *Los Angeles Times*, who told him he should go to Yugoslavia as a freelancer and write for anyone and that would publish his work. It sounded, said Brand, 'quite romantic and heroic; I pictured myself sitting, leaning against a battle-scarred concrete wall, a hail of bullets sailing inches over my head, and scribbling in my notebook—on the edge of death, and writing about it… but that was, in hindsight, rather naïve'.[73]

By November 1991, Brand's Eurorail pass had taken him, by bus, as far as Budapest, from where he bought a ticket for a, largely empty, train to Zagreb. The war there was at an end, at least for the time being, but rumours were abundant within the press corps that war in neighbouring Bosnia and Herzegovina was becoming increasingly inevitable; many were heading for Sarajevo. Brand did likewise, arriving in the city in late January 1992 to cover the immediate period preceding the independence

---

[72] Author's interview with Paul Harris (The Scotsman/Scotland on Sunday), August 2015.

[73] Author's interview with Joel Brand (The Times/Newsweek), November 2013.

referendum weekend of 29 February and 1 March. He would subsequently become *The Times* of London's resident correspondent in Sarajevo, while simultaneously stringing for *Newsweek*.[74] He was one of very few foreign correspondents based in the city throughout the siege and he became, alongside John F. Burns and Kurt Schork of Reuters, a near permanent fixture in the Holiday Inn throughout those years.

Many young photojournalists, too, made their way to Sarajevo; most were freelancers looking for their big break, others had established themselves covering the fall of the Berlin War and the Romanian Revolution before moving on to cover the disintegration of Yugoslavia. Paul Lowe, working for either *The Daily Telegraph* or *The European*, had followed this trajectory, and he went to Sarajevo already well established. Upon arrival in Sarajevo in July 1992, he checked into the Holiday Inn. While Lowe did cover his fair share of frontline combat, his photography evolved to focus on the experience of Sarajevans during the siege, capturing 'another facet of life under siege, the texture and fabric of the city itself'.[75] Thus his images captured more than simply the military and security aspects of the siege, but the soul of a city and its people experiencing the worst of times.[76]

Other, less experienced, young photojournalists eager to forge their careers also gravitated towards Sarajevo. The American photojournalist Robert King was among them. King, having just graduated from the Pratt Institute in Brooklyn, New York, and in recent receipt of a graduate grant, had headed for the Zagros Mountains in northern Iraq to do a story on Kurds. There he met two photojournalists who recommended he try his luck in Sarajevo. 'I didn't have an agent or even a press card', said King, 'but they called in a favour and got me a small job with an agency called JB Pictures and they provided my first accreditation that allowed me to get on a UN flight to Sarajevo'.[77] He was, by his own admission, 'pretty green' when he first arrived in Sarajevo (and the Holiday Inn) and had little idea of the dynamics of the war or how to operate in a war zone. 'I had absolutely no clue about the disintegration of Yugoslavia or war in Bosnia, so I had no idea who the political players were or who was shooting—when I got there

---

[74] Author's interview with Joel Brand (The Times/Newsweek), November 2013.
[75] Paul Lowe, 'Portfolio: The Siege of Sarajevo', *Photography and Culture*, Volume 8, Issue 1, March 2015, p. 135.
[76] See Paul Lowe, *The Siege of Sarajevo*, Sarajevo: Galerija 11/07/95, 2014.
[77] Author's interview with Robert King (Freelance photographer, JB Pictures), June 2015.

I just explored the Holiday Inn and the micro-world that existed there.'[78] A 2008 documentary film about King called *Killer Image: Shooting Robert King* shows him turning up at the hotel, which he could not afford to stay in, attempting to network with the journalists and photographers in the hotel and cheat the waiters when possible.[79] King soon left the 'Hollywood of the Holiday Inn, Sarajevo' to find cheaper accommodation, sometimes renting small rooms, staying with friends, or squatting, though he would return to the hotel on occasion to work with other journalists. Other freelancers or stringers who could not afford the room rates that could be paid by the larger agencies still hung around the lobby of the Holiday Inn—often to utilise, when possible, the satellite phone connections in the hotel or simply to network, to garner information, or to get work.[80] Some of the younger photojournalists who could not afford the room rates at the Holiday Inn would sneak into the upper floors, essentially camping out in otherwise uninhabitable rooms and hoping not to be discovered by staff.[81]

The hotel also became a home from home for many of locals who were employed as translators and stringers, many of whom worked in the offices of news agencies for much of the siege.[82] The vast majority of these were Sarajevans who 'simply fell into the job', after chance meetings with individual journalists or TV crews. Amra Abadžić and Sabina Ćosić both started working for Reuters in the summer of 1992. Originally employed as translators, they gradually became a crucial part of the Reuters bureau, which was based, until 1994, in the Holiday Inn. Džemal Bećirević's own trajectory to working for United Press International (UPI) and, later, *The Washington Post*, first came into contact with foreign journalists in May 1992, when he ran into the BBC's Martin Bell during the intense fighting. In June, he met Blaine Harden from *The Washington Post* and Jonathan Landay from UPI in the centre of Sarajevo and subsequently worked as a stringer and translator for them.[83]

---

[78] Author's interview with Robert King (Freelance photographer, JB Pictures), June 2015.
[79] See *Killer Image: Shooting Robert King*, Director: Richard Parry, Trinity Films, London, 2008.
[80] Lisa Smirl. 'Not Welcome at the Holiday Inn', Spaces of Aid, 2 February 2014, p. 4.
[81] Author's interview with Paul Lowe (The Daily Telegraph/The European), June 2015.
[82] Author's interviews with Amra Abadžić-Lowe (Reuters), May 2014, Sabina Ćosić (Reuters), June 2014, Džemal Bećirević (UPI/Washington Post), April 2015 and Samir Korić (Reuters), April 2015.
[83] Author's interview with Džemal Bećirević (UPI/Washington Post), April 2015.

Among the established and the young, aspiring journalists, photographers (and local translators and stringers), there were those who were curious about the war, had found their way to the Holiday Inn. They had no formal press accreditation and many of the more established journalists viewed them simply as 'war tourists'. According to the BBC's Jeremey Bowen, 'Some strange people washed up at the Holiday Inn...fantasists and desperadoes, soldiers and reporters, often lubricated by the leveller of drink.'[84] Similarly, Paul Harris (himself something of an oddity among correspondents based in the Holiday Inn), writing in *The Scotsman*, noted that the 'war tourists' were a mix of 'do-gooders' and 'thrill-seekers with battered copies of the warmonger's handbook *Soldier of Fortune*[85] stuffed into their flak-jacket pockets'.[86] Though they lacked the credibility that a press card would bestow, they added, if nothing else, an even more bizarre flavour to the strange atmosphere in the hotel, which had become, according to the writer and critic, Christopher Hitchens, 'the clearing-house for very kind of defector, rumour-monger, movie director and gun-runner'.[87] At any rate, the Holiday Inn became the operational base for many of the journalists (particularly those working for the press bureaus located there), though many would use Sarajevo's TV station while using the Holiday Inn as an 'accommodation and social base'.[88]

---

[84] Jeremy Bowen, *War Stories*, London: Simon & Schuster, p. 133. According to Paul Harris, there were indeed some unusual characters in the Holiday Inn. 'There was a young guy from Finland who was always hanging around the Holiday Inn hotel in Sarajevo. We called him Finnbar. We knew he represented some unpronounceable organ of the Finnish press. He was clearly on a tight budget because he slept in the laundry cupboard. It ultimately turned out, to everyone's embarrassment, not least to the UN's, that he was an enterprising 16 year-old schoolboy who had submitted a letter from UN press accreditation on the notepaper of the school magazine.' See Paul Harris, *More Thrills than Skills: Adventures in Journalism, War and Terrorism*, p. 145.

[85] 'Soldier of Fortune' (SOF), known also as 'The Journal of Professional Adventurers' was a monthly magazine published in the USA, which was widely read by soldiers, both by professionals and by mercenaries. The magazine became notorious in the 1970s when it launched a recruitment drive for mercenaries to fight for the Rhodesian Security Forces during the Rhodesian War of 1964–79. The magazine was known to be popular among 'war tourists' and other amateurs with an interest in warfare.

[86] *The Scotsman*, Edinburgh, 15 June 1998, p. 9.

[87] *The American Spectator*, Summer Reading Issue, June 2000, p. 115.

[88] Author's interview with Vaughan Smith (Frontline News), June 2015.

References

Calame, J., & Charlesworth, E. (2009). *Divided Cities: Belfast, Beirut, Jerusalem, Mostar and Nicosia*. Pennsylvania: University of Pennsylvania Press.

Donia, R. (2012). *Iz Skupštine Republike Srpske 1991–1996: Izvodi iz izlaganja poslanika skupštine Republike Srpske kao dokazni material ns medjunarodnom krivičnom tribunal u Hagu*. Sarajevo: University Press.

Glenny, M. (1996). *The Fall of Yugoslavia* (3rd ed.). London: Penguin.

Grebo, K. (1998). *Privreda u opkoljenom Sarajevu*. Sarajevo: OKO.

Hoare, M. A. (2004). *How Bosnia Armed*. London: Saqi Books.

Ingrao, C., & Emmert, T. (Eds.) (2013). *Confronting the Yugoslav Controversies: A Scholars' Initiative* (2nd ed.). West Lafayette, Indiana: Purdue University Press.

Lowe, P. (2014). *The Siege of Sarajevo*. Sarajevo: Galerija 11/07/95.

Lowe, Paul, 'Portfolio: The Siege of Sarajevo', *Photography and Culture*, Volume 8, Issue 1, 2015, pp. 135-142.

Lučarević, K. (2000). *The Battle for Sarajevo: Sentenced to Victory*. Sarajevo: TZU.

Maass, P. (1996). *Love Thy Neighbour: A Story of War*. London: Papermac.

Magaš, B., & Žanić, I. (Eds.) (2001). *The War in Croatia and Bosnia-Herzegovina 1991–1995*. London: Frank Cass.

CHAPTER 9

The Hazards of Living on the Frontline

It was immediately evident to correspondents reporting the siege of Sarajevo that the city was a very dangerous place to work, and this extended to the immediate vicinity of, and even *within* the hotel. The entire area around the Holiday Inn was exposed, subject to regular sniper fire and, albeit less frequently, fire from heavy weapons. Nearby buildings were testament to the dangers; the Bosnian parliament building and the UNIS towers had been badly damaged throughout May and June 1992.[1] The southern side of the Holiday Inn was hit numerous times in late June and the hotel was shelled again, shortly after reopening, on 28 July, adding to the existing damage on the southern side of the building.[2] Nowhere in Sarajevo was safe, however. After UNPROFOR had taken control of Sarajevo Airport on 29 June (one day after the French President Francois Mitterrand unexpectedly visited Sarajevo), most journalists flew into the city and then drove from there to the TV Station or the Holiday Inn. On this dangerous route, numerous journalists were either killed,[3] such

---

[1] UN-ICTY, Case No. IT-98-29/-T, 'The Prosecutor v. Dragomir Milošević': (D70033-D69927), 12 December 2007, p. 53.

[2] Miroslav Prstojević, *Sarajevo: ranjeni grad*, Sarajevo: Ideja, 1994, p. 110.

[3] A total of ten journalists were killed in Sarajevo during the siege (including two Serbian journalists—Miloš Vulević and Živko Filipović—in Ilidža). Among them were three *Oslobodjenje* journalists (Salko Hondo, Kasif Smajlović and Karmela Sojanović) and the Sarajevo correspondent for the Slovenian magazine *Mladina* (Ivo Standeker). One high-profile case (outside Sarajevo) involved the hardline editor-in-chief of Pale-based Bosnian Serb Televison, Risto

as the American Broadcasting Company's (ABC) news producer David Kaplan (who was accompanying the Yugoslav President, Milan Panić) was killed by a sniper's bullet on 13 August 1992, minutes after arriving in Sarajevo (he had opted not to wear a flak jacket for the journey from the airport to the city centre), or seriously injured, such as the CNN camerawoman Margaret Moth, who was shot through the jaw near the *Oslobodjenje* building in 'Sniper's Alley' on 23 July 1992.[4]

Reaching the relative safety of the Holiday Inn, described by the BBC's Malcolm Brabant, as a 'concrete cocoon', was not without significant danger.[5] Indeed, the journey from the airport to the hotel was known to journalists as 'one of the best laxatives known to mankind'.[6] The approach to the hotel required a hair-raising dash down *Vojvode Putnika* (now *Zmaja od Bosne*—Dragon of Bosnia) street (Sniper's Alley), which separated Serb forces in the Grbavica area from Bosnian government soldiers located in the Marindvor area.[7] John Sweeney, then working for *The Observer*, described the dangers of driving along 'Sniper's Alley' and what could potentially go awry:

> Askold Krushelnycky (from *The European* newspaper) and I were driving towards Holiday Inn in a very old BMW—a 'soft skin' of course. On the way there I realised he didn't know the way. We had missed the turn off and

Djogo, who was, allegedly, murdered at the Hotel Vidikovac (later the Hotel Sveti Stefan) in Zvornik. See Vreme News Digest Agency, No.156, 19 September 1994.p. 2.

[4] Margaret Moth worked as a photojournalist/camerawoman for CNN when she was injured in Sarajevo. She was a remarkable woman, who continued to cover conflicts around the world (including returning to Sarajevo in 1994) despite the horrific injuries she sustained in Sarajevo (for which she required extensive facial reconstruction surgery). She died of cancer in March 2010 at the age of 59. For an overview of her work and life see 'Margaret Moth: Fearless', CNN Documentary, broadcast on CNN, 22 September 2009.

[5] Author's interview with Malcolm Brabant (BBC), August 2015.

[6] *The Independent*, London, 2 April 2010, p. 29.

[7] The street has had a number of names throughout the twentieth century. During the period of the KSHS it was known as *Vojvode Putnika* (after the Serbian military leader, Radomir Putnik). During the occupation by the Ustaše (1941–45) it was known as *Ante Strarčević* street (after the Croatian nationalist philosopher, writer and politician) before being changed to the *Bulevar Crvene armije* (Soviet Red Army) in 1946. In 1952 its former name of *Vojvoda Putnik* was reinstated and remained in place until 1994, when it was renamed *Zmaja od Bosne*, after Husein-kapetan Gradaščević (the leader of the uprising against the Ottoman Empire in the 1830s). See Behija Zlatar et al., *Sarajevo: Ulice, trgovi, mostovi, parkovi i spomenici*, Sarajevo: Mediapress, 2007, p. 121.

we were driving straight along Sniper's Alley. I told him to turn as soon as he could, and he moved to take next left, lest we be exposed for too long. But in full view of the Serb snipers the car stalled. As he tried desperately to start the engine, I sat there for what seemed like a long time waiting for the bullets to hit the car. Needless to say, we felt very, very relieved to reach the Holiday Inn.[8]

Thus safe arrival at the Holiday Inn (based on the principle of 'the faster you drive, the lon ger you live') was best ensured by driving extremely rapidly towards it and then entering the basement car park of the hotel at breakneck speed (or, if on foot, at the rear of the hotel—its northern side).[9] Writing for the *New York Times*, John F. Burns noted that 'drivers must gun their vehicles, tires squealing to get down the ramp into the garage before the snipers can fire'. If returning to the hotel car park after nightfall, drivers must ensure that they turn their headlights off, lest they shine directly into Grbavica giving snipers a clear indication of one's location.[10] Accidents were, according to Joel Brand, 'the norm in such circumstances, particularly as the winter set in and the driver had to deal with the snow and ice'.[11] This was, of course, evidenced by the condition of the cars in the basement garage. There, according to John F. Burns, 'cars that have endured a few weeks of the siege look like wrecks from a stock-car race, riddled with bullet holes, their windshields and side windows shattered'.[12] Nevertheless, this route of entry became the favoured one (significantly preferable to entering the hotel on foot) as the dangers of the alternatives became increasingly evident.

Before the siege exiting through the front doors of the hotel would bring you to the pleasant fountain area and left onto the main thoroughfare

---

[8] Author's interview with John Sweeney (The Observer), July 2014.
[9] Giving evidence in the trial of Ratko Mladić in September 2013, the BBC journalist, Jeremy Bowen, described the approach to the hotel along 'Sniper Alley'. It was, he said 'Very dangerous because you could be shot by at by snipers from the Serb side. I would drive down it from the TV station to the [Holiday Inn] hotel and into the town in an armoured land rover. Before we had an armoured land rover, we had to take the roundabout route that avoided Sniper Alley. Even with the armour, I would drive fast because it is much harder to hit a moving target. During the siege many civilians were killed on the road by snipers. One sniper position overlooked the Holiday Inn.' UN-ICTY, Case No. IT-09-92-T, 'The Prosecutor v. Ratko Mladić'(Witness Statement: D70033-D69927), 13 September 2013, p. 5.
[10] Author's interview with Zoran Stevanović (Reuters TV), August 2015.
[11] Author's interview with Joel Brand (The Times/Newsweek), April 2014.
[12] *New York Times*, New York, 26 September 1992, p. 7.

towards the centre of the city. During the siege, however, leaving the hotel by this route was, bluntly, inviting death. Journalists generally left the building (as they had entered it) by car from the underground car park, at as much speed as their vehicles could muster. 'The screech of tyres', wrote Myers 'is the unfailing sign that a journalist is leaving the hotel'.[13] If on foot (or even on bicycle—this was the favoured mode of transport for the French photographer, Luc Delaheye), the main entrance of the hotel was exposed to sniper fire, and all guests were advised to avoid using this route—they tended to exit by the rear door and take the route behind the UNIS towers.

Guests were generally advised not to dally in the exposed areas around the hotel, dubbed by both locals and foreign correspondents as an *opasna zona* (danger zone), within which one was in sight of snipers and thus at serious risk of being targeted. 'You never, but never, left by the front door', said the Scottish freelancer Paul Harris, though without cars or armoured vehicles freelancers had to make a 'heart-stopping dash across a 100-yard space' from the back door towards cover (the first shelter being in the shadow of the UNIS towers).[14] Kevin Sullivan, then working for United Press International (UPI) had decided to move to the Holiday Inn in October 1992, when he arrived in Sarajevo. The UPI team had previously stayed at a small motel called *Monik* (near the Hotel Bristol—which was badly damaged in the early months of the siege), which belonged to the one-time Bosnian Minister of Interior Alija Delimustafić, and used the CENEX offices in Čengić vila to send their despatches. However, the CENEX offices were destroyed in early October, forcing the UPI team to find an alternative.[15] 'We had to move to the Holiday Inn' said Sullivan, 'because it had become impossible to use the satellite phone without our own generator; we had to warm up the car battery and use it to power the phone'.[16] Upon entering the Holiday Inn he made the potentially fatal mistake of attempting to enter the hotel through the front doors, possibly

---

[13] *The Guardian*, London, 14 July 1992, p. 21.
[14] Paul Harris, *More Thrills than Skills: Adventures in Journalism, War and Terrorism*, p. 183.
[15] Author's interview with Džemal Bečirević (UPI/Washington Post), April 2015.
[16] When Sullivan arrived in Sarajevo in October 1992, the UPI's equipment consisted only of 'a Volkswagen Golf with no windows and a satellite phone with no consistent access to electricity', so he opted to move to the Holiday Inn where there were distinct advantages. 'Being in the loop' he said, 'was the primary benefit. Information circulated, and people were generally collaborative'. Author's interview with Kevin Sullivan (UPI), April 2015.

in full view of snipers, and was met by a disgruntled member of staff who, recalled Sullivan, 'gallantly moved to a more exposed position, unlocked the door and ushered me in with the characteristically baroque formula of muttered oaths and indignation over the ineptness of strangers'.[17] On another day, an attempt to enter the hotel through the front door could have proved costly.

Inside the hotel, the reception area, with the reception desk on the right hand side, awaited. There the guests could arrange rooms and make payment. Christopher Hitchens noted 'the un-hypocritical way in which the management would demands payment in cash and in advance payment in cash, on the grounds that one never knew who would be the next to drive over a mine or be hit by a sniper'.[18] Kevin Myers, upon his arrival, writing for *The Guardian* (in a piece entitled 'Horror at the Holiday Inn'), stated that 'Large parts of the hotel are in ruins, and heaps of broken glass lie on corridor floors where blast damage or gunfire has scattered them. The lobby consists of dangling shards of sheet glass in front of a rest area. Everybody expects a shell to send the plate glass shredding through the lobby at any time.'[19] Joel Brand, upon his return to the hotel (he had previously stayed there during the referendum weekend of 29 February–1 March 1992), immediately noticed the abundance of glass and what it meant in a war context. An entire wall of the lobby, he noted, 'was sheet glass, which was not only a hazard in itself, but offered absolutely no protection from shrapnel or sniper fire'.[20] Maggie O'Kane of *The Guardian*, acutely aware of the danger noted that the Holiday Inn was the 'only war hotel where journalists keep their flak jackets on indoors'.[21]

Dangers aside, the new guests formed strong opinions about the Holiday Inn's aesthetic qualities upon their arrival.[22] The *New York Times*

---

[17] Author's interview with Kevin Sullivan (UPI), April 2015. On Kevin Sullivan's first evening at the Holiday Inn, he was introduced to an *Oslobodjenje* journalist, Marije Fekete, whom he later married. And despite being a distinctly unromantic place to meet a prospective partner, Sullivan was not alone. The CNN correspondent, Christian Amanpour, met her husband, James Rubin, then the US State Department spokesman, in the Holiday Inn. See *The Times*, London, 13 June 1998, p. 16.

[18] *The American Spectator*, Summer Reading Issue, June 2000, p. 115.

[19] *The Guardian*, London, 14 July 1992, p. 21.

[20] Author's interview with Joel Brand (The Times/Newsweek), April 2014.

[21] Peter Maass, *Love Thy Neighbour: A Story of War*, p. 122.

[22] The aesthetic qualities of the Holiday Inn were the subject of some debate between the wartime guests. Most thought the building to be rather ugly, and many of its more recent guests are of the same opinion. Indeed, the Holiday Inn was judged to be '10th ugliest hotel

journalist Roger Cohen, who resided in the hotel for several periods throughout the siege described the hotel as a 'hideous mustard coloured block'. 'During the war', he continued, the hotel:

> Acquired the distinction of the only Holiday Inn in the world where you could step outside and stand a fair chance of being shot. Beirut's Commodore Hotel was once aptly described as a functioning telex machine surrounded by four hundred broken toilets. The Sarajevo Holiday Inn [was] four hundred broken windows appended to a vast crepuscular atrium designed, it seemed, with the over-riding aim of chilling the soul.[23]

Peter Maass, upon his arrival, stated that, 'It would be hard to imagine an uglier building.' It was a pity, he lamented, that 'so many ancient monuments were shelled to their foundations in Sarajevo while the Holiday Inn survived'.[24] More charitable, perhaps, was the celebrated Spanish novelist and poet Juan Goytisolo, who wrote for the Spanish newspaper *El Pais*, noted that 'The battered, livid Holiday Inn, its floors looking over the entrance hall like galleries and cells in a large prison, is like a metaphor for the city, a luxury prison implanted in the midst of a vast concentration camp of open-category prisoners, the citizens of Sarajevo.'[25] The interior aesthetics were also the subject of derision. The BBC's Malcolm Brabant, for example, described the café section of the atrium as 'cavernous, kitsch....and purple'.[26]

Those journalists and agencies that had arrived early in the siege staked a claim to the best (safest) rooms on the northern side of the building, with those arriving later forced to take their chances in the more exposed parts of the building, at least until preferable alternatives materialised. After all, noted Miroslav Prstojević in the *Sarajevo Survival Guide*, 'The Holiday Inn...was one of the few hotels in which the most prized rooms were those without a view. A view of the mountains meant a view of the snipers' nests'. During the siege the rule was: if you see him, he sees you.'[27] Location of choice was a room (or if one worked for one of

in the world' (though judging by those hotels placed below, this may be a little harsh). See *Daily Telegraph* (Travel Section), 18 April, 2015, www.telegraph.co.uk/travel/picturegalleries/9672211/The-worlds-ugliest-hotels.html?frame=2395834 [last accessed 12 June 2015].

[23] Roger Cohen, *Hearts Grown Brutal: Sagas of Sarajevo*, New York: Random House, 1998, p. 120.

[24] Peter Maass, *Love Thy Neighbour*, p. 122.

[25] Juan Goytisolo, *Landscapes of War: From Sarajevo to Chechnya*, Oregon: City Lights Books p. 29.

[26] Author's interview with Malcolm Brabant (BBC), August 2015.

[27] Miroslav Prstojević, *Sarajevo Survival Guide*, Sarajevo: FAMA, p. 84.

the larger agencies, a suite) on the northern side of the hotel, facing the so-called *Karingtonka* (Carrington) apartment block, which was not exposed to sniper fire emanating from Grbavica and was by far the safest side of the building. The western side (facing the Maršal Tito barracks) was relatively safe, although snipers could still angle their shots into those rooms. Guests in these rooms could often hear bullets whizzing past their windows. There were, according to Remy Ourdan (then of *Radio Télévision Luxembourg*—RTL), who had moved into the Holiday Inn in August 1992, 'small parts of one's room which were exposed and were thus to be avoided' and it was necessary to 'manoeuvre around the room to avoid the dangers'.[28] When Anderson Cooper arrived in the hotel in early 1993 he observed that in his west-facing room 'tracer fire whipped past the windows' and as a result, 'I was afraid to sleep in my bed at the Holiday Inn. I kept thinking that some shrapnel would kill me during the night. So I'd lay on the floor, trying to sleep, listening to the dull thud of mortars landing on nearby buildings.'[29] But while less desirable than the north-facing rooms the west-facing rooms had benefits; those who used satellite dishes required that equipment be facing the west, where the best signal could be received.[30]

Other rooms in the hotel were available, but were less desirable. The eastern side was only used when the hotel was particularly busy.[31] Only the first five floors tended to be inhabited by the press, though rooms above the fifth floor were used during busy periods. Rooms on the upper floors facing the northern side were rented out, and they were cheaper (these were often taken by freelancers who could not afford the more desirable rooms).[32] The sixth floor was used by staff, many of whom (particularly those without familial obligations) would sleep in the hotel rather than run the risk of making the journey home between shifts.[33] Nobody was permitted to use the rooms on the southern (front) side of the building, which was exposed to sniper fire and occasional shelling, though these rooms, being empty and well ventilated, were occasionally used to store electricity generators (journalists were occasionally required to tread carefully into these exposed rooms to check

---

[28] Author's interview with Remy Ourdan (Le Monde), London, 5 November 2013.
[29] Anderson Cooper, *Dispatches From the Edge: A Memoir of War, Disasters and Survival*, p. 54.
[30] Author's interview with Joel Brand (The Times/Newsweek), May 2015.
[31] Author's interview with Joel Brand (The Times/Newsweek), May 2015.
[32] Author's interview with Vaughan Smith (Frontline News), June 2015.
[33] Author's interview with Holiday Inn (Sarajevo) employee, April 2015.

on them, particularly if they were not functioning properly—but had to be careful not to illuminate themselves with torchlight if doing so in the darkness, lest they become a target for snipers).[34] South-facing rooms were also, albeit infrequently, used by cameramen to capture images of night-time tracer fire, with the cameraman slipping in and out only to change tapes.

To see the 'action' venturing beyond the Holiday Inn was, on occasion, not necessary. From the relative safety of their rooms, journalists could observe at close proximity the horrors of the siege. As Jeremy Bowen noted, there was frequently sniper fire all around the building, with the exposed area around the car park being particularly dangerous. On one occasion, he witnessed someone being shot just outside the hotel.[35] He was, said Bowen, 'hit on the thigh and collapsed to the ground. I couldn't just leave him there, so I went downstairs to the cark park, got in the car and drove out there to help him. But when I got there he had gone, and I have no idea how he managed to extricate himself.'[36] Likewise, Vaughan Smith vividly recalled witnessing the work of the snipers within minutes of arriving in the hotel:

> I got to the Holiday Inn, very tired after a long journey. I went straight to my room, on the fourth floor on the safest [northern] side of the building, and threw my bags on the bed. It was summer and the room was stuffy, so I went to open the window and saw a woman with a child in hand scurrying across exposed ground. As I opened the window I heard the crack of a sniper's bullet and saw the woman fall to the ground. Very quickly, people came to her aid and I believe she survived. That was my introduction to the Holiday Inn.[37]

Such incidents were not uncommon. According to Peter Maass from *The Washington Post*, 'Even when you were in the hotel, there was a chance that you could see incidents from your room, if you had one of those facing the more exposed areas around the hotel.'[38] The Holiday Inn, said Maass, 'became a grandstand from which you could watch the snipers at work. A journalist could convince himself on a slow afternoon that he was

---

[34] Author's interview with Sean Maguire (Reuters), September 2013.
[35] UN-ICTY, Case No. IT-09-92-T, 'The Prosecutor v. Ratko Mladić'(Witness Statement: D70033-D69927), 13 September 2013, p. 9.
[36] Author's interview with Jeremy Bowen (BBC), March 2014.
[37] Author's interview with Vaughan Smith (Frontline News), June 2015.
[38] Author's interview with Peter Maass (The Washington Post), April 2015.

doing his job by peering through a window at people running for their lives....I could stand at my own window, out of the line of fire, and watch more drama unfold in five minutes than some might see in a lifetime. It was all there, within a 200-yard radius of my room at the Holiday Inn.'[39] On rare occasions, sniper fire would penetrate the windows of the building while journalists were at work. In August 1992, Malcolm Brabant, the BBC Radio correspondent, was in the Reuters office on the fifth floor (west side) of the building when 'a bullet came through the window and whizzed past me (about an inch above my head), virtually parting my hair'.[40]

Once settled in the Holiday Inn, the new clientele had to identify potential hazards and develop strategies for mitigating risk. There existed a general consensus that life in and around the hotel *was* dangerous. 'Sarajevo' said Kevin Myers was 'The worst posting any journalist here has experienced', and that despite the fact many had covered Beirut or even the wars in Vietnam or Sri Lanka, they all agreed that 'Sarajevo and the Holiday Inn is in a class of peril all of its own'.[41] Some journalists developed distinctive survival mechanisms, with the more superstitious among them developed and maintained a number of relatively complex rituals. For the BBC's Martin Bell (always adorned in his trademark white suit and green socks), this involved walking in and out of the hotel through the same (broken) window, walking to his room in a clockwise (never anti-clockwise) direction; carrying on his person a number of good luck charms, including a bullet, extracted from the wall of the Hotel Bosna, that had narrowly missed him while he was doing a live broadcast

---

[39] Peter Maass, *Love Thy Neighbour*, p. 148. Maass is not suggesting here that cameramen simply set up their equipment and waited for something to happen, but images could be captured from the confines of the Holiday Inn. This is not entirely novel—some of the most striking images of war or conflict have been captured from hotel balconies. Perhaps the most famous image of 'Tank Man' during the events was captured by the American photographer Jeff Widener (and published in a number of European newspapers) who worked for Associated Press (AP). Images were also captured by Charlie Cole of *Newsweek*, Stuart Franklin of Magnum Photos, and Arthur Tsang Hin Wah of Reuters. All the images were captured from balconies at the Hotel Beijing.

[40] Author's interview with Malcolm Brabant (BBC), August 2015.

[41] Myers also noted that 'To leave the hotel by the front door is to invite death—after all, the gardener was shot there. One leaves from the underground car park, bursting out of its entrance like a Grand Prix racing driver leaving pole position. One expects sniper fire immediately. If one is quick the sniper will be too rushed to be accurate. But if his main purpose is to scare, then he does his job well.' Ibid, p. 21.

for BBC Breakfast News during the battles in Ilidža, and listening every day to both sides of a cassette of 'The Love Songs of Willy Nelson on a daily basis'.[42] (The American singer–songwriter is, according to Bell, the 'troubadour of war correspondents'.)[43]

The dangers were such that many of the journalists were relatively limited in their ability to travel within the city. Martin Bell, for example, acknowledged that 'for weeks at a time, during the years of working from Sarajevo, we would venture no further than the airport in one direction and the Presidency in the other' and that 'our measure of Bosnia was approximately the length of a single street in its capital'.[44] Few dared to tread much beyond this well-beaten path—the airport, the TV building, the Holiday Inn, and the Presidency. Sarajevo, in the early months of the siege, was difficult to cover and journalists were limited in what they could report; many opted, according to Kevin Myers, for 'just a few darts here and there, no more than a mile or so from the [Holiday Inn] hotel, always at top speed, horn sounding, and always without exception attracting sniper or even machine gun fire'.[45] Jeremy Bowen also acknowledged the problems with leaving the Holiday Inn, particularly after dark when most journalists would bed down in the hotel. 'The city outside the hotel', he said, 'was always dangerous…at the beginning of the war, no journalist left the hotel at night unless they had a very good reason'.[46]

Even during daylight hours, operating in the exposed area around the Holiday Inn was perilous. Indeed, in early July 1992, an ITN crew that included the cameraman Sebastian Rich and the veteran reporter Michael Nicholson were returning from the Sarajevo TV building to the hotel after completing a live satellite feed for 'News at Ten'. But their efforts came to the attention of a sniper who, said Nicholson, 'obviously enjoyed this deadly sport'.[47] The crew attempted to sprint across the car park towards the hotel but were fired upon at every attempt. 'We waited there for an hour', said Nicholson, 'becoming ever anxious at the prospect of being left out on our own unprotected and at the mercy of all sides'.[48] A passing

---

[42] Martin Bell, *In Harm's Way*, pp. 85–86. See also Jeremy Bowen, *War Stories*, p. 130.
[43] Authors interview with Martin Bell (BBC), December 2013.
[44] Martin Bell, *In Harm's Way: Bosnia: A War Reporter's Story*, London: Penguin, 1996, p. 114.
[45] *The Guardian*, London, 14 July 1992, p. 21.
[46] Jeremy Bowen, *War Stories*, p. 136.
[47] Michael Nicholson, *Natasha's Story*, London: Macmillan, 1993, p. 12.
[48] *Ibid*, p. 12.

UNPROFOR armoured vehicle stopped, however, pointed its heavy machine gun towards the snipers nest allowing cover for the ITN crew to make the dash across the open space to the entrance to the Holiday Inn. Not content with the footage he had managed to cobble together under the sniper fire, Rich continued to attempt to garner footage of the snipers at work in Grbavica, but did so *within* the building. He bedded down in one of the south-facing first-floor rooms (room 106), which had been rendered uninhabitable by shell fire in the first months of the siege, and was filming when his camera was suddenly blown off his shoulder in a shower of plastic and metal. Rich then stumbled down to the lobby of the hotel where three colleagues dowsed his injuries with vodka, which was, said Nicholson, 'the only disinfectant we had with us'.[49] After a rather uncomfortable night, Rich was evacuated on a UN flight out of Sarajevo to Germany, and to hospital in Berlin the following day. Still reeling from his injuries he assessed his condition. The ITN crew were temporarily pulled out, and while Rich received medical treatment Nicholson was ordered by his superiors in London to return to Belgrade.

Incidents such as the one involving Sebastian Rich illustrated the evident dangers, and some sought to mitigate these when possible. Though he can hardly be regarded as risk averse, the BBC's Martin Bell nevertheless became acutely aware of the risks he and his fellow journalists were exposed to and sought to limit risk, where possible. He disliked what he referred to as 'hotel roof dish monkeys' (journalists who would rarely leave the hotels in which they were staying), but he recognised that the journalists, more precisely, the news agencies they worked for, were increasing their risk by competing with each other to garner the most sensational stories and the most powerful images (Image 9.1).[50] In order to circumvent this, he led the establishment of the Sarajevo Agency Pool (SAP), a collective which sought to minimise the risk to journalists and cameramen. The idea was simple: 'declare a voluntary pool of our coverage. It made arithmetical sense.' But, he said, 'it wasn't popular. It penalized the brave. It rewarded the indolent who did not leave the hotel or their bunkers at the TV station.'[51] Though Bell acknowledged that 'journalists are not by their nature team players', the SAP not only functioned well but undoubtedly saved lives.[52]

---

[49] Michael Nicholson, *Natasha's Story*, p. 13.
[50] Authors interview with Martin Bell (BBC), December 2013.
[51] Martin Bell, *In Harm's Way*, pp. 77.
[52] Authors interview with Martin Bell (BBC), December 2013.

Image 9.1 The view from the (uninhabitable) southern side of the Holiday Inn, circa 1993. Snipers located in the apartment blocks in Grbavica had a clear line of fire into the hotel. (Photo: Joel Brand)

But his sensible and pragmatic approach did not stop him from being wounded by shrapnel from a mortar which landed near where he was preparing to give a piece to camera. Bell had narrowly escaped being hit while reporting (live) from a balcony in the Hotel Bosna in Ilidža in May, but in August 1992, despite being driven in the BBC armoured vehicle (known as 'Miss Piggy')[53] and wearing a flak jacket, he was shot and wounded near the Maršal Tito barracks (a few hundred yards west of the Holiday Inn).[54]

Gradually, as the risks of reporting from Sarajevo became evident, the bigger news agencies would purchase armoured cars for their employees (the BBC and CNN were the first, but other soon followed), rather than have them traverse the city in 'soft skins'. The dangers of driving down 'Sniper's Alley' in a soft skin were apparent to all who made the journey. 'We took real chances taking the route from the airport to the Holiday Inn

---

[53] The use of armoured vehicles was controversial among the journalists. Some saw them as necessary, other saw their use as grotesque. They were resistant to bullets, but not fully bulletproof. Top-heavy, however, the Land Rovers were a mixed blessing, forever falling off mountains or rolling into ditches. See *New York Times*, New York, 19 June 1994, p. 14.

[54] Bell, *In Harm's Way*, pp. 92–93. See also *The Times*, London, 26 August 1992, p. 8.

in a soft skin', said Zoran Kusovac of Sky News, 'my car was like a sieve, having been hit many times'.⁵⁵ The basement car park of the Holiday Inn was full of cars in various states of disrepair, many riddled with bullet holes and missing windows, almost all with 'Press' or 'TV' painted on the doors or bonnets. Armoured cars, though they offered no real protection from heavy weapons, would protect the driver and passengers from sniper fire or machine-gun fire (on the down side, they were 'top heavy' and could be difficult to control). For some, acquiring them was deemed a necessary evil, but it was, equally, a 'barrier' between them and the ordinary citizens, who were afforded no such protection.

Likewise, the wearing (or not) of flak jackets was an issue that divided the press corps. For most, it was regarded as necessary, regardless of the risk of creating a barrier between the journalist and the ordinary citizen. According to Joel Brand, there was no dilemma among the majority.

> Most of us had a strict rule about never leaving the hotel without a flak jacket and helmet. If you wore them, it wasn't something that you put on as you started your journey, the way one might casually buckle up a seatbelt after you had begun driving. Stepping outside the door without a flak jacket and helmet felt very risky. It was dangerous enough inside the building, let alone outside.⁵⁶

But some journalists were critical of the shift towards the use of armoured cars, flak jackets, and helmets, the foremost among them the French radio reporter Paul Marchand. He had reported from (and lived in) Beirut before coming to Sarajevo, and had a number of 'strings', working for Canadian, Swiss, and Belgian radio stations, and though he did not have the clout of a big media organisation behind him, he became one of the best-known figures among the journalists in the Holiday Inn—largely for his eccentricity.⁵⁷ Almost always immaculately dressed, often donning a straw hat and constantly puffing on large Cuban cigars, he could be brusque and uncompromising. A self-declared 'artisan', he refused to wear

---

⁵⁵ Author's interview with Zoran Kusovac (Sky News), March 2015.
⁵⁶ Author's interview with Joel Brand (The Times/Newsweek), May 2015.
⁵⁷ For Paul Marchand's personal account of his journalistic endeavours in Beirut and Sarajevo see Paul Marchand, *Sympathie pour le diable*, Outremont: Lancot, 1997. A documentary film of with the same title was made in 2010 by the French film director Arthur Liminia.

a flak jacket because he could 'not find one that matched his clothes'.[58] Marchand not only drove a 'soft skin', but one with 'Don't shoot, you will waste your bullets, I'm immortal' written in large letters (in English) and 'For those about to die, we salute you!' emblazoned on the bonnet and rear end of his car. He would, according to John Burns, 'mock the flak jackets and helmets of his fellow reporters', while driving around Sarajevo in a battered car 'with doors that must be held shut and a broken exhaust system that advertises his arrival from a mile away'.[59] And this was merely one example of Marchand's idiosyncratic and eccentric behaviour—other antics included regular abseiling sessions from the highest points inside the atrium of the Holiday Inn and down the adjacent UNIS towers. On one occasion he even persuaded the conductor of the Sarajevo Philharmonic Orchestra (who played a concert in the hotel in 1993) to conduct while suspended from the roof.[60]

Marchand genuinely took risks, and was often scathing of what he regarded as journalists becoming detached from the reality of the conflict by traversing Sarajevo in armoured cars while wearing flak jackets and helmets. Interviewed by the filmmaker Marcel Ophuls in 1993, Marchand stated that armoured cars were merely 'status symbols' while railing against their use. 'I'll never get in an armored car' he said, 'I'm an artisan; I stay one. There are people who even wear a vest and flak protection [and drive] an armored car…it'll be a chain reaction—tomorrow a bodyguard, in a year, army protection. That's journalism?'[61] Marchand learned to adapt to the 'rules of the game' in and around the hotel and in Sarajevo. He took, no doubt, significant risks, but maintained that his approach was authentic and thus justified. But he, too, was badly injured in October 1993, after which he returned to France. He spent the subsequent years writing novels (he had to learn to write with his left hand after losing the ability to do so with his right), but struggled to cope with the reality of being unable to continue doing the work he loved. To some he was a bully and a show-off, to others he was highly regarded—a true maverick who took significant risks in the pursuit of his craft. In any event, the question of when, where,

---

[58] Paul Marchand, *Sympathie pour le diable*, p. 95.
[59] *New York Times*, New York, 26 September 1992, p. 7.
[60] *New York Times*, New York, 91 June 1994, p. 24.
[61] Interview with Paul Marchand in 'Veillées d'armes: Histoire du Journalisme en temps du guerre' ('The Troubles We have Seen: A History of Journalism in Wartime'), Second Journey, Director: Marcel Ophuls, Little Bear Productions, 1994.

and whether to wear flak jackets and armoured cars continued, but the risks associated with working in Sarajevo were clear.

Such debates aside, there developed a distinct comradery among the 'Holiday Inn crowd'. According to Emma Daly of *The Observer*, there existed 'a genuine sense of community within the press corps' based there. 'We became', she said, 'a dysfunctional family—it didn't mean that you had to like everyone else or want to hang out with them, but we were forced together; connected'.[62] But critics argued that this very connectedness had led to a form of 'journalism by consensus' that had led to biased reporting. Thus they were often accused by some of their peers of lacking objectivity, campaigning explicitly for armed intervention against the Bosnian Serbs, and conveying a one-dimensional caricature of the war, one which played into the hands of the Bosnian government. Among those critical of the journalists based for long periods in the Holiday Inn was the veteran BBC correspondent John Simpson, who covered the Bosnian War with far less regularity than some of his colleagues. He noted synergies between Western journalists and the Bosnian government, and argued that the Bosnian government 'regarded international opinion as their chief weapon' and 'the more the Western press based in the Holiday Inn reported on the savage horrors of the war, the more likely the Americans, British and French would intervene on their side'. 'Such reflections', he further noted, 'weren't welcome at the Holiday Inn'. The prevailing mood among the journalists based there was, he said, 'Profoundly partisan. If you share the sufferings of a city under siege, you instinctively side with the people in it; that's natural enough. But what many of the journalists based there did, and it has to be remembered that many of them were young and inexperienced, was to line up with the [Bosnian] government rather than with the people.'[63] Conversely, however, his BBC colleague Martin Bell (who saw the 'journalism of attachment' as unproblematic) defended the partisan reporting of some of his fellow journalists, stating that in the context of Sarajevo 'dispassionate and distant journalism...was simply not an option'.[64]

---

[62] Emma Daly, 'Dateline in the 1990s: In Sarajevo, Scant Rations but Abundant Black Humour', Overseas Press Club of America, 24 April 2014, https://www.opcofamerica.org/news/dateline-1990s-sarajevo-scant-rations-abundant-black-humor [last accessed 2 June 2015].

[63] John Simpson, *Strange Places, Questionable People*, London: MacMillan, 1999, p. 445.

[64] Martin Bell, 'Farewell to War', in Tony Grant (ed.), *From Our Own Correspondent: A Celebration of Fifty Years of the BBC Radio Programme*, London: Profile Books, 2005, p. 19.

Simpson was, however, by no means alone. Others questioned the objectivity and the motives of those journalists based at the Holiday Inn. Ljiljana Smajlović, once a journalist with *Oslobodjenje* but writing in the Serbian weekly *Vreme*, wrote a series of highly critical articles in which she bemoaned their lack of objectivity and the 'media consensus' that had emerged during the war in Bosnia and Herzegovina. While under the pretext that they wanted to help suffering citizens, she said, the foreign journalists had explicitly identified 'with one party to the conflict' and were manipulating stories 'for the purposes of the evening news'.[65] In subsequent articles she questioned the legitimacy of John Burns's and Roy Gutman's Pulitzer prizes, claiming that both had no dilemma about their sympathy for Bosnia's Muslims and their demonisation of the Serbs as those primarily responsible for the war.[66]

The most vitriolic assessment of the role of journalists staying in the Holiday Inn was, however, provided by Peter Brock, who argued that the hotel had 'a profoundly institutional effect on its guests/inmates, who daily churned out the victim idolatries of exploited tragedy obtained from government propagandists or overheard in its dining room and hallways. It was, in fact, the Bosnian government's de facto public relations annex that provided endless grist of misery and ready access to media-ready misery.'[67] 'The Sarajevo government' he added, 'plied their schemes and media mischief on the reporters billeted at the Holiday Inn who could be counted on to sensationalise'.[68] One of those singled out by Brock was John F. Burns, who defended his own reporting of the war, stating that there was a difference between 'impartiality and fairness':

> To have stuck then to the neutral view might have served the notional ends of impartiality, but not of fairness, or of truth. And much of the reporting of the time in English and American publications, it's safe to say, was not, in that narrow sense of the term, impartial....There are still those, particularly among Serb nationalists, but not alone among them, who condemn reporters of the time for having enlisted in the cause of the Bosnian Muslims, as

---

[65] Ljiljana Smajlović, 'Okrutno šminkanje krvavog rata', *Vrene*, Belgrade, 8 February 1993, in Helsinški odbor za ljudska prava u Srbiji, *Jezgro velikosrpskog projekta*, pp. 634–635.

[66] Ljiljana Smajlović, 'Dva "Pulicera" za jedan sat', *Vreme*, Belgrade, 5 April 1993 in *Ibid*, pp. 641–642.

[67] Peter Brock, *Media Cleansing, Dirty Reporting: Journalism and Tragedy in Yugoslavia*, Los Angeles: GM Books, 2006, p. 133.

[68] *Ibid*, p. 132.

though we had made a choice of our champions, and our villains, without troubling ourselves with the facts. But the overriding reality was that on any fair weighing of the facts as we knew them, there was a truth we owed to our readers, and most of us reported it that way.[69]

The geography of the Holiday Inn vis-à-vis the city of Sarajevo played a significant role in the nature of the reporting. It was a place where journalists, aid workers, and others could exchange information and assist one another. There was a natural tendency to converge there, if for no other reason than attempting to cover the story independently, particularly in the early days of the siege, was too dangerous. Located between the airport, the TV building, and the Presidency, journalists would often travel in convoys, in armoured cars, and visit only a few key city locations to be briefed by UNPROFOR or by Bosnian government officials. This generated a criticism of the so-called pack journalism of the Holiday Inn crowd who were all too easily manipulated by political elites that closely monitored their movements. As Lisa Smirl has argued, the Holiday Inn became 'constitutive of the conflict geography', shaping a dominant but flawed narrative of the war, a narrative manipulated by the Bosnian government. 'It seems almost certain' she said, 'that the hotel and its residents were considered, either implicitly or explicitly, officially or unofficially, to be an audience to be perform for, entertained, excited, horrified'.[70] In this respect, the hotel may indeed have created an institutionalising and homogenising effect on those that were based there.

Journalists, however, were not the only guests to visit the Holiday Inn during the siege. Two rooms in the hotel would, in 1993, be utilised as a temporary base for the US Embassy in Sarajevo (and thus the first port of call for a myriad of US diplomats), which was 'less than ideally suited' south-west corner of the building.[71] In addition to the US, the Turkish, and French governments maintained 'embassies' in the hotel.[72] Bill Clinton's special envoy, Richard Holbrooke, stayed when in Sarajevo,

---

[69] John F. Burns, 'Neutrality isn't the same as being fair', *The British Journalism Review*, London, Vol. 21, No. 3, 2010, p. 30.
[70] Lisa Smirl, 'Not Welcome at the Holiday Inn'.
[71] Robert Donia, *Sarajevo: A Biography*, p. 315.
[72] According to a Guardian article from April 1994, the British, too, were to set up an embassy (run by a chargé d'affaires rather than a full ambassador), initially from the Holiday Inn. But the chargé d'affaires, Robert Barnett, only spent one or two nights in the hotel before establishing his headquarters elsewhere. See *The Guardian*, London, 1 April 1994, p. 12.

though he found the Holiday Inn to be 'One of most peculiar hotels ever. Its cavernous lobby/atrium is freezing cold, dark and dismal. The upper stories are shot to hell, with gaping holes to the outside world. The upper stories are closed to guests.'[73] Nevertheless, it was the 'safest' accommodation to be found in the city, a factor that determined the US decision to establish their first embassy there in 1993, with Victor Jakovich (who had been appointed the USA's first ambassador to Bosnia and Herzegovina in May 1992) taking up residence in the hotel; staff came to know him as a polite and courteous guest with modest needs. Indeed, according to one member of staff:

> We prepared the biggest suite for him, which consisted of five rooms. He arrived with his staff and bodyguards, and after we had showed him the accommodation he decided that five rooms was excessive. He wanted only a simple room and an additional room for his office. He ended up staying in room 412 for a long time. He was a normal, down to earth gentleman who did not ask for anything special.[74]

But journalists, diplomats, and aid workers were not the only guests to grace the battered corridors and rooms of the hotel. Aspiring authors hung out with the journalists at the Holiday Inn, and the hotel attracted a number of Western artists and intellectuals.[75] As Peter Andreas noted, Sarajevo 'attracted not only a small army of journalists, but also a wide assortment of artists, intellectuals, and celebrities, such as Susan Sontag, Bianca Jagger, Bernard-Henri Levy (who was making a film entitled *Bosna!*), Vanessa Redgrave and Joan Baez', giving the city 'a hip, intellectually fashionable profile arguably unmatched in any war zone since the Spanish Civil War'.[76] They would pitch up at the Holiday Inn because they did not have an appropriate support network in Sarajevo—upon arrival, however, they could embed themselves in the hotel and utilise the knowledge and get logistical assistance from the journalists based there (such as gaining access to travel in an armoured car) who were well organised.[77]

---

[73] Richard Holbrooke, *To End a War*, New York: Random House, 1998, p. 48.
[74] Author's interview with Holiday Inn (Sarajevo) employee, April 2015.
[75] Phillip Hammond, *Media, War and Postmodernity*, New York: Routledge, 2007, p. 50.
[76] Peter Andreas, *Blue Helmets and Black Markets: The Business of Survival in the Siege of Sarajevo*, 2008, pp. 71–72.
[77] Author's interview with John F. Burns (New York Times), July 2015.

The American singer–songwriter Joan Baez visited Sarajevo in April 1993, making the Holiday Inn her base throughout her stay. She was in the city to attempt to bring attention to the US public the plight of the besieged city. While there she performed at the *Kino Imperijal* (Imperial Cinema) in a concert in which she sang, among other songs, Kemal Monteno's ode to Sarajevo and *Sarajevo ljubavi moja* (Sarajevo, my love). After the concert she returned to the Holiday Inn and socialised with the journalists. She was, recalled Džemal Bećirević, 'very relaxed and easy going'. 'After the concert', he said, 'we heard that John Burns received the Pulitzer Prize (and it was also his birthday). I asked her to come and she just put her dressing gown on and came long to Burns' room. She sang "Happy Birthday" to him, joined us for drinks—it was very pleasant and relaxed.'[78] (She later stood on a chair and sang a rendition of the Chilean songwriter Violeta Parra's *Gracias a la Vida*.)[79]

But perhaps the most famous 'celebrity' to reside at the hotel was the New York-based writer and theatre critic Susan Sontag, who had been persuaded to visit Sarajevo by her son, the American journalist David Rieff, who had been covering the Bosnian War and the siege of Sarajevo for, among others, *The Nation*. Convinced of the need to do something for the citizens of the besieged city, she subsequently arrived in Sarajevo in April 1993 (staying, of course, at the Holiday Inn) and worked on plans to direct her stage version of Samuel Beckett's *Waiting for Godot* (which was, she stated, 'the ultimate fringe production' which seemed 'written for, and about, Sarajevo').[80] The play took place in the *Pozorište mladih* (Youth Theatre) where there was no electricity, so it was staged by candlelight. In July, she returned accompanied by an entourage which included the photographer Annie Liebowitz, who was covering Sontag's stage production for *Vanity Fair* magazine.[81] Though staying in relative comfort (in comparison to her actors) in the Holiday Inn, she was known to conceal a few loaves of bread in her bag to give it to them.[82]

---

[78] Author's interview with Džemal Bećirević (UPI/Washington Post), April 2015.
[79] Author's interview with Allan Little (BBC), March 2015.
[80] See Susan Sontag, 'Waiting for Godot in Sarajevo' *Performing Arts Journal*, Vol. 6, No. 2, 1994, pp. 87–106.
[81] *The Guardian*, London, 25 July 1993, p. 13.
[82] Susan Sontag, 'Godot Comes to Sarajevo', *The New York Review of Books*, 21 October 1993. See also Janine di Giovanni, 'Siege Food: Bosnia', in Matthew McAllister, *Eating Mud Crabs in Kandahar: Stories of Food During Wartime by the World's Leading Correspondents*, California: University of California Press, 2011, p. 34.

Sontag and Baez were by no means the only high-profile figures to endorse Sarajevo's plight, but others were in Sarajevo to document, and offer a rather more serious critique of, the role of the media in covering the siege of Sarajevo and the journalists residing in the Holiday Inn.[83] The foremost of these was the renowned French filmmaker Marcel Ophuls, best known for *Le Chagrin et la pitié* (The Sorrow and the Pity)—the epic 1969 film documenting the Nazi invasion of France and the imposition of the Vichy regime, and *Hotel Terminus*—a documentary about the 'Butcher of Lyon', Klaus Barbie. He arrived in Sarajevo in January 1993 to film a documentary about the siege of Sarajevo and the life of the war correspondents documenting it. Parts of the documentary, released in 1994 and entitled *Veillées d'armes: Histoire du Journalisme en temps du guerre* (The Troubles We've Seen: A History of Journalism in Wartime), is filmed within the confines of the Holiday Inn and in its immediate environs. The film is characteristically eccentric though it is, equally, a very prescient analysis and evaluation of the role, motivation, and dilemmas faced by those attempting to document and convey the complexities of war in a way that is consumable to their (often fickle) domestic audiences.

Divided into two parts (or 'journeys'), based on two visits to Sarajevo, Ophuls's stated objective was to understand not just the motivations of the journalists covering the Bosnian War, but the contradictions of reporting war in the context of an increasingly fast-moving and whimsical media environment. The 'first journey', filmed in December 1992 and January 1993, focuses largely on Anglo-American journalists, with the BBC's John Simpson (and his crew which included the South African cameraman Nigel Bateson and the BBC's translator Vera Kordić) and the *New York Times*'s John Burns taking centre stage.[84] The latter part again focuses on the work of John Burns, but shifts towards focusing on the *France 2*

---

[83] With celebrity engagement risking trivialisation of the conflict, there existed a distinct unease at the celebrity endorsement of a 'Bosnian cause', of which many of the celebrity advocates knew very little, and they were derided as gimmicks by some. In an article in *The Guardian* in September 1993 entitled *Sarajevo? Been there. Done it*, Peter Beaumont caustically commented that 'Whatever the good intentions of all these stunts or exercises in consciousness-raising—call them what you will—a fundamental sense of uneasiness remains about the motivation.' See *The Guardian*, London, 20 September 1993 (Supplement), p. 4.

[84] See 'Veillées d'armes: Histoire du Journalisme en temps du guerre' ('The Troubles We've Seen: A History of Journalism in Wartime'), First Journey, Director: Marcel Ophuls, Little Bear Productions, 1993. See also John Simpson, *Strange Places, Questionable People*, London: MacMillan, 1999, pp. 451–457.

crew, led by Stephane Maniér and the cameraman Jean-Jacques Le Garrec, and their endeavours to capture the experience of Sarajevans (of all ethnic backgrounds) living through the daily depravations of the siege, though, as Stephane Maniér notes, 'when Marcel was there it was reasonably quiet, so it was a snapshot, and not really a representative one in the wider context of the siege'.[85] Many of the interviews with the journalists took place in the Holiday Inn (where Ophuls and his own crew stayed during their visits to Sarajevo) and they provide a fascinating insight into life in the hotel—though, ultimately, only a snapshot of the days in which Ophuls stayed in Sarajevo.

The 'second journey' continues in a similar vein, though the tone is markedly darker and more cynical, critiquing the role of the media in war zones. The focus remains firmly on French journalists, with a few exceptions. The film includes many interviews with French print and television journalists, including Remy Ourdan, Martine Laroche-Joubert, Stephane Maniér, Paul Marchand, and the French filmmaker Romain Goupil in either Sarajevo or Paris. Additional scenes were shot in Belgrade (where Ophuls conducts a slightly bizarre interview with Slobodan Milošević) and Pale, where Ophuls conducts an interview with both Radovan Karadžić and Nikola Koljević in which they berate the *New York Times* correspondent John Burns for 'writing against Serbs'. During the interview, Ophuls jokes with Karadžić and Koljević that their (Serb) snipers 'must know his room number' at the Holiday Inn, to which Koljević responds, 'I think you are not too well informed who is really counting on snipers—it's much more of a Muslim speciality', while Karadžić (in the background) mumbles that 'our snipers are too distant from Sarajevo'.[86]

The extensive interviews and scenes from Sarajevo are intercut with short images from, for example, the 1940 film *De Mayerling à Sarajevo* (From Mayerling to Sarajevo) directed by his father—the celebrated filmmaker Max Ophuls. *Veillées d'armes*, though perhaps one of Ophuls's lesser-known works, is an insightful analysis of the nature of war reporting, and the moral dilemmas faced by those journalists whose role it is to do so (though some critics claimed that the film was 'somewhat ragged' in

---

[85] Author's interview with Stephane Manier (France 2), April 2015.
[86] See 'Veillées d'armes: Histoire du Journalisme en temps du guerre' ('The Troubles We've Seen: A History of Journalism in Wartime'), Second Journey, Director: Marcel Ophuls, Little Bear Productions, 1994.

contrast to his previous work).⁸⁷ It provides a unique insight, or at least a snapshot, into the culture that had developed among journalists and other 'guests' within the Holiday Inn during the siege.

A more intimate (indeed, deeply personal) view into the lives of ordinary Sarajevans was provided by Bill Tribe, who arrived in Sarajevo, and the Holiday Inn, in late December 1992. But Tribe was, unlike Ophuls, no transient visitor. He knew Sarajevo well, having taught English at the University of Sarajevo for twenty-six years, and also knew a number of the SDS leadership (in particular Nikola Koljević) from his time there. He had been living in the city when the war broke out, but had returned to the UK in August 1992. The film, shown on the Channel Four in the UK (entitled originally *Urbicide: A Sarajevo Story*, though an updated version entitled *A Sarajevo Diary: From Bad to Worse* was released later), includes a section where Tribe surveys the square outside the parliament building from the eighth floor of the hotel. He recalls the events of 5 and 6 April, during which he was present, and the subsequent slide into the war, lamenting the suffering of the city he loved.⁸⁸

In addition to, hosting visiting filmmakers and celebrities, political activists, or human rights campaigners, the Holiday Inn would also host a number of important domestic events, though initially they were few and far between. The PEN Centre of Bosnia and Herzegovina was launched in the hotel on 31 October 1992, while, according to the academic and PEN Centre member Zdenko Lešić, 'while the hotel was shaking from the falling shells'. Dževad Karahasan, a resident of Marindvor, who in 1992 became the Dean of the Academy of Theatrical Arts at the University of Sarajevo, desperately tried to reach the Holiday Inn to attend the meeting. While living very close to the hotel, getting there safely involved a route that took much longer. 'There were no more than five hundred meters between my home and the hotel', he said, 'but that route could not be used because of the snipers. So I departed by way of the military hospital, which is a roundabout course, five times longer than the normal one, but somewhat safer—or at least providing an illusion of safety.'⁸⁹ Karahasan never reached the Holiday Inn. The sniping and shelling intensified and he was advised (or told in no uncertain terms) by a local solider not to proceed. Nevertheless, their founding assembly went

---

⁸⁷ See *Christian Science Monitor*, Massachusetts, 27 June 1994, p. 16.
⁸⁸ See 'A Sarajevo Diary: From Bad to Worse', Director: Dom Rotheroe, W.O.W Productions, 1993.
⁸⁹ Dzevad Karahasan, *Sarajevo: Exodus of a City*, p. 37.

on, accompanied by a recital from the Sarajevan pianist Liljana Pečanac. That the event went on gave Karahasan, 'a lesson in stubbornness as well as renewed confidence that goodness still prevails'.[90]

Other cultural events would take place throughout the coming year. In the summer of 1993, the Holiday Inn hosted the 'War Fashion Show', during which models strutted the catwalk to the sounds of Murray Head's 'One Night in Bangkok'. AP reported that the models wore designs often made using whatever meagre material was available but that the clothing 'would not look out of place in the most *avant garde* of European capitals'.[91] Guests at the event were, however, sharply reminded of the reality of living in a besieged city when they left the building; sniper fire rang out as people left the hotel, though no one (on that occasion) was injured. And, of course, political events also took place in the hotel. The *Drugi bošnjački sabor* (The Second Bosniak Congress) took place in the Holiday Inn in September 1993.[92] This meeting brought together representatives of Muslim organisations, who agreed after lengthy debates that the term *Bošnjaci* (Bosniak) was the most appropriate replacement for the designation *Muslimani* (Muslim).[93]

---

[90] *Ibid*, p. 40.

[91] Associated Press Archive, SD F05079304, Story No. w094045, 5 July 1993. Some write that in the winter of 1993 the 'Miss Besieged Sarajevo' contest took place in the Holiday Inn (an event that was to be made globally famous by the Irish rock band U2's song, *Miss Sarajevo*), where, according to Paul Harris, 'a couple of dozen girls, involuntarily slimmed down on EC rations, paraded in the Holiday Inn'. (The winner was Inela Nogić, a seventeen-year-old Sarajevan, though the result was less important than the image of the participants holding aloft a banner at the end of the event emblazoned with the words 'Don't Let Them Kill Us'.) The event did not, however, take place at the Holiday Inn but the Bosniak Cultural Centre.

[92] In one of the unresolved controversies of the Bosnian war, the one-time President of the SDP in Srebrenica (and then Police Chief in Srebrenica), Hakija Meholjić, claimed that he had met in the Holiday Inn with Alija Izetbegović during the 'Bosniak Congress' and that Izetbegović had informed him that the US President had offered him (NATO) military intervention, but that Srebrenica had to be sacrificed in order to provide a justification. According to Meholjić, the proposal was 'rejected without any discussion'. See *Dani*, Sarajevo, 22 June 1998, p. 5. Meholjić repeated these accusations in a controversial Norwegian documentary film *Srebrenica: izdani grad* (Srebrenica: A Town Betrayed). Interviewed drinking coffee in the lobby of the Holiday Inn he said, 'Whether Clinton offered it to him or not, I do not know.' The matter has never been resolved. Meholjić's interview can be seen in *Srebrenica: izdani grad* (Dir: David Hebditch), Fenris Fil, Oslo, Norway, 2012.

[93] The *Muslimansko nacionalno vijeće Sandžaka* (MNVS) similarly changed its name to the *Bošnjačko nacionalno vijeće Sandžaka* (BMVS) on 10 May 1998.

References

Andreas, P. (2008). *Blue Helmets and Black Markets: The Business of Survival in the Siege of Sarajevo.* Ithica and London: Cornell University Press.
Bell, M. (1996). *In Harm's Way: Bosnia: A War Reporter's Story.* London: Penguin.
Burns, J. F. (2010). Neutrality isn't the same as being fair. *The British Journalism Review, London, 21*(3), 27–31.
Cohen, R. (1998). *Hearts Grown Brutal: Sagas of Sarajevo.* New York: Random House.
Hammond, P. (2007). *Media, War and Postmodernity.* New York: Routledge.
Holbrooke, R. (1998). *To End a War.* New York: Random House.
Marchand, P. M. (1997). *Sympathie pour le diable.* Outremont: Lancot.
McAllister, M. (2011). *Eating Mud Crabs in Kandahar: Stories of Food During Wartime by the World's Leading Correspondents.* California: University of California Press.
Nicholson, M. (1993). *Natasha's Story.* London: Macmillan.
Simpson, J. (1999). *Strange Places, Questionable People.* London: MacMillan.
Sontag, S. (1993). Godot comes to Sarajevo. *The New York Review of Books.*
Sontag, S. (1994). Waiting for godot in Sarajevo. *Performing Arts Journal, 6*(2), 87–106.
UN-ICTY Case No. IT-09-92-T. (2013). The Prosecutor v. Ratko Mladić (Witness Statement: D70033-D69927).
Zlatar, B., et al. (2007). *Sarajevo: Ulice, trgovi, mostovi, parkovi i spomenici.* Sarajevo: Mediapress.

CHAPTER 10

Hostelry *in Extremis*

In an article entitled 'A Reporter's Handbook on How to Survive Wartime Hotel Siege', published in *Variety* magazine in 1974, Ernest Weatherall offered some sage advice to the correspondent locked down in a frontline hotel. 'Since whiskey doubles in price every hour during a siege until it disappears entirely', he said, 'bring along a good supply…then hide it in your hotel room and invited only the closest friends to drink'. And he also provided prudent advice regarding the maintenance of personal hygiene. 'Usually the pumping station in the city stops working', he added, 'and this means the water system is the first to go out. Be sure to fill up the bath tub—you'll need water from everything from mixing it with your whiskey to flushing the toilet.'[1] Such advice would have proved invaluable to the guests at the Holiday Inn during the siege of Sarajevo. For many staying in the hotel, at least that did not have the better rooms, staying at the hotel differed little from camping—plastic sheeting, provided by the United Nations High Commissioner for Refugees (UNHCR) replaced the glass in the atrium (and in most of the rooms), stopping shards of glass from injuring anyone but rendering them difficult to heat. The electricity supply was inconsistent, and there was rarely running water. The hotel management and their staff (those fortunate enough to work there) endeavoured to run the hotel as efficiently as possible under difficult circumstances—they also had to, at least attempt, to ensure that they themselves appeared clean and professional.

[1] *Variety* (New York), 31 July 1974, p. 1.

For staff, a job at the Holiday Inn was, despite the dangers, highly coveted; staff could largely avoid being drafted into the army and away from the frontlines (though some had already been 'drafted', and others forced to dig trenches, before the hotel reopened in July 1992).[2] Their professionalism was noted by the guests. Colin Smith, *The Observer* correspondent, for example, noted that, 'The Holiday Inn… functions amazingly well. They serve three meals a day, when there's water you can get your laundry done, the waiters—in evening dress with black ties—serve you lunch and dinner.'[3] The hotel staff serving the guests became highly respected by the guests for their endeavours. According to UPI's Kevin Sullivan, 'Staff friendly and helpful, there was a lot of camaraderie and most journalists were sensitive to the fact that the hotel staff *had* to be there, and didn't have the option of leaving.'[4]

SIEGE FOOD

While serving dinner, waiting staff always wore their green (and later brown) jackets, white shirts, and black bow ties.[5] They would, noted Allan Little, 'always endeavour to ensure the comfort of the guests while they were having dinner, even suggesting politely that at times when shelling was intense that the guest should sit nearer the centre of the room and away from the external wall, lest they be injured'.[6] Sabina Ćosić, who worked for Reuters, noted that 'the waiters were beautifully trained so they made a great show of serving everything properly, approaching you from the right side and so forth. They were absolutely professional, even though they were serving junk; the whole thing had a surreal aura to it.'[7] John Sweeney, meanwhile, noted that 'the juxtaposition between being served beautifully while the vibrations from the bombs outside made the

---

[2] Author's interview with Holiday Inn employee, April 2015.

[3] Interview with Colin Smith (The Observer) in BBC Television 'The Late Show Special: Tales from Sarajevo', First broadcast 21 January 1993.

[4] Author's interview with Kevin Sullivan (UPI), April 2015.

[5] The desire to appear 'normal' and to continue with daily life as much as possible was not only limited to the staff at the Holiday Inn but also common across Sarajevo. According to Ivana Maček, 'Making an effort to appear normal was important to Sarajevans, enabling them to feel less defeated by their circumstances than they may otherwise have done.' See Ivana Maček, *Sarajevo Under Siege: Anthropology in Wartime*, p. 63.

[6] Interview with Allan Little (BBC Radio) in BBC Television 'The Late Show Special: Tales from Sarajevo', First broadcast 21 January 1993.

[7] Author's interview with Sabina Ćosič (Reuters), June 2014.

cutlery and crockery rattle on the tables was striking—the waiters continued as if it was quite normal, demonstrating real grace under pressure'.[8] The waiting staff always endeavoured to keep the guests happy, despite the occasional setback. In the late summer of 1992, Kate Adie of BBC was having dinner in the restaurant when 'a thunderous explosion' that 'brought down the plaster and shook the foundations' hit the hotel; seconds later one of the hotel's chefs appeared to announce that dinner would be served as usual, albeit a bit late (as a consequence of the kitchen being damaged).[9]

Even within the hotel comfort was rather limited in the early months of the siege, but as the harsh winter of 1992–93 set in, conditions became more difficult. Regardless, the staff retained their professionalism and dignity. The veteran BBC correspondent John Simpson noted that 'in the dreadful winter of 1992 the waiters wore dinner jackets and white shirts with bow ties even though there was there was no water, no soap and no way of drying anything'.[10] He also noted, however, the charmed life for the guests in the Holiday Inn. 'It's very easy', he said, 'to start to live in the journalistic *milieu* and forget what the reality of life is—the reality of life [in Sarajevo] is not that there's light and a certain amount of limited, boring food. The reality of life is that people are chopping down trees to keep warm.'[11] And food, however limited or boring, was always available in the Holiday Inn, though the quality and quantity varied significantly. But it was available, and at a time when the vast majority of the residents of the city survived on meagre rations of humanitarian aid.[12] Since the beginning of the siege, a black market trade had emerged, one that crossed siege lines, and there was additional UN aid coming into the city.[13] The hotel's management were not immune to the economic dynamics of the siege and had to become highly proficient in dealing on the black market to make

---

[8] Author's interview with John Sweeney (The Observer), July 2014.
[9] Kate Adie, *The Kindness of Strangers*, p. 314.
[10] John Simpson, *A Mad World, My Masters*, London: MacMillan Press, 2000, p. 23.
[11] Interview with John Simpson (BBC) in 'Veillées d'armes: Histoire du Journalisme en temps du guerre' ('The Troubles We've Seen: A History of Journalism in Wartime'), First Journey, Director: Marcel Ophuls, Little Bear Productions, 1993.
[12] *The Spectator*, London, 23 January 1993, p. 12. Citing a 1992 article from *MacLeans*, Andreas notes that some of the best of the 'highest quality humanitarian aid items were showing up on the tables at the Holiday Inn'. See Peter Andreas, *Blue Helmets and Black Markets: The Business of Survival in the Siege of Sarajevo*, p. 183 fn. 178.
[13] Peter Andreas, 'The Clandestine Political Economy of War and Peace in Bosnia', *International Studies Quarterly*, 2000, No. 48, pp. 29–51.

the hotel function at even the most basic levels. A consistent supply of food was, after all, crucial to the hotel's ongoing viability (UN humanitarian aid in itself would not be sufficient), and to facilitate this the hotel's management developed their own 'micro-economic strategy', trading on the black market to ensure the supply of food, water, and fuel for the electrical generators.[14] They became rather effective in doing so, ensuring that the hotel could continue to be a viable operation. As Janine di Giovanni noted, the fact that the Holiday Inn managed to function at all under the circumstances was 'testament to the astonishing black-market contacts of the management'.[15]

Dinko Ćorić, one of the hotel's directors, became a pivotal link in ensuring the continuation of this symbiosis by forging a supply line through the neighbourhood of Stup (between Sarajevo and Ilidža) while nurturing trading contacts in both Croat-held Kiseljak and Serb-held Ilidža.[16] Ćorić had good relations with the Croatian Defence Council (*Hrvatsko vijeće obrane*—HVO) in Stup, who operated independently of the Bosnian government, and this supply line was vital to the hotel, at least until Bosnian government forces forced the HVO out of Stup in late 1992; in any event, food was somehow getting into the hotel.[17] According to one member of staff, Ćorić went to significant lengths to bring food to the hotel:

> Dinko bought from anyone and everyone who would sell—anyone from black-marketeers to farmers based on the outskirts of Sarajevo near the front lines. One of the truck drivers who used to bring supplies to the hotel told me an amusing story. They once went to pick up a live cow, and Dinko, always dressed in a suit and tie with dress shoes, was pulling this cow over the fields with a rope. He was very inventive in buying food and other supplies.[18]

Of course, food plays a significant role in all wars (and in a siege the difficulties in acquiring food are even more acute). Soldiers have to break from battle to replenish, a refugee mother still has to feed her children, often under impossible circumstances, and even correspondents have to

---

[14] Andreas, *Blue Helmets and Black Markets: The Business of Survival in the Siege of Sarajevo*, p. 73.

[15] Author's interview with Janine di Giovanni, 11 July 2013.

[16] Chuck Sudetić, 'Flow of Commercial Good into Sarajevo', quoted in Andreas, *Blue Helmets and Black Markets: The Business of Survival in the Siege of Sarajevo*, p. 74 and p. 183 fn. 176.

[17] *The Spectator*, London, 18 July 1992, p. 11. For an analysis of the struggle between the Bosnian government forces and the HVO and the role of the HVO in Sarajevo, see Mario Pejić, *HVO Sarajevo*, pp. 102–104.

[18] Author's interview with Holiday Inn (Sarajevo) employee, September 2013.

'fuel up'.¹⁹ The largely successful endeavours of the hotel's management, their access to hard cash, and good connections ensured that there was sufficient food to feed the guests at the Holiday Inn. It was a constant challenge, though, placed in the wider context, this was a challenge faced in a far more serious way by citizens of Sarajevo, who experienced significant difficulties in attaining the necessary nutrients to sustain physical existence.²⁰ Providing food, however, was more challenging—particularly when there was a lack of consistent electricity to power the refrigerators. Food had to be bought daily and this required significant endeavour and a sufficient amount of hard cash. The basics could be provided, with the hotel's basement bakery ensuring a daily (and vital) supply of bread for the guests.²¹ But basic provisions such as flour, eggs, and butter required to make the bread were highly prized and expensive, thus their cost was significantly (though artificially) inflated. The cost of even the most basic goods on the black market, which *within* siege lines (even UN aid) was controlled by Sarajevo's criminal gangs, increased dramatically as the siege tightened, subjecting citizens of Sarajevo to a 'siege within a siege'; one external (imposed by the VRS) and one internal (imposed by predatory criminals—often defenders of the city who were celebrated—and corrupt politicians).²²

NIN, the Belgrade weekly, noted that in the autumn of 1992, 'There are places in Sarajevo where it is possible to eat well...the Holiday Inn offers first-class meals even during the wartime days of general hun-

---

¹⁹ Matthew McAllister, *Eating Mud Crabs in Kandahar: Stories of Food During Wartime by the World's Leading Correspondents*, California: University of California Press, 2011, p. 3.

²⁰ Ivana Maček, *Sarajevo Under Siege: Anthropology in Wartime*, University of Pennsylvania Press, Philadelphia, 2009, p. 64.

²¹ Larry Hollingworth, *Merry Christmas, Mr. Larry*, p. 15. By 1993, there were other places in which food and drink could be found in Sarajevo. There was a bar/restaurant called *Jez* (hedgehog) in a basement near the Orthodox Cathedral which was run by gangsters and war profiteers. Hot food and alcoholic drinks were served, but only foreigners (with hard currency) and war profiteers could afford to dine or drink there.

²² *NIN*, Belgrade, 27 November 1992, p. 23. According to Peter Andreas, 'The murkier reality on the ground in Sarajevo included a less visible internal siege (made possible by the external siege conditions)—ranging from theft and looting by criminals-turned-combatants within the city, to profiteering by unit commanders on the frontline, to the political power grab by the SDA leadership in sacking competent officials and replacing them with party loyalists.' See Peter Andreas 'The Longest Siege: Humanitarians and Profiteers in the Battle for Sarajevo', in Benedek, Wolfgang (et al.), *Transnational Terrorism, Organized Crime and Peace Building: Human Security in the Western Balkans*, London: Palgrave MacMillan, 2010, p. 180.

ger in Sarajevo. There, if you have money, you can drink cognac and eat pastries, and also have a choice of cutlets.'[23] Likewise, Zlatko Dizdarević, the *Oslobodjenje* journalist, knowing the privations suffered by ordinary Sarajevans, was surprised by what he saw being served at the Holiday Inn when he visited the hotel in July 1992: 'In the restaurant the tables are laid with immaculate white tablecloths. The silver cutlery and the water and wine glasses are sparkling. Everything is perfect. The waiters look as if they have no inkling of what goes on outside. The menu offers steaks, French fries, beef stew, crêpes with chocolate sauce.'[24] But during the first winter of the siege, providing meals for the guests became increasingly problematic, even if sufficient food could be procured. If the generators were working and there was electricity, food could be cooked as normal; if not, kitchen staff would simply fire the barbeques and cook on an open fire.[25]

Under such circumstances, the food available in the Holiday Inn was never going to be of a very high quality. It was, recalled Kevin Sullivan of the UPI, 'pretty dodgy—meat, pasta and *ajvar*[26] with everything'.[27] 'War Soup', consisting of stock, rice or noodles, and small pieces of meat was on the menu frequently, much to the displeasure of the guests. Rice was part of the staple offering, though it could be made palatable with some added salt and, when available, a splash of Tabasco.[28] Nevertheless, the quality of the food in the hotel far outstripped that on offer in the rest of the city, as Di Giovanni noted, 'What we were eating at the Holiday Inn' was akin to 'Julia Child's *canard a l'ornage* compared to what was available in the city outside' where 'the civilian population of Sarajevo was subsisting on rice, macaroni, cooking oil, a small packet of sugar, and some tinned meat or fish'.[29] What was on offer was significantly better than one might have expected. The *Oslobodjenje* journalist, Zlatko Dizdarević, knowing the pri-

---

[23] *NIN*, Belgrade, 27 November 1992, p. 23.

[24] Zlatko Dizdarević, *Sarajevo: A War Journal*, New York: Fromm International, 1994, p. 104.

[25] Most Sarajevans, with little or no access to gas or electricity, cooked on a *Sarajevska konzerva* (Sarajevo tin can), which was constructed from a five-litre tin can of humanitarian aid. This implement would be used to boil water, heat coffee, or small foodstuffs. See Ivana Maćek, *Sarajevo Under Siege: Anthropology in Wartime*, p. 73.

[26] Ajvar is a relish made from garlic and red bell peppers (and sometimes chilli peppers), and can be used as a spread or as a dip/side dish. Often quite hot, it is a very popular condiment in the Balkan region.

[27] Author's interview with Kevin Sullivan (UPI), April 2015.

[28] Janine di Giovanni, 'Siege Food: Bosnia', p. 34.

[29] *Ibid*, p. 34.

vations suffered by ordinary Sarajevans, was shocked by what he saw being served at the Holiday Inn when he visited the hotel in July 1992:

> In the restaurant the tables are laid with immaculate white tablecloths. The silver cutlery and the water and wine glasses are sparkling. Everything is perfect. The waiters look as if they have no inkling of what goes on outside. The menu offers steaks, French fries, beef stew, crêpes with chocolate sauce.[30]

Of course, there was not always enough to ensure that this fare could be served every evening; Friday evening, however, was different. Without fail, a buffet dinner was served to the guests. Maggie O'Kane of *The Guardian* wrote that 'The best and most extraordinary thing about the Holiday Inn is the Friday-night buffet…the waiters put on their tuxedos and serve, and a pianist played to entertain the guests. How the food gets here we are not sure, but after the aperitifs we dine on Dalmatian ham and braised steak.'[31] Thus, though many of the guests at the Holiday Inn may not have dwelled too much on it, there was evidence that the 'highest quality humanitarian aid items were showing up on the tables at the Holiday Inn' and not in the homes of ordinary Sarajevans.[32] According to Vaughan Smith, then a freelance cameraman working for *Frontline News*, 'the calorific intake of the journalists at the Holiday Inn far outstripped that of most ordinary Sarajevans', and, he further noted, 'while journalists have to eat, it should not be at the expense of someone else's calorific intake, particularly in a siege situation where everything *should* be divided equally, but there would have been times when journalists, through the staff at the hotel, were being served food that was part of humanitarian rations'.[33]

A short, albeit fascinating, film entitled *Hotel na liniji fronta* (Hotel on the Front Line), produced in 1993 by SAGA Films Sarajevo, provides a fascinating glimpse into life in the hotel during the summer of that year.

---

[30] Zlatko Dizdarević, *Sarajevo: A War Journal*, New York: Fromm International, 1994, p. 104. Dizdarević was also shocked to see a notice board giving details of the Sarajevo itinerary of a UNHCR delegation that were due to arrive that evening, which included a meeting with Radovan Karadžić in Serb-held Lukavica. 'I must admit' he wrote, 'that I felt faint when I saw, in black and white, on a notice board in the centre of Sarajevo, that certain gentlemen have arranged a meeting with a criminal who has thrown the operation of this very hotel into disarray, who has killed people who have stayed in it, and who is personally responsible for demolishing the side of the hotel that faces the hills'. *Ibid*, p. 105.
[31] *The Guardian* (Features supplement), London, 14 July 1993, p. 2.
[32] Andreas, *Blue Helmets and Black Markets: The Business of Survival in the Siege of Sarajevo*, p. 74.
[33] Author's interview with Vaughan Smith (Frontline News), June 2015.

The external footage clearly shows the damage to the southern side of the hotel (facing Grbavica), which had absorbed at least six large hits from shells as well as significant damage to the façade by small arms fire. Almost every window on this side of the building had been shattered. Footage taken from within the hotel shows a strange mix of apparent normality and chaos; the shattered glass of the windows and doors near reception, the almost complete destruction of the *Nacionalni* restaurant, the *Hertz* car rental office, the *Putnik* travel agency, the burnt-out corridors on the seventh and eighth floors of the building, and the basement car park, full of cars in various states of disrepair. Conversely, the footage also reveals a busy working hotel, full of guests (journalists), with a working laundry service, an efficient and functioning kitchen, and a dining room (the tables resplendent with white table cloths, salt and pepper shakers, folded napkins, ashtrays, and jugs of water) where journalists were offered an alcoholic *aperitif* before dining on food, such as fresh bread, cheese, and *pršut* (dry-cured ham), that ordinary citizens of Sarajevo could only dream of.[34] (The existence of decent food in the hotel did not escape the local journalists, who would be more than happy to cover an event at the Holiday Inn in the knowledge that there might be something to eat there; they might even be able to bring home to their families—so being sent to cover an event at the Holiday Inn was, therefore, regarded as a choice assignment.) In any event, Žalica's film conveys the stark contrast between the normality and the chaotic context within which this 'normality' is preserved. It is, however, merely a snapshot, and perhaps captures a short period where everything appears to function well. Had the same crew visited the hotel in the winter of 1992–93, they would have found the guests staying in a far more challenging environment.

Even for those journalists who stayed in the Holiday Inn throughout the harsh winter of 1992–93, food was always available, albeit the quality and quantity of which varied significantly (Image 10.1). In any event, the lack of 'luxury' food items provided by the hotel could be circumvented by the guests bringing their own supplies, and some became increasingly creative in so doing. Food could be bought at a fraction of the price of that available within siege lines in Pale, Ilidža, or Kiseljak (where sup-

---

[34] SAGA Films Sarajevo, 'Hotel na prvoj liniji', Dir: Antonije 'Nino' Žalica, Sarajevo, 1993. For a succinct but powerful description of the quantities of humanitarian aid provided per citizen of Sarajevo, see Sulejman Grozdanić, *Bosna nije san*, Sarajevo; Svjetlost, 1995, pp. 146–151.

Image 10.1 Waiting staff preparing to serve the New Year buffet, circa December 1992. (Photo: The Holiday Inn, Sarajevo)

plies could be bought at the Hotel Continental, which was, according to the BBC's Kate Adie, a 'hub of veracious black-marketeering'),[35] and this could then be brought back into Sarajevo, though any supplies were likely to be depleted by having to provide small 'incentives' for those manning the various checkpoints between the source of food and the Holiday Inn. According to di Giovanni, the British brought (and shared) chocolate, the Italians brought pasta and (when possible) parmesan cheese, though the Americans, she said, 'as a rule, did not share…American newspaper reporters tended to operate like lone wolves: each man for himself'.[36] It was, however, the French contingent that was most successful in garnering desirable consumables, such as champagne, French mustard, and foie gras. Even Sarajevo's stray dogs, according to the *France 2* cameraman,

---

[35] Kate Adie, *The Kindness of Strangers: The Autobiography*, Headline Books, London, 2002, p. 303.

[36] Janine di Giovanni, 'Siege Food: Bosnia', p. 35. According to di Giovanni, one (unnamed) American correspondent, came down for breakfast one morning at the Holiday Inn with two eggs (a very rare and valuable commodity in Sarajevo) in his pocket. 'He removed them and asked the waiter to cook them. He did this in front of the rest of us, who probably had not tasted an egg for some time…Shamelessly, he ate the fried eggs, dipping hard bread into the yolk.' See *Ibid*, p. 35.

Jean-Jacques Le Garrec, knew that 'the best food was with the French'.[37] Utilising the so-called *Systeme D* (a term used to describe 'making do' during the Second World War), they succeeded in making life in the Holiday Inn bearable. In an article for *The Spectator* magazine, Janine di Giovanni described how it functioned:

> The French journalists are the experts, having narrowed down the best way to survive in the worst of conditions. They call it *Systeme D*... It meant that while the rest of us began to scratch and look decidedly seedy, the French seemed to grow more chic and elegant. They risked the harrowing airport rat-run to pick up packages containing necessary items such as crates of wine, tins of pâté, and slabs of good salami from Paris.[38]

Stephane Maniér from *France 2* TV remains unsure whether *Systeme D* was anything more than the French being well organised and having ensured before departure that enough 'luxury' food was packed in advance. For the *France 2* crew, the normal shift in Sarajevo was normally one month, so enough additional luxuries had to be brought to the city for that period. 'This was', said Maniér, 'more problematic when we had to reach Sarajevo by car because we needed to carry a lot of gear'. It was, however, easier when it was possible to enter Sarajevo by plane. 'We would then buy food in Paris and put it in large military-style cases—sometimes we would take sweets and even, on one occasion, a whole ham—enough to last one month, which was shorter than many who stayed at the Holiday Inn, but was our usual shift in the city.'[39] But the crew would also take trips out of Sarajevo to buy food, something which is impossible for ordinary citizens of Sarajevo. That food was something precious to the people of the city was brought home in the starkest terms to Maniér in the winter of 1992/1993, when interviewing a Bosnian soldier (a Serb from Sarajevo serving in the ARBiH) in the centre of the city. That morning, before the interview, Maniér and his crew had been to Kiseljak to purchase food and had not had time to drop it off at the Holiday Inn, and the food had remained in the back of their armoured car. After concluding the inter-

---

[37] Interview with Jean-Jacques Le Garrec (France 2) in 'Veillées d'armes: Histoire du Journalisme en temps du guerre' ('The Troubles We've Seen: A History of Journalism in Wartime'), First Journey, Director: Marcel Ophuls, Little Bear Productions, 1993.

[38] *The Spectator*, London, 23 January 1993, p. 13. In the same article Di Giovanni noted that the hotel management 'followed the same rule of thumb as the French journalists, though using *Systeme D* to the highest level.

[39] Author's interview with Stephane Manier (France 2), April 2015.

view, Maniér offered the soldier a lift home. The soldier accepted and entered the vehicle, and according to Maniér:

> When he opened the back door of the vehicle and saw all the food we had in the back he almost collapsed. He asked me if he could buy some eggs (which were then *very* expensive in Sarajevo) for his pregnant wife. Of course, we offered the eggs to him – we could never accept anything for them. As we were handing them over, one of the eggs fell on the floor and smashed. He got on the floor and ate the raw egg. That was really terrible, and a reminder of the privations that ordinary Sarajevans were suffering. We could got to Kiseljak or Pale and buy food…they could not.[40]

Indeed, while those fortunate enough to be staying in the Holiday Inn could consume decent food (or have the ability to bring it into Sarajevo), electricity, and some heat, for the ordinary citizens of Sarajevo it was an entirely different matter. Although many had settled into a routine of survival, the winter had made life far tougher. The UN was ensuring that humanitarian rations were being delivered into the city, but collecting water and firewood and keeping warm in homes that often had no windows (and were thus very exposed to the elements) remained the primary objective and the daily preoccupation of many.[41] People slept with their clothes on in an attempt to keep warm. The Bosnian government, unable to break the siege of the city 'above ground', began work (in May 1992) on the construction of an underground tunnel under Sarajevo's airport, which would connect government-held territory in Butmir and Dobrinja (Bosnian Serb forces held the territory on either side of the runway, in Lukavica and Ilidža) and allow them to weapons and other key supplies into Sarajevo, circumventing, to some extent, the UN arms embargo.[42] The tunnel, known as *Tunel spasa* (Tunnel of Life) which took nearly a year to construct and was 800 m in length, created a link between the besieged city and the outside world, had been built underneath Sarajevo's Butmir airport. Thus, by the summer of 1993 the supply of food was more consistent. Of course, there were more pressing concerns—arms and other military material took precedence, but slowly food was also brought into the city. According to Remy Ourdan:

---

[40] Author's interview with Stephane Manier (France 2), April 2015.
[41] *NIN*, Belgrade, 27 November 1992, p. 23.
[42] Peter Andreas, 'The Clandestine Political Economy of War and Peace in Bosnia', p. 39.

In 1992 and early 1993 there wasn't much food and what existed was of varying quality. Before the opening of the tunnel we had only black market goods and humanitarian aid. One can only presume that this humanitarian aid was being sold on the black market and bought by the hotel, with our money, in order to feed us. But after the opening of the tunnel things improved, not immediately in terms of food – obviously arms and fuel took precedence – but within a few months the food situation, too, had vastly improved.[43]

Visiting the Holiday Inn in December 1993, Paddy Ashdown, the then leader of the British Liberal Party (and later High Representative in Bosnia), enjoyed 'a good meal accompanied by some wine they'd found in the cellars, left over from before the war'.[44] Maggie O'Kane, *The Guardian* correspondent, noted that, by the summer of 1993 already, 'bottles of *cuvee* specially bottled in the Franciscan cellars' were on offer in the hotel.[45] Likewise, Jeremy Bowen noted that French UNPROFOR troops would appear at the rear of the hotel to unload cases of Bordeaux (which were issued as part of their rations) to journalists for the equivalent of approximately 50 US dollars per bottle.[46] The guests could consume wine largely because the hotel management were able to buy stocks from existing wine cellars in Sarajevo that otherwise had no outlet for selling their remaining stock.[47]

Alcohol, which helped to oil the wheels, was available at the right price to journalists who were awash with cash from their employers, and, claims Bowen, 'no-one, least of all those working for the big media networks, was in a mood to skimp on such luxuries'.[48] Beer was always available, though of varying quality. Indeed, the Sarajevo Brewery in Bistrik continued to produce their famed *Sarajevsko pivo* (Sarajevo beer), which was brewed using rice during the siege.[49] Those who smoked could purchase locally produced cigarettes—primarily *Drina* or locally made *Marlboro* from the *Fabrika duhana Sarajevo* (Sarajevo Tobacco Factory), and often

---

[43] Author's interview with Remy Ourdan (Le Monde), 5 November 2013.
[44] Paddy Ashdown, *The Ashdown Diaries: Volume One, 1988–1997*, London: Allen Lane, 2000, p. 245.
[45] *The Guardian*, London, August 1993, p. 1.
[46] Jeremy Bowen, *War Stories*, pp. 144–145.
[47] Author's interview with Holiday Inn (Sarajevo) employee, September 2014.
[48] Author's interview with Jeremy Bowen (BBC), London, March 2014.
[49] Author's interview with Džemal Bećirević (UPI/Washington Post), April 2015.

in plain packaging—from the newsagent kiosk inside the hotel, which, during wartime, served largely as a tobacco vendor (cigarettes were highly valued during the siege, becoming a parallel currency of sorts),[50] though they also sold *trafika* (postcards, small souvenirs, etc.).[51]

WATER, ELECTRICITY, AND HEATING

In addition to food and drink, the Holiday Inn was the only hotel in Sarajevo that could provide basic supplies such as water, a (reasonably) consistent supply of electricity, and, when required, heat. Water was hardly plentiful at the Holiday Inn, but cisterns of water were delivered by truck on a (more or less) weekly daily basis, allowing for a supply of water, albeit limited and, of course, cold. There were no such luxuries for ordinary Sarajevans for whom collecting water often meant embarking upon a treacherous journey (mainly on foot or by bike) carrying large and heavy jerry cans from the nearest available source of water to their homes.[52] That access to water was severely curtailed by the Bosnian Serbs was no surprise; that access to water was 'impeded from within' is more so.[53] According to Andreas, television images of Sarajevans carrying water for their families under sniper fire was 'highly visible evidence for a global audience that the civilian population was a victim of Serb aggression' and, additionally, the Bosnian government were obstructive when presented with potential solutions (such as the emergency water treatment system

---

[50] According to Peter Andreas, cigarettes were so valued in Sarajevo during the siege that the city's tobacco factory 'essentially played the role of a government mint. Well stocked before the siege with tobacco, meant to supply the entire region, the factory was officially designated a priority building and managed to operate throughout the war, maintaining about 20 % of its pre-war production capacity'. See Peter Andreas, *Blue Helmets and Black Markets: The Business of Survival in the Siege of Sarajevo*, p. 85.

[51] Author's interview with Holiday Inn employee, April 2015. For more on the wartime endeavours of the *Fabrika dunava* (Tobacco factory) in Sarajevo, see Kemal Grebo, *Privreda u opkoljenom Sarajevu*, pp. 94–97.

[52] Ivana Maček, *Sarajevo Under Siege: Anthropology in Wartime*, p. 71. For an overview of the ingenious ways in which Sarajevans collected water, see Armina Pilav, 'Before the War, War, After the War: Urban imageries for urban resilience', *International Journal of Disaster Risk Science*, Vol. 3, No. 1, 2012, p. 29.

[53] Peter Andreas, *Blue Helmets and Black Markets: The Business of Survival in the Siege of Sarajevo*, p. 102.

designed by the American disaster relief expert Fred Cuny,[54] to provide running water to citizens in their homes of Sarajevo):

> There are a number of potential explanations, involving both front-stage and backstage dynamics, for the Sarajevo government's unexpected obstructionism. A cynical front-stage explanation is that Bosnian government officials resisted and delayed turning on the taps because the globally televised images of the desperate and dangerous quests for water by ordinary Sarajevans would disappear – and such heart-wrenching imagery was important public relations tool in maintaining international sympathy and support. A plausible backstage explanation is that turning on the taps would remove a source of black market revenue.[55]

Whether subject to the political or economic dynamics of the siege, water was a valuable commodity. When there was no water supply in the city, and thus in the hotel, staff found ways of providing a limited supply for the guests, capturing the last of the remaining supply from the basement, where the little water that remained would drip slowly from the taps. Here it would be bottled and distributed to the hotel's guests, normally in empty wine bottles—the hotel had long exhausted their stocks of mineral water, so this bottled water would often be used, when absolutely necessary, as drinking water. But these rations had to be used sparingly, and for the most basic of functions. As Kevin Sullivan of UPI recalled, 'Water was infrequent, which meant there was a permanent miasma emanating from loos that were never properly flushed; water had to be kept for the essentials—basic washing and flushing toilets with the minimum amount of water possible.'[56] The photojournalist Paul Lowe described how, in the

---

[54] Fred Cuny would, after is endeavours in Sarajevo, work in Chechnya, where he was vocal in his criticism of the Russian government. In April 1995, he disappeared in Ingushetia. For an analysis of Cuny's work and his disappearance, see Scott Anderson, *The Man Who Tried to Save the World: The Dangerous Life and Mysterious Disappearance of Fed Cuny*, New York: Doubleday, 1999.

[55] *Ibid*, p. 102. Andreas underpins this argument by illustrating the case of Fred Cuny's water treatment system, which would channel water from the Miljacka River through the underground water system. Although he had the system rigorously tested by the World Health Organisation (WHO), among others, the Bosnian government was reluctant to allow the system to become operational, claiming that the water was not safe for consumption. They later allowed the system to be used for 'non-drinking purposes' but then (in April 1995) allowed the system to become fully operational (used for drinking water) and it remained so until the end of the siege.

[56] Author's interview with Kevin Sullivan (UPI), April 2015.

early days of the siege, 'journalists would venture up to the upper floors of the hotel to find empty, damaged rooms where the toilets had not been flushed' so that they could relieve themselves.[57]

The guests, too, would seek to collect and preserve their own water supply when it was viable to do so. 'There were rarely', according to Jeremy Bowen, 'protracted periods without *any* water, but it could be pretty irregular'. He maintained a supply in his own room by 'keeping the bath full of water so that I could immerse myself in it in an attempt to keep clean—and when it got too dirty I would use it to flush the toilet'.[58] But the water could be replenished periodically. According to Bowen's colleague, Allan Little, 'A water tanker would arrive at the hotel every couple of weeks or so and fill the cistern, but you had to make sure you were in so that you could fill your bath tub to the brim to last you till the next delivery.' But it was, he said, 'a catastrophe if you hadn't put the plug in properly and the water you'd carefully stored drained away slowly in the night'.[59] Bath plugs, therefore, became an essential item of kit to be packed in advance of departure to Sarajevo; a simple item that proved invaluable.

Bathing was, however, generally endured in cold water. This, according to Joel Brand, meant simply that one 'had a tough choice between a heart-stopping plunge into a bath full of cold water or adding another day's layer of adrenaline-laced sweat to our already unwashed bodies'.[60] Given that the water was generally cold, ways to circumvent the need to bathe in cold water were found. Some of the hotel's guests brought their own electric elements, which after a few hours would heat the water sufficiently to bathe more comfortably. But in the winter, when demand for electricity was high, these electric elements drained a lot of electricity, and their use became increasingly unpopular with the hotel management. The heating elements would, if discovered, be confiscated.[61] For the few 'in the know', there was, however, an alternative. There existed a 'secret' supply of hot water, which according to Džemal Bećirević of UPI, very few of the guests had access to. 'I knew some staff at the Holiday Inn', he said, 'and they told me there was a room in the basement which had

---

[57] Author's interview with Paul Lowe (The Daily Telegraph/The European), June 2015.
[58] Author's interview with Jeremy Bowen (BBC), March 2014.
[59] Author's interview with Allan Little (BBC), March 2015.
[60] Author's interview with Joel Brand (The Times/Newsweek), May 2015.
[61] Author's interview with Holiday Inn (Sarajevo) employee, May 2014.

extremely hot water (I think because of the proximity to the kitchens), so I used it on occasion, and, occasionally, told some of my colleagues about it'.[62] According to Kevin Sullivan, Bećirević's colleague at UPI, who used the shower (though rarely), 'Usually by the time we got there, the water had been reduced to a scalding trickle but it was still possible to soak a towel, allow it to cool a little and conduct tactical ablutions.'[63]

The real problem, particularly during the harsh winter of 1992–93, was not water, but heat. Cold penetrated the building and it was not a problem that could be easily solved. The snow and ice, known colloquially as *bijela smrt* (white death), had a significant impact on the lives of Sarajevans and, albeit to a lesser extent, the guests in the Holiday Inn. After an unseasonably mild early winter, temperatures had dipped significantly by December 1992. To provide fuel for heat, many trees in the centre of Sarajevo were felled to be used as firewood. Both water and electricity supplies had been inconsistent for months, largely because the VRS would not allow the transit of fuel into the city. Some burnt their treasured book collections just to generate some heat. Hamza Bakšić, the *Oslobodjenje* journalist, described powerfully the pain of burning his books. 'In order to be curious', he said, 'a man has to be alive. To stay alive I have to be warm enough, and to stay warm I have to burn books. Books are also some sort of memories. Shopping for books has always been a highly personal act for me. Burning them is a painful version of the same thing'.[64]

In terms of heat, the Holiday Inn provided a level of comfort marginally better than in most of Sarajevo. As temperatures dropped, the lack of fuel (and the quality of the fuel available on the black market) became a serious issue. Fuel would often be watered down and would have to be filtered before use.[65] To do this, jerry cans of fuel would be left outside so

---

[62] Author's interview with Džemal Bećirević (UPI/Washington Post), April 2015.
[63] Author's interview with Kevin Sullivan (UPI), April 2015.
[64] Hamza Bakšić, *Sarajevo više nema*, Sarajevo: Oslobodjenje, 1997, p. 17.
[65] According to John Burns, the journalists' own stock of fuel was kept (under lock and key) in the basement garage. What became evident, however (after several incidents in which cars did not function effectively after filling with fuel), was that the fuel was being watered-down. A group of journalists went to the hotel management to complain and request that they be given control over access to the fuel store. When this was refused, many simply stored it in their rooms. 'I had', said Burns, '2000 L of fuel—both gasoline and diesel—stored in one of my rooms. AP and CNN did the same thing. We all feared that the staff would have them removed, given the possible impact if the hotel was to be hit, but they did not.' Author's interview with John F. Burns (New York Times), September 2013.

that the water would freeze and thereafter separated from the fuel.[66] With fuel to run the generators, heat could be generated, but preserving heat *within* the building was quite another matter. According to one member of the reception staff, 'it was minus 17 degrees outside and with all of the windows blown away and covered with only plastic sheeting, the lobby was as dark and cold as a tomb—we dressed in our coats, gloves, scarfs…it was colder *at* the front desk than outside'.[67] The Holiday Inn's expansive atrium, intended to provide an environment akin to an 'indoor city' by the hotel's architect Ivan Štraus, was difficult to heat even when all the windows and doors were intact, but now that the majority of those windows and doors were no longer intact and the glass replaced by plastic UNHCR plastic sheeting, any heat generated soon dissipated.

Sleeping in such cold was uncomfortable. Paul Harris, who stayed in the hotel over the Christmas of 1992, simply slept with his clothes on. There was, he said, 'two reasons for doing so: to keep sufficiently warm and to be prepared to exit the room quickly should it be targeted and you had to be evacuated'.[68] Most journalists ensured that they purchased the most robust sleeping bags and down jackets to protect from the cold *within* their rooms. Amra Abadžić-Lowe, who worked as a translator and fixer for the Reuters bureau in the Holiday Inn, acknowledged that 'in comparison to the rest of Sarajevo, there was relative luxury in the hotel' but 'when winter arrived keeping warm became a major problem, even within the concrete walls of the Holiday Inn':

> We slept in temperatures of minus 20 degrees in that first winter, and the rooms had no heating. There was nothing we could do, short of taking panelling from the walls and making a campfire in the middle of the room. Of course, you had things that you would cover yourself with a sleeping bags or blankets, but you literally couldn't breathe and then you removed them from your face to find that it is too cold without them. You couldn't sleep, and that was the *real* privation in the Holiday Inn during that winter.[69]

Working in the cold was also challenging. Joel Brand wrote in his room (which had no windows, only plastic sheeting) under candlelight 'to be able to see the keyboard and to be able to keep my hands warm so that

---

[66] Author's interview with Vaughan Smith (Frontline News), June 2015.
[67] Author's interview with Holiday Inn (Sarajevo) employee, September 2013.
[68] Author's interview with Paul Harris (The Scotsman/Scotland on Sunday), August 2015.
[69] Author's interview with Amra Abadžić-Lowe (Reuters), May 2014.

I could type'.[70] When there was electricity in the hotel, the journalists could use small electric heaters, and Stephane Maniér of *France 2* recalled bringing several of these to the Holiday Inn for his colleagues. They were, however, not very energy efficient and thus drained the limited electricity supply. The hotel management, he said, 'soon realised that it was more viable to provide us with a small amount of heat through the central heating system rather than have these small electric heaters draining the electricity, which is what they eventually did'.[71] All such heaters, like the small heating elements, were subsequently confiscated by staff.[72]

Of course, lack of electricity for heat was less than ideal, but it was 'manageable'. Electricity in Sarajevo was scarce, with many citizens of Sarajevo going without it for long periods (and many reliant on candles or car batteries to power small light bulbs for light); most domestic appliances had not been in use since the beginning of the siege.[73] For journalists, however, electricity was not a luxury, it was a necessity. While some could adapt to the lack of water, heat, or decent food, they could not do without the electricity supply needed to run the equipment or recharge batteries (Image 10.2). The Reuters correspondent Kurt Schork noted that electricity was *the* most important of the scarce resources. Without it, he said, 'my computers don't work, my telex won't work and I cannot send my stories. I can do without water and I can do without food, but I need electricity.'[74] Many soon learned, too, that electricity could be cut at any time; thus the hotel's lifts were to be avoided. On a number of occasions, guests found themselves trapped in the lift and had to wait for hours before staff could come with a winch to manually pull the lift to the next floor.[75]

Providing a consistent supply of electricity in a city that was often without it was a constant challenge. The hotel did possess generators, though running them required fuel, most of which had to be procured on the black market at varying cost. Sabina Ćosić, who worked for *Reuters*, recalled that 'I often bought gasoline from black marketers who would come straight to the hotel garage and I would give them ten thousand

---

[70] Author's interview with Joel Brand (The Times/Newsweek), May 2015.
[71] Author's interview with Stephané Manier (France 2), April 2015.
[72] Author's interview with Holiday Inn (Sarajevo) employee, April 2014.
[73] Ivana Maček, *Sarajevo Under Siege: Anthropology in Wartime*, p. 65.
[74] Interview with Kurt Schork (Reuters) in 'Hotel na prvoj liniji', SAGA Films, Sarajevo, 1993.
[75] Author's interview with Paul Lowe (The Daily Telegraph/The European), June 2015.

Image 10.2 One of the CNN rooms at the Holiday Inn, complete with satellite phone, dish, plastic sheeting on the windows, and sleeping bag. (Photo: Nic Robertson)

deutschmarks for, say, anything between ten to forty marks a litre.'[76] Some of the French contingent also fixed deals with the Ukrainian and French UNPROFOR troops based in the Maršal Tito barracks to buy fuel to run the hotel's generators (some of the French UNPROFOR troops were later based *in* the hotel. In the early days, Paul Marchand was pivotal to this trade—the 'interlocutor' between the journalists and the UNPROFOR troops. (He was the fixer of many of these deals, agreements that would be crucial in assuring the ongoing functioning of the generators.)[77] If fuel

---

[76] Author's interview with Sabina Ćosić (Reuters), June 2014.
[77] On occasion, fuel acquired by the Holiday Inn would be 'donated' to the Bosnian Army. A Bosnian Army (ARBiH) document from 15 June 1993, signed by Mušan Topalović 'Caco' states that the Holiday Inn donated 50 L of oil to the Bosnian Army's 'Tenth Mountain

was available, the generators would run, though they had to be regularly serviced under circumstances where spare parts could not be easily acquired. Thus, with the generators being of real importance, the hotel's electrician, Milorad 'Šika' Šikman, became one of the Holiday Inn's most important members of staff. Without his knowledge and his ability to keep them running the entire operation may have been unviable.[78]

The privations suffered during the winter of 1992–93 represented something of a nadir. By the summer of 1993 conditions improved, albeit only slightly. The area around the hotel remained as dangerous as ever, but by April 1993, during the Vance–Owen Peace Plan (VOPP)[79] negotiations (the plan was eventually rejected by the Bosnian Serb Assembly during a long session in the Hotel Bistrica in Jahorina on 6 May 1993), the lobby bar was again serving alcoholic drinks until the early hours, and by the end of July the flow of consumables was increasing, due in part to the opening of the tunnel beneath Sarajevo airport which, though largely used to bring arms and other military and medical supplies, would also be used to bring in food (a second tunnel—higher, wider, and better equipped than the first—was completed in November 1995, just five days before the Bosnian War formally ended).

Posao je posao (Business Is Business)

Despite its frontline location, the Holiday Inn could provide all of the aforementioned services for its guests simply because of its well-paid clientele, many of whom had generous expense accounts and access to (reasonably) large amounts of cash. Nic Robertson, the CNN producer, recalled that he would come to Sarajevo with at least 30,000 US dollars (or the equivalent in Deutschmarks) for a one-month stint—much of which would have to be spent on hotel-related expenses.[80] The BBC's Kate Adie also noted that the hotel took 'wheelbarrows of deutschmarks from the foreign press for the privilege of having a bathroom with no water and dodging sniper fire to get to the bar in the reception'.[81] These guests, or rather the organisation they worked for, were willing to

---

Brigade'. Ref: Armija Republike Bosne i Hercegovine (10 Brdska 'Caco'), Inv. br. 1189/93, Sarajevo, 15.06.1993.g.

[78] Author's interview with Holiday Inn (Sarajevo) employee, May 2014.

[79] A range of primary materials relating to the VOPP can be found in David Owen (ed.) *Bosnia-Herzegovina: The Vance/Owen Peace Plan*, Liverpool: Liverpool University Press, 2013.

[80] Author's interview with Nic Robertson (CNN), August 2015.

[81] Kate Adie, *The Kindness of Strangers*, p. 314.

pay high prices for this 'frontline view' and the distinct advantages that being based in the hotel provided. For journalists it was not only a place to rest and be provided with food (negating the need to have to acquire food independently—as those journalists staying in private apartments had to do), but a place to network and to garner information. In addition to paying for this privilege, those international news agencies who located their own satellite dishes and generators in the hotel paid thousands of dollars per month.[82] A FAMA study estimated that the Holiday Inn had made 230,000 US dollars in two months as a result of their ability to service their foreign guests.[83]

In any event, hotel management were hardly unfamiliar with transacting large amounts of cash (the hotel had a working casino before the war), significant amounts of it were being generated, and, at least on the face of it, large profits were being made. The guests also speculated how the hotel continued to function in the midst of a besieged city. According to Paul Harris, 'the only way the hotel could keep going right on the frontline in the middle of a besieged city was by either paying off both sides or in alliance with organised crime'.[84] Janine di Giovanni also noted that the hotel 'could well be the most profitable Holiday Inn in the world'.[85] After all, the guests were, she said, paying 'handsomely to live in that third-rate university dormitory and someone, somewhere was making a huge profit'.[86]

There was, of course, a minimum price for accommodation and meals at the hotel that outstripped the standard peacetime price. Under the new circumstances the guests, a captive market, would pay a minimum 82 US dollars per person. For that price the guest could expect a bed in a room that may or may not be damaged, no guarantee of running water, but with two reasonable meals per day in the 'safe' dining room with no windows included in the price.[87] Prices were non-negotiable and bills had to be settled in cash, preferably deutschmarks though dollars were also acceptable. This harsh economic reality was made clear to the Canadian UNPROFOR soldiers (CANBAT) who arrived at the hotel shortly after it reopened in July 1992. Under the misapprehension that they had reached an agreement (albeit an oral one) with the then government of the Socialist

---

[82] *The Spectator*, London, 23 January 1993, p. 12.
[83] Suada Kapić, *The Siege of Sarajevo, 1992–1996*, Sarajevo: FAMA, 2000, p.
[84] Paul Harris, *More Thrills than Skills: Adventures in Journalism, War and Terrorism*, p. 184.
[85] *The Spectator*, London, 23 January 1993, p. 12.
[86] Janine Di Giovanni, 'Siege Food: Bosnia', p. 34.
[87] *The Spectator*, London, 18 July 1992, p. 11.

Federal Republic of Yugoslavia (which no longer existed) under which the Canadians would pay only overhead costs such as electricity, food, and water, they arrived at the Holiday Inn. Similar arrangements were previously made in Croatia, and their expectation was that this would be extended to the UNPROFOR mission in Bosnia. However, Dinko Ćorić (one of the hotel's two directors) refused to accept the 'agreement' (which was, as far as he was concerned, null and void), arguing instead that the cost of accommodation could be no lower than 38 US dollars per soldier, per night—and they would be sharing rooms. Upon receiving this information, Michel Jones, a Canadian Colonel, left his bunker at Sarajevo airport to remonstrate with Ćorić, but left an hour later citing a 'misunderstanding'. The CANBAT troops were permitted, temporarily, to stay in 'underground facilities' at the hotel but left soon after to establish an alternative base at a disused JNA facility, they dubbed 'Beaver Camp'.[88] Ćorić remained adamant. Why, after all, would he want UN troops at the Holiday Inn? The foreign journalists were paying (at least) double what he had asked from the Canadians, and that did not include the revenue generated from bar, laundry bills, and (for staff) the occasional tip. Moreover, he argued, if the UNPROFOR troops took rooms in the hotel, the existing staff could not cope—he would have to employ four times as many staff to cater for them. Ćorić said he felt sympathy for the Canadians but argued that he was 'running a business' and that he 'had to pay his staff', many of whom risked their lives on a daily basis to come to work to serve the hotel's guests.[89] Fred Eckhardt, an UNPROFOR spokesman, dryly commented that the oral agreement the Canadians *thought* they had reached with the hotel management 'must have clashed with some newly embraced capitalist principles'.[90]

These 'capitalist principles' almost certainly ensured that profits were made, but the hotel management was certainly running an enterprise that was, at best, cost intensive. Just to keep the hotel operational, money was diverted into the purchase of fuel, food, and other basic necessities, some of which could only be procured for hugely inflated prices on the black market. The Holiday Inn functioned within a specific set of economic

---

[88] Dawn M. Hewitt, *From Ottawa to Sarajevo: Canadian Peacekeepers in the Balkans*, Martello Papers No. 8, Centre for International Relations, Queens University, Kingston, Ontario, Canada, 1998, p. 39.

[89] *The Washington Post*, Washington, 4 July 1992, p. 3.

[90] *The Philadelphia Inquirer*, 4 July 1992, p. 2.

and political dynamics, and was subject to these forces. The stress of the job did, however, have its impact on those tasked with delivering a continued service. As the Muslim–Croat war intensified in late 1992,[91] Ćorić departed unannounced in late 1992, taking from the hotel an 'expensive armoured Mercedes owned by the Spanish newspaper *El País*'.[92] He was subsequently replaced by Avdija Hadrović, who continued to keep the hotel functioning to the best of his—and his staff's—abilities.[93]

Wherever the money generated by the hotel went, the fees for the franchise agreement with the Atlanta-based Holiday Inn Group remained unpaid throughout the war.[94] According to the *New York Times*, the hotel was failing to meet the commitments of its agreement and was unable to provide a service consistent with 'Holiday Inn standards', they began to put in motion processes that would lead to the revocation of the brand and the end of the franchise agreement signed in 1983.[95] As Anderson Cooper noted, 'Given the constraints imposed by the Serb stranglehold on Sarajevo, the hotel just couldn't maintain the high standards demanded by the parent corporation' and that 'the bed mints had run out a long time ago'.[96] Indeed, by mid-1993, rumours were abundant that corporate headquarters were to insist that the hotel change its name and that the huge Holiday Inn logos adorning the exterior of the building should be removed. Given, however, that any attempt to remove these would expose the individuals or individuals who might be bold enough

---

[91] The worsening Muslim–Croat conflict had implications for the defence of Sarajevo. A small section of the siege line was manned by the Croatian Defence Council (*Hrvatska vijeć obrane* - HVO) until relations between them and the Sarajevo government became untenable. See Peter Andreas 'The Longest Siege: Humanitarians and Profiteers in the Battle for Sarajevo', pp. 174–175.

[92] Paul Harris, *More Thrills than Skills: Adventures in Journalism, War and Terrorism*, p. 182.

[93] *The Scotsman*, Edinburgh, 15 June 1998, p. 9.

[94] According to Paul Harris, 'I wrote a very complimentary article about the Sarajevo Holiday Inn and the war for the business section of the *Scotland on Sunday*. It brought an incredibly sniffy response to the editor from the [Holiday Inn's] Franchising Department in Brussels who denied it was any longer part of the chain. Instead of being proud of one of their most resilient outfits, they chose to pull the plug from underneath it. Of course, they [the Holiday Inn, Sarajevo] probably weren't paying their franchise fee any longer, but that could hardly be regarded as surprising.' Paul Harris, *More Thrills than Skills: Adventures in Journalism, War and Terrorism*, pp. 183–184.

[95] *The New York Times*, New York, 19 June 1994, p. 25.

[96] Anderson Cooper, *Dispatches From the Edge: A Memoir of War, Disasters and Survival*, p. 54.

to attempt this to sniper fire, the management's response was thus: if the Holiday Inn wanted to send someone from HQ to remove their corporate logos, they were welcome to do so, at their own risk, of course.[97] Nobody came and the Sarajevo 'great sign' remained in place. Moreover, as the *New York Times* correspondent John Kifner noted, the company 'should have been proud'; The Holiday Inn, Sarajevo, ensured that the company brand appeared almost daily on news reports throughout the world.[98] It was perhaps not exactly the kind of advertising that the company would have wanted, but it was publicity nevertheless. But with the franchise fees unpaid the hotel, while known as 'The Holiday Inn' to all and sundry, was in fact operating under the name of 'HTP Sarajevo'.[99]

THE DRIFT FROM THE HOLIDAY INN

The Holiday Inn had managed to survive because of its guests, though the capacity of the hotel was only stretched on occasions when Sarajevo was a 'story' (during such times even the less desirable, more exposed, rooms were made available to guests). But occupancy fluctuated wildly throughout 1992 and 1993, with some distinctly quiet periods. As Joel Brand recalled, 'normally there would be thirty to forty journalists in the hotel, though this would increase depending on events'.[100] This changed somewhat after the Markale marketplace massacre on 5 February 1994, whereupon sixty-eight citizens of Sarajevo, vendors, and customers, innocently browsing through the outdoor market were killed by a single shell (the highest number of casualties caused by a single shell throughout the siege). The subsequent NATO ultimatum, which included threats to bomb the VRS if they did not withdraw their heavy weapons from a 20-km 'exclusion zone' from Sarajevo, forced the VRS to cease their attacks on the city with artillery shells. For the next year, Sarajevo was largely free from such attacks, though small arms and sniper fire remained a regular occurrence.[101] During the de facto ceasefire, the food supply into the city had become more consistent. On 16 February 1994, despite objections from the executive board of the IOC, its president, Juan

---

[97] Author's interview with Holiday Inn (Sarajevo) employee, May 2014.
[98] *The New York Times*, New York, 19 June 1994, p. 25.
[99] Robert O' Connor, 'Old Name Returns to Peaceful Sarajevo', *Hotel and Hotel Management*, Vol. 10, No. 213, June 1998, p. 6.
[100] Author's interview with Joel Brand (The Times/Newsweek), May 2015.
[101] Robert Donia, *Sarajevo: A Biography*, p. 328.

Antonio Samaranch, returned to Sarajevo to visit some of the sites that he had seen constructed (including the Holiday Inn) in preparation for the 1984 Winter Olympics.[102]

And as time went on, the Holiday Inn became a less popular destination for foreign journalists, with occasional exceptions. The subsequent NATO ultimatum had brought something in the region of 400 journalists to the hotel, all in anticipations of NATO air strikes on the surrounding VRS forces around Sarajevo.[103] The 'Holiday Inn crowd'—those journalists that had stayed regularly in the hotel during the siege—became increasingly frowned upon by many Sarajevans. As they became more disappointed with Western reluctance to intervene and break the siege, they began to view representatives of the West (including the journalists in the Holiday Inn) with near contempt.[104] They became increasingly cynical about their presence and the conditions in which they lived and worked.[105] The Bosnian weekly *Dani* noted that 'The citizens of Sarajevo, mainly hungry and frost-bitten, sometimes hated the hotel',[106] while, the Belgrade independent weekly *Vreme* wrote that, 'Humanitarian workers, diplomats, international bureaucrats, military officers, wheeler-dealers and one or two dumbfounded intellectual-humanists...They [the journalists] drive around town in armoured white Land Rover's with air-conditioning. Even then they are in radio contact with somebody back at the Holiday Inn...The citizens of Sarajevo look on them with a mixture of scorn and disappointment.'[107]

An even more cynical assessment was that these media professionals were akin to vultures feeding their own career ambitions on the misery of Sarajevo. Increasingly, the Holiday Inn (and its guests) became strangely detached—in the city, but not *of* it. Some of the press corps, particularly those that did not stay in the hotel for long periods, concurred with this assessment. Anthony Loyd, *The Times* correspondent, noted that 'Too many simply walked into the basement of the Holiday Inn each day, drove out in an armoured car to a UN headquarters, grabbed a few details, filled them with the words of "real people" acquired for them by local

---

[102] Jason Vuić, *The Sarajevo Olympics: A History of the 1984 Winter Games*, p. 162.
[103] *The Los Angeles Times*, Los Angeles, 22 March 1994, p. 21.
[104] Ivana Maček, *Sarajevo Under Siege: Anthropology in Wartime*, p. 133.
[105] *Dani*, Sarajevo, April 2008, p. 87.
[106] *Ibid*, p. 87.
[107] *Vreme News Digest Agency*, Belgrade, No. 154, 5 September 1994, p. 6.

fixers, and then returned to their sanctuary to file their heartfelt vitriol with scarcely a hair out of place.'[108]

By 1994, however, many of the Holiday Inn's regular journalists were no longer residing in the hotel (a report in *Oslobodjenje* noted that the hotel's reception and lobby was 'half empty' and no longer packed with guests).[109] By then, the majority of them knew the city well, had established strong networks and a capacity to operate within the city more independently.[110] For many of the journalists, this was driven by a need to escape the detachment of the Holiday Inn and live among the citizens of Sarajevo.[111] To facilitate this, they soon moved to cheaper hotels, such as the Hondo, while many opted instead to rent private apartments in the city (*Reuters*, e.g. who had for two years rented the fifth-floor 'Olympic Suite' in the Holiday Inn moved in 1994, to an apartment in Bjelave, opposite the Sarajevo orphanage), thereby avoiding the high costs incurred by staying at the Holiday Inn. Those prices had risen steadily throughout the siege and were driving even the best-funded agencies out (though the BBC retained a minimal presence in the hotel).[112]

Technological advancements also played a part in the gradual flight from the hotel. Generators had reduced in size significantly as had become far more portable, while satellite communications devices also became far smaller and thus more portable. This meant that journalists no longer had a need to use the satellite phones and dishes located in the hotel—or pay a premium for having them installed there. Electricity, too, was more consistent in Sarajevo, and landlines functioned more frequently and effectively. So those journalists with access to the latest equipment need no longer rely on the heavy static generators based in the Holiday Inn. Aware of these technological advances, Remy Ourdan asked his employers to purchase this equipment, which they duly did. Thus, said Ourdan, 'We no longer needed to use those BBC and Reuters generators and satellite phones in the Holiday Inn, meaning we could work more independently in an apartment; it became a far more streamlined, and ultimately a less

---

[108] Anthony Loyd, *My War Gone By, I Miss It So*, p. 179.
[109] *Oslobodjenje*, Sarajevo, 27 February 1995, p. 10.
[110] *Oslobodjenje*, Sarajevo, 27 November 1995, p. 10.
[111] Author's interview with Allan Little (BBC), March 2015.
[112] *Oslobodjenje*, Sarajevo, 27 November 1995, p. 10. According to Paul Harris, it was estimated by some that 'the BBC paid out more than £100,000 a year for the privilege of this frontline seat'. See Paul Harris, *More Thrills than Skills: Adventures in Journalism, War and Terrorism*, p. 182.

costly, operation.'[113] Others followed, as it became easier for journalists to operate independent of the Holiday Inn. According to Džemal Bećirević, then working for the *Washington Post*:

> Early in the siege it was difficult for journalists to operate anywhere other than the Holiday Inn. But by 1994, and certainly by 1995, it became easier to work independently. You could buy more food in Sarajevo than had been the case and the option to buy food in Pale or in Kiseljak remained. You could work in a small apartment, use a portable generator and satellite phone, and, what's more, journalists knew the city better, they had contacts, and, of course, it was much cheaper to live somewhere other than the Holiday Inn.[114]

Even in the absence of some of those journalists that had frequented the Holiday Inn, the hotel was still busy with visiting journalists, diplomats, and aid workers when events in Bosnia were front-page headlines. And for those that stayed, while the cost remained high, the facilities improved. By 1994, after telecommunication cables had been laid through the airport tunnel, some journalists had access to landline telephones in their hotel rooms, circumventing the need to use telex or satellite phone.[115] The drift from the Holiday Inn had begun, though the hotel would be busy with journalists again in late August 1995, following the second Markale market bomb (which killed thirty-seven people), the NATO bombing of Bosnia Serb positions and as fighting intensified through the late summer of 1995, during which Muslim/Bosniak and Croat forces attempted to break the siege.

References

Adie, K. (2002). *Kindness of Strangers: The Autobiography*. London: Headline Books.
Anderson, S. (1999). *The Man Who Tried to Save the World: The Dangerous Life and Mysterious Disappearance of Fed Cuny*. New York: Doubleday.
Ashdown, P. (2000). *The Ashdown Diaries: Volume One, 1988–1997*. London: Allen Lane.
Bakšić, H. (1997). *Sarajevo više nema*. Sarajevo: Oslobodjenje.

---

[113] Author's interview with Remy Ourdan (Le Monde), London, 5 November 2013.
[114] Author's interview with Džemal Bećirević (UPI/Washington Post), April 2015.
[115] Author's interview with Joel Brand (The Times/Newsweek), April 2014.

Benedek, W., et al. (2010). *Transnational Terrorism, Organized Crime and Peace Building: Human Security in the Western Balkans.* London: Palgrave MacMillan.
Dizdarević, Z. (1994). *Sarajevo: A War Journal.* New York: Fromm International.
Grozdanić, S. (1995). *Bosna nije san.* Sarajevo: Svjetlost.
Hewitt, D. M. (1998). *From Ottawa to Sarajevo: Canadian Peacekeepers in the Balkans,* Martello Papers No. 8, Centre for International Relations, Queens University, Kingston, Ontario, Canada.
Kapić, S. (2000). *The Siege of Sarajevo: 1992–1996.* Sarajevo: FAMA.
Maček, I. (2009). *Sarajevo Under Siege: Anthropology in Wartime.* Philadelphia: University of Pennsylvania Press.
Owen, D. (Ed.) (2013). *Bosnia-Herzegovina: The Vance/Owen Peace Plan.* Liverpool: Liverpool University Press.
O'Connor, R. (1998). Old name returns to peaceful Sarajevo. *Hotel and Hotel Management, 10*(213).
Pilav, A. (2012). Before the war, war, after the war: Urban imageries for urban resilience. *International Journal of Disaster Risk Science, 3*(1), 23–37.
Simpson, J. (2000). *A Mad World, My Masters.* London: MacMillan.

CHAPTER 11

The Targeting of the Holiday Inn

Despite the fact the Holiday Inn remained relatively undamaged in comparison to adjacent buildings, the hotel *was*, nevertheless, regularly targeted. According to one member of staff who worked at the hotel throughout the siege, 'We were, fortunately, somewhat spared from the worst of the shelling—and it was, I think, because the hotel was full of journalists, and those shelling Sarajevo did not want to draw more attention to their attacks on the city by targeting the place where journalists were staying.'[1] Yet a perception grew that those within the Holiday Inn were protected, and those within it enjoyed something of a charmed life, at least compared to ordinary Sarajevans. And, of course, local media organisations were not extended such benevolence; the building of the daily newspaper *Oslobodjenje* was destroyed in August 1992, while the Sarajevo TV Station came under regular attack (though this solid concrete building proved quite resilient in comparison).[2] Rumours were abundant that the Holiday Inn was protected by a shady deal which maintained this status quo. So the fact that the hotel was not targeted as often as it could have been fuelled significant speculation about why this was the case and whether the hotel's preservation was agreed upon by the warring parties.[3] As the *Washington Post* correspondent Peter Maass observed:

[1] Author's interview with Holiday Inn (Sarajevo) employee, June 2015.
[2] Robert Donia, *Sarajevo: A Biography*, p. 315.
[3] Peter Andreas, *Blue Helmets and Black Markets: The Business of Survival in the Siege of Sarajevo*, p. 74. See also Paul Harris, *More Thrills than Skills: Adventures in Journalism, War and Terrorism*, p. 182.

It was surprising that the Serbs hadn't shelled the hotel to the ground, but there was a reason for their oversight. War causes inconveniences for both sides, but some can be overcome with mutually beneficial consequences. It goes like this: the Serbs have a building that they want to preserve, perhaps an old church, and the Bosnians have a building that they want to preserve, perhaps the Holiday Inn. The two sides cut a deal on shortwave radio in which the Serbs agree not to wreck the Holiday Inn, and the Bosnians agree not to wreck the church. It can be simpler than that, too: the Bosnians simply pay the Serbs not to shell the Holiday Inn. A time is set to meet at a quiet part of no-man's land, and a sack of Deutschmarks is handed from Bosnian to Serb. That, and the presence of the foreign press, helps explain the hotel's survival.[4]

Anthony Loyd also speculated that there could perhaps have existed 'a tacit understanding within the Serb command that the hotel was the focal point of the media in Sarajevo and should be left untouched' or, moreover, that a deal had been struck 'to ensure its security'.[5] Of course, the Bosnian government had an interest in keeping the international press, and agencies such as the UN, comfortable in the Holiday Inn. By keeping them in relative comfort in the hotel, they could file their stories and *Sitreps* (situation reports). Certainly, the hotel was not targeted as frequently or aggressively as might have been the case, though the Serb gunners on Trebević could have destroyed (with incendiary shells) the Holiday Inn, as they had destroyed the neighbouring UNIS towers (also designed by Ivan Štraus, the architect of the Holiday Inn) and the Bosnian parliament building, both a matter of metres from the hotel.

This was not lost on those journalists who travelled across the frontline to see Sarajevo from beyond the limits of siege lines. Janine Di Giovanni observed that, 'When I visited the friendly Serb gunners on the hills above Sarajevo, they very kindly pointed out the Holiday Inn and laughed at what easy target practice it could be. I could see my own room from their position.'[6] Similarly, Kevin Sullivan of UPI travelled through Serb lines to Ilidža through to Lukavica and then toward Grbavica where, he said, 'We ended up at a spot about 300 metres from the Holiday Inn. You could see very clearly where our rooms were.'[7] Adding to their existing

---

[4] Peter Maass, *Love Thy Neighbour*, p. 122.
[5] Anthony Loyd, *My War Gone By, I Miss It So*, p. 179.
[6] *The Spectator*, London, 23 January 1993, p. 12.
[7] Author's interview with Kevin Sullivan (UPI), April 2015.

concerns were rumours that the Holiday Inn had been militarised; utilised by Bosnian government snipers to fire into Serb-held Grbavica. The upper floors, access to which was strictly forbidden, were, according to some witnesses, used as snipers' nests, though very few of the staff or the resident foreign correspondents claimed to be aware of the existence of these nests.[8] There *were* Bosnian government sniping positions in the nearby UNIS towers and the Bosnian parliament building, but there exists no evidence that there were permanent (or even regularly utilised) snipers' nests in the hotel, though, as Zoran Kusovac noted, 'there were all sorts of military people coming and going from the hotel—that was normal', but 'I was never aware that snipers had used the building, never saw any sniper fire coming from the hotel, so I'm pretty certain the building did not have a military purpose'.[9]

Of course, while it may have been uncomfortable to become aware of just how exposed one was in the Holiday Inn, most journalists were equally aware that their presence in the hotel may have rendered a major assault on it unlikely. The killing of journalists would have been catastrophic for the Bosnian Serbs.[10] Thus, it would have been too politically dangerous for the VRS to do much more than hit the hotel occasionally, as doing so was almost always international news, and would, again, be negative public relations for the Bosnian Serbs (though they, throughout the war, showed little regard for Western public opinion). Džemal Bečirević of UPI concurs with this, stating 'the Serbs knew that there were many foreigners in the Holiday Inn, and they knew there would be international condemnation and potentially bad consequences, so they more or less let it be'.[11]

The presence of senior UN staff may have been an additional factor, though perhaps not a pivotal one. By late 1992, the UN were using parts of the hotel as operational spaces, while Aleksander Ivanko, the UN spokesman, was a regular fixture in the hotel, and when not holding briefings in the PTT building, the UN would hold them in the Holiday

---

[8] Author's interview with Janine Di Giovanni, July 2013. See also Janine Di Giovanni, 'Life During Wartime: Remembering the Siege of Sarajevo', *Harper's Magazine*, April 2013, pp. 82–87 and (by the same author), *The Quick and the Dead: Under Siege in Sarajevo*, London: Phoenix House, 1994.
[9] Author's interview with Zoran Kusovac (Sky News), March 2015.
[10] FAMA, *Sarajevo Survival Guide in* Suada Kapic, *The Siege of Sarajevo 1992–1996*, Sarajevo: FAMA, p. 130.
[11] Author's interview with Džemal Bečirevič (UPI/Washington Post), April 2015.

Inn.¹² Another, more mundane, reason that the Holiday Inn remained relatively unscathed was that many of the apartments behind the Holiday Inn belonged to Serbs, and some of them to JNA officers (the area around the Holiday Inn is close to both the Maršal Tito barracks and the military hospital).

Regardless of the factors that weighed in the hotel's favour, however, it was hit on numerous occasions. In August 1992, the Holiday Inn came under significant fire, with grenades and mortar bombs being, according to Kurt Schork of Reuters News Agency, 'rained down on the area between the Holiday Inn and the Maršal Tito army barracks to its west. Some two-dozen rocket-propelled grenades [RPGs] exploded within half an hour, about one hundred yards from the hotel.'¹³ Schork also noted that 'The bombardment appeared to come from Serb forces retaliating against Muslim snipers.'¹⁴ In November 1992, an Egyptian UNPROFOR soldier was injured while attempting to repair a water utility next to the hotel.¹⁵ And sporadic attacks continued, with the hotel being hit by two RPGs and machine-gun fire on 13 November 1994—the worst incident of such a kind since 1992.¹⁶ The area around the hotel was subject to continuing RPG attack and sniper fire throughout November 1994 and though this ebbed and flowed, the attacks reached their greatest intensity towards the end of the month.¹⁷ Nevertheless, despite incidents such as these, rumours were abundant that the hotel was fast becoming a 'protected space'.¹⁸ Sabina Ćosić of Reuters also speculated that a deal to protect the hotel may have been in place:

---

¹² General Sir Michael Rose, *Fighting for Peace: Lessons from Bosnia*, London: Harvill Press, 1998, p. 102.

¹³ *The Guardian*, London, 21 August 1992, p. 7.

¹⁴ *Ibid*, p. 7. Although most of the journalists staying at the Holiday Inn claimed they had no knowledge of Muslim (Bosnian government) snipers in the Holiday Inn, most acknowledged that they never ventured beyond the fifth floor of the hotel. Writing for *Harper's Magazine* in 2013, Janine Di Giovanni recalled that when she first checked into the Holiday Inn, she was instructed by a member of staff not to go up to the seventh floor of the building. 'The seventh floor', she said, 'was where the Bosnian snipers defending the city were positioned'. See *Harper's Magazine*, April 2013, p. 84.

¹⁵ UNPROFOR (SMO Sector Sarajevo), 'Senior Military Observer's End Month Report: November 1992', 1 December 1992, File Ref: 11008965, p. 1.

¹⁶ *Oslobodjenje*, Sarajevo, 14 November 1994, p. 1. See also *The Herald*, Glasgow, 14 November 1994, p. 7.

¹⁷ *Oslobodjenje*, Sarajevo, 27 November 1994, p. 12.

¹⁸ Lisa Smirl. 'Not Welcome at the Holiday Inn', Spaces of Aid, 2 February 2014. p. 4.

Image 11.1 The western and southern sides of the Holiday Inn hotel, circa January 1996. (The Holiday Inn, Sarajevo)

> There was no safety *per se* but we felt safe during the shelling of the general area. We would be in our offices filing or photographers were taking pictures of shells landing in the neighbourhood (that you could see with your own eye) and yet, we weren't hit. Occasionally a sniper would hit our satellite dish and yes there were occasional shells that would hit the building forcing everybody to run for cover, but by and large I had a feeling, from the moment I set foot in the Holiday Inn, that I was protected by the presence of foreign journalists—so there was a feeling of safety that the hotel was an oasis in the middle of the shelling and mayhem that's going on outside.[19]

In any event, the Holiday Inn *was* hit on hundreds of occasions, either by shell or by small arms fire (Image 11.1). In April 2002, giving evidence at the trial of the Stanislav Galić (a former JNA officer and commander of the Sarajevo-Romanija corps of the VRS)[20] at the ICTY in The Hague, Mesud Jusufović of the Sarajevo Fire Service (a number of whose firefighters were based permanently in the hotel) claimed that 'The Holiday Inn was a very popular target. They [the Serbs] were constantly targeting the Holiday Inn.'

[19] Author's interview with Sabina Ćosić (Reuters), June 2014.
[20] Stanislav Galić was the commander of the Sarajevo-Romanija corps until August 1994, whereupon he was replaced by Dragomir Milošević.

He went on to explain how the Sarajevo Fire Service[21] dealt with fires at the hotel caused by shelling and mortar fire:

> The Holiday Inn is in an open area, so when there was a fire there it was very difficult to reach it. We went there I don't know how many times, and then we had to flee and go back. For that reason we set up a fire brigade team which throughout this period [September 1992 to July 1994] was there all the time. Fire-fighters were in the Holiday Inn, and there was a fire engine in the basement. And throughout the hotel we distributed hoses, so that when it caught fire from an incendiary shell, the fire-fighters would put it out immediately, and they intervened around 500 times.[22]

The shelling of the building continued throughout the siege. The hotel was targeted in November 1994, whereupon three to four RPGs crashed into the lower floors of the hotel and set off a fire. An UNPROFOR fire-fighter who rushed to the scene was subsequently shot in the leg as sniper fire intensified around the hotel.[23] Similarly, the Holiday Inn was targeted again in January 1995, when an RPG fired from Grbavica hit the southern front of the hotel.[24] The hotel continued to be an occasional target as hostilities resumed and the relationship between UNPROFOR and the VRS became increasingly combative,[25] with damage being incurred as late as December 1995, after the signing of the DPA.[26]

Equally, drivers of the trams in Sarajevo dreaded approaching the Holiday Inn (the most exposed and dangerous part of the 18-mile tram system), knowing that they could be targeted at any time.[27] The company that tendered the services of the trams, GRAS, had been a target throughout the siege. Indeed, one of the first shells to hit Sarajevo (on 6 April 1992) fell on the premises of the company.[28] Sarajevo's tram system

---

[21] For a short (and fascinating) account of how the Sarajevo Fire Service endeavoured to deal with the results of daily shelling (including an account of how they dealt with large fires in the Marindvor area, including the Holiday Inn and the UNIS towers), see Kreševljaković (ed.), *I oni brane Sarajevo*, 1998, pp. 65–72.

[22] UN-ICTY Case No. IT-98-29-T, 'The Prosecutor V Stanislav Galić', 3 April 2002, p. 6508.

[23] AFP, Paris, FBIS-AU1311171894, 13 November 1994. p. 1.

[24] Sarajevo Radio, Bosnia and Herzegovina, Sarajevo, FBIS-AU0201193995, 2 January 1995.

[25] For an overview of the increasingly hostile relationship between UNPROFOR and the VRS, see Robert Donia, *Sarajevo: A Biography*, pp. 330–331.

[26] UPI Archives, 'Sarajevo hotel shelled', 14 December 1995.

[27] *Christian Science Monitor*, Massachusetts, 3 November 1994, p. 6. For a short overview of the role of the trams during the siege, see Muhamed Kreševljaković (ed.), *I oni brane Sarajevo*, pp. 101–104.

[28] Kemal Grebo, *Privreda u opkoljenom Sarajevu*, p. 111. See also *Oslobodjenje*, Sarajevo, 10 October 1994, p. 11.

had been designed by the Austro-Hungarians and officially launched in 1885, and originally operated by horses before being fully electrified in the 1960s.[29] The tram lines were extended towards Ilidža in 1961, linking this western suburb with both Baščaršija and Skenderija. When operational, the trams, during the siege, were targeted frequently, particularly around the exposed areas close to the Holiday Inn.[30] These trams were often packed, with the occasional passenger running the significant risk of riding on the outside of the trams on the bumpers.[31] Casualties were inevitable. On 8 October 1994, three bursts of gunfire hit a tram just outside the Holiday Inn, killing one civilian and injuring eleven.[32] (In a subsequent meeting between General Rose and General Mladić, the latter denied that the VRS were involved, claiming instead that the shooting had come from the Holiday Inn, and that the whole incident had been staged by Bosnian government forces.)[33] On 27 February 1995, four passengers were injured (one seriously) when a tram came under sniper fire as it approached the hotel.[34]

Sniper fire, the vast majority of which emanated from the Jewish cemetery in Vraca (on the western slopes of Mount Trebević), remained a significant problem in the area surrounding the Holiday Inn throughout the three-and-a-half-year siege. The area around the Holiday Inn was dubbed 'Sniper's Corner', notorious for sniper fire and with civilians being killed or injured on a regular basis.[35] Faud Babić, the commander of the Bosnian TO in Sarajevo, stated that the area around the Holiday Inn was 'the most difficult crossing to protect from snipers' because 'the Marindvor crossing was very elongated…the people who lived there simply couldn't go anywhere'.[36] By early 1994, according to General Michael Rose, the UNPROFOR Commander, part of the Serb line in Vraca, was held by a group of mercenaries called 'The Heroes', who had volunteered their services to the Bosnian Serbs. Among the ranks of the 'Heroes', he said, were

---

[29] For a brief history of the GRAS company, see *Slobodna Bosna*, Sarajevo, 20 February 2014, pp. 42–45.
[30] *Oslobodjenje*, Sarajevo, 26 January 1995, p. 3.
[31] AFP, Paris, FBIS-AU2411170294, 24 November 1994.
[32] UNPROFOR (Zagreb) Daily Sitrep, 8 October 1994, File Ref: SR091100, p. 3.
[33] UNPROFOR Office of Civil Affairs (Zagreb), 'Subject: Meeting with General Mladić in Jahorina', 10 October 1994, File Ref: CCA-BHC-363, p. 2.
[34] UPI Archives, 'Sarajevo streetcar under sniper fire', 27 February 1995.
[35] See, for example, *Oslobodjenje*, Sarajevo, 25 November 1994, p. 12.
[36] Interview with Faud Babić in Sauda Kapić, *The Siege of Sarajevo 1992–1996*, Sarajevo: FAMA, 2000, p. 812.

people 'not much interested in money or ideology, only in killing people' and they included 'Japanese, Russians and even an American'.[37]

Sniper fire was a significant problem in the area surrounding the Holiday Inn. Numerous incidents occurred throughout 1994. Despite an 'anti-sniping agreement' being signed by both sides, sniping on civilians and UNPROFOR peacekeepers remained commonplace.[38] By year end, these were near daily occurrences. On 6 December 1994, when two civilians were injured outside the Holiday Inn, UNPROFOR reported that the shots had emanated from the direction of Grbavica.[39] Four days later, one civilian was killed and one wounded outside the hotel.[40] The car of the US Ambassador, Victor Jakovich, which had been parked outside the Holiday Inn, was hit by three sniper bullets on the 25 March 1995, though he was not in the car at the time.[41] The problem was deemed serious enough for Ukrainian (and later French) UNPROFOR troops, including the 'anti-sniping unit' to be deployed around the Holiday Inn (some were even accommodated at the hotel).[42] They were occasionally targeted. On 26 October 1994, a grenade was thrown at the Ukrainian battalion (UKRBAT) stationed outside the Holiday Inn, though there were no injuries.[43]

For a ten-month period between late 1994 and 1995, the French battalion (FREBAT) would often be called into action to repel sniper fire coming from Grbavica, with the number of sniping incidents around the

---

[37] General Sir Michael Rose, *Fighting for Peace: Lessons from Bosnia*, London: Harvill Press, 1998, p. 95. According to Saud Kapić, 'In some European newspapers one could read reports about "war tourism" which included sniping [at] the citizens of Sarajevo. The Russian avant-garde writer Eduard Limonov was caught on camera indulging in this "enjoyable sport".' See Suada Kapić, *The Siege of Sarajevo 1992–1996*, p. 116. The astonishing footage of Limonov discussing poetry and politics with Radovan Karadžić before firing a sniper rifle into Sarajevo can be seen in Paul Pawlokowski's documentary film 'Serbian Epics'.

[38] UNPROFOR (Zagreb) Daily Sitrep, 14 August 1994, File Ref: SR151100, p. 4. Violations of the 'Sarajevo Anti-Sniping Agreement' were relatively commonplace, much to the annoyance of UNPROFOR. On 12 September 1994, UNPROFOR sent a letter to the UN Under-Secretary General, Kofi Annan, stating that these violations were occurring frequently. The list of incidents reported included the wounding of a civilian by Bosnian Serb sniper on 30 August at location 'Grid BP 917558' (Holiday Inn). See UNPROFOR (Zagreb), 'Outgoing Code Cable: Violations of the Sarajevo Anti-Sniping Agreement', 12 September 1994, Number: UNPROFOR Z-1398.

[39] UNPROFOR (Zagreb) Daily Sitrep, 6 December 1994, File Ref: SR071100, p. 4.

[40] UNPROFOR (Zagreb) Daily Sitrep, 10 December 1994, File Ref: SR111100, p. 4.

[41] *Oslobodjenje*, Sarajevo, 26 March 1995, p. 16.

[42] Lisa Smirl. 'Not Welcome at the Holiday Inn', Spaces of Aid, 2 February 2014. p. 4.

[43] UNPROFOR (Zagreb) Daily Sitrep, 26 October 1994, File Ref: SR271100, p. 8.

Holiday Inn increasing.[44] In January 1995, with relative quiet in the city, the hotel hosted an event which brought 'more than 240 guests from every part of the world' (including the mayors of a number of European cities) to mark 1000 days of the siege.[45] There, at the Holiday Inn, the mayors were provided with a presentation on Sarajevo as a 'united and undivided city'.[46] But by March 1995, the anti-sniping team came under consistent sniper fire, though they often responded robustly.[47] The following month, however, a French UNPROFOR soldier was shot dead by a sniper, directly across the road from the Holiday Inn while operating a forklift which was erecting containers (used to shield civilians against sniper fire).[48] In May 1995, another French UNPROFOR soldier was shot and wounded by sniper fire while standing guard outside the front doors of the hotel.[49] Indeed, such were the number of sniping incidents around the hotel, (and despite the presence of the anti-sniping teams) *Oslobodjenje* described the area as a 'Sniper's Safari'.[50] Matters worsened in late May 1995, during the 'Battle of Vrbanja Bridge' (where Suada Dilberović and Olga Sučić had been killed on 5 April 1992), after the VRS took control of both sides of the bridge and held twelve French UNRPOFOR peacekeepers hostage (though they were later released). The French responded robustly, and after an intense, hand-to-hand, battle, forced the VRS off the bridge. Thereafter, the VRS ceased their attacks on FREBAT, though sniping incidents in the area they policed (around the Holiday Inn) remained a constant.

So the Holiday Inn was not immune to the dangers of sniping and shelling throughout the siege, even in the latter days of the siege. Whether there was a deal (or otherwise) to protect it remains a matter of conjecture, but there exists no paper trail, and thus while a deal *may* have been possible, there is no evidence one existed. More likely, it was the presence of the journalists, and to a lesser extent UNPROFOR staff, that assured it was a *relative* safe place to reside in the context of the wider city of Sarajevo. As the siege was broken and the frontline, which had been static since May 1992, began to dissolve, the Holiday Inn was reaching the end of its three and a half years as a frontline hotel.

[44] *Oslobodjenje*, Sarajevo, 14 December 1994, p. 16. See also *Oslobodjenje*, Sarajevo, 5 March 1995, p. 1.
[45] *Oslobodjenje*, Sarajevo, 26 January 1995, p. 1.
[46] AIM Press, Paris, 'Thousand Days of the Siege of Sarajevo', 5 February 1995.
[47] *Oslobodjenje*, Sarajevo, 5 March 1995, p. 1.
[48] *Oslobodjenje*, Sarajevo, 16 April 1995, p. 16.
[49] UPI Archives, 'Sarajevo sniper hits French peacekeeper', 11 May 1995.
[50] *Oslobodjenje*, Sarajevo, 1 May 1995, p. 1.

References

Di Giovanni, J. (1994). *The Quick and the Dead: Under Siege in Sarajevo*. London: Phoenix House.
Kapić, S. (2000). *The Siege of Sarajevo: 1992–1996*. Sarajevo: FAMA.
Kreševljaković, M. (Ed.) (1998). *I oni brane Sarajevo*. Sarajevo: Zlatni ljiljani.
Rose, M. (1998). *Fighting for Peace: Lessons from Bosnia*. London: Harvill Press.
UNPROFOR (Zagreb) Daily Sitrep, 14 August 1994, File Ref: SR151100.
UNPROFOR (Zagreb) Daily Sitrep, 8 October 1994, File Ref: SR091100.
UNPROFOR (Zagreb) Daily Sitrep, 26 October 1994, File Ref: SR271100.
UNPROFOR (Zagreb) Daily Sitrep, 6 December 1994, File Ref: SR071100.
UNPROFOR (Zagreb) Daily Sitrep, 10 December 1994, File Ref: SR111100.

CHAPTER 12

The Rebirth and Demise of Sarajevo's Holiday Inn

The 'General Framework Agreement for Peace in Bosnia & Herzegovina', better known as the DPA, was signed in Paris in November 1995. Three months later, in February 1996, the siege of Sarajevo formally ended. Since the shootings of Suada Dilberović and Olga Sučić on 5 April 1992, more than 11,000 citizens of Sarajevo had been killed.[1] Dayton Bosnia created a one country with two entities—the Bosniak–Croat Federation and Republika Srpska (both of which possessed many of the 'attributes of a state') that were divided along the 'Inter-Entity Boundary Line (IEBL)'.[2] The terms of the DPA dictated that the SDS had failed in their stated objective vis-à-vis Sarajevo—to divide the city. The vast majority of Sarajevo was incorporated into the Bosniak–Croat Federation, with small parts of the east of the city (known as *Istočno Sarajevo*—Eastern Sarajevo) falling within the territory of Republika Srpska. Radovan Karadžić, the leader of the party that had launched the 'war of the barricades' from their headquarters at the Holiday Inn and had escaped from the hotel after the shootings on 6 April 1992, wrote a letter to the US President Bill Clinton, expressing his dissatisfaction. 'At the stroke of a pen', he said, 'Serbs now living in the wider region of

---

[1] UN ICTY, 'Death Toll in the Siege of Sarajevo, April 1992 to December 1995: A Study of Mortality Based on Eight Large Data Sources', Expert report prepared for the Case of Slobodan Milošević—Bosnia and Herzegovina, Case No. IT-02-54.

[2] Paddy Ashdown, *Swords and Ploughshares: Building Peace in the 21st Century*, London: Phoenix Press, 2008, p. 221.

Sarajevo have found themselves facing the prospect of life under the Muslim regime...If they were to leave they would be leaving behind the graves of those who have died for Serb Sarajevo, and not just their properties and land.' He then suggested to Clinton that a 'separate document' be adopted for Sarajevo that would allow the Serbs a level of autonomy and prevent the 'Muslim authorities' gaining access to hitherto Serb-held areas.[3]

But there was to be no special arrangement, and by March 1996, when the 'border' between Bosnian government and Serb positions was opened, many of those Serbs who had remained in areas like Grbavica, Rajlovac, and Ilidža had departed, in some cases driven out by Serb paramilitaries— the very people who had claimed to be their erstwhile defenders.[4] They were replaced, in part, by Muslim/Bosniak IDP's from eastern Bosnia and their ethnic kin from the Sandžak, as the ethnic dynamics in Sarajevo again shifted.[5] Bosnia and Herzegovina was subsequently administered by IFOR (NATO-led 'Implementation Force'), which took over the role of UNPROFOR, while civilian aspects of peace implementation were handled by the Office of the High Representative (OHR) which was responsible not directly to the UN but to the Peace Implementation Council (PIC).[6] The Holiday Inn was no longer a hotel on the frontline.

The reconstruction of Sarajevo, and other Bosnian towns and cities began (though much of the international aid was dedicated to reconstructing the capital). Despite all the damage incurred during the siege, the Holiday Inn fared rather better than many of the buildings constructed for the 1984 Winter Olympics, and reconstruction was relatively straightforward with reconstruction work ongoing throughout late 1997 and 1998. Some of Sarajevo's other iconic buildings had, however, been destroyed during the siege. The Vijećnica, which housed the national library, was completely gutted, as was the Olympic Museum in central Sarajevo, the Zetra Sports Hall (where Jane Torvill and Christopher Dean had performed their gold medal-winning *Bolero* routine),

---

[3] Central Intelligence Agency (CIA), Letter: Karadžić to President Clinton Accepting the Dayton Agreement, 02 December 1995, Document No. No. (FOIA)/ESDN (CREST): 5235e00d935294098d5174.

[4] For the Serb departures from previously Serb-held parts of Sarajevo see Robert Donia, *Sarajevo: A Biography*, pp. 337–339.

[5] See Xavier Bougarel, 'Urban Exile: Locals, Newcomers and the Transformation of Sarajevo', in Bougarel, Helms & Duijzings (eds.), *The New Bosnian Mosaic*, Ashgate Publishing, Aldershot, 2007, pp. 72–73.

[6] The PIC was established in London in December 1995. The Steering Board of the PIC (which operates under the chairmanship of the High Representative) is the executive arm of the PIC and includes the USA, UK, France, Germany, Canada, the Presidency of the EU, the European Commission, Japan, Russia, Italy, and the Organisation of the Islamic Conference (represented by Turkey).

which was completely destroyed and was used as a makeshift morgue during the siege; the skiing facilities on Bjelašnica and Mount Igman and those on Jahorina were also badly damaged and out of service for many years, while the bobsleigh and luge track on Trebević was rendered beyond repair. Much of Dobrinja, built to house journalists during the games, was also devastated. Among other important structures in Sarajevo, the *Oslobodjene* building, the *robna kuća* (department store), *Sarajka,* and the *Dom penzionera* (Hotel Rainbow) were completely gutted. The two major hotels in Baščaršija, the Europa and the Central, were badly damaged and the Hotel Bristol, located just off *Zmaja od Bosne,* likewise. Damaged as it was, the Holiday Inn still stood and it continued to function, and within a marketplace where it had little competition. The hotel was now managed into the new post-war era by Ibrahim Čolakhodžić, who oversaw much of the renovations.

It remained the only large hotel in Sarajevo to be fully functioning in the latter days of the Bosnian War and the early days of the fragile post-Dayton peace agreement.[7] Towards the end of the siege, the hotel was used less frequently by foreign journalists and more often as accommodation for members of the Bosnian government (*the Oslobodjenje* journalist Edina Kamenica, for example, described the Holiday Inn as 'the Hotel for Ministers').[8] But in the early post-war period, the service economy improved significantly, as a small army of international bureaucrats arrived in Bosnia to enforce the DPA.[9] In the hotel they replaced the foreign correspondents that, by 1996, had moved on to other wars. Many international organisations moved into, or held briefings at, the Holiday Inn. The NATO Implementation Force (IFOR), 'Press and Information Centre', held daily briefings at the hotel.[10] But doing so was costly; it was estimated that the lease for the hotel space amounted to 11,000 Deutschmarks per month.[11]

The British film director Michael Winterbottom brought his crew to Sarajevo (and to the Holiday Inn) in the early summer of 1996 to film *Welcome to Sarajevo,* a film depicting the lives of journalists covering the war in Bosnia and Herzegovina (in which the exterior of the Holiday Inn is one of the central locations, though not the interior), loosely based on the experiences of the ITN correspondent Michael Nicholson.[12] (Stephen Dillane, the

[7] For an overview of the status of Sarajevo's city-centre hotels in the last months of the siege, see *Oslobodjenje,* Sarajevo, 18 October 1995, p. 11.
[8] *Oslobodjenje,* Sarajevo, 26 August 1995, p. 5.
[9] Robert Donia, *Sarajevo: A Biography,* p. 344.
[10] Stephen Badsey, *The Media and International Security,* London: Frank Cass Publishers, 2000, p. 135.
[11] International Crisis Group (ICG), 'Media in Bosnia and Herzegovina: How International Support Can Be More Effective', ICG Bosnia Report No. 21, 18 March 1997, p. 15.
[12] See Michael Nicholson, *Natasha's Story,* London: Macmillan, 1993.

lead role in the film, rather colourfully described the Holiday Inn as 'yellow and famous...bright yellow, like a dizzy canary caught in the crossfire'.)[13] In September 1997, the Irish rock band U2 stayed in the hotel, though it was still undergoing renovations, during the preparations for their concert (part of their 'PopMart' tour) at the Koševo stadium. Their engagement with Bosnian issues, though regarded as cynical by many, stretched back to 1993 whereupon they broadcast satellite transmissions from Sarajevo during their 'Zooropa' tour.[14] Upon arriving in the Holiday Inn in September 1997, the band's drummer Larry Mullen recalled how his room at the Holiday Inn had 'mortar shrapnel embedded in the walls and bits of the floor missing'.[15] Two months later, in November 1997, Yusuf Islam (the artist formerly known as 'Cat Stevens') stayed in the hotel during his performance in the Zetra Centre in Sarajevo (parts of which were still under reconstruction)—the first artist to play there since the 'Yutel for Peace' concert in July 1991.

The hotel continued to be used as a *political space*, largely hosting large conferences such as the 1999 'Balkan Reconstruction Summit' and 'Stability Pact' meetings (the latter held at the Zetra Centre)—attended by the US President Bill Clinton and high-level delegations from sixty-two countries.[16] When the ICTY sent delegations to Sarajevo, they would only stay at the Holiday Inn (the expansive space around the hotel could be secured to provide appropriate security). And when officials from Republika Srpska were required to stay in Sarajevo, they would tend to do

---

[13] *The Guardian*, 7 November 1997 (Supplement), p. A5.

[14] For more on U2's concerts which included the Sarajevo live links, see Bill Carter, *Fools Rush In*, pp. 243–87.

[15] Neil McCormick, *U2 by U2*, London: HarperCollins Entertainment, 2008, p. 344.

[16] AIM Press, Paris, 'Thousand Days of the Siege of Sarajevo', 28 July 1999. The Holiday Inn was not the only hotel in Bosnia & Herzegovina to be utilised by the international community. In Mostar, the Hotel Ero (known locally as 'the pensioners hotel'), located just behind the front line on Šanticeva Street, had served as a base for the HVO during the Muslim–Croat conflict, but was subsequently repaired and utilised by the European Union Administration of Mostar (EUAM), who used the hotel as their base thereafter. The hotel brought together all kinds of people—from EU administrators and local politicians to soldiers and local crooks. Yet it proved to be no safe haven. On 12 September 1994 the room of Hans Koschnick, the EUAM chief, was hit be a rocket propelled grenade. He, however, had been at the lobby bar having finished a late dinner with EUAM staff, and escaped injury. Koschnick was again subject to an attack on 7 February 1996, when Bosnian Croats, angered by the EUAM's plans to push through a decree on the administration of the city (creating three Croat and three Bosniak majority municipalities as well as a shared 'central zone'), rioted outside the hotel and trapped Koschnick in his (bulletproof) car which took several bullets. He resigned one week later. See Sumantra Bose, *Bosnia after Dayton: Nationalist Partition and International Intervention* , London: Hurst & Co., 2000, p. 107; John R. Yarwood, *Rebuilding Mostar: Reconstruction in a War Zone* , Liverpool: Liverpool University Press, 1999, pp. 13–35; and International Crisis Group (ICG), 'Reunifying Mostar: Opportunities for Progress', ICG Balkans Report No. 90, April 2000, p. 9.

so at the Holiday Inn (the symbolism of this was not lost on anyone familiar with Sarajevo's modern history). And business seemed to be thriving. Despite foreign investment in Bosnia and Herzegovina being hampered by political uncertainty, a new franchising agreement was reached with the Holiday Inn (which had been bought by the UK-based Bass PLC in 1998, a company that was, in March 1998, to acquire the Intercontinental Hotels Group [IHG]).[17] This was a sign that they saw a future for their Sarajevo franchise.[18] Signed in January 1998 by the hotel's director Ibrahim Čolakhodžić, the agreement would be regarded by his successor, Senad Fetahagić, as problematic and costly. As part of the agreement, IHG sought to recoup some of the franchise fees they did not receive during the siege, when the hotel traded under the Holiday Inn brand.[19] The reconstruction of the hotel was not paid for by IHG, as the financial risks were 'assumed locally'. This model worked, as very few investors were looking to own hotels in Sarajevo. One hotel industry analyst noted that:

> Nobody wants to put capital in there. If anybody who is in the hotel business in Sarajevo wants to invest in the hotel market themselves and either offer a franchise, as with this [Sarajevo] Holiday Inn, or a management contract to any of the international chains, they will probably take it, if the hotel conforms to brand specifications.[20]

Over time, the hotel returned to normal, hosting guests for both business and, increasingly, tourism. The reconstruction of the war-damaged hotel was completed in late 1998. The reconstruction (and formal reopening) of the Holiday Inn was, in the words of the hotel's spokesperson Azra Aličić, 'an important psychological step for Sarajevo', while IHG's development director Peter Vermeer, said he expected demand to be high. 'There are a lot of visits here', he said, 'and there is not an oversupply of hotel rooms'.[21] Normal guests began to return and many of the journalists who

---

[17] For a history of the Intercontinental Hotels Group prior to 1998 see James Potter, *World of Difference: 50 Years of Intercontinental Hotels and Its People*, London: Weidenfeld Nicholson, 1996.

[18] A 1999 International Crisis Group (ICG) report noted that while foreign investment had been rather slow, the hospitality and tourism sector was not one which was 'likely to grow as long as the Balkan region as a whole remains politically volatile' but that some parts of the infrastructure for the 1984 Winter Olympics could serve as the basis for future development. The Holiday Inn, to some extent, bucked this trend because it hosted a large number of 'internationals'. See International Crisis Group (ICG), 'Why will no one invest in Bosnia and Herzegovina?', ICG Balkans Report No. 64, 21 April 1999.

[19] *Dani (Specijalni prilog)*, Sarajevo, 20 December 2002, p. 6.

[20] Robert O' Connor, 'Old Name Returns to Peaceful Sarajevo', p. 6

[21] Robert O' Connor, 'Old Name Returns to Peaceful Sarajevo', p. 6.

had stayed during the siege would also revisit it and find it transformed. Not all of them felt a warm glow upon their respective returns. As Peter Maass observed when he returned to the hotel in 1999, 'I had remembered it as a cold and grubby place filled with weary journalists, now it was rather pedestrian. There were aid officials, businessmen, politicians, and (amazingly) some tourists—but it was quite different from the last time I had set foot in the building.'[22] Upon her return to the hotel, for the sake of nostalgia in 2001, Janine di Giovanni found a place 'gloomier than during the siege'. In the bedrooms, they had not, she said, 'changed the depressing dark furniture or the curtains'.[23] Nevertheless, many of the journalists who stayed in the hotel during the siege continue to have an emotional attachment to it. The BBC's Martin Bell, for example, left a very complimentary message in the hotel's *knjiga utisaka* (guest book) which said, 'The Holiday Inn in Sarajevo is quite simply the greatest hotel in the world. It has a history unlike any other. It provided shelter and hospitality to those who stayed here during three and a half years of war.'[24]

Some of the journalists who stayed at the hotel during the siege returned in April 2012 for the twentieth-anniversary events (organised, in the main by Remy Ourdan) that marked two decades since the beginning of the siege, assembling at the Holiday Inn for what was mockingly described by some as a 'high school reunion'.[25] There they discussed the siege, the hotel, and some of those who had frequented it when many of them first arrived in Sarajevo to cover the 1992 independence referendum, such as the members of the SDS leadership that frequented the Holiday Inn before the outbreak of war in April 1992. After thirteen years of being on the run, Radovan Karadžić was arrested in Belgrade in August 2008, though many were convinced that he was being protected by the Serbian Orthodox Church in their extensive network of monasteries. Astonishingly, however, he had been living openly in the Serbian capital under the pseudonym of 'Dr Dragan Dabić', a practitioner in alternative medicine. His SDS colleagues, Momčilo Krajišnik and Biljana Plavšič, the latter of whom broke ranks with Karadžič in 1996, were both jailed by the ICTY (Krajišnik was released in 2013, having served seven years while Plavšič was released in 2009, having

---

[22] Author's interview with Peter Maass (Washington Post), April 2015.
[23] Janine Di Giovanni, *Madness Visible: A Memoir of War*, p. 260.
[24] Holiday Inn, Sarajevo, 'Knjiga utisaka, 2003', Holiday Inn (Sarajevo) archive.
[25] RFE/REFL, 'Sarajevo Notebooks: For Journalists' the Story of their Lives', 6 April 2012, http://www.rferl.org/content/sarajevo_siege_anniversary_reporters_notebook/24540320.html.

served a similar term). Karadžić's trial is, at the time of writing, ongoing but reaching a conclusion. Their erstwhile colleague Nikola Koljević committed suicide in Belgrade in January 1997.

Among the journalists, there were a few of the 'Holiday Inn crowd' conspicuous by their absence. Some were unable to attend, some chose not to, while others had passed away. But two of the central figures among the journalists in the Holiday Inn during the siege were unable to attend. Paul Marchand, one of the most colourful characters among them, committed suicide in June 2009 at the age of just 48, while Kurt Schork, the Reuters correspondent, had been killed in Sierra Leone in 2000. For those who had stayed in the Holiday Inn during the siege, the hotel is imbued with symbolic significance.

Yet the hotel's rich history and symbolic importance to myriad people from diverse backgrounds and professions have proved no guarantor of its future. The rot had already set in long before the sale of the hotel in 2003. In 2000 a majority share of the hotel was set to be sold to a local businessman called Nedim Ćaušević with strong political connections (who was the sole bidder) before the bid was blocked by representatives of the USA, EU, the IMF, and the World Bank, due largely to the fact that Ćaušević was planning to pay for the hotel partially using 'privatisation certificates' (that were relatively worthless), thereby purchasing the hotel at a fraction of its value.[26] According to Timothy Donias, 'The strong scent of corruption and cronyism that permeated the Holiday Inn sale from the very beginning ... led to its annulment in February 2001, even though many in the international community continued to insist that the sale was "technically" legal.'[27]

By October 2001 the hotel had a new director, Senadin Fetahagić. He took the reins at a time, immediately post-September 11, when tourism in Bosnia and Herzegovina had taken a downturn. In his first few days there he could see that improvements were needed. In an interview for *Dani* in 2002 he said, 'On reception there were three or four receptionists, and in the hotel one or no guests at all, and in the gloomy and empty hall there were three of four bored waiters. That was the Holiday Inn in the first days of October 2001.'[28] While acknowledging that the Holiday

[26] See AIM Press, Paris, 'Why was the great privatisation in FBiH annulled?', 26 April, 2000.
[27] See Timothy Donais, 'The Politics of Privatization in Post-Dayton Bosnia', *Southeast European Politics*, Vol. III, No. 1, June 2002, p. 7.
[28] *Dani* (*Specijalni prilog*), 20 December 2002, pp. 4–5.

Inn was 'a treasure', it was clear to him that new investment was needed. The botched sale in 2000 led to the hotel being again open to bidders, a process which began in earnest in 2002. And in December of that year a round table, 'The Holiday Inn: A Possible New Model of Privatisation', which was attended by economic and legal experts and representatives of the World Bank, among others, took place. The conclusion reached was that the hotel would not be sold at a knockdown price and that the tendering process and any subsequent sale would be transparent.[29]

The hotel was eventually purchased by the sole bidder, an Austrian company *Alpha Baumanagement* (a construction and development company which had been formed in 1988 in the Austrian city of Villach), with the signing of the sales contract taking place in April 2004. Its director, Jakob Kuess, used some creative accounting techniques (using the hotel, which he did not yet own, as security against the loan to purchase it). All seemed well. In a ceremony at the hotel, he promised that major investment would be forthcoming. But the investment he had promised (which was an obligation and part of the agreement on purchase arranged in cooperation with the Sarajevo Privatisation Agency) failed to materialise.[30] According to the Bosnian weekly *Slobodna Bosna*, all that remained of this grandiose project was the foundation stone laid in 2004.[31] In the immediate years after Kuess purchased his 74 % share he allegedly used the hotel as cover to conduct corrupt business transactions, during which little or no money was invested. Thus having committed in 2003, upon purchasing the hotel, to invest at least a million Bosnian marks (KM), Alpha Baumanagement simply failed to deliver.[32] In 2007, the company revealed plans for the development of the hotel and its immediate environs (the much-lauded 'Grand Media Centre'), but no money was invested and the plans were never realised.[33]

With no investment, therefore, and in the context of an increasingly competitive hotel market in Sarajevo (both the Europa and the Bristol,

---

[29] *Dani* (*Specijalni prilog*), 20 December 2002, p. 3.

[30] An article in the Bosnian magazine *Start* stated that the Holiday Inn would be fully upgraded with the latest technologies being made available in guests' rooms—including a Sony Playstation for children. See *Start*, Sarajevo, 20 April 2004, p. 34.

[31] *Slobodna Bosna*, Sarajevo, 29 June 2015, www.slobodna-bosna.ba/vijest/22295/hotel_holiday_kriminal_sa_medjunarodnim_predznakom.html [last accessed 3 July 2015].

[32] *Dnevni Avaz*, Sarajevo, 22 April 2008, p. 8. See also *Oslobodjenje*, Sarajevo, 19 May 2008, p. 19.

[33] *Oslobodjenje*, Sarajevo, 23 April 2012, p. 7.

to name only two major hotels in the city, by now provided a level of accommodation much higher in standard to that on offer at the Holiday Inn). The hotel began to lose money. After much speculation that the Serbian businessman Miroslav Mišković (owner of Delta Holding) was to buy the Holiday Inn, a much publicised bid by the Serbian company MPC Holding (owned by the Belgrade-based businessman, Petar Matić), in partnership with the US investment bank Merrell Lynch, to buy the hotel appeared to represent the most favourable option.[34] Interested less in the hotel and more in the valuable land upon which the Holiday Inn was built, their plan was to knock down the existing building to build a new hotel complex with additional amenities. Staff, deeply concerned about the bid and what it meant for their livelihoods, threatened to strike. Even the hotel's architect, Ivan Štraus, entered the fray, expressing the hope that the hotel would survive. Speaking to *Slobodna Bosna*, he said the hotel 'is not my property, but [the building] is is my work'.[35] Commenting on the character of the sale the Bosnian daily *Dnevni avaz* described the Holiday Inn as 'a monument to unsuccessful privatisation' (Image 12.1).[36]

Image 12.1 Design for the much-lauded 'Grand Media Centre' that was never realised. (Photo: Kenneth Morrison)

[34] *Dani*, Sarajevo, 22 February 2008, p. 14.
[35] *Slobodna Bosna*, Sarajevo, 10 April 2008, p. 29.
[36] *Dnevni avaz*, Sarajevo, 23 April 2008, p. 8.

Moreover, the Holiday Inn was no longer the destination of choice for tourists who could now choose from larger international chain hotels or small boutique hotels nearer Baščaršija. And though the Marindvor area would later become revitalised, it not only came too late for the Holiday Inn, but also changed the character of the area to one focused on consumption (shopping). Thus, over the years, the Holiday Inn became heavily indebted, and, as a consequence, staff pension contributions remained unpaid and, at times, their salaries went unpaid for months on end, a state of affairs that was, ultimately, untenable.[37]

In February 2013, the hotel lost (or, rather, opted out of) the right to use the label 'Holiday Inn', after no agreement on franchising fees was reached between IHG and their Sarajevo franchise. Seeking to limit the reputational damage incurred by the loss of the Holiday Inn brand, the hotel's director, Senadin Fetahagić, told *Oslobodjenje* that the hotel would continue to 'give every guest quality, regardless of the name'.[38] Thus, in light of the failure to agree to new terms with IHG, the Holiday Inn then changed its name to the 'Olympic Hotel Holiday Sarajevo', though the use of the term 'Holiday' (and even in the case of the website domain name—www.holidaysarajevo.com) was the source of objection from IHG.[39] The hotel's management argued that the costs of maintaining the franchise agreement outweighed the benefits, and that they would, nevertheless, continue to maintain the standards that they had endeavoured to adhere to over the past thirty years and that, in any event, the Holiday Inn brand was 'not what it used to be' and thus not worthy of the expensive franchise fees.[40]

Thereafter, there was little improvement in the situation. Occupancy rates remained stubbornly low and later in 2013 the hotel was once again in the headlines for the wrong reasons. Two notorious underworld figures, Željko Lekić and Mensur Aljićević (known as 'Merso'), were arrested by the Bosnian police in the hotel on the basis of allegations that they had been using it to run an elite prostitution racket—that involved prostitutes

---

[37] *Oslobodjenje*, Sarajevo, 23 April 2012, p. 7.

[38] *Oslobodjenje*, Sarajevo, 27 February 2013, p. 6.

[39] For more on the IHG's objection to the use of the term 'Holiday' see World Intellectual Property Organization (WIPO), Arbitration and Mediation Centre: 'Administrative Panel Decision. Six Continents Hotels Inc. v Triptih d.o.o', Case No. D2012-1600, 12 October 2012.

[40] Klix.ba, 'Hotel Holiday Inn promijenio ime u Holiday', 26 February 2013, http://www.klix.ba/biznis/hotel-holiday-inn-promijenio-ime-u-holiday/130226069 [last accessed 1 June 2015].

visiting clients in their rooms at the hotel—alongside other criminal activities such as dealing in narcotics and stolen art. The investigative television programme *Mreža* (Network) reported that the hotel had been used by numerous members of the Bosnian underworld and would regularly host some of the most dangerous criminal elements in the country, such as Mersed Hadžić (also known as 'Mirso the Swiss').[41]

For staff there was constant flux and uncertainty. In February 2014 matters came to a head and workers again went on strike or 'a suspension of work', during which they staged a sit-in protest in the hotel's atrium. They were doing so because they had not received their salaries for several months and had not had their pension contributions paid for years. Their own protest had been eclipsed by the violent protests in Sarajevo and other Bosnian towns and cities during the same period, but the underlying dynamics that fuelled the protests throughout the country applied in the case of the hotel. But the citizens' *plenums* that emerged from the demonstrations argued that the privatisation of the Holiday Inn should be one of the cases reviewed.[42] The workers complained that the hotel management 'only occasionally' came to the hotel and that the staff feared what would happen once the manager, Senad Fetahagić, whose contract was due to expire on 30 June 2014, leaves. They requested that bankruptcy proceedings be launched against the hotel's owners.[43]

In April 2014, with the hotel seemingly doomed, it was then, rather unexpectedly, taken over by a Sarajevo-based businessman, Alen Čengić, the owner of the well-known *Park Prinčeva* restaurant (which boasts enviable views of Sarajevo), who claimed to have agreed to lease and manage the hotel from Jakob Kuess.[44] Though there remained ambiguity over the nature and legality of the deal Čengić had concluded with Kuess, the new

---

[41] See Mreža (Federalna televizija), 8 November 2013, www.federalna.ba/bhs/vijest/79961/08112013 [last accessed 2 May 2014].

[42] Balkan Insight, 19 February 2014, http://www.balkaninsight.com/en/article/bosnians-shape-up-demands-as-protests-continue [last accessed 23 June 2014]. For the function of the plenums and the issues upon which they focus see Damir Arsenijević, *Unbribable Bosnia & Herzegovina: The Fight for the Commons*, Baden-Baden: Nomos 2014.

[43] During a visit to the hotel in April 2014, the author discussed a number of issues with the workers staging a sit-in protest in the hotel's atrium. One recurring theme was the frustration with the owners and their apparent inability to address the problems. Some expressed hope that Alpha Baumanagement would do so, but there was an evident dejection and absolute loss of trust between the workers and the hotel's owners. Others expressed a sense of betrayal—that their work, in some cases three decades of work, was not fairly acknowledged.

[44] Osservatorio Balcani e Caucuso, 'The slow decay of the Holiday Inn', 11 March 2015, www.balcanicaucaso.org/eng/Regions-and-countries/Bosnia-Herzegovina/Sarajevo-the-slow-decay-of-the-Holiday-Inn-159953 [last accessed 2 June 2015].

management set about steadying the ship. By June 2014, by which time the hotel was being run by Čengić, who was the new 'general director' and was now known simply as the 'Hotel Holiday', Alpha Baumanagement had gone into liquidation and the hotel was left with outstanding debts of 2.5 million KM. Receivers were appointed thereafter. In an effort to cut costs, some staff became redundant, but those that remained were paid their backdated salaries. Utility debts (electricity, gas, and so forth) were also settled, the hotel's decaying atrium was transformed, and the new management announced that they intended to seek new partners, reverse the negative image that the hotel had acquired, and re-establish the 'Hotel Holiday' as one of Sarajevo's greatest hotels. Čengić went on a public relations offensive and in an interview for *Business Magazine* he conveyed his motivation for wanting to manage the hotel:

> I wanted to make a concrete contribution and help the city where I was born and in which I live. My purpose is to bring the Hotel Holiday, which is not only one of Sarajevo's top hotels but one synonymous with the Olympics and with one of the most beautiful periods in this city's history. I hope it will once again become a symbol of unity and multiculturalism in the city.[45]

'Nothing other than the hotel's name', he added, had changed, and 'the history, excellent location and identity of the hotel remains'.[46] Initially, all appeared well. Improvements made to the interior of the building brought guests back, and the hotel was occasionally at full to capacity (during the 2014 Sarajevo Film Festival, for example).[47] The hotel also held a large donor conference (to raise funds for reconstruction after the 2014 floods), partially organised by the Organization for Security and Co-operation in Europe (OSCE) and the United National Development Program (UNDP), and the 2015 'Sarajevo Business Forum'. The Oscar-winning Bosnian film director Danis Tanović filmed parts of a new film, entitled *Smrt u Sarajevu* (Death in Sarajevo) in the atrium of the hotel in June 2015. The hotel's staff, or those that were retained, praised Čengić for the changes that he made.[48] The receivers, tasked with enforcing the terms of the bankruptcy proceedings,

---

[45] *Business Magazone*, Tešanj, 12 May 2015, p. 12.
[46] *Ibid*, p. 12.
[47] *Slobodna Bosna*, Sarajevo, 11 September 2014, p. 21.
[48] Radio Slobodna Evropa, 'Radnici se pitaju: Kome smeta što je Holiday vračen u život', www.slobodnaevropa.org/content/radnici-se-pitaju-kome-smeta-sto-je-holiday-vracen-u-zivot/27080943.html [last accessed 12 July 2015].

claimed, however, that they experienced problems conducting their investigations. Matters came to a head on 15 June 2015 when the hotel was closed down by Bosnia's State Investigation and Protection Agency (SIPA) on the basis of an investigation by tax authorities, the Prosecutor's Office of the Sarajevo Canton, and by order of the Municipal Court of Sarajevo. Guests staying in the hotel at the time (around 150 of them) were instructed, bluntly, to find alternative accommodation.[49] Businesses that had rented out spaces in the hotel as premises were instructed to do likewise. The staff again staged a sit-in and two workers at the hotel, Vahid Alić and Adis Skorupan, who refused to leave the building, were arrested by police but later released.[50] After three days of barricading themselves inside the hotel, those staff still in the building, who had no access to water or food, left on their own initiative. The hotel was thereafter closed indefinitely and, according to *Slobodna Bosna*, legal proceedings began against Jakob Kuess and the former manager Senadin Fetahagić, for, allegedly, using a complex series of financial transactions (through a company called L.H. Investments) to systematically steal money from the hotel over several years.[51] The Sarajevo daily *Dnevni avaz* claimed that the new management was also being investigated for alleged tax evasion.[52]

At the time of the completion of the book in August 2015, the downward trajectory appeared inexorable. The hotel remained closed, a status seemingly irreversible. Sadly, the prospects for the staff, many of whom have worked there since the day the hotel opened its doors on 6 October 1983 in advance of the Sarajevo Winter Olympics and had worked throughout the siege for little or no pay, seemed equally so. They lamented the closure of the hotel and expressed hope that the situation could be resolved soon, though that seems unlikely.[53] Some, or at least those fortunate enough to find it, had already moved on to other employment. Thus two decades

---

[49] *Slobodna Bosna*, Sarajevo, 29 June 2015, www.slobodna-bosna.ba/vijest/22295/hotel_holiday_kriminal_sa_medjunarodnim_predznakom.html [last accessed 3 July 2015].

[50] Klix, 'Radnici hotela Holiday Vahid Alić i Adis Skorupan pušteni na slobodu', www.klix.ba/vijesti/bih/radnici-hotela-holiday-vahid-alic-i-adis-skorupan-pusteni-na-slobodu/150725064 [last accessed 4 July 2015].

[51] *Slobodna Bosna*, Sarajevo, 29 June 2015, www.slobodna-bosna.ba/vijest/22295/hotel_holiday_kriminal_sa_medjunarodnim_predznakom.html [last accessed 3 July 2015].

[52] *Dnevni avaz*, Sarajevo, 16 June 2015, p. 10.

[53] Radio Slobodna Evropa, 'Radnici se pitaju: Kome smeta što je Holiday vraćen u život', www.slobodnaevropa.org/content/radnici-se-pitaju-kome-smeta-sto-je-holiday-vracen-u-zivot/27080943.html [last accessed 12 July 2015].

after the end of the Bosnian War, and having survived the siege of the city it seemed that Sarajevo's frontline hotel, a building that played a significant role in the city's modern history, could survive the shells and the sniping but could not survive the shady privatisation process, corruption, and mismanagement that heralded its demise. One can only hope that it does survive and overcome yet another major obstacle in its remarkable thirty-two-year history, and, moreover, that Ivan Štraus's design (whether the building remains a hotel or otherwise) can be preserved. If the hotel was to close permanently and the building destroyed, however, Sarajevo will have lost one of its most important symbols. And that, regardless of the nature of the events that have led to its demise, is lamentable.

References

Arsenijević, D. (2014). *Unbribable Bosnia & Herzegovina: The Fight for the Commons*. Baden-Baden: Nomos.

Ashdown, P. (2008). *Swords and Ploughshares: Building Peace in the 21st Century*. London: Pheonix Press.

Badsey, S. (2000). *The Media and International Security*. London: Frank Cass Publishers.

Bougarel, X. (2007). Urban exile: Locals, newcomers and the transformation of Sarajevo. In X. Bougarel, E. Helms, & G. Duijzings (Eds.), *The New Bosnian Mosaic* (pp. 72–73). Aldershot: Ashgate Publishing.

Death of Yugoslavia Archive, Transcript of interview with General Lewis MacKenzie, UBIT, 1995.

Donais, T. (2002). The politics of privatization in post-dayton Bosnia. *Southeast European Politics, III*(1), 3–19.

International Crisis Group (ICG). (1997). Media in Bosnia and Herzegovina: How international suport can be more effective, ICG Bosnia Report No. 21.

International Crisis Group (ICG). (1999). Why will no one invest in Bosnia and Herzegovina?, ICG Balkans Report No. 64.

McCormick, N. (2008). *U2 by U2*. London: HarperCollins Entertainment.

Nicholson, M. (1993). *Natasha's Story*. London: Macmillan.

Potter, J. (1996). *World of Difference: 50 Years of Intercontinental Hotels and Its People*. London: Weidenfeld Nicholson.

REFERENCES

Abraham, A. J. (1996). *The Lebanon War*. Westport: Praeger Publishers.
Aburish, S. (1989). *Beirut Spy: International Intrigue at the St. George Hotel Bar*. London: Bloomsbury Press.
Adie, K. (2002). *The Kindness of Strangers: The Autobiography*. London: Headline Books.
Ahrens, G. H. (2008). *Diplomacy on the Edge: Containment of Ethnic Conflict and the Minorities Working Group of the Conferences on Yugoslavia*. Washington: Wilson Centre Press.
Ajnadžić, N. (2002). *Odbrana Sarajeva*. Sarajevo: Sedam.
Akhavan, P. (Ed.) (1995). *Yugoslavia: The Former and the Future—Reflections by Scholars from the Region*, Geneva: The Brookings Institute, Washington, and the United Nations Research Institute for Social Development.
Alić, D., & Gusheh, M. (1999). Reconciling nationalist narratives in socialist Bosnia & Herzegovina: The Baščaršija Project, 1948–1953. *Journal of the Society of Architectural Historians, 58*(1), 6–25.
Alispahić, N. (2010). *Priče o Sarajevo*, Sarajevo.
Allcock, J. B. (2000). *Explaining Yugoslavia*. London: Hurst & Co..
Andjelić, N. (2003). *Bosnia-Herzegovina: The End of a Legacy*. London: Frank Cass.
Anderson, S. (1999). *The Man Who Tried to Save the World: The Dangerous Life and Mysterious Disappearance of Fed Cuny*. New York: Doubleday.
Andreas, P. (2004). The clandestine political economy of war and peace in Bosnia. *International Studies Quarterly, 48*, 29–51.
Andreas, P. (2008). *Blue Helmets and Black Markets: The Business of Survival in the Siege of Sarajevo*. Ithica and London: Cornell University Press.
Andreas, P. (2010). The Longest Siege: Humanitarians and Profiteers in the Battle for Sarajevo. In W. Benedik et al. (Eds.), *Transnational Terrorism,*

Organized Crime and Peace Building: Human Security in the Western Balkans (pp. 169–189). New York: Palgrave MacMillan.

Andrijašević , Ž. (1999). *Nacrt za ideologiju jedne vlasti*. Bar: Conteco.

Arhitektonski Fakultet u Sarajevo/Sarajevo Green Design (2011). *Arhitekt Ivan Štraus*. Sarajevo: Sarajevo Green Design.

Arnautović, S. (1996). *Izbori u Bosni i Hercegovini '90: Analaiza izborni procesa*. Sarajevo: Promocult.

Arnett, P. (1994). *Live from the Battlefield*. New York: Touchstone.

Arsenijević, D. (2010). *Forgotten Future: The Politics of Poetry in Bosnia & Herzegovina*. Baden-Baden: Nomos.

Arsenijević, D. (2014). *Unbribable Bosnia & Herzegovina: The Fight for the Commons*. Baden-Baden: Nomos.

Ashdown, P. (2000). *The Ashdown Diaries: Volume One, 1988–1997*. London: Allen Lane.

Ashdown, P. (2008). *Swords and Ploughshares: Building Peace in the 21st Century*. London: Pheonix Press.

Avdić, S. (2008). Karadžićev obavještajni stožer. *Slobodna Bosna*, 18–21.

Bačanović, V. (2011). Strategija istrebljenja. *Dani*, Sarajevo 30–31.

Badsey, S. (2000). *The Media and International Security*. London: Frank Cass Publishers.

Bakšić, H. (1997). *Sarajevo više nema*. Sarajevo: Oslobodjenje.

Banac, I. (1984). *The National Question in Yugoslavia; Origins, History, Politics*. Ithica and London: Cornell University Press.

Banac (1987). *With Stalin Against Tito: Cominformist Splits in Yugoslav Communism*. Ithica and London: Cornell University Press.

Bećirević, E. (2009). *Na Drini genocid: istraživanje organiziranog zločina u istočnoj Bosni*. Sarajevo: Buybook.

Bell, M. (1996). *In Harm's Way: Bosnia: A War Reporter's Story*. London: Penguin.

Benedek, W., et al. (2010). *Transnational Terrorism, Organized Crime and Peace Building: Human Security in the Western Balkans*. London: Palgrave MacMillan.

Bennett, C. (1995). *Yugoslavia's Bloody Collapse*. London: Hurst & Co..

Bennett, C. (2015). *Bosnia's Paralysed Peace*. London: Hurst & Co..

Berić, G. (1994). *Sarajevo: Na kraju svijeta*. Sarajevo: Oslobodjenje.

Bojić, M. (2001). *Historija Bosne i Bošnjaka (VII–XX vijek)*. Sarajevo: TKD Šahinpašić.

Boano, C., & Chabarek, D. Memories of War in the Divided City, Open Security, 18 April 2013, retrieved June 17, 2014 from https://www.opendemocracy.net/opensecurity/camillo-boano-dalia-chabarek/memories-of-war-in-divided-city.

Bogdanović, B. Murder of the City, *New York Review of Books*, 27 May 1993.

Bogdanović, B. (2001). *Glib i krv*. Beograd: Zagorac.

Bose, S. (2002). *Bosnia after Dayton: Nationalist Partition and International Intervention*. London: Hurst & Co.
Bougarel, X. (2003). Bosnian Muslims and the Yugoslav Idea. In D. Djokić (Ed.), *Yugoslavism: Histories of a Failed Idea*. London: Hurst & Co.
Bougarel, X. (1996). Bosnia and Hercegovina—State and Communitarianism. In D. A. Dyker, & I. Vejvoda (Eds.), *Yugoslavia and After: A Study in Fragmentation, Despair and Rebirth*. London: Pearson Education.
Bougarel, X. (2007). Urban Exile: Locals, Newcomers and the Transformation of Sarajevo. In X. Bougarel, E. Helms, & G. Duijzings (Eds.), *The New Bosnian Mosaic* (pp. 72–73). Aldershot: Ashgate Publishing.
Bowen, J. (2006). *War Stories*. London: Simon & Schuster.
Bowman, T. (2007). *Carson's Army: The Ulster Volunteer Force, 1910–1922*. Manchester: Manchester University Press.
Bowyer Bell, J. (1997). *The Secret Army: The IRA*. New Jersey: Transaction Publishers.
Bringa, T. (1995). *Being Muslim the Bosnian Way: Identity and Community in a Central Bosnian Village*. New Jersey: Princeton University Press.
Brock, P., & Binder, D. (2006). *Media Cleansing, Dirty Reporting: Journalism and Tragedy in Yugoslavia*. Los Angeles: GM Books.
Bruce, S. (1989). *God Save Ulster! Religion and Politics of Paisleyism*. Oxford: Oxford University Press.
Bruce, S. (1992). *The Red Hand: Protestant Paramilitaries in Northern Ireland*. Oxford: Oxford University Press.
Bulatović, L. (Ed.) (2002). *Radovan*. Belgrade: EVRO.
Burić, A. (2008). Casablanca pored snajperske raskrsnice. *Dani* (specialno izdanje), Sarajevo.
Burg, S. L., & Shoup, P. (2000). *The War in Bosnia-Herzegovina: Ethnic Conflict and International Intervention*. New York: M.E. Sharpe.
Burns, J. F. (2010). Neutrality isn't the same as being fair. *The British Journalism Review*, London, 21(3), 27–31.
Buturović, A. (2005). Godišnjica prvog zasejdanja Karadžićevih Srba. *Slobodna Bosna*, 22–25.
Calame, J., & Charlesworth, E. (2009). *Divided Cities: Belfast, Beirut, Jerusalem, Mostar and Nicosia*. Pennsylvania: University of Pennsylvania Press.
Calhoun, C. (2010). The Idea of Emergency: Humanitarian Action and Global (Dis) Order. In D. Fassin, & M. Pandolfi (Eds.), *Contemporary States of Emergency: The Politics of Military and Humanitarian Interventions*. New York: Zone.
Campbell, D. (1999). Apartheid cartography: The political anthropology and spatial effects of international diplomacy in Bosnia. *Political Geography*, 18(4), 395–435.
Carter, B. (2005). *Fools Rush In*. London: Corgi Books.

Central Intelligence Agency (CIA). Directorate of Intelligence, *Yugoslavia: Key Questions and Answers on the Debt Crisis: An Intelligence Assessment*, Document No. (FOIA)/ESDN (CREST): 0005361799.
Central Intelligence Agency (CIA). CIA Directorate of Intelligence Memorandum: Bosnia & Herzegovina on the Edge of the Abyss, 19 December 1991, Document No. (FOIA)/ESDN (CREST): 5235e50c9329405d174d7.
Central Intelligence Agency (CIA). Letter: Karadžić to President Clinton Accepting the Dayton Agreement, 02 December 1995, Document No. (FOIA)/ESDN (CREST): 5235e00d935294098d5174.
Central Intelligence Agency (CIA). Intelligence Report, DCI Interagency Balkan Task Force, *Bosnia & Croatia: The Costs of Reconstruction*, 20 November 1995, Document No. (FOIA)/ESDN (CREST): 5235e00d93294098d517537.
Central Intelligence Agency (CIA). Intelligence Report, DCI Interagency Balkan Task Force, *Sarajevo: Serbs More Likely to Flee Than Fight*, 17 December 1995, Document No. (FOIA)/ESDN (CREST): 5235e50c99324093d517406.
Cobban, H. (1985). *The Making of Modern Lebanon*. London and New York: Hutchinson.
Cohen, L. J., & Dragović-Soso, J. (2008). *State Collapse in South-Eastern Europe: New Perspectives on Yugoslavia's Disintegration*. West Lafayette, Indiana: Purdue University Press.
Cohen, L. J., & Lampe, J. R. (2011). *Embracing Democracy in the Western Balkans: From Postconflict Struggles toward European Integration*. Washington D.C.: Woodrow Wilson Center Press Baltimore: John Hopkins University Press.
Cohen, R. (1998). *Hearts Grown Brutal: Sagas of Sarajevo*. New York: Random House.
Collings, A. (2010). *Capturing the News: Three Decades of Reporting Crisis and Conflict*. University of Missouri Press.
Cooper, A. (2006). *Dispatches from the Edge*. New York: Harper Collins.
Coward, M. (2009). *Urbicide: The Politics of Urban Destruction*. New York: Routledge.
Craggs, R. (2012). Towards a political geography of hotels: Southern Rhodesia, 1958–1962. *Political Geography, 31*, 215–224.
Crnobrnja, M. (1996). *The Yugoslav Drama*. London: IB Tauris.
CSCE. (1992). The Referendum on Independence in Bosnia-Herzegovina, February 29–March 1, 1992, CSCE report.
Čaušević, S., & Lynch, P. (2013). Political (in)stability and its influence on tourism development. *Tourism Management, 34*, 145–157.
Čekić, S. (2005). *The Aggression against the Republic of Bosnia & Herzegovina: Planning, Preparation, Execution (Book One)*. Sarajevo: Institute for the Research of Crimes Against Humanity and International Law.
Čekić, S. (2005). *The Aggression against the Republic of Bosnia & Herzegovina: Planning, Preparation, Execution (Book Two)*. Sarajevo: Institute for the Research of Crimes Against Humanity and International Law.

Čolović, I. (2002). *The Politics of Symbol in Serbia*. London: Hurst & Co.
Daadler, I. (2000). *Getting to Dayton*. Washington: Brookings Institute.
Dallaire, R. (2004). *Shake Hands with the Devil: The failure of Humanity in Rwanda*. London: Arrow Books.
Death of Yugoslavia Archive, Transcript of interview with Radovan Karadžić (SDS), UBIT 177, 1996.
Death of Yugoslavia Archive, Transcript of interview with Momčilo Krajišnik (SDS), UBIT 050, 1996.
Death of Yugoslavia Archive, Transcript of interview with Milutin Kukanjac (JNA), UBIT 166 (2), 1996.
Death of Yugoslavia Archive, Transcript of interview with General Lewis MacKenzie, UBIT, 1995.
Demetriou, O. (2012). The militarization of opulence: Engendering a conflict heritage site. *International Feminist Journal of Politics*, 1(14), 56–77.
Demick, B. (2012). *Besieged: Life Under Fire on a Sarajevo Street*. London: Granta.
Didion, J. (1982a). In El Salvador. *The New York Review of Books*.
Didion, J. (1982b). In El Salvador: Soluciones. *The New York Review of Books*.
Didion, J. (2006). *Salvador*. London: Granta Books.
Di Giovanni, J. (1993). *All Systeme D at the Holiday Inn*. London: The Spectator.
Di Giovanni, J. (1994). *The Quick and the Dead: Under Siege in Sarajevo*. London: Phoenix House.
Di Giovanni, J. (2004). *Madness Visible: A Memoir of War*. London: Bloomsbury.
Dillon, M. (2003). The Europa hotel: A symbol. *The European Magazine*, London, 66–70.
Dizdarević, Z. (1994). *Sarajevo: A War Journal*. New York: Fromm International.
Djokić, D., & Ker-Lindsay, J. (2011). *New Perspectives on Yugoslavia: Key Issues and Controversies*. New York & London: Routledge.
Donia, R. J., & John, V. A. (1994). *Fine, Bosnia-Herzegovina: A Tradition Betrayed*. London: Hurst & Co..
Donia, R. J. (1981). *Islam under the double-headed eagle: The muslims of Bosnia and Hercegovina 1878–1914*. Boulder: Eastern European Monographs.
Donia, R. J., & Fine, J. (1994). *Bosnia & Herzegovina: A Tradition Betrayed*. London: Hurst & Co..
Donia, R. J. (2006). *Sarajevo: A Biography*. London: Hurst & Co..
Donia, R. (2012). *Iz Skupštine Republike Srpske 1991–1996: Izvodi iz izlaganja poslanika skupštine Republike Srpske kao dokazni material ns medjunarodnom krivičnom tribunal u Hagu*. Sarajevo: University Press.
Donia, R. J. (2015). *Radovan Karadžić: Architect of the Bosnian Genocide*. Cambridge: Cambridge University Press.
Donais, T. (2002). The politics of privatization in post-dayton Bosnia. *Southeast European Politics*, III(1), 3–19.

Dragović-Soso, J. (2002). *Saviours of the Nation: Serbia's Intellectual Opposition and the Revival of Nationalism.* London: Hurst & Co..

Bezrob, D. P., & Marie, A. (2004). *Sarajevo Roses: War Memoir of a Peacekeeper.* Paarl: Oshun Books.

Dyker, D. A., & Vejvoda, I. (1996). *Yugoslavia and After: A Study in Fragmentation, Despair and Rebirth.* London: Pearson Education.

Efendić, H. (1999). *Ko je branio Bosnu.* Sarajevo: Udruženje gradjana plemićkog porijekla BiH.

Fazlić, M. (2014). Pri(h)vatizacija Holiday Inna: Plajačka stoljeća. *Slobodna Bosna*, Sarajevo, 32–34.

Fialka, J. J. (1992). *Hotel Warriors: Covering the Gulf War.* Washington DC: Woodrow Wilson Center.

Fisk, R. (2002). *Pity the Nation: The Abduction of Lebanon* (4th ed.). New York: Nation Books.

Frei, M. (1993). *The Mafia Move In.* London: The Spectator.

Franklin, S. (2007). *Hotel Afrique.* London: Dewi Lewis Publishing.

Fregonese, S. (2008). The urbicide of Beirut? Geopolitics and the built environment in the Lebanese Civil War (1975–1976). *Political Geography*, *28*, 309–318.

Fregonese, S. (2012). Between a refuge and a battleground: Beirut's discrepant cosmopolitanisms. *The Geographical Review*, *102*(3), 316–336.

Fregonese, S., & Ramadan, A. (2015). Hotel Geopolitics: a research agenda. *Geopolitics*, *20*(4), 793–813.

Friedman, F. (2000). The muslim slavs of Bosnia and Herzegovina (with reference to the Sandžak of Novi Pazar): Islam as national identity. *Nationalities Papers*, *28*(1), 165–180.

Friedman, T. (1995). *From Beirut to Jerusalem.* New York: Doubleday.

Ganić, E. (2007). *Razgovori i svjedočenja 1990–1994.* Sarajevo: Svijetlost.

Garcia, S., & Kotzen, B. (2014). Re-constructing Sarajevo: Negotiating sociopolitical complexity, LSE Cities/The Ove Arp Foundation.

Gjelten, T. (1995). *Sarajevo Daily: A City and Its Newspaper Under Siege.* New York: HarperCollins.

Glenny, M. (1992). Yugoslavia: The Revenger's Tragedy, *The New York Review of Books.*

Glenny, M. (1993a). What Is To Be Done? *The New York Review of Books.*

Glenny, M. (1993b). Bosnia: The Tragic Prospect. *The New York Review of Books.*

Glenny, M. (1996). *The Fall of Yugoslavia* (3rd ed.). London: Penguin.

Glenny, M. (1999). *The Balkans 1804–1999.* London: Granta Books.

Gow, J. (2003). *The Serbian Project and Its Adversaries.* London: Hurst & Co.

Goytisolo, J. (2001). *Landscapes of War: From Sarajevo to Chechnya.* Oregon: City Lights Books.

Grandits, H., & Leutloff, C. (2003). Discourses, actors, violence: The organisation of war-escalation in the Krajina region of Croatia, 1990–1991. In J. Koehler, & C. Zürcher (Eds.), *Potentials of Disorder* (pp. 23–45). Manchester and New York: Manchester University Press.

Grandits, H., & Taylor, K. (Eds.) (2010). *Yugoslavia's Sunny Side: A History of Tourism in Socialism (1950s–1980s)*. Budapest: Central European University Press.

Grant, T. (Ed.) (2005). *From Our Own Correspondent: A Celebration of Fifty Years of the BBC Radio Programme*. London: Profile Books.

Grayson, R. S. (2009). *Belfast Boys: How Unionists and Nationalists Fought and Died Together in the First World War*. London: Continuum.

Greble, E. (2011). *Sarajevo, 1941–1945: Muslims, Christians and Jews in Hitler's Europe*. Ithica and London: Cornell University Press.

Grebo, K. (1998). *Privreda u opkoljenom Sarajevu*. Sarajevo: OKO.

Greene, G. (1966). *The Comedians*. London: The Bodley Head.

Grozdanić, S. (1995). *Bosna nije san*. Sarajevo: Svijetlost.

Gül, M., & Dee, J. (2015). Sarajevo—A city profile. *Cities*, *43*, 152–166.

Hadžić, K. (1998). *Sarajevo '94*. Sarajevo: Medjunarodni centar za mir.

Hadžihasanović, A. (2010). *1984: Olimpijada trijumfa i šansi*. Sarajevo: Rabic.

Hadžifejzović, S. (2002). *Rat užvo: Ratni teevizijski dnevnik*. Mladinska Kniga: Ljubljana.

Hadjithomas, M. T. (2012). *Le Phoenicia, un hôotel dans l'Histoire*. Beirut: Tamyras.

Hammond, P. (2007). *Media, War and Postmodernity*. New York: Routledge.

Harris, P. (2009). *More Thrills than Skills: Adventures in Journalism, War and Terrorism*. Glasgow: Kennedy & Boyd.

Harris, R. (2006). *Dubrovnik: A History*. London: Saqi Books.

Haugbolle, S. (2010). *War and Memory in Lebanon*. Cambridge: Cambridge University Press.

Hawton, N. (2009). *The Quest for Radovan Karadžić*. London: Hutchinson.

Helsinški odbor za ljudska prava u Srbiji (2004). *Izbeglice—žrtve etničkog inženinga*. Svedočanstva Br. 21, Knjiga 1, Beograd: Zagorac.

Helsinški odbor za ljudska prava u Srbiji (2006). *Kovane antijugoslovenske zavere*. Svedočanstva Br. 26, Knjiga 1, Beograd: Zagorac.

Helsinški odbor za ljudska prava u Srbiji (2006). *Jezgro velikosrpskog projekta*. Svedočanstva Br. 27, Beograd: Zagorac.

Henn, F. (2004). *A Business of Some Heat: The United Nations Force in Cyprus Before and During the 1974 Turkish Invasion*. Barnsley: Pen and Sword Military.

Hewitt, D. M. (1998). *From Ottawa to Sarajevo: Canadian Peacekeepers in the Balkans*, Martello Papers No. 8, Centre for International Relations, Queens University, Kingston, Ontario, Canada.

Hiro, D. (1993). *Lebanon, Fire and Embers: A History of the Lebanese Civil War.* London: Weidenfeld and Nicolson.
Hirst, D. (2010). *Beware of Small States: Lebanon, Battleground of the Middle East.* New York: Nation Books.
Hitchens, C. (2010). *Hitch-22: A Memoir.* London: Atlantic Book.
Hoare, M. A. (2004). *How Bosnia Armed.* London: Saqi Books.
Hoare, M. A. (2007). *The History of Bosnia.* London: Saqi Books.
Holbrooke, R. (1998). *To End a War.* New York: Random House.
Hollingworth, L. (2006). *Merry Christmas, Mr Larry.* London: William Heinemann Ltd.
Imamović, M. (1976). *Pravni položaj i unutrašnji politički razvitak Bosne i Herzegovina 1878 do 1914.* Sarajevo: Svijetlost.
Inalcik, H. (1973). *The Ottoman Empire: The Classical Age, 1300–1600*, trans. Praeger, New York and Washington: Norman Itzkowitz and Colin Imber.
Inalcik, H., & Donald, Q. (eds.) (1994). *An Economic and Social History of the Ottoman Empire, 1300–1914*, CUP.
Ingrao, C., & Emmert, T. (Eds.) (2013). *Confronting the Yugoslav Controversies: A Scholars' Initiative* (2nd ed.). West Lafayette, Indiana: Purdue University Press.
International Crisis Group (ICG). (1997). Media in Bosnia and Herzegovina: How international suport can be more effective, ICG Bosnia Report No. 21.
International Crisis Group (ICG). (1999). Why will no one invest in Bosnia and Herzegovina?, ICG Balkans Report No. 64.
Izetbegović, A. (2003). *Inescapable Questions: Autobiographical Notes* (pp. 66–74). Leicester: The Islamic Foundation.
Jameson, L. (2010). The changing face of hotel security, *Hotel Industry Magazine.*
Jergović, M. (1997). *Sarajevo Marlboro.* London: Penguin Books.
Jestrović, S. (2013). *Performances, Space, Utopia: Cities of War, Cities of Exile.* Basingstoke: Palgrave MacMillan.
Jović, B. (1996). *Poslednji dani SFRJ.* Beograd: Prizma.
Jović, D. (2001). The disintegration of Yugoslavia: A critical review of explanatory approaches. *European Journal of Social Theory*, 4(1), 101–120.
Jović, D. (2009). *Yugoslavia: A State that Withered Away.* West Lafayette, Indiana: Purdue University Press.
Jovičić, M. (2011). *Two Days Till Peace: A Sarajevo Airport Story.* Bloomington: Author House.
Judah, T. (2009). *The Serbs: History, Myth and the Destruction of Yugoslavia* (3rd ed.). New Haven: Yale University Press.
Jukić, I. (1974). *The Fall of Yugoslavia.* New York and London: Harcourt Brace Jovanovich.
Kalyvas, S. N. (2004). The urban bias in research on civil wars. *Security Studies*, 13(3), 160–190.
Kapić, S. (2000). *The Siege of Sarajevo: 1992–1996.* Sarajevo: FAMA.

Kapuscinski, R. (2007). *The Soccer War* (3rd ed.). London: Granta.
Karup-Druško, Dženana, 'Rat nije počeo u Sarajevu', *Dani*, Sarajevo, 12 March 2010, pp. 39-41.
Karahasan, D. (1994). *Sarajevo, Exodus of a City*. Tokyo & London: Kodansha International.
Kassir, S. (2010). *Beirut*. Berkeley: University of California Press.
Kecmanović, D. (2002). *Ethnic Times: Exploring Ethno-nationalism in the Former Yugoslavia*. London: Praeger.
Keen, D. (1998). *The Economic Functions of Violence in Civil Wars*. London: International Institute for Strategic Studies.
Keshishian, K. K. (1990). *Nicosia: Capital of Cyprus Then and Now*. Nicosia: The Moufflon Book and Art Centre.
Khalaf, S. (2002). *Civil and Uncivil Violence in Lebanon: A History of the Internationalization of Communal Conflict*. New York: Columbia University Press.
Khalaf, S. (2006). *Heart of Beirut: Reclaiming the Bourj*. London: Saqi Books.
Khazen, F. E. (2000). *The Breakdown of the State in Lebanon 1967-1976*. London: IB Tauris.
Knightley, P. (2003). *The First Casualty of War: The War Correspondent as Hero, Propagandist and Myth Maker from Crimea to the Gulf War II* (3rd ed.). London: Carlton Books.
Kobašić, A., et al. (1997). *100 godina suvremenog hotelijerstva u Dubrovniku*, Dubrovnik.
Koštović, N. (1998). *Srajevo između dobrotvorstva i zla*, Rijaset Islamske zajednice i Mladi Muslimani 39, Sarajevo.
Kreševljaković, M. (Ed.) (1998). *I oni brane Sarajevo*. Sarajevo: Zlatni ljiljani.
Kulić, V., et al. (2013). *Modernism In-Between: The Mediatory Architectures of Socialist Yugoslavia*. Zagreb & Vienna: Jovis.
Kurspahić, K. (1997). *As Long as Sarajevo Exists*. Connecticut: The Pamphleteers Press.
Laffin, J. (1985). *The War of Desperation: Lebanon 1982-1985*. London: Osprey Press.
Lampe John, R. (2005). *Balkans into Southeastern Europe: A Century of War and Transition*. London: Palgrave Macmillan.
Lampe, J. R. (2000). *Yugoslavia as History: Twice there was a Country* (2nd ed.). Cambridge: Cambridge University Press.
Le Bor, A. (2006). *'Complicity with Evil': The United Nations in the Age of Modern Genocide*. New Haven and London: Yale University Press.
Brigette, L. N. (2014). *Designing Tito's Capital: Urban Planning, Modernism, and Socialism in Belgrade*. Pittsburgh: University of Pttsburgh Press.
Levander, C. F., & Guterl, M. P. (2015). *Hotel Life: The Story of a Place Where Anything Can Happen*. Chappel Hill: University of North Carolina Press.
Lisle, D. (2013). Frontline leisure: Securitizing tourism in the war on Terror. *Security Dialogue, 44*(2), 127-146.

Little, A., & Sibler, L. (1997). *The Death of Yugoslavia*. London: Penguin Books.
Lodge, R. (1992). *Changing Guard at the Holiday Inn*. London: The Spectator.
Lowe, P. (2014). *The Siege of Sarajevo*. Sarajevo: Galerija 11/07/95.
Lowe, Paul, 'Portfolio: The Siege of Sarajevo', *Photography and Culture*, Volume 8, Issue 1, 2015, pp. 135-142.
Loyd, A. (1999). *My War Gone By, I Miss It So*. London: Random House.
Lucianović, L. (2008). *Dubrovačke plaže—nekad*. Dubrovnik: Alfa 2 Press.
Lučarević, K. (2000). *The Battle for Sarajevo: Sentenced to Victory*. Sarajevo: TZU.
Lyon, J. (2014). Habsburg Sarajevo 1914: A social picture, *Prilozi/Contributions*, Institut za istoriju u Sarajevu, 43, Sarajevo, 23–40.
Maček, I. (2009). *Sarajevo Under Siege: Anthropology in Wartime*. Philadelphia: University of Pennsylvania Press.
Maass, P. (1996). *Love Thy Neighbour: A Story of War*. London: Papermac.
MacKenzie, L. (1993). *Peacekeeper: The Road to Sarajevo*. Vancouver/Toronto: Douglas & McIntyre.
MacKenzie, L. (2009). Canada's army—Post peacekeeping. *The Canadian Journal of Military and Strategic Studies*, 12(1).
Magaš, B. (1993). *The Destruction of Yugoslavia*. London: Verso Press.
Magaš, B., & Žanić, I. (Eds.) (2001). *The War in Croatia and Bosnia-Herzegovina 1991–1995*. London: Frank Cass.
Mahmutćehajić, R. (2000). *Bosnia the Good: Tolerance and Tradition*. Budapest and New York: Central European University Press.
Malcolm, N. (1994). *Bosnia: A Short History*. London: MacMillan Press.
Manević, Z., et al. (1986). *Arhitektura XX vijeka*. Beograd: Prosveta.
Marchand, P. M. (1997). *Sympathie pour le diable*. Outremont: Lancot.
Markowitz, F. (2010). *Sarajevo: A Bosnian kaleidoscope*. Chicago: University of Illinois Press.
Mazzeo, T. J. (2014). *The Hotel on Place Vendome: Life, Death and Betrayal at the Hotel Ritz in Paris*. New York: HarperCollins.
McCormick, N. (2008). *U2 by U2*. London: HarperCollins Entertainment.
McGurn, W. (1998). Putting on the Rex. *American Spectator*, 31(2).
McNeill, D. (2008). The hotel and the city. *Progress in Human Geography*, 32(3), 383–398.
McSmith, A. (2010). *No Such Thing as Society: A History of Britain in the 1980s*. London: Constable Press.
McAllister, M. (2011). *Eating Mud Crabs in Kandahar: Stories of Food During Wartime by the World's Leading Correspondents*. California: University of California Press.
Mišina, D. (2013). *Shake, Rattle and Roll: Yugoslav Rock Music and the Poetics of Social Critique*. Farnham: Ashgate Press.
Moll, N. (2014). An integrative symbol for a divided country? Commemorating the 1984 Sarajevo winter Olympics in Bosnia and Herzegovina from the 1995 war until today. *Croatian Political Science Review*, 1(5), 127–156.

Morgan, T. (2010). *A Sweet and Bitter Island: A History of the British in Cyprus*. London: IB Tauris.
Morrison, K. (2010). The State-Criminal Symbiosis in the Yugoslav Wars of Succession. In A. Colas, & B. Mabee (Eds.), *Mercenaries, Pirates, Bandits and Empires: Private Violence in Historical Context*. London: Hurst & Co.
Morrison, K., & Roberts, E. R. (2013). *The Sandžak: A History*. London: Hurst & Co..
Myers, G. (1996). The inscription of difference: News coverage of the conflicts in Rwanda and Bosnia. *Political Geography, 15*(1), 21–46.
Nagel, C. (2002). Reconstructing space, re-creating memory: Sectarian politics and urban development in post-war Beirut. *Political Geography, 21*, 717–725.
Neidhardt, T. (2004). *Sarajevo Through Time*. Sarajevo: Bosanska Riječ.
Neill, W. J. V., et al. (1995). *Reimagining the Pariah City: Urban Development in Belfast and Detroit*. Aldershot: Avebury.
Neuffer, E. (2002). *The Key to my Neighbour's House: Seeking Justice in Bosnia and Rwanda*. London: Bloomsbury Press.
Nicholson, M. (1993). *Natasha's Story*. London: Macmillan.
Nicholson, M. (2012). *A State of War Exits: Reporters in the Line of Fire*. London: Biteback.
Northedge, R. (2007). *Half a Million Rooms to Choose From*. London: The Spectator.
Organizacionog komiteta XIV zimskih olimpijskih igara Sarajevo (1984). *Završni izvještaj—Organizacionog komiteta XIV zimskih olimpijskih igara Sarajevo, 1984*. Sarajevo: Oslobodjenje.
Owen, D. (1995). *Balkan Odyssey*. London: Victor Gollancz.
Owen, D. (Ed.) (2013). *Bosnia-Herzegovina: The Vance/Owen Peace Plan*. Liverpool: Liverpool University Press.
Owen, J. (Ed.) (2009). *International News Reporting: Frontlines and Deadlines*. Chichester: Wiley-Blackwell.
O'Ballance, E. (1998). *The Civil War in Lebanon, 1975–1992*. London: MacMillan Press.
O'Connor, R. (1998). Old name returns to peaceful Sarajevo. *Hotel and Hotel Management, 10*(213).
O'Rourke, P. J. (1988). *Holidays in Hell*. New York: The Atlantic Monthly Press.
Palavestra, V. (2003). *Legends of Old Sarajevo*. Zemum: Most Art.
Pavlović, S. (2005). Reckoning: The Siege of Dubrovnik and the consequences of the 'War for Peace'. *Spaces of Identity, 5*, 1–47.
Pavlović, S., & Živković, M. (Eds.) (2013). *Transcending Fratricide: Political Mythologies, Reconciliations, and the Uncertain Future in the Former Yugoslavia*. Baden-Baden: Nomos.
Pećanin, S. (2007). *Skandirao sam: Bosna, Bosna!* Sarajevo: Dani.
Pedelty, M. (1995). *War Stories: The Culture of Foreign Correspondents*. Abingdon: Routledge.

Pejić, M. (2008). *HVO Sarajevo*. Sarajevo: Libertas.
Petrović, R., & Blagojević, M. (1992). *The Migration of Serbs and Montenegrins from Kosovo and Metohija*: Results of the Survey Conducted in 1985–1986, Serbian Academy of Arts and Sciences (SANU), Demographic Studies, Volume III, Belgrade, (English translation).
Pettifer, J. (2005). *Kosova Express: A Journey in Wartime*. London: Hurst & Co..
Pilav, A. (2012). Before the war, war, after the war: Urban imageries for urban resilience. *International Journal of Disaster Risk Science*, 3(1), 23–37.
Pinson, M. (1993). The The Muslims of Bosnia-Herzegovina: Their Historic Development from the Middle Ages to the Dissolution of Yugoslavia, Harvard University Press.
Plavšić, B. (2005). *Svedočim: Knjiga pisana u zatvoru*. Banja Luka: Trioprint.
Potter, J. (1996). *World of Difference: 50 Years of Intercontinental Hotels and Its People*. London: Weidenfeld Nicholson.
Prstojević, M. (1992). *Zaboravljeno Sarajevo*. Sarajevo: Ideja.
Prstojević, M. (1992). *Sarajevo Survival Guide*. Sarajevo: FAMA.
Prstojević, M. (1992). *Sarajevo: Ranjeni grad*. Sarajevo: Ideja.
Prstojević, M., Razović, M., & Wagner, A. (Eds.) (1993). *Sarajevo Survival Guide*. Sarajevo: FAMA.
Pullan, W. (2011). Frontier urbanism: The periphery at the centre of contested cities. *The Journal of Architecture*, 16(1), 15–35.
Ragaru, N. (2013). Missed encounters: Engaged French intellectuals and the Yugoslav wars. *Südosteuropa*, 61(4), 498–521.
Ramet, S. (2002). *Balkan Babel: The Disintegration of Yugoslavia from the Death of Tito to the Fall of Milošević*. Boulder, Colorado: Westview Press.
Radević, M. (2013). *Štraus: Bosansko-Srpski akademik* (pp. 62–65). Sarajevo: Slobodna Bosna.
Ramadan, A. (2008). Destroying Nahr el-Bared: Sovereignty and urbicide in the space of exception. *Political Geography*, 28, 153–163.
Ravi, S. (2008). Moderntiy, imperialism and the pleasures of travel: The continental hotel in Saigon. *Asian Studies Review*, 32, 475–490.
Ristić, M. (2011). *Sarajevo Warscapes: Architecture, Urban Spaces and Ethnic Nationalism*, Unpublished Ph.D. thesis, University of Melbourne, Australia.
Rohde, D. (1997). *A Safe Area, Srebrenica: Europe's Worst Massacre Since the Second World War*. London: Simon & Schuster.
Rose, M. (1998). *Fighting for Peace: Lessons from Bosnia*. London: Harvill Press.
Rusesabagina, P. (2006). *An Ordinary Man: The True Story Behind Hotel Rwanda*. London: Bloomsbury Press.
Rusher, W. A. (1995). Hotel Highs (and Lows), *The National Review*.
Rusinow, D. (1977). *The Yugoslav Experiment 1948–1974*. London: Hurst & Co..
Rusinow, D. (2008). *Yugoslavia: Oblique Insights and Observations*. Pittsburgh University Press.

Russell, A. (1993). *Prejudice and Plum Brandy: Tales of a Balkan Stringer*. London: Michael Joseph Press.
Salibi, K. S. (1976). *Crossroads to Civil War: Lebanon 1958–1976*. London: Ithica Press.
Scoular, C. (2003). *In the Headlines: The Story of the Belfast Europa Hotel*. Belfast: Appletree Press.
Serotta, E. (1994). *Survival in Sarajevo: How a Jewish Community Came to the Aid of Its City*. Budapest: CECRD.
Sharro, K. (2013). Warspace: Geographies of conflict in Beirut, Open Security, retrieved June 15, 2014 from https://www.opendemocracy.net/opensecurity/karl-sharro/warspace-geographies-of-conflict-in-beirut.
Shawcross, W. (1980). The end of Cambodia. *The New York Review of Books*.
Sibler, L., & Little, A. (1996). *The Death of Yugoslavia*. London: Penguin Books.
Simpson, J. (1999). *Strange Places, Questionable People*. London: MacMillan.
Simpson, J. (2000). *A Mad World, My Masters*. London: MacMillan.
Smirl, L. (2011). Not welcome at the Holiday Inn: How a Sarajevo landmark influences political relations, Unpublished Paper.
Softić, E. (1996). *Sarajevo Days, Sarajevo Nights*. Saint Paul, Minnesota: Hungry Mind Press.
Sontag, S. (1993). Godot comes to Sarajevo. *The New York Review of Books*.
Sontag, S. (1994). Waiting for godot in Sarajevo. *Performing Arts Journal*, 6(2), 87–106.
Sönmez, S. F. (1998). Tourism, terrorism and political instability. *Annals of Tourism Research*, 25(2), 416–448.
Sparks, M. (2014). *The Development of Austro-Hungarian Sarajevo, 1878–1918: An Urban History*. London & New York: Bloomsbury Press.
Stewart, C. S. (2007). *Hunting Tiger: The Fast Life and Violent Death of the Balkans' Most Dangerous Man*. New York: St. Martin's Press.
Stratfor Global Intelligence. (2009). Special security report: The militant threat to hotels.
Sučić, A., et al. (1984). *Sarajevo '84*. Sarajevo: Oslobodjenje.
Sudetić, C. (1999). *Blood and Vengeance*. London and New York: Penguin Books.
Swain, J. (1996). *The River of Time*. London: Minerva Books.
Sweet, M. (2011). *The West End Front: The Wartime Secrets of London's Grand Hotels*. London: Faber & Faber.
Šarkinović, H. (1997). *Bošnjaci od nacertanije do memorandums*. Podgorica: MNVS.
Štraus, I. (1991). *Arhitektura Bosne i Herzegovine, 1945–1995*. Sarajevo: Oko.
Štraus, I. (1995). *Arhitekt i barbari*. Sarajevo: Medjunarodni centar za mir.
Tanner, M. (2010). *Croatia: A Nation Forged in War* (3rd ed.). New York: Yale University Press.
Taylor, P. (1997). *The Provos: The IRA and Sinn Fein*. London: Bloomsbury Press.
Tebbit, N. (1988). *Upwardly Mobile: An Autobiography*. London: Weidenfeld and Nicolson.

Terzani, T. (1975). Vietnam: The first year. *The New York Review of Books*.
Thatcher, M. (1993). *The Downing Street Years*. London: HarperCollins.
Thomson, M. (1992). *A Paper House: The Ending of Yugoslavia*. London: Vintage Books.
Thompson, M. (1994). *Forging War: The Media in Serbia, Croatia and Bosnia-Herzegovina, Article 19*, London.
Tomašević, B. (2008). *Life and Death in the Balkans: A Family Saga in a Century of Conflict*. London: Hurst & Co..
Traboulsi, F. (2007). *A History of Modern Lebanon*. London/Ann Arbour: Pluto Press.
Trifunovska, S. (1994). *Yugoslavia Through Documents: From Its Creation to Its Dissolution*. Dordecht; London: Martinus Nijhoff.
Udovički, J., & Ridgeway, J. (2000). *Burn This House: The Making and Unmaking of Yugoslavia*. London: Duke University Press.
UN-ICTY Case No. IT-95-5/18-T. (1992). The Prosecutor V. Radovan Karadžić (ET SA01-1505-SA01-1571.doc), Club of Parliament Representatives, Serb Democratic Party, Bosnia and Herzegovina: Transcript from the meeting of the Club, Sarajevo.
UN-ICTY Case No. IT-95-5/18-T. The Prosecutor V. Radovan Karadžić (ET SA03-0331-SA03-03311.doc).
UN-ICTY Case No. IT-95-5/18-T. The Prosecutor V. Radovan Karadžić: Revised Notification of Submission of Written Evidence Pursuant to Rule 92 *ter*: Aleksandar Vasiljević (KW527).
UN-ICTY Case No. IT-09-92-T. (2012). The Prosecutor v. Ratko Mladić, Prosecution 92 *TER* MOTION: RM114 (Colm Doyle).
UN-ICTY Case No. IT-09-92-T. (2013). The Prosecutor v. Ratko Mladić (Witness Statement: D70033-D69927).
UN-ICTY, Case No. IT-04-79. (2008). Mićo Stanišić and the Bosnian Serb Leadership 1990–1992 (Addendum to the Bosnian Serb Leadership, 1990-1992), Patrick J. Treanor, Research report prepared for the case of Mićo Stanišić (IT-04-79).
UN-ICTY Document. (1992). Socialist Republic of Bosnia & Herzegovina: Ministry of the Interior State Security Service, Sarajevo, Security Information in Relation to the Events of 01.03/02.03 and 303.03/04.03.1992 in Sarajevo, ET 0323-7746-0323-7757.
UN Final Report of the United Nations Commission of Experts. (1994). Study of the Battle and Siege of Sarajevo, Part 1/10, S/1994/674/Add.2 (Vol. II).
UN ICTY: Robert D. (2006). From Election to Stalemate: The Making of the Siege of Sarajevo, 1990–1994, Statement of Expert Witness in Case IT-98-29-1, The Prosecutor V. Dragomir Milošević.
UN ICTY. (2003). Death Toll in the Siege of Sarajevo, April 1992 to December 1995: A Study of Mortality Based on Eight Large Data Sources, Expert report

prepared for the Case of Slobodan Milošević—Bosnia & Herzegovina, Case No. IT-02-54.
UNPROFOR (Zagreb) Daily Sitrep, 14 August 1994, File Ref: SR151100.
UNPROFOR (Zagreb) Daily Sitrep, 8 October 1994, File Ref: SR091100.
UNPROFOR (Zagreb) Daily Sitrep, 26 October 1994, File Ref: SR271100.
UNPROFOR (Zagreb) Daily Sitrep, 24 November 1994, File Ref: SR251100.
UNPROFOR (Zagreb) Daily Sitrep, 6 December 1994, File Ref: SR071100.
UNPROFOR (Zagreb) Daily Sitrep, 10 December 1994, File Ref: SR111100.
UNPROFOR (Zagreb), Outgoing Code Cable: Violations of the Sarajevo Anti-Sniping Agreement, 12 September 1994, Number: UNPROFOR Z-1398.
UNPROFOR Office of Civil Affairs (Zagreb), Subject: Meeting with General Mladić in Jahorina, 10 October 1994, File Ref: CCA-BHC-363.
UNPROFOR (SMO Sector Sarajevo), Senior Military Observer's End Month Report: Novermber 1992, 1 December 1992, File Ref: 11008965.
UNPROFOR (SMO Sector Sarajevo), Senior Military Observer's End Month Report: Novermber 1992, 1 January 1993, File Ref: 11008977.
UNPROFOR (SMO Sector Sarajevo), Senior Military Observer's End Month Report: Novermber 1992, 2 February 1992, File Ref: 11008990.
UN Security Council. (1994). Final Report of the United Nations Commission of Experts Established Pursuant to Security Council Resolution 780: Annex XI.A: The Battle of Dubrovnik and the Law of Armed Conflict,' S/1994/674/Add. 2 (Vol. V).
United Nations Security Council, 'Final Report of the United Nations Commission of Experts Established Pursuant to Security Council Resolution 820: Annex IV – The Policy of Ethnic Cleansing', S/1994/674/Add.2 (Vol.1), 28 December 1994.
United Nations Security Council, 'Final Report of the United Nations Commission of Experts Established Pursuant to Security Council Resolution 780, S/1994/674/Add.2 (Vol.1), 28 December 1994.
Vaill, A. (2014). *Hotel Florida: Truth, Love and Death in the Spanish Civil War.* London and New York: Bloomsbury Press.
C. M., V. (2010). *The Land of Blood and Honey: The Rise of Modern Israel.* New York: St. Martin's Press.
Vladisavljević, N. (2008). *Serbia's Antibureaucratic Revolution: Milošević, the Fall of Communism and Nationalist Mobilisation.* Basingstoke: Palgrave MacMillan.
Vuić, J. (2015). *The Sarajevo Olympics: A History of the 1984 Winter Games,* University of Massachusetts Press.
Vulliamy, E. (1994). *Seasons in hell: Understanding Bosnia's War.* New York: St. Martin's Press.
Wessenlingh, I., & Valerin, A. (2005). *Raw Memory: Prijedor, Laboratory of Ethnic Cleansing.* London: Saqi Books/The Bosnian Institute.
West, R., Graham Greene and the Quiet American (1991). *The New York Review of Books.*

Wharton, A. J. (2001). *Building the Cold War: Hilton International Hotels and Modern Architecture*. Chicago: University of Chicago Press.
Whitehouse, R. (2007). *Are We There Yet? Travels with My Frontline Family*. London: Reportage Press.
Wilson, K. (1996). *Half Luck and Half Brains: The Kemmons Wilson, Holiday Inn Story*. Memphis: Hambleton Hill.
Wise, N., & Mulec, I. (2014). Semblances of war tourism in Sarajevo, post-2005. *The American Journal of Tourism Management*, 3(1B), 1–9.
Woodward, S. (1995). *Balkan Tragedy: Chaos and Dissolution after the Cold War*. Brookings Institute, Washington, DC: Brookings.
World Intellectual Property Organization (WIPO). (2012). Arbitration and Mediation Centre: Administrative Panel Decision. Six Continents Hotels Inc v Triptih d.o.o, Case No. D2012-1600.
Zimmermann, W. (1996). *The Origins of a Catastrophe*. New York: Random House.
Zlatar, B., et al. (2007). *Sarajevo: Ulice, trgovi, mostovi, parkovi i spomenici*. Sarajevo: Mediapress.
Žanić, I. (2007). *Flag on the Mountain: A Political Anthropology of War in Croatia and Bosnia*. London: SAQI Books.
Zulfikarpašić, Adil (in dialogue with Milovan Djilas and Nadežda Gaće) (1998). *The Bosniak: Adil Zulfikarpašić*. London: Hurst & Co.

Newspapers, Periodicals and News Agencies

Oslobodjenje (Sarajevo), Naši dani (Sarajevo), Dani (Sarajevo), Dnevni avaz (Sarajevo), Start (Sarajevo), Danas (Belgrade), Vreme (Belgrade), NIN (Belgrade), Feral Tribune (Zagreb), Slobodna Dalmacija (Split), Novi Tednik (Ljubljana), Monitor (Podgorica), Pobjeda (Podgorica), The Guardian (London), The Times (London), The Independent (London), The Daily Mail (London), The European (London), The Daily Telegraph (London), The Spectator (London), The Observer (London), The Scotsman (Edinburgh), The Irish Times (Dublin), The People (Dublin), The Belfast Telegraph (Belfast), The New York Times (New York), The Washington Post (Washington D.C.), The Philadelphia Enquirer (Philadelphia), The San Francisco Chronicle (San Francisco), Newsweek (New York), Time Magazine (New York), New York Review of Books (New York), Reuters (New York), Associated Press (New York), Balkan Insight (Belgrade), Osservatorio Balcani e Caucuso (Trento), AIM Press (Paris/Zurich).

Documentary Films

'A Sarajevo Diary: From Bad to Worse', Director: Dom Rotheroe, W.O.W Productions, London, 1993.
'Cinema Komunisto', Dir: Mila Turajlić, Dribbling Pictures, Belgrade, 2010.
'Godot-Sarajevo', Director: Pjer Žalica, SAGA Films Sarajevo, 1993.
'Hardboard Hotel', BBC Radio Four Productions, September 1998.
'Hotel na prvoj liniji' (Hotel on the Front Line), Director: Antonije 'Nino' Žalica, SAGA Films Sarajevo, 1993.
'Killer Image: Shooting Robert King', Director: Richard Parry, Trinity Films, London, 2008.
'Margaret Moth: Fearless', CNN Documentary, 22 September 2009.
'Serbian Epics', Director: Paul Pawlokowski, BBC TV, 1992.
'Tales from Sarajevo: A Late Show Special' Director: Roland Keating, BBC, London, 1993.
'The Reckoning', Director: Kevin Sim, Channel 4 'True Stories' 1998.
'Veillées d'armes: Histoire du Journalisme en temps du guerre' ('The Troubles We've Seen: A History of Journalism in Wartime'), First Journey, Director: Marcel Ophuls, Little Bear Productions, 1993.
'Veillées d'armes: Histoire du Journalisme en temps du guerre' ('The Troubles We've Seen: A History of Journalism in Wartime'), Second Journey, Director: Marcel Ophuls, Little Bear Productions, 1994.

Index[1]

A
Abadžic-lowe, Amra, 181, 181n69
Abdić, Fikret, 78–9
Adie, Kate, 167, 167n9, 173, 173n35, 184, 184n81
Ahrens, Geert Hinrich, 81, 81n41
Alcazar Hotel, 13
alcoholic beverages, 61, 118, 169n21, 176, 184
Alić, Vahid, 215
Alliance of Reform Forces (SRSJ), 78
Alpha Baumanagement, 3, 210, 214
Al Rashid, Baghdad, 8
American Broadcasting Company's (ABC), 142
The American Spectator, 139n86, 145n18
Andjelić, Neven, 71n1, 74n12, 75, 75n17, 78n32, 79n35
Andreas, Peter, 158, 158n76, 168n14, 171n31, 175n42, 177, 177n50, 177n53
anti-bureaucratic revolution, 67
anti-communist activities, 72
anti-Serb' 1974 constitution, 67
Arkanovi tigrovi, 103
Armija Republike Bosne i Herzegovine (ARBIH), 119
Army of Republika Srpska, 119
Arnautović, Suad, 78n33
Ashdown, Paddy, 176, 176n44
attacks
 bombing (*see* bombing)
 with rockets, 37
 on Sarajevo TV Station, 173

B
Babić, Milan, 68
Baez, Joan, 158, 159
Bakšić, Hamza, 180, 180n64
Balkan reconstruction Summit (1999), 206
Battle of Hotels, Beirut, 10
Beæirević, Edina, 78n30

---

[1] Note: Page number followed by 'n' refers to footnotes.

Becirević, Džemal, 138, 138n82, 138n83, 144n15, 158, 159n78, 176n49, 179, 180, 180n62, 191, 191n114, 196
Bećirević, Edina, 77, 78n30, 81, 81n42
Bečka kafana (Viennese café), 64
Bell, Martin, 128, 150, 150n42, 150n43, 152, 152n50–152n52, 152n54, 155, 155n64
bijela smrt (white death), 180
black market, 167–9, 176, 178, 180, 183
Blagojević, Marina, 66n68
Bogdanović, Bogdan, 53
bombing
  Baščaršija, 118
  Europa Hotel, Belfast, 14–15
  of FRY, NATO, 42
  King David Hotel, Jerusalem, 14
  Semiramis Hotel by Jewish paramilitary organisation, 14
Boras, Franjo, 78
Bosnia and Herzegovina, 79, 84–6, 95, 99, 101, 106
  capital, Sarajevo, 1
  deployed UN peacekeeping force, 81
  Elektropriveda BiH, Electric Company of, 52
  foreign investment, 206
  Muslim-dominated, 72
  PEN Centre of, 162
  politics in, 71
  republic's first multiparty elections, 72
  tourism, 209
  war in, 3, 5, 6, 8n4
Bosniak–Croat Federation, 203
Bosnian League of Communists/Social Democratic Party (SK-SDP), 78
Bosnian Serb, 77, 99, 114n50, 115, 121–2, 155, 177, 196, 199, 200n38

armed intervention against, 155
  forces, 65n65, 175
  and JNA, heavier fighting broke between, 118–19
  killed von Hohenberg, Sophie, 1
  Knežević, Milan, 125
  Koljević, Nikola, 78
  leaders, 93
  MUP, 104n4
  Plavšić, Biljana, 78
  positions, 44, 191
Bosnian Serb Army (*Vojska Repulike Srpske* (VRS)), 47
Bosnian Serb Assembly (BSA), 112n41, 184
Bosnian Serb Leadership (1990–1992), 85n10
Bosnian war, 7, 5, 48, 87n16, 122n24, 155, 159, 160, 163n92, 184, 205, 216
Bowen, Jeremy, 143n9, 148, 148n36, 151, 151n46, 176, 176n46, 179, 179n58
Brabant, Malcolm, 142, 142n5, 146, 146n26, 149, 149n40
Brand, Joel, 90n28, 90n32, 123n27, 136, 136n73, 137n74, 143, 143n11, 145, 147n30, 147n31, 153, 153n56, 179, 179n60, 181, 182n70, 188, 188n100, 191n115
bratstvo i jedinstvo (brotherhood and unity), 65
British Broadcasting Corporation (BBC), 43, 123, 124, 129, 129n48, 129n50, 132
  Adie, Kate, 167, 173, 179n59, 184, 190n111
  armoured vehicle, 'Miss Piggy,' 152
  Bell, Martin, 44, 124, 138, 150, 150n42, 150n43, 152, 152n50–152n52, 152n54, 155, 155n64, 208

INDEX   237

Bowen, Jeremy, 40, 129n50, 130n52, 130n55, 139, 143n9, 148, 151, 151n46, 176n48, 179n58
Brabant, Malcolm, 129n48, 142, 142n5, 146, 146n26, 149, 149n40
Breakfast News, 150
Drake, Chris, 39
Glenny, Misham, Radio journalist, 124
Little, Allan, 128, 128n47, 159n79, 166n6
News, 24n69, 29n85, 43n45, 43n47
'Serbian Epics,' documentary, 75
Simpson, John, 40, 155, 155n63, 160, 167
translator, Kordi, Verač, 160
British Liberal Party, 176
Brock, Peter, 156, 156n67
Bulatović, Momir, 67
Bulić, Branko, 53
Burns, John F., 132, 133, 133nn65–7, 134, 134n68, 134n69, 137, 143, 154, 156, 156n69, 158n77, 159–61, 180n65
Bush, George, 42

C
Canadian UNPROFOR soldiers (CANBAT), 185, 186
Caravelle, Saigon, 8
Carlton Citadel Hotel, 43
Carrington–Cutileiro plan negotiations, 98
Ćausević, Nedim, 209
Cazeau, Pierre, 34
Central Intelligence Agency (CIA), 65n66, 81, 81n40, 204n3
Cirkusplatz, 54
Clinton, Bill, 203–4, 206

Code Communication System, 100n65
Cohen, Roger, 146, 146n23
Cold War, 40, 58n40
Commission on Security and Cooperation (CSCE), 81
Commodore, Beirut, 8
Commodore Hotel, Beirut, 117
Communist Information Bureau (COMINFORM), 56
Communist Party Of Yugoslavia (KPJ), 61n54
conflict(s), 8, 10, 15, 17, 25, 26, 28, 29, 73, 74, 127, 130, 135, 154, 157
armed, 9, 95, 101, 103, 104
Muslim–Croat, 187n91
between TORS and JNA, 68
zone, press hotels (*see* press hotels)
Constitution of the Serb Republic of Bosnia & Herzegovina, 86
construction, Holiday Inn (Olympic Hotel)
accommodation for 'Olympic Family,' 60, 62, 62n55
atrium of, 55–7
bazen (pool), 65
Bosnia and Herzegovina, economic crisis, 65–6
Bulgaren Äcker, plot of land, 54
business/leisure travel, 60
casino, 61
city's 'war hotel,' 48
clothing boutiques, 61
commencement (1981), 53
commercial art gallery, 61
comparison between existing modernist buildings and, 51
under construction (June 1983), 53
corporate logo, 'Great Sign,' 59
design, 54–5
Diskoteka '64 at basement, 61

238 INDEX

construction, Holiday Inn (Olympic Hotel) (*continued*)
economic reforms, 50
effective infrastructure, 50
esteemed guests from world, 62–3
exterior and interior visual, 47
franchise chain hotel, 59
Gallagher, Rory, 64
hairdressing salon, 61
HOLIDEX booking system, 59
iconic symbol of siege, 48
John, Elton, 64
Marindvor, 51
multifunctional building, 57
named after Holiday Inn movie, 58
newspaper/tobacco shop, 61
occupancy ratings, 59
Olympic symbols in entrance pillar, 48, 49
opened in Memphis (1952), 58–9
'Presidential Suite,' Samaranch, Juan Antonio, 60–1
professional building firms and volunteers SORA, 54
providing post-games legacy, 50–1
scale model for outline vision, 55
souvenir shop, 61
standards of time, 61
Štraus, Ivan, Bosnian architect, 47n1, 52–7, 52n17, 52n18, 53n19, 54nn24–6, 55n27, 55n31, 55n32, 56n34, 57n35, 61, 61n52
travel agency, 61
used in domestic films, 65
Winter Olympics (1984), 63–4
Continental Palace, Saigon, 8
Continental shelf
location, 35
Radio Catinat, 35
Cooper, Anderson, 147, 147n29, 187, 187n95
Ćorić, Dinko, 125, 126, 168, 186, 187

Ćosić, Dobrica, 77
Ćosić, Sabina (Reuters), 138, 166, 166n7, 183, 183n76, 197, 197n19
'counter-revolutionary acts,' 72
Crawshaw, Steve, 101
Croatian Democratic Community (*Hrvatska demokratska zajednica* (HDZ)), 68
Croatian Democratic Community of Bosnia and Herzegovina (*Hrvatska demokratska zajednica Bosne i Hercegovine* (HDZ-BiH)), 74, 74n13, 75, 79, 80
Croatian Democratic Union (HDZ), 74
Cuny, Fred, 178, 178n54, 178n55

D
Daly, Emma, 154, 155n62
Dani, 189, 189n105, 189n106
Dayton agreement, 5
Dayton Peace Agreement (DPA), 1, 203
Death of Yugoslavia Archive, 88n19, 89n25, 97n53, 97n56
de facto ceasefire, 188
Delaheye, Luc, 144
De Mayerling à Sarajevo (1940), 161
Di Giovanni, Janine, 159n82, 168, 170, 170n28, 173, 173n36, 174, 185, 185n86, 194, 195n8, 197n14
Dilberović, Suada, 203
Dizdarević, Zlatko, 170, 170n24, 171n30
Djukanović, Milo, 67
Dom mladih, Skenderija, 74, 75
Dom vojske (Army Hall), Derventa, 52
Donia, Robert, 51, 51n13, 61n54, 75n16, 75n20, 76n21, 76n25, 77n26, 80n37, 81n38, 89n26, 95n46, 107, 107n17, 108n23, 112, 112n40, 119n7, 120n14, 127, 127n44, 157n71, 188n101, 193n2, 198n25, 205n9

Drina, 176
Drugi bošnjaèki sabor (The Second Bosniak Congress), 163
Duraković, Nijaz, 71, 78
Dursun, Danilo, 84, 122, 122n24, 125n33
Dutina, Todor, 98, 98n58, 102

E
Eckhardt, Fred, 186
Ekmeèiè, Milorad, 76
electric elements, 179
electric heaters, 182
Elektropriveda BiH (Electric Company of Bosnia and Herzegovina), New Sarajevo, 52
El Pais, Spanish newspaper, 146, 187
emergency water treatment system, 177–8
Europa Hotel, Belfast, 8, 14, 15, 15n37, 17, 19, 65n65, 114, 114n50, 117, 121

F
Fabrika duhana Sarajevo (Sarajevo tobacco Factory), 176
Farabundo Marti National Liberation Front (FMlN), 39, 40
Federal Republic of Yugoslavia (FRY), 42, 119n8
fierce fighting, 118
Filipovi, Živko, 141n3
Filipović, Muhamed, 74, 75
firefighters, 197, 198
First Indochina War (1946–1950), 35
Fisk, Robert, 9, 18, 39, 39n32
Fleiner, Thomas, 81
Florida Hotel, Plaza de Callao, 34
14th Winter Olympic Games (*Zimskih Olimpijskih Igara* (ZOI)), 48

freelance journalist, 127
French Peacekeeping Battalion in Bosnia and Herzegovina (FREBAT), 200, 201
Friedman, Thomas, 37, 38
Frontline News, 132, 132n63, 135n71, 139n88, 147n32, 148n37, 171, 171n33, 181n66

G
Galić, Stanislav, 197, 197n20
Gallagher, Rory, 64
Ganić, Ejup, 78
Gardović, Nikola, 87
General Framework Agreement for Peace in Bosnia & Herzegovina, 203
generators, 170, 185
  BBC and Reuters, 190
  electrical, 168
  fuel, 181, 183–4
  heavy static, 190
  portable, 191
Glenny, Misha, 124, 124n29
Good Friday Agreement, 17
Goupil, Romain, 161
Goytisolo, Juan, 146, 146n25
Grand Media Centre, 3, 210
Grand Metropolitan Hotels, 15n36
Greene, Grahame, 35
The Guardian, London, 12n21, 12n22, 13n26, 13n28, 13n30, 19, 19n48, 19n50, 19n51, 25n70, 25n72, 26n77, 35n8, 35n9, 37n21, 38n28, 39n35, 100, 100n67, 124n31, 144n13, 145, 145n19, 151n45, 159n81, 171, 176, 176n45, 196n13, 206n13, 590n30
Gulf War (1990), 127
Gutman, Roy, 156

H

Hadžihasanović, Aziz, 50n10
Hadrović, Avdija, 187
Halepović, Nermin, Bosnian Muslim, 125
Harris, Paul, 8, 126, 127n42, 136, 139, 139n84, 181, 181n68, 185, 185n84, 187n92, 187n94, 190n112
heating elements, 179, 182
Hébrard, Ernest, 34
Hewitt, Dawn M., 186n88
Hilton, Conrad, 57, 58, 58n40
Hitchens, Christopher, 145
The Holiday Inn, 63
  author's interview with
    Abadžić-Lowe, Amra, 138n82, 181n69
    Bećirević, Džemal, 138n83, 159n78, 176n49, 182n62, 191n114
    Bowen, Jeremy, 176n48, 179n58
    Brand, Joel, 137n74, 179n60, 182n70, 188n100, 191n115
    Burns, John F., 180n65
    Ćosić, Sabina (Reuters), 166, 166n7, 183n76
    Di Giovanni, Janine, 168n15, 170, 170n28, 185, 185n86
    employee, 118n2, 166n2, 168n18, 176n47, 177n51, 179n61, 181n67, 182n72, 184n78
    Harris, Paul, 181n68
    King, Robert, 137n77, 138n78
    Little, Allan, 159n79, 166, 166n6, 179n59
    Lowe, Paul, 138n81, 179n57, 183n75
    Manier, Stephané, 160n85, 174n39, 175n40, 182n71
    Ourdan, Remy, 176n43, 191n113
    Robertson, Nic, 184n81
    Smith, Colin (BBC Television), 166n3
    Smith, Vaughan, 139n88, 171n33, 181n66
    staff, 118n2
    Sullivan, Kevin, 166n4, 178, 178n56, 180n63
    Sweeney, John, 166, 167n8
  Bosnian Territorial Defence, meeting place and operational centre, 118
  business
    adorning logos, 187–8
    agreement failure, 187
    Atlanta-based Holiday Inn Group, 187
    capitalist principles, 186
    cash settlement, 185
    cost for accommodation, 185
    double pay, foreign journalists, 186
    functioning with economic and political dynamics, 187
    hotel management, 185
    large amount of cash transaction, 185
    non-negotiable prices, 185
    paying overhead costs, 186
    underground facilities for CANBAT, 186
  centre for Bosnian Territorial Defence, 118
  city's 'war hotel,' 2, 117
  construction (see Construction, Holiday Inn (Olympic Hotel))
  damaged interior building, 117
  demise, 3
  drift from
    increased occupancy, 188
    journalists, NATO air strikes, 189
    Markale market bomb, 191
    press corps detachment, 189

Sarajevo visit by Samaranch, Juan Antonio, 189
technological advancements, 190–1
withdrawal of journalists, 190
electricity supply, 177, 182–4
external and internal features, 2
fuel generators, 183–4
hazards of living, frontline, 141–63
heat elements, 177
  burning books, 180
  firewood, 180
  fuel availability, 180–1
  generators, 181
  plastic sheeting, 181
history, 3–4
hosted 'War Fashion Show,' 162
hotel-related expenses, 184
idiosyncratic appearance, 2
Karadžić, Radovan and SDS residence
  accommodation for SDS members, 83
  Assembly of the Serbian People of Bosnia & Herzegovina, 84, 86
  conference and meeting facilities, 83
  housekeeping staff, 100n64
  Orthodox New year celebration (1992), 85
  SDA and HDZ-BiH, 83
  staff interview, 83, 83n1
  sweeping function rooms, 84–5
lobby bars, 184
looting, 118
Oslobodjenje, daily news paper, 193
Party of Democratic Action (SDA), 5
privatisation process, 3
reopening (1992), 117
SDS activities centre, 117
siege food
  availability during harsh winter, 172–3

basic provisions, 169
black market trade emergence, 167–8
buffet dinner, 171
first-class meals during wartime, 169
high quality food, 170
local cigarettes, 176–7
meal with wine, 176
menu, 170
rice, 170
serving preparation, 172, 173
supply through neighbourhood of Stup, 168
System D, 174
varied quality and quantity, 167
waiters dress code, 166
'War Soup,' 170
during siege of Sarajevo, 4
sleeping bag, 181, 182
water supply, 177–9
Hollingworth, Larry, 169n21
Hondo hotel, 190
'hostile propaganda,' 72
Hotel Aletti, Algiers, 8
Hotel Bistrica, Jahorina, 112
Hotel El Aurassi, Algiers, 8
Hotel na liniji fronta (Hotel on the Front line), 172
Hotel Onogošt, Nikšić, 52
Hotel Panorama, 112
Hotel Pelegrin, 42
hotels
  Aletti, Algiers, 8
  Al Rashid, Baghdad, 8
  Commodore, Beirut, 8
  Continental Palace and Caravelle, Saigon, 8
  El Aurassi, Algiers, 8
  Europa, Belfast, 8
  Holiday Inn, Beirut, 8
  Ledra Palace, Nicosia, 8

hotels (*continued*)
  mundane as, 7
  paying guests' needs, provider for, 7
  prestige/political target, 14–29
  Rixos, Tripoli, 8
  sanctuaries, 29–30
  St George's, Beirut, 8
  as strategic assets, 9–13
  during war
    barracks, 7–8
    press hotels, 8
    targets for terrorist groups, 9, 28
Hotel Slano, Osmine, 52
Hotel Srbija (Hotel Serbia), 111, 112
Hrvastska republika Herceg-Bosna (the Croatian Republic of Herceg-Bosna), 74
Hrvatsko vijeće obrane (HVO), 168, 187n91
The Hunting Party, 65
Hyatt, 42

I
The Independent, London, 9, 9n9, 15n35, 36n14, 39, 44n48, 44n50, 59n43, 110n28, 113n48, 126n36, 128n45, 130n53, 142n6
  Crawshaw, Steve, 101
  Fisk, Robert, 9, 38n26, 39
  Tanner, Marcus, 109, 128
Independent Nasserite Movement (INM), 12
Intercontinental and Hyatt hotels, Belgrade, 57
Intercontinental Hotels, 42
Intercontinental Hotels Group (IHG), 207
Intercontinental, Zagreb, 57
Inter-entity Boundary Line (IEBL), 203
internally displaced people (IDPs), 30

International Association Of Holiday Inns (IAHI), 59
International Committee of the Red Cross (ICRC), 43
International Criminal Tribunal for the Former Yugoslavia (ICTY), 88n18
International Crisis Group (ICG), 205n11, 207n18
International Monetary Fund (IMF), 50
International Olympic Committee, 5
The Irgun, 14
Irish Republican Army (IRA), 17
Islamic Community (*Islamska zajednica*—IZ), 73
Islamska deklaracija (Islamic Declaration), 72, 73, 73n8, 74, 75, 78
Istoèno Sarajevo, 203
Izetbegović, Alija, 5, 72, 73, 73n7, 73n8, 74, 75, 78, 89, 120

J
Jagger, Bianca, 158
Janković, Živorad, 53
Jeftanović, Gligorije, 64
Jestrović, Silvija, 64, 64n63
Jez (hedgehog), 169n21
John, Elton, 64
Jones, Michel, 186
journalists
  Burns, John F (*see* Burns, John F.)
  foreign, 26, 87, 90, 101, 113, 123, 132, 138, 156, 186, 189, 197, 205
  Friedman, Thomas, 37
  Harris, Paul (*see* Harris, Paul)
  networking hub, Europa, 15
  Ryder, Chris, 15
  Schanberg, Sydney, 36
  Swain, Jon, 36

Journal of Professional Adventurers, 139n85
Jovićić, Mile, 120, 120n12
Judah, Tim, 113, 114n49

K
Kapić, Suada, 185n83
Karadžić, Radovan, 7, 5, 75, 75n16, 75n19, 75n20, 76, 76n21, 76n25, 77, 77n26, 78, 80, 81, 84, 120, 161, 171n30, 203, 208
Karahasan, Dževad, 65n65, 162, 162n89
Kataeb Regulatory Forces (KRF), 12
Kattan, Abdal Moshin, 10
Kaye, Sidney, 16
Kifner, John, 188
Killer Image: Shooting Robert King (2008), 138
The Killing Fields, 37
King, Robert, 137, 137n77, 138n78
Kino Imperijal (Imperial Cinema), 158
Kljuić, Stjepan, 74n15, 78
Knežević, Milan, 125, 126
knjiga utisaka, 208
Koljević, Nikola, 78, 114, 161, 162
Krajišnik, Momčilo, 77, 84, 86, 107, 108n19, 114, 115n54
Kristl, Stanko, 53
Kučan, Milan, 68
Kukanjac, Milutin, 113
Kurspahić, Kemal, 89
Kusovac, Zoran, 152, 152n55, 195, 195n9

L
Lagumdžija, Zlatko, 77n28, 79n34
Laroche-Joubert, Martine, 161
laundry service, 38, 172
League of Communists of Serbia (*Savez komunista Srbije* (SKS)), 66

Le Chagrin et la pitié (The Sorrow and the Pity) (1969), 160
Le Commodore (the Commodore), 37
  damage, 39
  foreign correspondents, 37
  hotel management, 38
  West Beirut, 37
Ledra Palace Hotel, Nicosia, 8, 117
Le Garrec, Jean-Jacques, 174
Leova, Slavko, 76
Le Royal (The Royal), 36
Levy, Bernard-Henri, 158
Lisabonski sporazum (the Lisbon Agreement), 99, 101
Little, Allan, 11n34, 128, 128n47, 159n79, 166, 166n6, 179, 179n59, 190n111
Lodge, Robin, 128
The Los Angeles Times, 127n43, 189n103
Lowe, Paul, 137, 137n75, 137n76, 138n81, 178, 179n57, 183n75
Loyd, Anthony, 189, 190n108, 194, 194n5
Lučarević, Kerim, 118
Lyon, James, 51n12, 54n23

M
Maass, Peter, 117, 117n1, 145n21, 146, 146n24, 148, 148n38, 149n39, 193, 194n4
MacKenzie, Lewis, 110–11, 111n33
Maček, Ivana, 166n5, 169n20, 177n52, 183n73, 189n104
Magaš, Branka, 50n8, 68n72
Maguire, Sean, 148n34
Malcolm, Noel, 72n6
Malreaux, André, 35
Manevič, Zoran, 55n28
Maniér, Stephané, 160, 161, 174, 182
Marchand, Paul, 153, 153n57, 153n58, 154, 154n61, 161
Marlboro, 176

Marović, Svetozar, 67
McAllister, Matthew, 169n19
'Meetings of truth,' Montenegro, 67
Memorandum, 66
Mikulić, Branko, 60
Milošević, Slobodan, 66–8, 90
Mitterand, François, 127
Mladi Muslimani (Young Muslims), 72
Mladina (Ivo Standeker), 141n3
modernist buildings, 51
Monik, 144
Moth, Margaret, 142, 142n4
Mullen, Larry, 206
Muslim Bosniak Organisation (MBO), 74
Muslim–Croat war, 187
Muzej avijacije (Museum of Aviation), 52
Myers, Kevin, 145, 150, 151n41

N

Nacionalni (National), 61
National Broadcasting Company (NBC), 63n61
Neidhardt, Juraj, 54
The New York Times, 36, 37, 143, 143n12, 145, 154n59, 154n60, 160, 161, 187, 187n95, 188n98
Nicholson, Michael, 151, 151n47, 151n49
nightclubs, 12, 19
Nikola Koljević, 86
NIN, Belgrade, 77n29, 78, 78n31, 169, 169n22, 170n23, 175n41
The *Noćni* (Night), 61
Northern Ireland Civil Rights Association (NICRA), 17, 18
Novi Beograd (New Belgrade) hotel, 42
Novi Tednik, 101, 101n68
Šučić, Anton, 60

O

The Observer, London, 27, 27n78, 27n80, 35, 35n7, 36n13, 36n16, 122n22, 142, 154, 166
O' Connor, Robert, 188n99
Office of the High Representative (OHR), 204
O'Kane, Maggie, 176
Olympic Committee (IOC), 60
Olympic Press Centre, Bjelašnica, 52
Omladinska radna akcija (ORA), 54
Operation Peace in Galilee, Israel, 37
Ophuls, Marcel, 154, 154n61, 160, 160n84, 161, 161n86
Organization for Security and Co-operation in Europe (OSCE), 214
O'Rourke, P.J., 60, 60n47
Oslobodjenje, 84n2–84n4, 87, 87n13, 87n15, 89, 91, 91n34, 92n36, 93, 93n43, 96n49, 96n50, 97, 97n54, 190, 190n109, 190n110, 190n112
destroyed (August 1992), 193
journalists
Bakšić, Hamza, 180, 180n64
Dizdarević, Zlatko, 170, 171
Hondo, Salko, 141n3
Smajlović, Kasif, 141n3
Smajlović, Ljiljana, 155
Sojanović, Karmela, 141n3
Sullivan, Kevin, 145n17
Ourdan, Remy, 131, 131n58, 147, 147n28, 161, 190, 191n113, 208

P

Palestinian Liberation Organisation (PLO), 11, 13, 37, 38
Paris Peace Accord, 36
Party of Democratic Action, 74n13
Pašić, Adnan, 52n16, 55n29

Peace Implementation Council (PIC), 204
Pečanac, Liljana, 162
Pedrotty, Kate Meehan, 48n4, 50n9, 64, 64n62
Perinović, Davorin, 74
Petrović, Ruža, 66n68
The Philadelphia inquirer, 186n90
photojournalist
   King, Robert, 137
   Lowe, Paul, 128n47
   Reid, Andrew, 133n47
Plavšić, Biljana, 78
Politics, Holiday Inn
   Bosnian parliament session, 80
   Brozović, Dalibor, HDZ, 74
   'Constituent assembly' SDA, 73
   Izetbegović, Alija, 73–4
   Karadžić, Radovan, 75–8
   meetings and party launches, 72
   SDS/SDA/HDZ-BiH coalition, 79
   SFRJ, 79
   'Statement of the Forty,' 73
   Variant A and Variant B, 80–1
   'Vrbas Hall,' 72
PopMart tour, 206
Portman, John (American Architect), 54
Potter, James, 57n37
Praznik u Sarajevu (Holiday in Sarajevo), 65
press hotels, 5
   Alexandre Hotel, East Beirut, 37–8
   bars, 33
   Continental shelf, 35
   day's events, 34
   Hotel Florida, Plaza de Callao, 34
   Le Commodore (the Commodore), 37, 38
   Le Royal, 36
   Palace Continental hotel, 34–5

Provisional Irish Republican Army (PIRA), 14
Prstojević, Miroslav, 121n18, 141n2, 146, 146n27

Q
The Quiet American, 35

R
Radio Télévision Luxembourg (RTL), 147
Raèan, Ivica, 68
Ravel, Maurice, 63n61
Ravnikar, Edvard, 53
reconstruction, Holiday Inn
   brand, 207
   Colakhodžić, Ibrahim, 207
   hosting guests, 207
   Mullen, Larry, 206
   1984 Winter Olympics, 204
   reopening, 207
Redgrave, Vanessa, 158
Republika Srpska, 203
Rex Hotel, 35
Rhodesian Security Force, 139n85
Rhodesian War (1964–1979), 139n85
Rich, Sebastian, 151
Rixos, Tripoli, 8
Rizk Tower, 12
Robertson, Nic, 184
Rocket-propelled grenades (RPGs), 196–8
Royal Ulster Constabulary (RUC), 18

S
Salvadoran Foreign Press Corps Association (SPECA), 39
Samaranch, Juan Antonio, 60, 189

Sarajevo
  Bašèaršija, 1
  capital of Bosnia and Herzegovina, 1
  iconic Holiday Inn (*see* The Holiday Inn)
  1 May holiday, 1
  outbreaks of war, 103–15
Sarajevo Agency Pool (SAP), 152
Sarajevo Business Forum (2015), 214
Sarajevo ljubavi moja (Sarajevo, my love), 158
Sarajevski proces (The Sarajevo Trials), 72
Sarajevsko pivo (Sarajevo beer), 176
satellite dishes, 185
satellite phones, 182, 190, 191
Savez komunista Bosne i Hercegovine (SK-BIH), 71
Schork, Kurt, 183
The Scotsman, 135n70, 136, 139, 139n86, 181n68, 187n93
SDA *(Stranka demokratske akcije)*, 72, 73
Selesković, Sabahudin, 57, 57n39
Selimić, Sabahudin, 61n50
Serbian Academy of Arts and Sciences (*Srpska akademija nauka i umetnosti* (SANU)), 66, 66n68
Serbian Democratic Party (SDS), 5, 75–7, 77n27, 77n28, 78–81, 81n38, 103–8, 110–14
Serbian Republic of Bosnia & Herzegovina, 84
Šešelj, Vojislav, 99
Silajdžić, Haris, 81
Simpson, John, 155, 155n63, 160, 167
Skorupan, Adis, 215
Sky News, 152, 152n55
Slobodna Bosna, 55n30, 88n18, 89n22, 210, 210n31, 211, 211n35, 214n47, 215, 215n49

Slovenian League of Communists (*Zveza komunistov Slovenije* (ZKS)), 68
Slovenian Territorial Defence (*Teritorialna obramba Republike Slovenije* (TORS)), 68
Smajlović, Kasif, 141n3
Smajlović, Ljiljana, 155, 156n65, 156n66
Smirl, Lisa, 157, 157n70
Smith, Colin, 166
Smith, Vaughan, 147n32, 148, 148n37, 171
Social Democratic Party of Croatia (*Socijaldemokratska partija Hrvatske* (SDP)), 68
Socialist Federal Republic Of Yugoslavia (SFRJ), 48, 71, 79
Socialist Federal Republic of Yugoslavia (SFRJ) disintegration of, 66, 66n67
Sojanović, Karmela, 141n3
Soldier of Fortune (SOF), 139, 139n85
Sontag, Susan, 158, 159, 159n80, 159n82
Spanish Civil War, 158
The Spectator, London, 100, 100n66, 128n46, 168n17, 174, 174n38, 185n82, 185n85, 185n87, 194n6
Srebrov, Vladimir, 77
Srpska radikalna stranka (SRS), 99
Srpske autonomne olbasti (SOA), 81
Srspka Sparta (Serbian Sparta), 76
'Stability pact' meetings, 206
Stambolić, Ivan, 66
Stambolić, Petar, 66
State Investigation and Protection Agency (SIPA), 215
Stevanović, Zoran, 143n10
St George's, Beirut, 8, 13

Štraus, Ivan, 47n1, 52, 52n17, 52n18, 53, 53n19, 54, 54nn24–6, 55, 55n27, 55n31, 55n32, 56, 56n34, 57, 57n35, 61, 61n52, 95n45, 181
street battles, 118
Sudetić, Chuck, 168n16
Suči, Olga, 105, 201, 203
Sullivan, Kevin, 144, 144n16, 145, 145n17, 166, 166n4, 170, 170n27, 178, 178n56, 180, 180n63, 194, 194n7
Sunday Times, 36
Sweeney, John, 142, 143n8, 166, 167n8

T
Tanjug Domestic Service, Belgrade, 72n4, 74n12
Tanović, Danis, 214
targeting Holiday Inn
   French battalion, 200–1
   killing civilian, 199
   Loyd, Anthony, 194
   Maass, Peter, 193–4
   protection, shady deal, 193
   Sarajevo Fire Service, 198
   Sarajevo's tram system, 198–9
   Serb gunners on Trebević, 194
   shot dead, UNPROFOR soldier, 201
   sniper fire, 199
   UNPROFOR, 96–102, 198
   UN staff, 196
   western and southern sides of, 195
Territorio Comanche, 65
terrorist
   attacks
      bombing (*see* bombing)
      Intercontinental Hotel, Kabul, 28
      The Irgun, 14

Pearl Continental Hotel, Peshawar, 28
groups, 9, 14
Time Magazine, 59–60, 60n46
The Times, London, 49n5, 59n44, 59n45, 81n39, 189
Tito, Josip Broz, 48–50
Tunel spasa (Tunnel of Life), 175

U
Ukrainian Battalion (UKRBAT), 200
Ulster Freedom Fighters (UFF), 17
Ulster Transport Authority (UTA), 15n37
Ulster Unionist Party (UUP), 17, 18
Ulster Volunteer Force (UVF), 17, 18
United Investment and Trading Company (UNITIC) towers, 52, 52n15
United National Development program (UNDP), 214
United Nations assistance Mission in Iraq (UNAMI), 28
United Nations High Commissioner for Refugees (UNHCR), 165
United Nations Peacekeeping Force in Cyprus (UNFICYP), 26–7
United Nations Protection Force (UNPROFOR), 95–102, 204
   guard, 120
   and Kaadžić, Clan, 96–102
   Sarajevo airport control under, 127
   soldiers, 125
   staff, 124, 201
   troops, 200
United Press International (UPI), 138
   Bećirević, Džemal, 138, 138n82, 138n83, 144n15, 158, 159n78, 176n49, 179, 180, 180n62, 191n114

United Press International (UPI) (*continued*)
  equipment, 144n16
  Landay, Jonathan, 138
  Sullivan, Kevin, 144, 144n16, 145, 145n17, 166, 166n4, 170, 170n27, 178, 178n56, 180, 180n63, 194, 194n7
UN Security Council Resolution, 713, 118
Župa Sveti Franje Catholic church, Zovik, 52
Uvalić, Milica, 50n7
Uzelac, Uglješa, 60

V
Vance–Owen Peace Plan (VOPP), 184, 184n79
Variety (1974), 165, 165n1
Veillées d'armes: Histoire du Journalisme en temps du guerre (The Troubles We've Seen: A History of Journalism in Wartime) (1994), 160, 161, 161n86
Vermeer, Peter, 207, 208
Vešović, Marko, 76
Vietnam War, 34–6
Vladisavljevic, Nebojša, 67n70
Vojska Republika Srpsk (VRS), 119, 119n9
Vrbas Hall, 72
Vreme News Digest Agency, 189, 189n107
Vuić, Jason, 51n11, 52n14, 57n39, 62n56, 63, 63n60, 189n102
Vulević, Miloš, 141n3

W
war hotels, 8, 9. *See also* The Holiday Inn
The Washington Post, 138, 148, 186n89, 191
Welcome to Sarajevo, 65, 206
Wilson, Kemmons, 58, 58n41, 58n42, 59
Winterbottom, Michael, 206
Winter Olympic Games (1984), 2, 5, 63–4, 112, 117
Woollacot, Martin, 35
World Health Organisation (WHO), 178n55

Y
The Yoghurt Revolution, 67
Youth Voluntary Labour Association (*Savez omladinska radna akcija* (SORA/ORA)), 54
Yugoslav Army (JNA), 67, 68, 119
Yugoslav counter-intelligence service (*Kontra-obavještajana služba* (KOS), 104
Yugoslav League of Communists (*Savez komunista Jugoslavije* (SKJ), 48, 65
Yutel za mir (Yutel for Peace) concert, 79

Z
Žabljak Constitution, 119n8
Zelen, Ljlijana, 76
Zetra sports hall, 51, 64, 80, 205
Zooropa tour, 206
Zulfikarpašić, Adil, 73, 73n9

The manufacturer's authorised representative in the EU is Springer Nature Customer Service Centre GmbH, Europaplatz 3, 69115 Heidelberg, Germany. If you have any concerns regarding our products, please contact ProductSafety@springernature.com

Printed and bound by CPI Group (UK) Ltd, Croydon, CR0 4YY
23/03/2026
02076459-0003